Unix Networking
Clearly Explained

Richard Petersen

MORGAN KAUFMANN PUBLISHERS, INC.

San Francisco, California

This book is printed on acid-free paper. ∞

Copyright © 1999 by Academic Press.
All rights reserved.
No part of this publication may be reproduced or
transmitted in any form or by any means, electronic
or mechanical, including photocopy, recording, or
any information storage and retrieval system, without
permission in writing from the publisher.

Morgan Kaufmann Publishers, Inc.
340 Pine Street
San Francisco, CA 94104
www.mkp.com

Library of Congress Catalog-Card Number: 98-49378
International Standard Book Number: 0-12-552145-6

Printed in the United States of America
99 00 01 02 03 IP 9 8 7 6 5 4 3

Unix Networking
Clearly Explained

To my nephews
Justin, Christopher, and Dylan

Contents

Section I

Electronic Mail

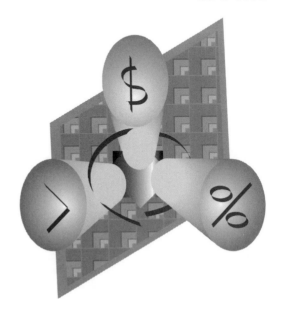

Introduction

Unix systems can be connected by a network. A network is a group of computers connected by a communications line. The line may connect a few computers or many. It may connect computers in a localized area or across global distances. In the case of networked Unix systems, each computer usually has its own Unix system. The different Unix systems then communicate across a network connecting the different computers. Using a network, you can send messages to users on other Unix systems, transfer files from one system to another, post news and discussion items that can be read by users on other systems, and locate information such as programs and articles on another system and transfer it to your own.

This book introduces you to four different kinds of Unix networking applications: mailers, newsreaders, network and Internet tools, and remote access commands. Mailers are utilities you use to send and receive messages. You use newreaders to read and post Usenet news articles. Unix supports a wide range of tools you can use to access network resources such at Telnet for remote logins, Ftp for file transfers, Gopher menus, and Web browsers that provide an easy-to-use interface. The remote access commands are used to execute commands on remote systems that you enter on your own system.

This book focuses on user interaction with a network, not network administration. It is meant for the normal Unix user working in a network environment, presenting a range of networking applications available for use on Unix systems.

Client/Server

Before the development of networks, most computing was performed on mainframe computers to which terminals were connected. Users used terminals to connect directly to the mainframe computer and issue commands. With the development of the PC, users began having the mainframe perform difficult tasks and then downloading the results to their PC for more customized processing like incorporating data into a report with a word processor or spreadsheet. With the development of local area networks and minicomputers, a network could be set up to link several PCs and minicomputers. Minicomputers would perform intensive tasks for the PCs. Instead of logging separately into a mainframe to have a task performed, a user could request it directly from a connected minicomputer. The results would then be automatically sent to the requesting PC. On such a network, the PCs became known as the clients making requests, and the computers receiving and performing the requested tasks became known as servers. In this client/server relationship, the client sends requests to servers, which then process the requests, sending the results back to the client. Workstations have since replaced most minicomputers as servers on networks. A workstation is a hybrid combining the versatility of a PC with the power of a minicomputer.

The Unix operating system became the operating system of choice for many client/server networks. Because of its multi-user and multi-tasking capabilities, Unix systems can receive and process requests from many different clients at the same time. Unix was expanded to support networking needs, integrating network functions such as file sharing and identifying other connected systems. In addition, many of the original network tools for communicating across networks such as Ftp for file transfer were first developed on Unix systems.

A server is a system or part of a system that performs tasks requested by other users on a network. The server is designed to perform certain tasks such as printing files or accessing a database. It receives requests for one of these specified tasks from a system connected on the network. The request is initiated by a user on that system. The server then performs the task for the requesting system and returns the results. After printing a file, the server would send a response saying that the file was printed. In the case of accessing a database, it would send back database records. This kind of structure avoids a great deal of duplication. For example, instead of each computer having its own printer, you only need one printer on the network with the server connected to it to perform the actual printing. Other systems on the network simply ask the server to print a document, sending it the document or telling it where it is. The same is true for files. Instead of each system having its own copy of the same database, you could have one server with the database and other systems sending requests to it to query or update the database.

Clients are systems or applications that send requests to a server. The terms *client* and *server* originally applied to hardware components on a network. These were the computers that sent requests and those that received and processed the requests. These terms have evolved to apply more to specialized software programs on the system. Requests and processing are actually performed by programs. A Unix operating system running on a computer can function as a server, receiving requests and running server programs to process those requests. Requests are sent by corresponding client programs running on a computer from which the request is sent. For example, a mail client is a mail program with which a user composes a message and then sends it to a mail server with a request that it be transmitted to a designated user on the network. The mail server is a server program run by the server's operating system that can locate a user on the network and transmit the message. Another example is a Web browser and a Web server on a Web site. The Web browser is the client program that sends requests for Web pages to a Web server operating at a particular Web site. The Web server is a server program that can detect browser requests and return the requested Web page.

In this respect, a server may not actually take up an entire computer or even operating system. It may be a program that uses only part of a system. For example, the same Unix system could support a Web server, a Gopher server, and an Ftp server all at once. A Web server would consists of a Web server program running alongside of a Gopher server program and a Ftp server program. The Web server program would provide access to Web pages located on that Unix system's file system, as would the Gopher server for Gopher directories, and the Ftp server for publicly accessible files. The implementation and maintenance of server software is primarily a network administration task and is beyond the scope of this book. This book focuses on client programs that a user makes use of in a network environment.

TCP/IP and UUCP

A network connects the systems on it by means of communication protocols. There are two different types of network connections that Unix systems can use, each with its own protocols, Transmission Control Protocol/Internet Protocol (TCP/IP) and Unix-to-Unix Communications Protocol (UUCP). The TCP/IP protocols used with the Internet can also be used for local networks. Networks using TCP/IP often have dedicated connections, such as Ethernet connections or remote dial-in connections. Most Unix systems are configured to connect into networks that use the TCP/IP protocols.

TCP/IP consists of different protocols, each designed for a specific task in a TCP/IP network. The two basic protocols are the Transmission Control Protocol (TCP), which handles receiving and sending communications, and the Internet Protocol (IP), which handles transmitting communications. Other protocols provide various network services. The Domain Name Service (DNS) provides address resolution. The File Transmission Protocol (Ftp) provides file transmission, and Network File Systems (NFS) provides access to remote file systems.

TCP/IP protocols are not limited to Unix systems. They are designed to operate with any kind of operating system, whether it is a minicomputer running VMS, a mainframe running an IBM system, or a personal computer running Windows. This is one reason the Internet uses the TCP/IP protocols. However, the TCP/IP protocols were first developed on Unix systems and are used for most Unix networks.

UUCP is an alternative set of protocols that provides network communication between Unix systems only. It is an older protocol that was designed to operate between systems that were not already connected on a network. With UUCP, one system can connect directly to another across phone lines at a predetermined time, sending a batched set of communications all at once. UUCP is very helpful for making a direct connection to a particular system, transferring data, and then ending the connection.

Electronic Mail

Unix systems have electronic mail capabilities that allow you to send and receive messages to other users on your network. You can send messages to anyone on your system, on a system connected to your network, or to anyone on the Internet. On a network such as the Internet, each user has an email address. The address consists of the user name combined with the address of the system at which they are located. If a network is made up of several other networks, then these networks will also have an address, as is the case with the Internet. The network address is added to the system name to form a fully qualified domain name that can be used to locate any system on the network.

You send and receive messages on Unix using a electronic mail utility called a *mailer*. Several commonly used mailers are available on
most Unix systems. Though they perform the same basic tasks of
receiving and sending messages, they have very different interfaces. This book presents four different mailers: mailx, Elm, MH,
and Pine. Each has a distinctive interface and all are very powerful
mailers with extensive sets of features and options. mailx has become a standard utility found almost all Unix systems. It uses simple command-line interface that is not all that easy to use, but has
very powerful features. The Elm mailer has a cursor-based full-
screen interface that makes managing messages a simple matter of
moving the cursor and pressing single letter commands. The Mail
Handler, MH, takes a very different approach. Email operations are
integrated into your standard Unix interface as Unix commands
that you can execute from your Unix command line. You do not
start up a separate application with its own environment. With simple Unix commands you can check your mail or send a message.

Pine is a popular mailer that has been implemented on many different operating systems. There are versions of Pine for Windows,
Macintosh, and Unix systems. Pine uses MIME protocols to enable
you to attach binary files to your messages. With Pine you can
send a binary file such as an image file along with a message, and
have that file received and displayed by another user with Pine.
Pine also has Usenet news functions, which allows you use it as a
newsreader.

The mailers described here are either cursor-based or line-by-line
mailers that you can run from your Unix command line. They are
not X-Window mailers. Many of the X-Window GUI interfaces
such as Motif and Open-Look provide easy-to-use X-Window
mailers. Also, the Web browsers, Netscape Communicator and
Mosaic, provide X-Window-based mailers. You can use any one of
these to send and receive messages, but they may not have the extensive set of features found in the cursor-based or line-by-line
mailers like MH or Pine.

Other forms of communication supported by Unix are also discussed. With `write` you can send an instant message to another
user logged into your system. `talk` lets you set up two-way com-

munication with another user, where both of you can type messages at the same time on a split screen displayed on both your terminals.

Newsreaders

Newsreaders are designed to read Usenet news articles. Articles are organized into newsgroups that you can use a newsreader to subscribe to. The newsreader will download and display the article for your subscribed newsgroups. Many newsreaders are available. Most Web browsers such as Netscape Communicator and Mosaic also have newsreaders. The chapters in this book describe cursor-based newsreaders used on Unix systems: rn, trn, tin, and nn. rn was one of the first newsreaders developed. It uses a simple line-by-line interface but contains powerful search and selection capabilities. Articles are displayed using a pager that operates like the **more** or **pg** commands.

trn is a threaded newsreader that provides a full-screen display for selecting articles (though not newsgroups). Articles are organized into threads where replies and follow-ups to an article are listed along with it. A cursor-based thread tree lets you move easily from one follow-up article to another, as well as to other articles on the same subject.

The **tin** newsreader implements full-screen cursor-based interfaces for both the newsgroup list and article lists. Like trn, it supports threads, listing articles with their follow-ups and replies. tin provides an extensive set of options and features. nn is another full-screen cursor-based newsreader similar to tin but without the extensive set of features.

Network and Internet Resources

On Unix systems, client/server software was developed for accessing certain kinds of resources available on networks using TCP/IP protocols. A resource could be a file, a remote login to another system, locations of files on the network, or menus and pages that list or reference other resources. The software that provides access to these resources can be thought of as providing a service. A user uses the client software to request a service and it is performed by the receiving server running the corresponding server software. The services commonly available on networked Unix systems are Telnet, Ftp, Archie, WAIS, Gopher, and the Web. This book discusses the clients. Server operation is a network administration topic.

Telnet will connect to a remote system and let you log in to an account there as if you were using a terminal connected to it. With Ftp you can connect to a remote system, log in, and then transfer files to and from it. Though you can use Ftp to connect to any system that supports it, it is commonly used to download documents and software packages from Ftp sites. Archie is a utility that searches for directories and files and returns a list of the Ftp sites on which they are located. You can use patterns with regular expressions to locate sites that have files you are looking for. You can then use Ftp to download the file. WAIS (Wide Area Information Service) is another search service that lets you locate any kind of document whether it be on an Ftp, Gopher, or Web site. WAIS indexes documents, allowing them to be searched easily.

Gopher is a menu-based interface that provides easy access to network resources. You use a Gopher client to connect to Gopher sites, which then display Gopher menus listing the resources available on that site or links to resources on other sites. A Gopher menu can link to other Gopher menus or to other network resources such as an Ftp site or Telnet connection. You can easily search for Gopher menus entries, displaying the results in the form of another Gopher menu listing all the matching Gopher entries.

The World Wide Web (WWW or Web) is a network of Internet sites that use a HyperText interface for easily accessing Internet resources throughout the world. A HyperText document can display images and forms, as well as formatted text. Those used on the World Wide Web are known as Web pages. A Web page can contain the Internet addresses of other Internet resources. Such embedded addresses are known as HyperLinks or just links. Using Web pages with links you can access Internet resources such as Ftp or Gopher sites, Telnet connections, or other Web pages. In this respect, Web pages can form an interlocking web of connections, where accessing one can lead to another, and that one to yet another, and so on.

The kind of client program that you use to access and display a Web page is called a Web browser. With a Web browser you can display Web pages located on different Web sites. Several browsers are available for use on Unix systems. Netscape Communicator and Mosaic are X-Window-based browsers with buttons, menus, and windows that can display images and run Java applets. Lynx is a cursor-based browser that does not run on X-Windows and cannot display images. It is essentially a text-based browser with an interface similar to that of Pine.

Remote Access

Remote commands are used to perform operations on remote systems connected to your network. You execute these commands from your Unix command line as you would any other Unix command. For systems on TCP/IP networks, you can use remote commands to perform operations such as logging into another system or copying files to and from it. Common command names are preceded by an **r** to indicate that their operations are remote. For example, `rcp` is the command to copy a file remotely from one system to another. With `rlogin` you can log in to an account on another system, much like with Telnet. With the `rsh` command you can execute a command on a remote system. Certain commands are used to determine the status of a system. `ping` will check to see if a system is connected to the network and running. These remote commands have the advantage of performing real-time operations. For systems on your network that allow you access, you can copy files and execute commands, and the operations will be carried out almost immediately. Keep in mind though that these commands work only on systems connected to networks that use the TCP/IP protocols.

A UUCP network has a different set of remote commands that you can use to perform operations on remote systems. With the `uucp` command you can transfer files from one system to another. uname will display all the systems accessible to you through UUCP connections, essentially all of those on your UUCP network. uux will execute a command on a remote system. Many of the UUCP commands correspond to the TCP/IP remote access commands. uucp operates much like rcp and uux like rsh.

In a UUCP network, commands are batched and sent out all at once to other systems on the network. Transmissions are often sent by modem over standard communication lines. The remote systems execute the received commands and later send the results. For example, a request to copy files from the remote system to your own is first batched with other commands and sent to the remote system. The copy command is executed along with any others and the "copied" files are sent back in the next scheduled transmission to your system.

How to Use This Book

The book arranges the different kinds of Unix networking applications into four sections. In Section I, Unix mailers are discussed. Section II discusses newsreaders used to retrieve and display Usenet news articles. Section III discusses tools to access network resources such as those used on the Internet. It covers such topics as remote login with Telnet, Gopher menus, Ftp sites, Web browsers, and Web pages. Section IV discusses remote access commands that can be entered from your Unix command line but executed on a remote system. Section V is a reference section.

The first chapter in each section presents basic information about that particular category. For example, Chapter 10, the first chapter in Section III, discusses the essentials of network addressing used by the applications discussed in the later chapters. Each chapter contains extensive tables. The last chapter, Chapter 19, is a command reference that takes all the tables and places them together, integrating some into larger tables for easy reference. You can use the reference to obtain listings of all the network applications with their commands and options.

Electronic Mail

Your Unix system has electronic mail utilities with which you can send and receive messages. You can send messages to anyone on your system, on a system connected to your network, or to anyone on the Internet. On your own system, each user has an address that is the same as his or her login name. To send a message to another user, you only need to know that user's login name. For other users to send you messages they need to have your address—your login name. To send messages to users on other systems, you need to know their network address. This usually consists of a user's login name along with the name of the system and the system's location. Given a user's address you can send messages to that user no matter where their system is located.

You send and receive messages on Unix using an electronic mail utility called a *mailer*. Several commonly used mailers are available on most Unix systems. Though they perform the same basic tasks of receiving and sending messages, they have very different interfaces. You can send and receive messages in very different ways, depending on the mailer you use. This text presents four different mailers: mailx, Elm, MH, and Pine, each with a very different type of interface. mailx uses a simple command line interface operating within its own shell. It is found on most Unix systems and is considered a standard. Elm has a full-screen interface and employs single key commands much like those used for the Vi editor. MH defines a set of Unix commands that directly receive and send messages within the user's own shell. Instead of operating from within a special mail utility, MH commands can be executed like any Unix command. Pine also uses a full-screen interface, but integrates other capabilites such as a newsreader.

You can also send binary files through Unix electronic mail provided they are first encoded as text files. The received message can then be decoded, translating it into a binary file. In addition, the `write` and `talk` Unix utilities allow you to send and receive real-time messages with users currently logged into your system. These are not mail utilities. Rather they set up direct connections between users much like a radio or telephone.

This chapter discusses the network addresses, the basic electronic mail operations for sending and receiving messages with mailx, the methods for sending binary files, and the utitlites for real-time communications between logged in users. The different electronic mail utilities will be handled in depth in the following chapters.

User Network Addresses

Users on a Unix system are given his or her own electronic mail address. To send a message to another user, you need to use that user's email address. Currently, most Unix systems are connected to networks that use Internet addressing. Each user's mailing address would consist of their user name and their system's internet address. For the user **justin** on the **violet.berkeley.edu** system his address would be **justin@violet.berkeley.edu**. Unix supports alternative methods of addressing. Users on the same system only have to use another user's user name (login name) as the address (much like users on America Online). Other users on the same system as **justin** need only use the address **justin**. However, when sending messages to users on other systems, you need to know not only their user name, but also the address of their system. Unix also supports an older method of addressing that uses UUCP. This is designed for a more rudimentary kind of network where messages are passed from one system to another either through network connections or dial-up modem connections.

For users on other systems to be able to communicate with each other, those systems need to be connected to a network. The network may in turn be connected to other networks at different locations across the country, which in turn may be connected to other networks in other parts of the world. The systems are indirectly connected to each other through the network connections. One system is connected to another system, which in turn is connected to yet another system and so on. You can reach a system on the far end of a network by sending a message that is then passed along by intermediately connected systems. If the **violet** system is connected to the **stan** system, which in turn is connected to the **bell** system, then a user on **violet** can reach a user on **bell** through **stan**. A message is actually sent as part of a batched collection of messages that are sent from one system to another, being delivered as they reach their addressed systems.

Addresses on networks require that the system address be uniquely identified. Each system will have its own name as well as names that may specify the location of the system or the owner of the system. You can then use such a complete network address to send mail to users on any system on the global network. In the case of the Internet, you can send messages to systems around the world.

Two different forms of addressing are available: domain and path. The domain form of addressing was originally developed for use with Arpanet, now known as the Internet. Domain addressing is widely used for communicating across the Internet. For the System

login-name@ system.domain	Domain mail addresses (Internet)
	`chirs@violet.rose.edu`
system!login-name	Path mail address for System V (UUCP)
	`rose!violet!justin`
system\!login-name	Path mail address for C-Shell (UUCP). Escape the exclamation point.
	`rose\!violet\!justin`

Table 2.I Network Mail Addresses: Domain and Path

V version of Unix, AT&T developed another network communications package called the Unix-to-Unix Communications Protocol (UUCP). A UUCP network usually uses the path form of addressing. The two forms of addressing can be intermixed, though the domain form has become the standard form for Internet and Intranet networks.

Domain (Internet) addressing handles messages across networks by designating a unique address for each system. Path addressing, on the other hand, requires that you know and specify all the intermediate connecting systems between yours and the one you are trying to reach. This makes path addressing far more complicated than domain addressing. Both forms of addressing are described in Table 2.I.

Domain Addressing: Internet

Domain addressing was developed to simplify the process of locating a user on another system. Domain addressing assigns a system a domain address which, combined with the system name, gives the system a unique address. Once the user specifies this unique address, the network then tracks it down.

The domain name address consists of the host name, the name for your system, a domain name, the name that identifies your network, and an extension that identifies the type of network. Each component is separated by a period. Here is the syntax for domain addresses:

host-name.domain-name.extension

The login name of the user on a particular system, combined with the domain address forms the complete Internet mail address.

login-name @ host-name.domain-name.extension

To send a message to **justin** on the **violet.berkeley.edu** system, you simply add the domain name to the user name: **justin@ violet.berkeley.edu**. In the following example, the domain address references a computer called **violet** on a network referred to as **berkeley**, and it is part of an educational institution, as indicated by the extension **edu**.

```
$ mailx justin@violet.berkeley.edu < mydata
```

Paths Addressing: UUCP

The path form of addressing uses only system addresses, not domain addresses. The system address is placed before the user name and separated by an exclamation point. Below is the syntax for path addressing.

```
system!login-name
```

In the next example, the mailx utility sends a message to the user **justin** on the Unix system called **violet. chris**'s address is represented using a path format: **violet!justin.**

```
$ mailx violet!justin < mydata
```

Within the C-shell, the path form of addressing requires that a backslash be placed before the exclamation point. The exclamation point by itself in the C-shell denotes the history command. The backslash will escape the exclamation point treating it as a exclamation point character, not as a history command. Below is the syntax for a C-shell path address, as well as an example of the C-shell path used in a mailx command.

```
system\!login-name
% mailx violet\!justin < mydata
```

On networks using a path form of addressing, the address of a user on another system consists of the intermediate systems you have to go through to get to that user's system. Each intermediate system is written in the address sequentially before the user's system and separated by an exclamation point. If you are on **violet** and want to send a message to **chris** on the **bell** system, then you have to specify any intermediate systems through which the message is to be sent. With an intermediate system named **bell**, the address would be **stan!bell!chris**. There may be any number of intermediate systems. If, to send a message to **dylan** at **rose**, you have to go through three intermediate systems, you have to specify those three intermediate systems in the address. In the next examples, messages are sent through an intermediate system to reach a final destination. In the first command a message is sent to the stan system, which then passes it on to bell where chris is located. In the second command, the message is first sent to lilac which passes it on to sf. sf then passes it on to rose where dylan is located.

```
$ mailx stan!bell!chris < mydata
$ mailx lilac!sf!rose!dylan < mydata
```

Sending and Receiving Mail

To send and receive electronic mail messages you use a mailer such as mailx or Elm. This section describes the basic operations for sending and receiving messages. mailx is used since mailx has become a standard utility found on most Unix systems.

To send a message, enter the mailx command followed by the address of the user to whom you are sending the message. After pressing **enter**, you will be prompted for a subject. Enter a brief description of the message (one or more words), and press **enter**. You are then are placed in an input mode where anything you type is taken as the contents of the message. Pressing **enter** will add a newline to the message. When finished, type a **Ctrl-d** on a line of its own (press **enter** and then hold down the Ctrl key while pressing 'd'). The **Ctrl-d** ends and sends the message. You will see the

characters EOT (end-of-transmission) displayed after you enter the
Ctrl-d. In the next example, the user sends a message to another
user whose address is `dylan`. The subject of the message is 'Game'.
After typing in the text of the message, the user presses a **Ctrl-d**.

```
$ mailx dylan
Subject: Game
                 Hockey is the best
                 not tennis.
^D
EOT
$
```

Messages sent to a user are placed in a special file called the user's
mailbox. Messages sent to you are placed in your mailbox until
you retrieve them. To retrieve these messages you also use the
mailx command, but this time with no address. Just the mailx command itself. This starts up the mailx interface, which then dispalys
a list of header summaries for each message you have received. A
header summary holds brief information about a message. Summary information is arranged into fields beginning with that status of the message and the message number and followed by the
date, size, and subject of the message. The status of a message is indicated by a single uppercase letter, usually **N** or **U**. The letter **N**
indicates a new message, and the letter U identifies previously unread messages. Message numbers are used to reference messages
in mailx commands. They follow the status field.

```
$ mailx
Mailx version 5.5. Type ? for help.
"/usr/mail/justin": 3 messages 3 new
>N 1 Justin Mon May 11 11:31:19 5/44 "Car"
 N 2 Larisa Tue May 12 9:14:05 28/537 "Homework"
 N 3 chris  Fri May 15 10:43:51 4/76 "Game"
?
```

Simply entering in the number of the message by itself at the mail
prompt will display that message. The message will then be output screen by screen. Press the **spacebar** or the **enter** key to continue on to the next screen. If you enter the number 1 at the mail
prompt, the first message will be displayed for you.

```
Mailx version 5.5. Type ? for help.
"/usr/mail/dylan": 3 messages 3 new
>N 1 Justin     Mon May 11  11:31:19 5/44   "Car"
 N 2 Larisa     Tue May 12   9:14:05 28/537 "Homework"
 N 3 chris      Fri May 15  10:43:51 4/76   "Game"

? 3
From chris Tue May 15 10:43:51 PST 1998
To: dylan
Subject: Game
Status: R
We have to figure out how to play hockey on a train

                    Chris

?
```

Entr q at the mail prompt to quit mailx. Saved messages are automatically saved in a file called **mbox** in your home directory. You can use mailx with the -F options to redisplay them.

```
$ mailx -F mbox
```

Notifications of Received Mail: from **and** biff

As messages are received, they are placed in a file that operates like a mailbox. Each user has his or her own mailbox that holds waiting messages. You are not automatically notified when you receive a message. However, you can use the from and biff utilities to notify you if you have any mail waiting.

The from utility lists the messages you have received that are waiting to be read. Each entry displays the sender's address and time the message was received. To use from, you type the command from and press **enter**.

```
$ from
1 From justin Mon May 11 11:31:19 1998
  Subject: Car
```

```
2 From larisa Tue May 12 9:14:05 1998
  Subject: Homework
3 From chris Fri May 15 10:43:51 1998
  Subject: Game
$
```

The biff utility notifies you immediately when a new message is received. It is helpful when you are expecting a message and want to know as soon as it arrives. The notification includes the message header and the first few lines of message. You turn on biff using the biff command with the y argument: biff y. To turn it off you enter biff n. Using the biff command with no arguments will tell you whether biff is on or not. biff displays a message notification whenever a message arrives, no matter what you may be doing at the time. You could be in the middle of an editing session and biff will interrupt the editing session to display message notification on your screen. In the next example, the user first sets biff on. Then biff notifies the user that a message has been received. The user then checks to see if biff is still on.

```
$ biff y
$
New mail for dylan has arrived:
—Date: Wed Mar 17 10:15:20
From: larisa
To: dylan
Subject: Vacation
      Dylan,
         Tell Justin his idea was brilliant???
...more...
$
$ biff
is y
$
```

If you don't want to be interrupted, you can temporarily block biff by using the mesg n command to prevent any message displays on your screen. mesg n will not only stop any write and talk messages, it will also stop biff and notify messages. You can then later unblock biff with a mesg y command. A mesg n command comes in handy should you not want to be disturbed while working on some project.

Receiving Mail Automatically: vacation

Should you be unavailable, say on vacation, and you are not able to log in and read your mail for a certain period, then you can have your mail saved automatically for you in your mailbox and a message sent to senders that you are unavailable and have not yet read it. The vacation command will perform these operations, reading and saving your mail and sending 'vacation' messages to the senders. Messages received are placed in a file in your home directory called **.mailfile**, **$HOME/.mailfile**. A log of senders is kept in the **.maillog** file. The standard reply message is found in the system's **/usr/lib/mail/std_vac_msg** file.

The vacation command has several options as listed in Table 2.II. The -m option lets you specify a particular mailbox file where want messages saved. You could then simply access this file to list all the messages sent while you were away. The -M option lets you compose your own vacation messges. The default one just says that you are on vacation. The -M option takes as its argument a text file from which it will read the message. You use an editor to create this text file and compose your message. In the following example, the text in the file named **vacplans** is used as the reply message by vacation and any messages received are saved in the file named **vacmsgs**.

```
$ vacation -M vacplans -m vacmsgs
```

To disable vacation you enter the following command.

```
$ mail -F ""
```

Mailing Binaries and Archives:
uuencode, tar, MIME

Messages sent through electronic mail connections are treated as text messages. Messages consist of a sequence of characters. Binary files such as compiled programs cannot be sent through the mail utilities. If you do send binary files, they will arrive corrupted and unusable. The same is true for archived or compressed files. A set

-d	Append the date to the logfile
-F *user*	If mail can't be sent to mailfile, forward mail to specified user.
-l *filename*	Save names of senders who were sent the vacation reply in the specified file (default is **$HOME/.maillog**)
-m *mailbox-filename*	Save received messages in specified file (default is **$HOME/.mailfile**)
-M *mesg_file*	Use the text in *mesg_file* as vacation's automatic reply message (default is **/usr/lib/mail/std_vac_msg**).

Table 2.II vacation Options

of files that you archive into one file using an archive utility like tar or a file that you compressed using zip, cannot be sent via electronic mail. However, you can encode binary, archived, and compressed files into character text equivalent files that can then be sent through electronic mail. The uuencode utility translates a binary file into a character equivalent. You can then send this character file of encoded binary data through a mail utility such as mailx or Elm. The person receiving such an encoded file can then convert it back to a binary file using the uudecode utility.

As an alternative to encoding and decoding binaries manually, many mailers support MIME extensions that allow a mailer to send and receive binary files as attached files that are then automatically encoded and decoded for you. MIME support is particularly useful for multimedia files such as image or sound files. Pine has built-in MIME support whereas Elm relies on a program called metamail to provide it.

Encoding Binaries: uencode *and* uudecode

uuencode works on either the standard input or on a particular file. In either case you have to provide a name for the file that will be created when the encoded data are converted back to binary. uuencode outputs the encoded binary data to the standard output. uuencode has the following syntax where *name* is the name to be given to the decoded binary data and *file* is the name of a binary file to be encoded. Keep in mind that since uuencode sends the encoded data to the standard output, you should redirect this output to a file. Then you can send that file.

```
uuencode file name
```

The uudecode program takes as its argument the file that holds text data encoded by uuencode. It will generate a binary file using the name provided in the uuencode operation. The basic steps are shown in the following example. A file is encoded with the encoded data redirected to another file, *encoded-file*. *name* is the name that will be used for the binary file created when it is decoded. It is then mailed as a message by the mailx utility. When that message is received in the mailx utility, it is saved as a file (encoded-file). That file is then then decoded with uudecode, generating a binary file called name.

```
uuencode file name > encoded-file
mailx address < encoded-file
& s msg-num encoded-file
uudecode encoded-file
```

In the next example, the user encodes the picture file called **justin.gif**. Picture files such as gif and jpeg files are binary files and have to be translated to character format before they can be mailed. In this case the name of the binary file and the name to used for the decoded version of the file are the same. The encoded output is redirected to a file called **justypic**.

```
$ uuencode justin.gif justin.gif > justypic
```

justypic is a file that contains only character data, though this character data are encoded binary data. The user can then send **justypic** through the mail system.

```
$ mail justin@ix.com < justypic
```

Once received, you simply use uudecode to convert the encoded data back to its binary form. uudecode will create a binary file, giving it the name specified when it was encoded by uuencode.

In the following example, the data from **justypic** file has been received as a message. The receiver then saves this message as **justypic**. uudecode then converts this message to the original binary format and places it in a file called **justin.gif.** The name that the receiver saves the message as does not have to be the same as the one the sender used.

```
$ mail
Mail version 5.5-kw 5/30/95. Type ? for help.
"/var/spool/mail/justin": 1 message 1 unread
>U 1 chris                      Mon Apr 8 00:06 236/14104
& s 1 justypic
"justypic" [New file]
& q
$ uudecode justypic
$ ls
justin.gif
```

You can apply the same process to archived and compressed files. You could send several gif picture files in the same message by first combining them into one archive file and compressing it. Then you could encode the compressed archived file with uuencode and mail it as a message. The person receiving it can decode the message to a compressed archive file, which can then be decompressed and gif pictures extracted from the archive. You can also do this for entire directories and their subdirectories. In the next examples the entire **birthday** directory is archived by tar and compressed with zip. The compressed archive is then encoded into character data and saved in a file called **birthdaydir**. The name given to the binary data is **birthday.tar.Z.** The file is sent as a message through **mailx**. The receiver saves this message in a file called **birthd**. uudecode then decodes the **birthd** file, generating the **birthday.tar.Z** file, which can then be decompressed and extracted to create the **birthday** directory in its entirety.

```
$ tar cvf birthday.tar birthday
$ zip birthday.tar
$ uuencode birthday.tar.z birthday.tar.z > birthdaydir
$ mail dylan@pango1.com < birthdaydir
```

```
$ mail
Mail version 5.5-kw 5/30/95. Type ? for help.
"/var/spool/mail/justin": 1 message 1 new
>N 1 chris                    Mon Apr 8 00:10 236/14162
& s 1 birthd
"birthd" [New file]
& q
$ uudecode birthd
```

Since the uuencode program can receive binary data from the standard input, you could combine the archive, compression, encoding, and mailing operations in one pipe sequence as shown here. The – in the tar operation represents the standard output and will instruct tar to send its output to the standard output instead of a file. Notice that the name to be used for the decoded binary file is still included as an argument to uuencode. uudecode, when applied to this message, will generate a binary file called **birthday.tar.Z.**

```
$ tar cf - birthday | zip | uuencode birthday.tar.z | mail
dylan@pango1.com
```

MIME

MIME stands for Multi-purpose Internet Mail Extensions and is used to enable mailers to send and receive multimedia files and files using different character sets such as those for different languages. Multimedia files can be images, sound, or even video. Mailers that support MIME can send binary files automatically as attachments to messages. MIME- capable mailers maintain a file called **mailcap** that maps different types of MIME message to applications on your system that can view or display them. For example, an image file will be maped to an application that can display images. Your mailer can then run that program to display the image message. A sound file will be mapped to an application that can play sound files on your speakers. Some mailers such as Pine already have MIME capabilites built in and use their own version of the **mailcap** file. Others like Elm use a program called metamail that adds MIME support.

Online Communications: write **and** talk

With the write and talk utilities you can set up direct communcation with other users that are logged in at the same time. The write utility operates like the instant messages used on online services like America Online. It allows you to contact someone also logged in and display a message on their screen. The talk utility operates like the chat rooms used on on-line services. It allows you to have a direct two-way conversation with another user somewhat like a telephone.

Direct Connections: The write *Utility*

With the write utility you can send a real-time message to another user. write operates a bit like two people communicating over a radio. The message the sender types is immediately displayed on screen of the user receiving the message. In this way, write is guaranteed to get someone's immediate attention.

Keep in mind that write does not operate like the standard mail operation. You should not think of it as actually sending a message like those placed in a mailbox file. It simply displays characters making up the message directly on another user's screen. A user receives no physical message that can be saved or read later.

To send a write message you enter the write command with a user's user name (usually the login name). This opens up a connection to that user. You then type text that will be displayed on that user's screen. To end the message, enter a **Ctrl-d** on a line of its own. The user, meanwhile, will first have a notice displayed on his or her screen saying that a message was sent by you and giving the date and time, and then the message is displayed. In the next example, a user writes a message to dylan. After entering in the message, the user presses a **Ctrl-d** to cut the connection.

```
$ write dylan
How are you today?
^D
```

dylan then receives a message header followed by the message.
The **Ctrl-d** entered by the sender shows up as EOT, end-of-transmission.

```
Message from chris [Tues July 5 11:31]
How are you today
EOT
```

You can use the write utility to establish two-way communication
between you and another user. You can send a message with the
write command, and the receiving user can send a response
using the write command and your user name. The messages
sent back and forth by you and the other user are displayed on
both terminal screens.

Such interactive write communication should be handled as if
you were talking over a radio. First one user sends a message and
then indicates that the message is finished, and then the other user
responds with a reply. A common convention adopted by many
Unix users is to indicate the end of a message with the letter o, for
'over'. The letters oo, over and out, are used when you are finished
communicating and wish to sign off. You physically end the connection with a **Ctrl-d**. However, both users must enter a **Ctrl-d**.
Your **Ctrl-d** cuts your connection with the other user, and the other
user's **Ctrl-d** ends that user's connection with you.

Figure 2.1, **chris** initiates a write communication with **dylan.** A
message notice is displayed on **dylan**'s screen along with **chris**'s
first message. **dylan** responds with a write command of his own
and **chris**'s login name. A message notice is displayed followed by
dylan's first response. They then talk back and forth line by line
waiting for the other to finish before responding. **chris** then indicates that he is finished talking by entering oo and then presses
Ctrl-d. This appears on **dylan**'s screen as EOT (end of transmission).
dylan responds with his own sign off message and then also
presses **Ctrl-d** displaying an EOT symbol on the **chris**'s screen.

A write communication will be displayed on your screen even if
you are in the middle of some other task such as editing a file. If
you do not want to be interrupted by write messages suddenly
being displayed on your screen, you can suppress them with the

```
$ write dylan                              Message from chris [Tues July 5 10:31]
How are you today?                         How are you today?
Message from dylan [Tues July 5 10:33]      $ write chris
I am fine chris o                          I am fine chris o
Did you really take the train o            Did you really  take the train o
Of course,  all the way here o             Of course,  all the way here o
Ok bye oo                                  Ok bye oo
^D                                         EOT
$                                          It was fun, bye oo
It was fun, bye oo                         ^D
EOT                                        $
```

         chris's screen   dylan's screen

Figure 2.1. Two users use the write command to carry on a two-way conversation. The o at the end of each line stands for over, and the oo at the end stands for over and out. A user presses a Ctrl-d to end the connections, and this shows up on the other screen as EOT.

mesg command. The mesg command takes two possible options, y or n. mesg -n suppresses any reception of a write message. mesg -y restores reception of write messages. In the next example, the mesg -n command suppresses any messages sent to you from other users using write.

```
$ mesg -n
```

Interactive Communication:The talk Utility

With the talk utility you can set up an interactive two-way communication between you and another user. Unlike write, both you and the other user can type in messages simultaneously. The talk utility operates more like a phone call where two people are constantly talking back and forth to each other. It is similar to chat rooms where multiple users are communicating, entering text at the same time.

You establish a talk connection by entering the talk command followed by the other user's user name. A message is displayed on that user's screen asking if he or she wants to talk and giving your user name. The user then responds with a talk command of his or her own using your user name. Both your screen and the other user's screen then split into two segments. The top segment

displays any characters that you type, and the bottom segment
displays any characters that the other user types. Either user can
end the session with an interrupt character, usually a **Ctrl-c**.

    % **talk chris**

In Figure 2.2 **Chris** and **Dylan** communicate with each other using
the `talk` command. Each is free to type in a response at any time
on their own part of the screen.

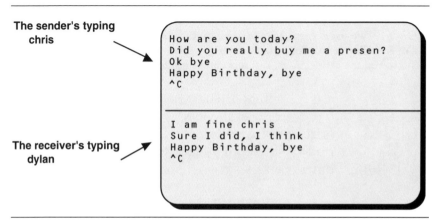

The sender's typing chris

```
How are you today?
Did you really buy me a presen?
Ok bye
Happy Birthday, bye
^C
```

The receiver's typing dylan

```
I am fine chris
Sure I did, I think
Happy Birthday, bye
^C
```

Figure 2.2. The `talk` command splits the screen into two sections. The same
split screen is displayed for both users. Each user types what they want,
when they want. In this figure, Chris has initiated a talk session with dylan.
What Chris types appears in the top half of the screen, and what Dylan types
appears at the bottom. They end the session with a Ctrl-c.

mailx *Mailer*

With the `mailx` utility you can easily send and receive messages to and from other users. Sending a message is as simple as typing in a login name followed by the text of the message. Receiving messages is merely a matter of selecting a message from a list of received messages.

The `mailx` utility is a very flexible and complex program offering many different features. When sending messages there are commands for modifying the message text and what is known as the message header. When receiving messages you can reply to them, save them in files, or simply delete them. A special initialization file, **.mailrc**, configures your mail utility with special features such as aliases. The `mailx` utility also has an addressing capability that operates across networks. You can easily send a message across a network to a user on another Unix system.

The Unix `mailx` command may go by slightly different names in different versions of Unix. What is known now as the `mailx` utility was originally created for BSD Unix by Eric Allman and called simply `mail` (early versions of System V had a simplified mail utility that was also called `mail`). Later versions of System V as well as a System V, release 4, adopted the BSD mail utility and renamed it `mailx`. BSD `mail` and System V `mailx` are virtually equivalent.

Sending Messages: `mailx`

You can send a message to any user by using the `mailx` command. The message can be something you type in at the keyboard or it can be the contents of a file. While you are entering in a message at the keyboard, you can edit it using special tilde commands. These commands allow you to save a message, redisplay what you have written, or invoke an editor with which to edit the message.

To send a message, type in the word `mailx` along with the address of the person to whom you are sending the message. Upon pressing **enter**, you will be prompted for a subject. Enter the subject of the message and then press **enter**. At this point you are placed in an input mode. Anything typed in is considered part of the message. Pressing the **enter** key adds a newline to the text. When you have finished typing in your message, type in a **Ctrl-d** on a line of its own. The **Ctrl-d** ends and sends the message. You will see the characters EOT (end-of-transmission) displayed after you enter the **Ctrl-d**. In the next example, the user sends a message to another user whose address is `dylan`. The subject of the message is 'Game'. After typing in the text of the message, the user presses a **Ctrl-d**.

```
$ mailx dylan
Subject: Game
  We have to figure out how to play hockey on a train
    Chris

^D
EOT
$
```

Standard Input and Redirection

`mailx` receives input from the standard input. By default the standard input is taken from what the user enters with the keyboard. However, with redirection, standard input can be taken from a file. With redirection, you can use the contents of a file as the message for the `mailx` program. You can create and edit a text file with an editor and then use that text file as redirected input for the `mailx` utility. In effect, the file is sent to the address. In the next example as well as in Figure 3.1, the file **myidea** is redirected input for the `mailx` utility and sent to the user called `dylan`.

```
$ mailx dylan < myidea
```

When you mail a file using redirection, you are not prompted to enter a subject for the mail message. If you want to specify a subject, you use the `mailx -s` option that allows you to enter the subject of a message on the command line. This subject will then show up as the subject in the header list of that message. (`mailx` options are listed in Table 3.I.) In the next example, **chris** sends the file **complist** and specifies the subject as **computer**.

```
$ mailx -s computer dylan < complist
```

Sending Mail to Several Users

To send a message to several users at the same time, you only have to list those users' addresses as arguments on the command line. In the next example, a user sends the same message to both `dylan` and `justin`.

```
$ mailx dylan justin
Subject: Game
  We have to figure out how to play hockey on a train
    Chris

^D
EOT
$
```

```
$ mailx -s computer dylan < complist
```

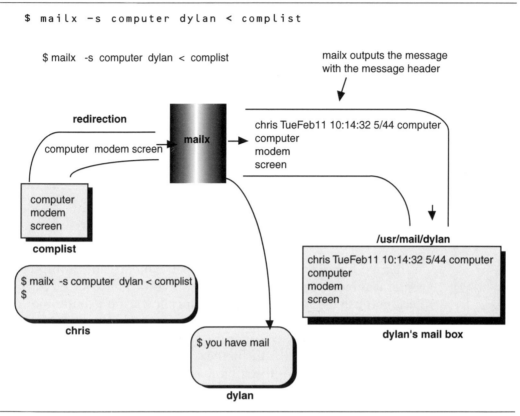

Figure 3.1. Redirecting the standard input from a file to `mailx`**. The contents of the file are then sent as a message to the user.**

You can also use redirection to send the contents of a file to several users at once. In the next example, the contents of the **myidea** file is sent to both **dylan** and **justin**.

```
$ mailx dylan justin < myidea
```

Copying a Message to a File

Should you want to save a copy of a message that you are sending to a particular file, you only have to list that file name on the command line after the addresses. The file name has to be a relative or full path name, containing a slash in its name. A path name identifies

-f *mailbox-filename*	Invoke the `mailx` utility to read messages in a mailbox file in your directory rather than your mailbox of waiting messages.
-H	Display only the list of message headers.
-s *subject*	When sending messages, this option specifies the subject.
-F	Save message in a file with the name of the first recipient.

Table 3.I. mailx Command Options

an argument as a file name to which `mailx` will save a copy of the message being sent. In the next example, the user saved a copy of the message to a file called **birthnote**. A relative path name is used with the period denoting the current working directory: **./gamenote.**

```
$ mailx dylan ./gamenote
Subject: Game
  We have to figure out how to play hockey on a train
    Chris

^D
EOT
$ cat gamenote
Subject: Game
  We have to figure out how to play hockey on a train
    Chris
$
```

You can specify a file name even when using redirection and multiple addresses.

```
        $ mailx justin dylan < myidea ./gamenote
```

Editing Mail Messages: The Tilde Commands

A mail message has two components: the header and the text. The header contains information about the message such as the addresses of people to whom the message is to be sent and the subject of the message. You normally enter the addresses as arguments to the `mailx` command. `mailx` then prompts the user to enter the subject of the message. After entering the subject, you then enter the message.

`mailx` has set of commands known as *tilde commands* that allow you to perform editing operations both on the header and the text of the message while you are composing it. A tilde command consists of a one-character command preceded by a tilde and entered on a line of its own. The tilde functions as a special character, indicating a tilde command. The tilde and the command are not taken as part of the message. Instead, they execute various file or editing commands. Tilde commands for the header allow you to change address and subject information. The tilde commands for the text allows you to redisplay, save, and use an editor to modify the text. (Should you need to enter the tilde as a character in the message, you can do so by entering two tildes next to each other, ~~.) The commonly used tilde commands are listed in Table 3.II. You can also obtain a listing of the tilde commands with the ~? tilde command.

Tilde Commands for the Message Text

Once you have entered the subject and pressed **enter**, you are placed into an input mode in which you enter the text of the message. This input mode has no editing capabilites execept for a simple character deletion using the **backspace** key. You are simply typing in a stream of data. The **backspace** key will erase the character to the immediate left of the cursor on that line.

Should you want to use an editor to compose your message, you can invoke the Vi editor from within the `mailx` input mode. You do so using a the ~v tilde command. The ~v command is entered in on a line by itself, after which you press the **enter** key. Once you have started up the Vi editor, you can edit your message as you would any other text. Any part of the message you have typed in so far will be displayed as text to be edited.

When you are finished composing your message, you exit the editor with the save and quit command such as `ZZ` or `:wq` for the `Vi`

TILDE COMMANDS FOR MESSAGE HEADER

~h	Prompts the user to enter in addresses, subject, and carbon copy list.
~s *subject*	Enter a new subject.
~t *addresses*	Add addresses to the address list.
~c *addresses*	Add addresses to the carbon copy list.
~b *addresses*	Add addresses to the blind carbon copy list.

TILDE COMMANDS FOR MESSAGE TEXT

~v	Invoke the Vi editor. Changes are saved to the message text.
~p	Redisplay the text of the message.
~x	Quit the message and leave the `mailx` utility.
~w *filename*	Save the message in a file.
~r *filename*	Read the contents of a file into the message text.
~e	Invoke the default text editor.
~ |*filter*	Pipe the contents of a message to a filter and replace the message with the ouptut of that filter.
~m *message-list*	When sending messages or replying to received mail, this command inserts the contents of a received message. The contents are indented. Used when receiving messages.
~f *message-list*	When sending messages or replying to received mail, this command inserts the contents of a received message. Unlike ~m, there is no indentation. Used when receiving messages.

GENERAL TILDE COMMANDS

~?	Display a list of all the tilde commands.
~~	Enter a tilde as a character into the text.
~! *command*	Execute a shell command while entering a message.

Table 3.II. Mailx Tilde commands for Sending a Message

editor. You will return to the `mailx` input mode. However, the text of the message will not be redisplayed. Instead the word *continue* in parentheses is displayed on the screen. You could, if you wish,

then enter in more text, execute other tilde commands, or end and
send the message with a **Ctrl-d**.

Other mailx tilde commands can also be used while in the input
mode to perform operations such as redisplaying a message, saving the message to a file, or reading in text from another file to add
to the message. The ~p tilde command can redisplay your message, and the ~p command sends your message to a printer for
printing. When you enter the ~p command on a line by itself and
press **enter**, your entire message is displayed on your screen. With
he ~w tilde command your can save your message to a file, and
with the ~r command you can read in text from another file. You
enter the ~w command with the name of the file the message is to
be written to. The command ~r reads the contents of a file and
inserts it into the message, making it part of the message. Like the
~w command, you enter the ~r command with the name of the file
to be read. In the next example, ~w mydata saves the input message to the file **mydata**. The ~r command then reads the contents
of the file **mynames** and inserts it into the mail message.

```
$ mailx dylan
Subject: Files
          This is a list of all the
          students in my class.
~w mydata
"mydata" 2/48
~r mynames
"mynames" 3/15
~p
_____
Message contains:
To: dylan
Subject: Files
          This is a list of all the
          students in my class.
larisa
aleina
christopher
justin
(continue)
^D
EOT
$
```

Should you decide not to send a message after composing it, you can quit `mailx` with either the ~x or the ~q tilde commands. The message is deleted and you return to the Unix shell. With the ~q command, the message is saved in a file called **dead.letter** should you want to view it later.

You can also process the text of your message through any Unix filter. You can use the current text of your message as input to a filter whose output will then replace the text of your message. For example, if your message consisted of a list, you could pipe the list to the `sort` filter and then have the contents of the message replaced by the sorted output. The ~| tilde command allows you to pipe your text through a filter. ~| takes as its argument a filter. The text of the message becomes the standard input that is piped into the filter. The output of the filter then replaces the message.

The `fmt` filter in particular is very useful for formatting mail messages. Often when you are entering a message, the lines of text are not of an even length, as they are in a word processor. The `fmt` filter will format your lines so that they all have a standard length of approximately 72 characters. Lines beginning with spaces or tabs are taken as the beginning of paragraphs. In the next example, the user makes use of `fmt` to format the message.

```
$ mailx george
Subject: Title
George,
                Have you thought of a new
title for the
project we were discussing
last month?
It should have a new theme based on
the realistic expectations of
our target audience.
~| fmt
(continue)
~p
```

```
Message contains:
To: george
Subject: Title
George,
```

```
        Have you thought of a new title for
the project we were discussing last month? It
should have a new theme based on the realistic
expectations of our target audience.
(continue)
^D
EOT
$
```

Tilde Commands for the Message Header

There are also `mailx` tilde commands designed to let you change components of a message header. A message header has four possible components: the address list, the subject, the carbon copy list, and the blind carbon copy list. Both carbon copy components are optional. An address list is required for each message and you will always be requested to enter a subject.

The address list is the list of addresses to whom the message is being sent. Though you initially enter this list on the command line when you invoke `mailx`, you can add to it with the ~t tilde command while composing your message.

With the ~s command you can change the subject entry for your message, replacing it with a new one. You enter the ~s command with the new subject text on the same line. In the next example both the subject and the address list are changed. The address **justin** is added to the address list. Now the message will be sent to both **justin** and **chris**. Then the subject is changed from 'Files' to 'Class Roster'.

```
$ mailx chris
Subject: Files
This is a list of all the
students in my class.
~t Justin
~s Class Roster
_____
Message contains:
To: chris justin
Subject: Class Roster
        This is a list of all the
        students in my class.
```

```
(continue)
^D
EOT
$
```

You may want to send a copy of a message to someone other than the main recipient. Such a copy would contain the address of the person it was sent to. In effect, you are giving someone a carbon copy of a message you sent out, including the header, not just the text. To send carbon copies with mailx you need to set up a carbon copy list of addresses. A copy of your message will be sent to those listed in the carbon copy list. You create a carbon copy list with the ~c command. With the ~c command you enter the list of addresses that will receive the copy of the message on the same line.

In the case of a carbon copy, those receiving the copy and those receiving the original message will have the carbon copy list of addresses printed at the end of the message. This will be a list of all those receiving a carbon copy. If you do not wish to have a person's address printed in the carbon copy list, yet still want that person to receive a carbon copy of the message, you can send the carbon copy using a blind carbon copy list. The blind carbon copy list operates the same way as the carbon copy list, except that the addresses in the blind carbon copy list are not printed at the end of the message. Only those addresses on the normal carbon copy list are listed. You create a blind carbon copy list with the command ~b entered with a list of blind carbon copy addresses.

Should need to change all the header components, you can use the ~h command to change them all at once. You will first be prompted for a new address list, then a new subject, and finally a new carbon copy list.

Receiving Mail: The Mail Shell

When messages that have been sent to you arrive at your Unix system they are placed in your mailbox until you are ready to read them. A mailbox is really a file filled with recently received messages. You retrieve messages in your mailbox using a mail utility such as mailx.

As noted previously you invoke `mailx` by entering the word `mailx` by itself on the command line. The `mailx` utility has its own shell with its own set of commands and prompt. Upon invoking the `mailx` utility, you enter that mail shell. From within the mail shell you can receive messages, reply to messages, and even send new messages. Commonly used `mailx` message listing conventions and commands are listed in Tables 3.III and 3.IV, respectively.

Upon entering the mail shell, a list of header summaries for each message is displayed. Summary information is arranged into fields beginning with the status of the message and the message number. The status of a message is indicated by a single uppercase letter, usually N or U. N indicates a new message, and U identifies previously unread messages. The next field shows the message number. Message numbers reference messages in `mailx` commands. After the message number, the address of the sender is displayed, followed by the date and time it was received, and then the number of lines and characters in the message. The last field shows the subject the sender gave for the message.

message-number	Reference message with message number.
num1-num2	Reference a range of messages beginning with num1 and ending with num2.
.	The current message.
^	The first message.
$	The last message.
*	All messages waiting in the mailbox.
/pattern	All messages with *pattern* in the subject field.
address	All messages sent from user with *address*.
:*c*	All messages of the type indicated by *c*. Message types are as follows:
n	newly received messages
o	old messages previously received
r	read messages
u	unread messages
d	deleted messages

Table 3.III. Message List

After the header summaries, the mail shell displays its prompt. In early versions of System V as well as System V, release 4, the `mailx` prompt is a question mark, ?, whereas in BSD Unix, the mail prompt is an ampersand, &. At the mail prompt, you enter mail commands that operate on the messages.

```
$ mailx
Mailx version 5.5. Type ? for help.
"/usr/mail/dylan": 3 messages 3 new
>N 1 Justin  Mon May 11 11:31:19 5/44   "Car"
 N 2 Larisa  Tue May 12 9:14:05 28/537 "Homework"
 N 3 chris   Fri May 15 10:43:51 4/76  "Game"
?
```

If you do not have any messages waiting in the mailbox, a notice saying that there is no mail will be displayed. You will only enter the mail shell if messages are waiting. In the next example, since there are no messages waiting, a simple notice is displayed, and the user remains in the Unix shell.

```
$ mailx
Sorry, no mail
$
```

Message Lists and the Current Message Marker

`mailx` references messages either through a message list or through the current message marker. The greater-than sign, >, is the current message marker and is placed before a message that is considered the current message. The current message is referenced by default when no message number is included with a mail command. For example, in the header summaries above, if no message number is given in the command, then message 1 will be referenced since it is the current message. When a message is referenced in a command, it automatically becomes the current message and the current message marker moves to its header. If you were to display message 2, then message 2 would become the new current message.

You can also reference a message using a message list. A message list is a reference to a particular message or messages. A message list often consists of message numbers. A message number is the number displayed in a message's header summary. Specifying the message number in a `mailx` command will reference that message. Many mail commands can also operate on several messages. You reference several messages in a mail command using a message list consisting of several message numbers. You just list the message numbers of the messages you want. You can also specify a range of messages by entering the number of the first message in the range followed by a dash and then the message number of the last message in the range. Given the messages above, the number 2 will reference the second message. The numbers 1 and 3 will reference messages one and three. And the range 1–3 will reference messages one, two, and three.

There are ways other than message numbers with which you can reference messages in message lists. Special characters reference certain messages. The ^ references the first message. For example, `^-3` specifies the range of messages from the first message to the third message. The $ references the last message. `4-$` would reference messages from 4 to the last message. $ by itself just references the last message. The period, ., references the current message. And the asterisk, *, references all messages. For example, to display all messages you could use the command `p *`. You can also select a group of messages based on the addresses of senders, or the message's subject. An address by itself consititutes a message list that references all messages sent by the user with that address. A slash followed by a pattern references all messages whose subject field contains that pattern. For example, `/birthday` is a message list referencing all messages with the subject birthday. `justin` is a message list referencing all messages sent by `justin`.

You can also reference messages according to their status by entering a colon followed by a character representing the status of the messages you want. The characters are lowercase versions of the uppercase status codes used in the header summaries. For example, `n` represents new messages that are inidicated with a status code N in header summaries. `:n` is a message list that references all new messages. The command `p :n` would display all new messages. `:u` would reference all unread messages, those with a status code of U.

Displaying Messages

Several different methods are available for displaying messages. The simplest way is to type the number of the message and press **enter**. The message is displayed screen by screen. Press the **spacebar** or the **enter** key to continue on to the next screen. For example, if you enter the number 1 at the mail prompt, the first message is displayed.

To look at several messages in sequence, you enter their message numbers at the mail prompt. You can also reference and display messages according to their position with respect to the current message in the list of headers. To display the message before the current message, you use the – command. A number used with the – command references a message positioned that number of messages before the current message. For example, if message 8 were the current message, the -3 would reference message 5. You use the + command to reference messages after the current message in the header list. A number used with the + command references a message positioned that number of messages before the current message. The + command alone displays the next message after the current message. The n command also displays the next message.

With the p and t commands you can display a range of messages. In the message list for these commands, you can specify a set of messages to be referenced or a range of messages, as well as a single message. To specify a set of messages, you list their numbers one after the other, separated by a space. 2 5 will reference messages two and five. command p 2 5 will display message two and message 5. To specify a range you enter the first message number in the range, a dash, and then the last message number. 1-3 will reference the range of messages 1, 2, and 3. p 1-3 will display messages 1 through 3.

If you use the p or t commands without a message list, then the current message is displayed, >. A + used with these commands will display the previous message, and a – will display the next message. In the next example the p command is entered without a message number to print the current message, message 1. Then the second message is then displayed using the p command and the message number.

STATUS CODES

N	Newly received messages.
U	Previously unread messages.
R	Read messages in the current session.
P	Preserved messages, read in previous session and kept in incoming mailbox.
D	Deleted messages. Messages marked for deletion.
O	Old messages.
*	Messages that you have saved to another mailbox file.

DISPLAY MESSAGES

h	Redisplay the message headers.
z+ z-	If header list takes up more than one screen you can scroll header list forward and backward with the + and −.
t *msge-list*	Displays a message referenced by the message list. If no message list is used, then the current message is displayed.
p *msge-list*	Displays a message referenced by the message list. If no message list is used, then the current message is displayed.
n	Displays next message.
+	Displays next message.
−	Displays the previous message
top *message-list*	Displays the top few lines of a message referenced by the message list. If no message list is used, then the current message is displayed.
=	Displays the number of the current message

Table 3.IV. Mailx Commands for Displaying Messages

```
Mailx version 5.5. Type ? for help.
"/usr/mail/dylan": 3 messages 3 new
>N 1 Justin      Mon May 11 11:31:19 5/44   "Car"
 N 2 Larisa      Tue May 12 9:14:05 28/537 "Homework"
 N 3 chris       Fri May 15 10:43:51 4/76   "Game"

? p
From justin Mon May 11 11:31:19 PST 1998
To: dylan
Subject: Car
Status: R

Can I borrow your car tonight?

    Please

            Justin

? p 2
From larisa Tue May 12 9:14:05 PST 1998
To: dylan
Subject: Homework
Status: R

Thanks for the help with the homework

            Larisa
?
```

Shown here are several command examples of p using differently composed message lists. The special characters, ^, $, and *, are used to reference the first, last, and all messages. The : references special types of messages. You can also reference by addresses or subject.

```
p $          Display the last message
p *          Display all messages.
p ^-3        Display from the first to the third message
p .-$        Display from the current message to the last
             message
p n          Display the next message, not the current one.
p +2         Display second message down from the current
             message.
```

p /budget	Display messages with the pattern "budget" in their subject field.
p dylan	Display messages sent by the user with the address "dylan".
p :n	Display newly received messages.
p :u	Display previously unread messages.
p :r	Redisplay the messages you have already read.

You can display the header at any time with the h command. h stands for headers. In the next example, enter the h command to redisplay the list of message headers.

```
?h
>N 1 Justin Mon May 11 11:31:19 5/44    "Car"
 N 2 Larisa Tue May 12 9:14:05 28/537 "Homework"
 N 3 chris  Fri May 15 10:43:51 4/76   "Game"
?
```

If you have a great many messages, then the header list will likely take up more than one screen on your terminal. In this case the h command displays only the first screen of headers. To see the next screens you use the z+ command. z+ moves you forward to the next screen, and z- moves you backward to previous screen of headers. If you know the number of the particular message header you want, you can use the h command with that number to display the header. h15 will display the header for message 15, as well as the headers before and after it.

Deleting and Undeleting Messages

When you quit mailx, messages you have read are automatically saved. If, instead, you want a message erased, you can delete it using the delete command, d. To delete a particular message you use the d command with that message number. The command d3 deletes message 3. To delete several messages at once, you can list either a set or a range of message numbers. d 2-4 deletes messages 2, 3, and 4. The d command entered without a message number deletes the current message, >. In the next example the user deletes the third message.

```
Mailx version 5.5. Type ? for help.
"/usr/mail/dylan": 3 messages 3 new
>N 1 Justin      Mon May 11 11:31:19 5/44   "Car"
 N 2 Larisa      Tue May 12 9:14:05 28/537 "Homework"
 N 3 chris       Fri May 15 10:43:51 4/76   "Game"
?d 3

?h
>N 1 Justin      Mon May 11 11:31:19 5/44   "Car"
 N 2 Larisa      Tue May 12 9:14:05 28/537 "Homework"
?
```

If you change your mind and want a deleted message to be saved, you can undelete the message using the u command. The u command restores messages that have been deleted within a mail session. Keep in mind that the delete command does not immediately remove a message. It merely marks a message for deletion when you quit mailx. The u command will unmark a message for deletion. With the u command you can specify several messages or a range of messages. The command u3 restores message 3. u 2-4 restores messages 2, 3, and 4. Table 3.V summarizes the delete commands.

```
?h
>N 1 Justin      Mon May 11 11:31:19 5/44   "Car"
 N 2 Larisa      Tue May 12 9:14:05 28/537 "Homework"
?u 3

?h
>N 1 Justin      Mon May 11 11:31:19 5/44   "Car"
 N 2 Larisa      Tue May 12 9:14:05 28/537 "Homework"
 N 3 chris       Fri May 15 10:43:51 4/76   "Game"
?
```

Replying to Messages and Sending New Messages: R, r, m, and v

While working in the mail shell, you can compose and send your own messages. You can either reply to messages that you have just received or send entirely new messages. In replying to a message, mailx allows you automatically to make use of the header information in a received message. You need only specify the message that you are replying to and then type the text of your reply.

d *message-list*	Delete a message referenced by the indicated message list from your mailbox.
u *message-list*	Undelete a message referenced by the indicated message list that has been previously deleted.
q	Quit the `mailx` utility and saves any read messages in the mbox file.
x	Quit the `mailx` utility and does *not* erase any messages you deleted. This is equivalent to executing a u command on all deleted messages before quitting.
pr *message-list*	Preserve messages in your waiting mailbox even if you have already read them.

Table 3.V. Deleting and Restoring Messages

You use the R and r commands to reply to a message immediately from within the mail shell. The R command entered with a message number will generate a header for sending a message and then place the user into the input mode to type in the message. The header will consist of the address of the sender and the subject specified by the sender. The subject header will also have the added title Re:, to indicate a reply. Simply type in your reply and end with a **Ctrl-d** on a line of its own. The reply will then be sent to the sender.

```
Mailx version 5.5. Type ? for help.
"/usr/mail/dylan": 3 messages 3 new
>N 1 Justin     Mon May 11 11:31:19 5/44    "Car"
 N 2 Larisa     Tue May 12 9:14:05 28/537   "Homework"
 N 3 chris      Fri May 15 10:43:51 4/76    "Game"
? R 2
To: larisa
Subject: RE: Homework
  It was fun, anytime
^D
EOT
?
```

Many times you will receive a message that has been sent by the sender to several users including you. You can, if you wish, use the r command to send your reply not only to the sender, but also

to everybody the message was originally sent to. Be careful of the
r command. You may not want your reply sent to all the people
who received the message. If you want your reply sent to the
sender alone, you need to use the R command.

To compose and send a new message, use the m command. In the
next example the user sends a new message to aleina.

```
Mailx version 5.5. Type ? for help.
"/usr/mail/dylan": 3 messages 3 new
>N 1 Justin      Mon May 11 11:31:19 5/44   "Car"
 N 2 Larisa      Tue May 12 9:14:05 28/537  "Homework"
 N 3 chris       Fri May 15 10:43:51 4/76   "Game"

? m aleina
Subject: Car
Justin's car broke down again
Can he use yours?
^D
EOT
?
```

As with any mail message, you can use the tilde commands for
composing message replies and new messages. With the ~v tilde
command you can edit a message reply in an editor. Upon sending
the reply with a **Ctrl-d** you return to the mail shell prompt.

When composing a message, you can include the contents of one
of the messages that you have received. For example, in composing a reply to someone, you may want to include the text of the
message that the user sent you. You could also include the message
your received from one person in a reply to another, in effect
forwarding the message. With the ~m and ~f tilde commands, you
can read in the contents of a different message into the message
you are sending. The ~m and ~f tilde commands take as their
argument a message list, usually a message number. For example,
the tilde command ~m 2 reads in the contents of the second message into the new message you are currently composing. The ~m
and ~f commands differ in that the ~m command will indent each
line of the message it reads in, distinguishing it from the rest
of your message. The ~f command performs no indentation,
inserting the message as is.

You can also, if you wish, use the v command to edit directly a message that you received. For example, you might want to annotate a message with your own comments before you save it. Or you might want to add your comments directly to the message and then use ~m to use it in a reply or to send to someone else. To edit a specific message, you simply specify the message number after the v command. v 3 will edit the third message. Table 3.VI summarizes the send commands.

Quitting the Mail Shell

You use the q command to quit from the mailx utility, returning you to the login shell command line. When you quit, messages that you have read are saved in a file called **mbox** in your home directory. mailx will display a short notice telling you how many messages were saved in your **mbox** file. Your read messages will also be removed from your incoming mailbox. Should you want a message to remain in your incoming mailbox, use the pr command with the message number before you quit.

When you quit, unread messages remain in your incoming mailbox file. The next time you enter the mail shell, these messages are displayed in the message list with the letter U placed before them rather than an N. The U indicates that they are previously received messages that are as yet unread.

```
Mailx version 5.5.  Type ? for help.
"/usr/mail/dylan": 3 messages 3 new
 U 1 chris       Fri May 15 10:43:51 4/76 "Game"
 N 2 aleina      Fri May 15 11:30:05 2/10 "mycar"
?q
Saved 1 message in mbox
$
```

Messages that you have marked for deletion are not removed from your incoming mailbox until you quit. Read messages marked for deletion are not saved in the mbox file and deleted unread messages are removed from the incoming mailbox. Should you change your mind and decide that you do not want any of these messages

r	Send a reply to all persons who received a message.
R	Send a reply to the person who sent you a message.
m *address*	Send a message to someone while in the `mailx` utility.
v *message-list*	Edit a message with the `vi` editor.

Table 3.VI. Sending and Editing Messages

deleted, you can use the x command instead of the q command to quit. Think of the x command as a generalized undo for delete operations. It quits the mail shell without deleting any messages.

Saving and Accessing Messages in Mailbox Files: s *and* S

With the s command, you can save a message to a file of your choice, rather than to your mbox file. The s command includes the message header and message when it saves it. This has the effect of creating another mailbox file. Any file that contains message headers can be read by the mailx utility and is considered to be a mailbox file. You can use mailx to access the messages in such a file, just as you would the mbox file or newly received messages.

To save a message with the s command, you type s with the message number followed by the name of the file to which the message is to be saved. If the file does not exist, it will be created. If it already exists, it will be appended to the end of that file. In the next example, the command s2 family_msgs saves the second message to the **family_msgs** file. You can save several messages at a time by specifying a set or range of message numbers. s1-3 family_msgs saves messages 1, 2, and 3 to the file **family_msgs**.

```
Mailx version 5.5. Type ? for help.
"/usr/mail/dylan": 3 messages 3 new
>N 1 Justin    Mon May 11  11:31:19 5/44   "Car"
 N 2 Larisa    Tue May 12   9:14:05 28/537 "Homework"
 N 3 chris     Fri May 15  10:43:51 4/76   "Game"
? s 2 family_msgs
```

The s command gives you the flexiblity to save particular messages to specific files. This capability allows you to organize messages using different mailbox files. One mailbox file may contain
messages from a particular sender, another on a particular topic.
The name of the mailbox file can incorporate the classification of
the messages. For example, all messages from chris could be
saved in a file called **chris**.

You may find it helpful to organize messages by sender, setting up
a mailbox file for each sender. For this kind of organization, you
can use the S command instead of the lowercase s command. The
S command will automatically save a message to a mailbox file
that bears the name of the sender. The S command takes as its argument a message list, but no file name. The S command followed
by a message number will save that message to a file that has the
name of the message's sender. If the file does not exist, S will create it. In the next example, the user saves message 3 to a file named
after the message's sender, in this case chris.

```
Mailx version 5.5. Type ? for help.
"/usr/mail/dylan": 3 messages 3 new
>N 1 Justin     Mon May 11 11:31:19 5/44    "Car"
 N 2 Larisa     Tue May 12 9:14:05 28/537  "Homework"
 N 3 chris      Fri May 15 10:43:51 4/76   "Game"
? S 3
? q
$ ls
mbox chris
$
```

The s and S commands save both messages and their message headers to a file. The message headers in effect create a mailbox file that
you can read and manage using the mailx utility. The headers provide the mailx utility with all of the information it needs to access a
message. With the header information, mailx can perform any mail
operation such as referencing messages by a message number,
displaying a header list, or deleting messages. You can access a mailbox file by invoking the mailx utility with the -f option and the
mailbox file name. Also, while running mailx, you can switch to a
mailbox file by execting the folder command. In effect, you can
switch mailx from one mailbox file to another, checking mail you
have read, and then switch back to the mbox mailbox file for newly

received messages. For example, the command `mailx -f family
_msgs` accesses the mailbox file **family_msgs**. Each message in the
family_msgs mailbox file will then be displayed in a message list.
The mail commands such as d and p will work on these messages.

```
$ mailx -f family_msgs
Mailx version 5.5. Type ? for help.
"family_msgs": 1 message
 > N 1 Larisa        Tue May 12 9:14:05 28/537 "Homework"
?
```

`mailx` is designed to operate on any mailbox file that you specify.
By default, when you invoke `mailx`, you automatically begin to
operate on your incoming mailbox where the system places newly
received mail. You can, however, at any time switch to another
mailbox file and operate on the messages there. You switch to yet
another mailbox file and so on as you wish, or switch back to your
incoming mailbox. To switch to another mailbox file, you enter the
`folder` command followed by the name of the mailbox file. The
header summaries for this mailbox file will be displayed and you
can then operate on those messages. To switch back to your incoming mailbox, you use the `folder` command followed by the symbol %, which represents the name of your incoming mailbox. You
can also switch back and forth between two mailboxes using the #
symbol for the mailbox file name. # represents the previous mailbox file accessed. In the next example, the user begins `mailx` with
the incoming mailbox and then uses the folder command to switch
to the **family_msgs** mailbox file. The user then switches back to the
incoming mailbox with the `folder %` command.

```
$ mailx
Mailx version 5.5. Type ? for help.
"/usr/mail/dylan": 2 messages 2 new
>N 1 Justin      Mon May 11  11:31:19 5/44 "Car"
 N 2 chris       Fri May 15  10:43:51 4/76 "Game"
? folder family_msgs
Held 2 messages in /usr/mail/chris
"family_msgs": 1 message
 > N 1 Larisa    Tue May 12  9:14:05 28/537 "Homework"
? folder %
"/usr/mail/dylan": 2 messages 2 new
>N 1 Justin      Mon May 11  11:31:19 5/44 "Car"
 N 2 chris       Fri May 15  10:43:51 4/76 "Game"
```

When you quit from the mail shell, the messages that you have read
are saved with their headers in a file called **mbox**. If the **mbox** file already exists, then the new messages are appended onto the end. The
mbox file is a collection of all your previously read messages. You
may want to go back and access a previously read message saved in
mbox. Since the **mbox** file contains the message headers, it is a mailbox file that you can access with the `mailx` utility. You can access
the **mbox** file either by invoking `mailx` with a `-f` option followed
by the name **mbox**, `mailx -f mbox`, or by switching to **mbox** using
the `folder` command and the symbol `&`, which represents the
name of the file used to save your read messages, `folder &`. A list
of header summaries for all your previously read messages is displayed with the headers. `mailx` commands such as `p` and `d` can display or delete them. You can even send replies to messages using the
`R` command. In the next example the user invokes `mailx` to access
the `mbox` file in order to access previously read messages.

```
$ mailx -f mbox
Mailx version 5.5. Type ? for help.
"/home/dylan/mbox": 2 messages
> 1 Justin     Mon May 11    11:31:19 5/44  "Car"
  2 chris      Fri May 15    10:43:51 4/76  "Game"
?
```

Saving Message Text in Files: Sending and Receiving Files

You use the `w` command to save a message without its mail header.
The `w` command has the same syntax as that of the `s` command.
(Table 3.VII summarizes the save commands.) For example,
`w 1 newbudget` writes message 1 without its header to the file
newbudget. The file **newbudget** is only a standard text file. It is
not a mailbox file and cannot be accessed by the mail utility.

```
Mailx version 5.5. Type ? for help.
"/usr/mail/dylan": 3 messages 3 new
>N 1 Justin     Mon May 11  11:31:19 5/44   "Car"
 N 2 Larisa     Tue May 12   9:14:05 28/537 "Homework"
 N 3 chris      Fri May 15  10:43:51 4/76   "Game"
? w 3 newgame
```

It is possible to use the `w` command to send and receive large text
files instead of just messages. By invoking `mailx` with a redirection

SAVING MESSAGES

s *message-list filename*	Save a message referenced by the message list in a file, including the header of the message.
S *message-list*	Save a message referenced by the message list in a file named for the sender of the message.
w *message-list filename*	Save a message referenced by the message list in a file without the header. Only the text of the message is saved.
c *message-list filename*	Copy a message referenced by the message list to a file without marking it as saved.
folder *mailbox-filename*	Switch to another mailbox file.
%	Represents name of incoming mailbox file.
	folder % Switch to incoming mailbox file.
#	Represents name of previously accessed mailbox file.
	folder # Switch to previous mailbox file.
&	Represents name of mailbox file used to automatically save your read messages, usually called mbox.
	folder & Switch to **mbox** file.

GENERAL COMMANDS

?	Display a list of all the mail commands.
! *command*	Execute a user shell command from within the mail shell.
alias *name address-list*	Create an alias for a list of addresses.
	alias myclass chris aleina larisa
	$ mailx myclass

Table 3.VII. Saving and General Commands

operation from the file you want to send, you can send a text file to any user you want. You can use the w command to receive and save a text file sent to you by another user.

To send a text file through the `mailx` utility, you need to make use of redirection. The `mailx` utility's input mode accepts standard input. Standard input, in turn, can be redirected to receive input from a text file. In the next example the user sends file **complist** to `chris`.

        $ **mailx chris < complist**

When you receive the text file, a mail header is attached to it. To save the file without the mail header, you need to use the w command. If the **complist** file was received as message 1, then the command w1 `complist` saves the message as a text file without the mail header. In effect, a user has sent you a document instead of just a message.

```
$ mailx
Mailx version 5.5. Type ? for help.
"/usr/mail/chris": 1 messages 1 new
>N 1 dylan      Tue Feb 11 10:14:32 5/44
? w 1 complist
```

Sending files through `mailx` has one major limitation. You can only send character files, not binary files. The `mailx` utility will corrupt a binary file in the transmission process as well as insert a header. However you can first encode a binary file using `uuencode` as described in Chapter 2. When received it can be decoded back to a binary file using `uudecode`. You can also use the file transfer utility `ftp` to send binary files. ftp is discussed in Chapter 12. ftp is far more reliable than mail for transferring very large files as well as binary files.

`mailx` **Aliases, Options, and the Mail Shell Initialization File: .mailrc**

`mailx` has its own initialization file called **.mailrc**, which you can use to customize mailx, adding features and defining aliases. Each time you invoke `mailx` either for sending or receiving messages, mail commands in the **.mailrc** file are read and executed. The **.mailrc** file is commonly used to set options that add different mail features such as changing the prompt or saving copies of sent messages. It also usually holds mail alias definitions, particularly those used to broadcast a message to several users at once. Mail aliases are very helpful for broadcasting a message to users that are part of a group such as a class or project.

`mailx` *Aliases*

In some situations, you may need to send the same message to the members of a particular group. In this respect, you are broadcasting a message to specific group of users. For example, suppose you are teacher for a class where each student has her or his own Unix account. You may need to send the same message to every student in the class, such as an updated reading list. The students, in effect, define a group of users to which you need to broadcast the same message. You could send the same message to each student by typing each student's email address when you compose the message. Alternatively, you can take advantage of the fact that in `mailx` you can define an alias for a set of addresses. You could define an alias for all of the addresses for the students in your class. Then, instead of listing all addresses each time you compose a message you intend to broadcast to a group of users, you merely type the alias name. The `mailx` utility will automatically replace the alias name with its associated list of addresses, sending the message to all those users.

You define a mail alias using the `alias` command. You enter the `alias` command followed by the alias name you have chosen and then the list of addresses it represents. `mailx` aliases have to be defined within the mail shell, not in a user shell such as the BASH shell. This means that you cannot define a mail alias in a shell initialization file like **.profile** or **.bashrc.** Each time you leave and then reenter the mail shell you need to redefine the alias. You can have this done automatically by placing the alias definition in the mail shell initialization file, the **.mailrc** file. The **.mailrc** file is a simple text file that you can edit using a text editor like `vi` or `Emacs`, just as you would edit a shell initialization file like **.profile**. Within the **.mailrc** file, enter the `alias` command, followed by the alias name and the list of

addresses. The alias command, name, and list of addresses all have
to be on the same line. If you have a very long list of addresses be
sure keep them on that same line (i.e., do not press **enter**). In the next
example, the alias `myclass` is defined in the **.mailrc** file.

`.mailrc`

```
alias myclass  justin chris dylan aleina larisa marisa leslie
```

Whenever you invoke the `mailx` utility, the **.mailrc** file is automatically read and any alias comamnds in it are executed, defining
those alias names. Keep in mind that the `mailx` command you use
when sending a message reads and executes the **.mailrc** file. This
means that you can use a mail alias name on the command line
when you use `mailx` to send a message. The alias name replaces
the list of addresses you would have ordinarily have had to enter
on the command line. Of course when you are running the `mailx`
interface, say, when you are listing received messages, you can also
use mail aliases for sending messages. The **.mailrc** file would have
already been read and executed, defining the alias. In the following `mailx` command, the `myclass` alias is used in place of the addresses. The contents of the file **homework** is sent to all the users
whose addresses are aliased by `myclass`.

$ **mailx myclass < homework**

`mailx` *Options*

`mailx` has options that you can use to set different mail features.
These also you can place in the **.mailrc** file, automaically defining
them whenever you use mailx. Table 3.VIII lists several of the more
common `mailx` options. You use the set command to set a `mailx`
option. The `set` command is followed by the option name. If the option requires a value, you add an equal sign and a string representing
that value. For example, suppose that you want to change the mail
prompt to be an asterisk instead of a question mark. The `prompt`
option is used to change the prompt and it is assigned the prompt
symbol you want to use. The command `set prompt="*"` will set
the `mailx` prompt to an asterisk. To have the prompt set each time
you use `mailx`, place the set prompt command in the **.mailrc** file.

The `sign` option is a popular mail option. With the `sign` option you can specify a signature that you can insert into the end of a message when you finish composing it. A signature usually consists of your name, and may include other information such as your phone number or network address. The next example sets the signature to "Justin and Chris."

set sign="Justin and Chris"

The ~a tilde command will insert whatever string you assign to the `sign` option as your signature. When finished composing a message, use the ~a tilde command to insert your signature.

```
$ mailx chris
Subject: Breakfast
Lets have some chocolate chip pancakes
OK?
~a
Justin Petersen
^D
EOT
$
```

Another common mail option is the `record` option. With this option you can have any messages that you compose and send automatically saved, making copies of all your sent messages. The `record` option requires that you specify a mailbox file in which to save the copies of your sent messages. In the next example, the user sets the `record` option and has sent messages saved in a file called `sentbox`. As part of the mailbox file name, you can specify an absoulte path, indicating a specify directory. If no absolute path name is specified, then the file is placed in your home directory.

set record="sentbox"

Organizing Your Mailbox Files: `folder,` MBOX*, and* `outfolder`

Keeping track of mailbox files can be confusing. Unless you specify a directory, mailbox files that you create with the s command for your saved messages are placed in your current working directory, whatever that may be at the time you invoke `mailx`. Mailbox files created in this way can end up scattered in different directories. Your **mbox** file used for received messages and mailbox files created with the `S` command, are placed in your home directory. The directory used for sent messages is whatever you specified in the record option. Instead of your home directory or working directory, you can use the `folder`, `MBOX`, and `outfolder` options to place your mailbox files for incoming, saved, and sent messages all in one specified directory.

To the `folder` option you assign the path name of the directory in which you want your mailbox files placed. Any mailbox files that you create using the `S` command will be placed in the directory assigned to `folder`. This directory is commonly referred to as the folder directory. This directory can be referenced in file names with the + symbol. Preceding a mailbox file name with a + effectively references the mailbox file in the `folder` option specified directory. For example, when using the s command, you can precede a mailbox file name you want to use with the + symbol to save it to the folder directory. When using the `folder` command to switch to another mailbox file, you can precede the file name with a + symbol so that `mailx` will search for the file in the folder directory.

In the next example, the user has created a directory called **/home/dylan/mail** and has assigned this path name to the variable folder. Now any mailbox files that the user creates using the `S` command are placed in that directory.

> **`set folder="/home/dylan/mail"`**

In the following example, the user saves message 2 to a mailbox file called **family_msgs**. The file name is preceded by a + symbol which references the folder directory. Given the setting of the folder option in the previous example, the file name `+family_msgs` will save the **family_msgs** mailbox file to the directory `/home/dylan/mail`, along with any other mailbox files. Then the user switches to another mailbox file in the folder directory, making sure to pecede the mailbox filename with a + symbol so that `mailx` will search for it in the folder diretory, and not the current working directory.

```
Mailx version 5.5. Type ? for help.
"/usr/mail/dylan": 3 messages 3 new
>N 1 Justin      Mon May 11 11:31:19 5/44 "Car"
 N 2 Larisa      Tue May 12 9:14:05 28/537 "Homework"
 N 3 chris       Fri May 15 10:43:51 4/76 "Game"
? s 2 +family_msgs
"/usr/mail/justin/mail/family_msgs" [Appended]
? folder +family_msgs
Held 2 messages in /usr/mail/chris
"+family_msgs": 1 message 1 new
> 1 Larisa     Tue May 12 9:14:05 28/537 "Homework"
```

The MBOX option lets you specify a directory and file name for your **mbox** file. By default your **mbox** file is placed in your home directory. With the MBOX option you can have it placed in another directory, such as the same one you specified in your folder option. A simple way assign the folder direcory to the MBOX option is to use the + sign to represent the folder directory. Simply precede the **mbox** file name with the + sign: +mbox, as shown here.

set MBOX=+mbox

To have the mailbox file that you use for saving sent messages placed in the the folder directory, you set the `outfolder` option. You need to have already set the record option, specifying a file for sent messages.

set outfolder

You could also simply assign to the record option, the file name for your outgoing messages preceded by a + symbol.

set record=+sentbox

With these three options, all your mailbox files can be kept in one designated directory. All option settings should be placed in your **.mailrc** file. A sample **.mailrc** file follows, incorporating mail aliases and option settings.

.mailrc

```
alias myclass  justin chris dylan aleina larisa marisa leslie
set sign="Dylan Petersen"
set folder="/home/dylan/mail"
set MBOX=+mbox
set record=outbox
set outfolder
set prompt="*"
```

Table 3.VIII. mailx Options

append	Place messages saved in your mailbox at the end, rather than the beginning (disabled by default).
asksub	Prompt for subject.
	`set asksub`
askcc	Prompt for carbon copy addresses.
	`set askcc`
autoprint	When deleting messages, shows the next message after the last one deleted (disabled by default).
cmd=*cmd*	Specify default command to use with pip operation should no command be given (disabled by default).
crt=n	For messages that are *n* or more lines, displays them using your PAGER program (disabled by default).
dbug	Debug mode with detailed descriptions of actions taken, but there is no actual delivery of messages (disabled by default).
dot	Allows you to end a message by entering a dot on a line by itself, instead of **Ctrl-d** (disabled by default).
escape=*c*	Specify c as the escape character in the input mode.
flipr	Switch the R and r commands so the R sends a reply to senders of several specified messages and r sends a response to all other recipients of a message you received (disabled by default).
folder=*directory*	Save any mailbox files created by the s or S command to the directory assigned to it.
	`set folder=$HOME/mail`
header	Show header sumary when starting up (default).
hold	Keep read messages in your incomming mailbox, instead of **mbox** (disabled by default).

`ignore`	Ignore interrupts when composing messages (disabled by default).
`ignoreeof`	Disables the use of **Ctrl-d** to end input when composing messages. Should have dot enabled so you can end messages with just a . on a line by itself, or use ~. to end messages (disabled by default).
`indentprefix=`*string*	Specify string (characters) to be placed at the beginning of each line of a copied message included within a response you are composing (disabled is tab).
`keep`	Keep mailbox files when they become empty (disabled by default).
`keepsave`	When you save a message to a particular mailbox file, also save a copy to your standard mailbox file, usually **mbox** (disabled by default).
`metoo`	Allows you to send a copy of a message to yourself that you are also sending to others. By default your name would automatically be deleted from a list of addresses (disabled by default).

`outfolder`	Place record file in folder directory. In the following example, `outbox` will be a file in the directory defined by `folder`.
	
	`        set record=outbox`
	
	`        set outfolder`

`page`	When piping several messages through a pipe command, this option inserts a formfeed after each so that each message will start on its own screen (disabled by default).
`prompt=`*string*	Redefine `mailx` prompt `        set prompt="&"`
`record=`*filename*	Automatically saves a copy of any message that you create and send. Messages are saved in a file specified when you set the record option. `        set record=$HOME/outbox`
`save`	Save incomplete or interrupted messages in your dead letter file (disabled by default).
`screen=`*n*	Set the number of lines of the header displayed on your screen (default is 5).
`sendwait`	Wait for background mailer to finish processing before resuming with `mailx`.
`showto`	For messages shown in the header summary for which you are the sender, shows the recipient's name instead of yours (disabled by default). *(continued)*

Table 3.VIII. mailx Options *(continued)*

---

sign=*string*	Define string to be inserted by the ~a tilde command into a message that you are inputting (empty by default).
	`set sign="Justin and Dylan"`
Sign=*string*	Define string to be inserted by the ~A tilde command into a message that you are inputting (empty by default).
toplines=*n*	Specifies how many lines the top command will show of the header summary (default is 5).
quit	Do not show identification line (disabled by default)

MAILX CONFIGURATION VARIABLES

MBOX=*filename*	Holds the name of the **mbox** file to which read messages are automatically saved. By default, **mbox** is placed in your home directory. To put it in the folder directory, place a + sign before the mbox name.
	`set MBOX=+mbox`
DEAD=*filename*	Specifies the dead letter file where incomplete and interrupted messages are placed.
LISTER=*cmd*	Specify the command to use to list the contents of the folder directory (default is ls).
EDITOR=*cmd*	Specify the editor to use when invoked with the ~e command (default is Ed, a line editor).
VISUAL=*cmd*	Specify the editor to use when invoked with the ~v command (default is Vi).
PAGER=*cmd*	Specify the pager program to use (default is pg or more).
sendmail=*cmd*	Specify the the mail transport agent for your mailer (default is usually sendmail or rmail, include full path names).

Elm Mailer

Elm is one of the more popular mailers used on Unix systems. It is a public domain mail utility developed by Dave Taylor. Elm performs much like `mailx` but has a screen-oriented user-friendly interface that makes mail tasks easy to execute. Messages are displayed one screen at a time, and you can move back and forth through the message screen by screen. Elm use single letter commands much like those used in the Vi editor or the pg display utility. Table 4.I lists the basic Elm commands.

elm *login-name*	Send a message using Elm.
	s Send the message.
	e Edit the message.
	f Forget the message; quit and do not send.
	h Edit the header of the message.
elm	Invoke the Elm utility.
?	Help. Press key used for a command to display information about that command.
	? Display a list of all commands.
	. Return to Elm index.
q	Quit the Elm utility with prompts for saving read and unread messages, and deleting messages marked for deletion.
Q	Quit the Elm utility with no prompts.
x and **Ctrl-q**	Quit the Elm utility leaving your mail as you found it. No deletions are made or messages saved. Messages remain as you found them.

Table 4.I. Basic Elm Commands

Sending Mail Using Elm

To send a message using Elm, you use the elm command. You can compose the message within Elm or send a text file that you have already created. If you compose a message, Elm will invoke a standard editor such as Vi or Emacs for you to use. You will have all use of capabilites of that editor in composing your message. To send a message, type in the command elm followed by the address of the person to whom you are sending the message. Upon pressing the **enter** key, Elm will display the name of the person to whom you are sending the message, and then prompts you for the subject. Elm attempts to display the actual name of the person, not the address. This is usually obtained from on-line information much in the same way that the finger command can obtain the name of a user.

```
$ elm justin
```

Instead or entering the elm command with the user's name, you can enter the elm command by itself. This will start the Elm mailer and display a menu with several options. One will be the m option for mailing a message. You then press them key and you will be prompted for the user to whom you want to send the message.

```
You can use any of the following commands by pressing the
first character;
d)elete or u)ndelete mail, m)ail a message, r)eply or
f)orward mail, q)uit
To read a message, press <return>. j = move down,
k = move up, ? = help
Command: m
```

Elm prompts you to enter a subject at the the subject prompt, and then prompts you to enter a carbon copy list. This list would include the addresses of other users you want to copy on the message. If you do not want any copies sent out, you can simpley press **enter**. At this point, you are placed in the standard editor, usually Vi or Emacs. You then use the editor to compose your message. If you are using Vi, recall that you have to first enter the input mode with either the command a or i before you can enter text. You press the **escape** key to return to the Vi command mode. When finished composing your message, you save and exit Vi with the ZZ command.

```
                    Send only mode [ELM]
           Send the message to: Justin Saturn
           Subject of message: Vacation
           Copies to:


           Invoking editor...
```

After composing the message, Elm then displays a message menu listing different commands to send the message, quit without sending, edit the message again, or edit its headers. Each option is executed with a single letter command. The commands are displayed with a following parenthesis. Simply press the key to execute the command. There is no command line in which you enter the letter and press **enter**. Merely press the desired key. For example, to send a message, press the 's' key; to edit a message, press the 'e' key.

```
Please choose one of the following options by
parenthesized letter:
e)dit message, edit h)eaders, s)end it, or f)orget it
```

Figure 4.1 displays the different steps you take to send an Elm message and shows how the screen changes at each step. The user sends a message to another user whose address is robert. The subject of the message is 'Birthday'. The user then uses Vi editing commands to enter the message, and then, at the Elm menu, presses s to send the message.

Should you want to edit the header of your message, you can press the h command. Upon pressing the h key, a message header edit screen is displayed listing a prompt for each header field. To edit or add values to a header field, enter the first character of the header prompt. At the bottom of the screen you will be prompted with the name of the field and you can then enter a new value. Upon pressing the **enter** key, the new value is displayed in the

```
              Message Header Edit Screen
   T)o: justin (Justin Saturn)
   C)c:
   B)cc:
   S)ubject: Vacation
   R)eply-to:
   A)ction:                  E)xpires:
   P)riority:                Precede(n)ce:
   I)n-reply-to:
Choose header, u)ser defined header,
d)omainize, !)shell, or <return>.
Choice: s
Enter value for the header.
Subject: Trip
```

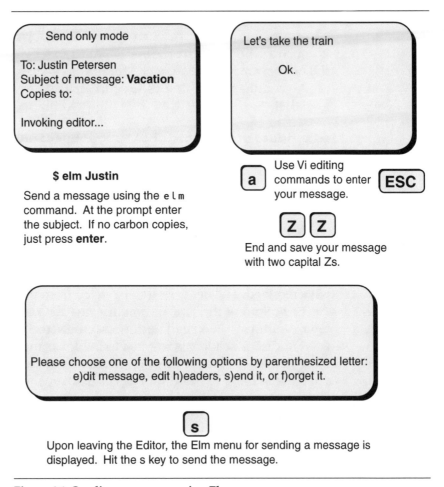

Figure 4.1. Sending a message using Elm.

header field. For example, to change the subject press the s key and you will be prompted to enter a new subject. After entering the new subject and pressing return, the new value for the subject field is displayed in the header. You can then edit another header field.

To leave the message header edit screen, you just press **enter**, instead of the first character of a header prompt. This places you back at the message menu. The next example show a sample of the Menu Header Edit Screen. In this case, the user presses the s key to change the subject field, and then is prompted to enter a new subject.

When you enter elm on the command line you can also add the
-s option with which you can specify the subject. This is helpful
if you are sending a text file and want to specify a subject for it. In
the next example, the subject "Tonight's celebration" is specified
on the command line and redirection is used to send the text file
guestlist.

```
$ elm justin -s "Tonight\'s celbration" <guestlist
```

Receiving Mail Using Elm

To receive mail using Elm, you need to invoke the Elm utility. You
invoke Elm by entering elm by itself on the command line. The Elm
utility then displays a list of message headers for messages you
have received. The headers are displayed from the top of the screen.
At the bottom of the screen is an information menu listing the different commands you can perform on the screen of message headers. This list of headers is referred to in Elm as the *index*. If you have
more than one screen of message headers, you can move to the next
screen with the + key, and move back a screen with the – key.

The Elm message headers have much the same format as the mailx
headers. An Elm header displays the status, message number, the
date, the name of the sender, the number of lines in the message, and
the subject. As in mailx, the message status is represented by a letter code. An N indicates a newly received message, and O indicates
an old message, one that is still unread. The message number can be
used to reference the message in Elm commands. An example of an
Elm message header is shown next. All the messages are newly received. The first message is from Justin Saturn and was sent on May
11. It contains 5 lines and its subject is "Car." Notice that the full
name of the sender is displayed, not simply the address.

The current header is either preceded by an arrow, ->, or highlighted by the background. To perform an operation on a message, you need to make that message's header the current header.
You can do this using message references or movement commands. An easy way to make a particular message the current
header is to enter its message number and press **enter**. If you type

```
Mailbox is '/usr/spool/mail/dylan' with 3 messages [ELM]
    ->N 1 Justin Saturn      May 11 (5)   "Car"
      N 2 Larisa Petersen    May 12 (28)  "Homework"
      N 3 Chris Neil         May 15 (4)   "Game"



You can use any of the following commands by pressing
the first character;
d)elete or u)ndelete mail, m)ail a message, r)eply or
f)orward mail, q)uit

To read a message, press <return>. j = move down,
k = move up, ? = help
Command:
```

a 3 and then **enter**, then the third header becomes the current message header. You can also make a header the current header by moving to it on the screen using the movement commands. The movement commands j and k move from one header to another (Figure 4.2). j moves up to the previous header, and k moves down to the next header. You can also use the up and down arrow commands. The arrow or highlight indicating the current header will move as you press the j or k commands, moving to the next or previous message header. If the first header is the current header, then pressing the j key twice will make the 3rd header the current header.

To display the current message, you simply press the **enter** key. To display a specific message, either move to that message with the k or j keys, or enter the message number and then press the **enter** key. A new screen will appear in which the message is displayed. If the message is larger than a screen, you can move to through the message screen by screen using the same commands as those found in the pg or more utilities. Pressing the **spacebar** moves you to the next screen and pressing b move you back a screen. You can even search for particular patterns in the message.

Once you have examined your message, you can use the i command to return to the header screen. Simply press the i key. The i stands for index, which is the term Elm uses to refer to the list of headers.

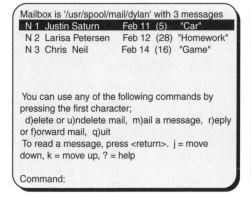

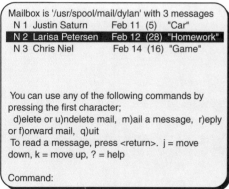

On many systems, the current message is
indicated by a highlighted header.

 or

The user hits j to to move down to the next
header, making it the current message and
highlighting it. You can move up and down
using the k and j keys.

Figure 4.2. Moving from one header to the next using the j **or** k **keys.**

You can print messages using the p command. Press the p key to
print the message for the current message header, or press a message number followed by the p key to print a particular message.

If you want to perform an operation on several messages at once,
you can first tag them using the t command and then the next
command will operate on all of them. To tag a message, you
move to that message header and press the t key. A + sign will
appear before that message header. After tagging the messages
you want to operate on, you then enter an Elm command. That

```
Message 1/3 From Justin Saturn      May 11, 98 11:31:19 am

Subject: Car
To: dylan (Dylan Petersen)
Date: Mon, 11 May 1998 11:31:19 (PDT)
   Can I borrow your car tonight?
     Please
           Justin
     Command ('i' to return to index):
```

command is performed on all the tagged messages. Suppose you want to print several messages. You could tag the headers for those messages using the t command, and then press the p key to print them. In the next example, the user has tagged the first two messages. If the user then presses the p key, messages 1 and 2 will both be printed.

```
+N 1 Justin Saturn     May 11 (5)   "Car"
+N 2 Larisa Petersen   May 12 (28)  "Homework"
 N 3 Chris Neil        May 15 (4)   "Game"
```

Elm also allows you select a current header by using pattern searches. There are several Elm commands that search different parts of a message for a specified pattern. The / command searches the address and subject fields of a header for a particular pattern. A double slash command, //, searches the text of a message for a pattern. If you enter a / command, you are then prompted to enter a pattern. Upon pressing **enter**, Elm searches address and subject fields in each message for that pattern. It stops at the first occurrence it finds and makes that header the current header. For example, if you searched for a header that has the pattern "work" you would locate and make message 2 the current header. A // command will search the text of your messages for a pattern. You enter in a // command and then Elm prompts you to enter in a pattern. Then it searches the text of all your messages and makes the header of the first message with that pattern in its text, the current header. For example, if the user enters in a // and the pattern 'borrow', then Elm will match on the pattern 'borrow' in the text of the first message, making that the current header.

```
->N 1 Justin Saturn     May 11 (5)   "Car"
  N 2 Larisa Petersen   May 12 (28)  "Homework"
  N 3 Chris Neil        May 15 (4)   "Game"
```

Other search commands perform specific operations such as the **Ctrl-t** command that tags headers that have a certain pattern, or the **Ctrl-d** command that deletes headers with a pattern. You can use the **Ctrl-t** command to tag easily all messages from a certain user or messages that deal with a certain topic. You could then perform an operation on those messages such as printing them. For example, to print all messages that deal with the subject 'Game,'

+	Display next index screen if headers take up more than one screen.
−	Display previous index screen if headers take up more than one screen.
j	Move down to the next message header, making it the current message.
k	Move up to the previous message header, making it the current message.
msge -number **enter**	Make the header whose message number is *msge-number* the current message.
/*pattern*	Search for the pattern in the subject or address headers, making the first header with a match the current message.
/ /*pattern*	Search for the pattern in the text of messages, making the first message with a match the current message.
t	Tag the current message. A + sign appears before the message. You can tag several messages and then perform an operation on them all at once.
Ctrl-t	Search address and subject headers for a pattern and tag all messages that match.

Table 4.II. Selecting Messages in Elm

you first enter a **Ctrl-t** and the pattern 'Game' to tag all messages that deal with birthdays, and then press the p command to print those messages. Table 4.II summarizes Elm's commands for selecting messages.

Quitting the Elm Utility

You can quit the Elm utility by pressing the q key. Before you leave Elm, you will be asked whether or not you wish to save your read messages in your received mailbox file. The received mailbox file holds read messages. The name of the file is contained in the Elm variable called `received`.

You will also be asked if you want to keep unread messages in your incoming mailbox so that you can read them later. If not, they will be deleted. Also, if you have deleted any messages during this session, you will be asked to confirm the delete. In the next example, the user confirms deleted messages, saves read messages in the received mailbox, and keeps unread messages for later access.

```
Delete message? (y/n) n
Move read messages to "received" folder? (y/n) y
Keep unread messages in incoming mailbox? (y/n) y
Keeping 2 messages and storing 1
```

There are several other commands that you can use to quit Elm. A Q command will quit without any prompts for received and unread messages. Preset defaults will be used to determine whether messages are to be saved or not. The x and **Ctrl-q** commands will quit the Elm utility, leaving the incoming mailbox as you found it. Any deletions, read or unread messages, will be ignored.

Deleting and Undeleting Messages: d and u

To delete messages, you first mark them for deletion. Then, when you quit Elm, the messages are removed. This means that you can undelete a message anytime before you quit, no longer marking it for deletion. You use the d key to mark a message for deletion. The d key by itself marks the message of the current header. The status field of that message will change to a D. When you exit the Elm utility it will be deleted. To delete another message, you first select its header, making it the current header, and then press the d key. For example, to delete message 4, press 4 and then d. If you want to delete several messages as a group, you can first tag them with the t command and then press the d key. In the next example, the user has deleted the second message. Its status is now marked with a D.

```
   N 1 Justin Saturn   May 11 (5)   "Car"
->D 2 Larisa Petersen May 12 (28)  "Homework"
   N 3 Chris Neil      May 15 (4)   "Game"
```

You can also delete groups of messages selected according to their subjects or addresses. The **Ctrl-d** command lets you mark messages for deletion that contain a specified pattern in their address or subject fields. You can use this command to select and delete messages from a certain user or messages that deal with a specific topic. In the next example, the user decides to delete all messages from Aleina. The user presses a **Ctrl-d** and is prompted for a pattern, in this case "Aleina." The fourth message is matched in its address field and then marked for deletion.

```
    N 1 Justin Saturn    May 11 (5)   "Car"
    D 2 Larisa Petersen May 12 (28)  "Homework"
    N 3 Chris Neil       May 15 (4)   "Game"
 ->D 4 Aleina Petersen May 16 (32)  "Party"
```

If, before you quit, you change your mind and decide not to delete a message you have already marked for deletion, you can unmark it with the u command. First select or reference the message header and then press the u key. The status field of the message will change from D to U, indicating an undelete. Whereas the u key undeletes the current message or tagged messages, the **Ctrl-u** command will undelete any messages with a certain pattern in their address or subject fields. **Ctrl-u** works the same way as **Ctrl-d** does.

Replying to Messages

You can compose and send a reply to any message whose header is displayed. The header information is used to determine the address of the sender and the subject. You use the r command to compose and send a reply. To reply to a particular message you first make its header the current header, or enter its message number, and then press the r key. Upon pressing r, Elm first asks if you want to include a copy of the message in your reply. Elm then opens up a screen with the sender's name and subject displayed at the top. The cursor is positioned at the subject so that you can modify it if you wish. Press **enter** to continue. You are then prompted for any carbon copies that you want to send. Upon pressing **enter**, you then enter a standard editor such as Vi or Emacs where you enter the text of your reply. When you save your message, the menu for sending messages is displayed. You then press the s key to send the message.

Sending Messages from within Elm

You not only can receive messages in Elm, you can also compose and send new ones. To compose and send a new message, use the m command. You are prompted for the address of the user and the subject of the message. After entering the subject you are asked if you want to send any carbon copies. If not, press **enter**. You are then placed in an editor where you compose your message. When you save the message, the menu for sending messages is displayed. Press the s key to send the message.

Saving messages

Elm automatically saves your read and sent messages into two mailbox files. The mailbox files are referenced in the Elm variables received for read messages and sent for sent messages. The received mailbox file operates like the mbox file in mailx. Messages that have been read are automatically saved in this file when you exit Elm. The sent file usually holds messages that have been sent.

You can also save messages to a particular mailbox file. A mailbox file is a file of messages that include header information and can be read using a Unix mailer like Elm or mailx. To save a message to a mailbox file, use the s command. Select the header, or enter the message number, and then press the s key. At the bottom of the screen, Elm displays a Save prompt with a default mailbox file name. The default name is the name of the sender of the message. Elm assumes that you may want to organize the messages that you save into different mailbox files according to the person who sent them. To save a message in the mailbox file for the sender displayed at the save prompt, just press **enter**. You can, however, specify a particular mailbox file of your own choosing. At the save prompt, enter an = sign followed immediately by the name of the mailbox file. You can use a mailbox file you have already set up or enter a new name, creating a new mailbox file. For example, if you want to save your message in the file "birthdays," you would enter =birthdays. If you want to save several messages to the same mailbox file, first tag the message headers and then press the s key. You can also save a message to the `received` mailbox file by entering a > at the save prompt. A <will save the message in the `sent` mailbox. These Elm operations are summarized in Table 4.III.

Reading Mailbox Files with Elm

By default, Elm reads your system-maintained mailbox file for your incoming messages. You can, if you wish, switch over to another mailbox and display its messages, instead of the one with your incoming messages. Elm refers to mailbox files as folders. You change to another mailbox file using the change folder command, the c key, which displays a "Change folder" prompt. To select a folder (mailbox file), press the c key and a prompt appears for the name of the folder you want. Initially, the prompt will display the name of the folder used to hold received messages from the sender in the current message header. You can specify your own folder by entering the name of the file preceded by a = sign. =`birthdays` will specify the `birthdays` mailbox file (folder). You can change back to the incoming mailbox folder by entering a !. > will change to the received files folder, and < to the sent files folder.

In the next example, the current header is a message sent by the user called `chris`. When the user presses the c command, the Change folder notice is displayed at the Command prompt, and, as a default, the name of the user who sent the current message is displayed at the folder prompt. In this case the user name is `chris`.

```
Command: Change folder
Change to which folder: =chris
```

The user then enters in the folder name =newgames at the folder prompt, overwriting =chris.

```
Command: Change folder
Change to which folder: =newgames
```

OPERATIONS ON MESSAGES

enter	Display the current message.
	i Return to headers (index).
p	Print the current message.
d	Delete the current message. The header is marked with a D and deleted when you exit Elm.
Ctrl-d	Search address and subject headers for a pattern and delete all messages that match.
u	Undelete the current message.
Ctrl-u	Search address and subject headers for a pattern and undelete all messages that match.
r	Reply to the current message. The address and subject are taken from the current message's header. You then compose and send your reply as with any other message.
s	Save the current message or tagged messages in a mailbox file. By default, the message is saved to a mailbox file using the address of the user who sent the message. You can specify your own mailbox file by entering the name of the file preceded by an = sign.

=mailbox-filename

You can also save the message to a received or sent mailbox files using the following commands.

>   Save message to received mailbox file.

<   Save message to sent mailbox file.

ELM OPERATIONS

m	Send a message from within the Elm utility. You compose and send a message.
c	Use Elm to operate on a specific mailbox file. The command switches from incoming mail to any other mailbox file with messages.
a	Manage Elm aliases. Upon pressing the a command, the alias menu is displayed with the following options.

a   Create an alias using the name and address of the current message.

m   Create an alias using a name and address that you enter.

d   Delete an alias.

l   List aliases.

p   Display the name and address of a particular aliases.

s   Display any system aliases.

r   Return to Elm main menu.

Table 4.III. Elm Operations

Once you have changed to the other folder, the headers for all the messages in this mailbox file will then be displayed and you can perform Elm operations on those messages. You can display the messages, delete them from the file, or send replies. The folder's name will be displayed at the top to the screen. In Figure 4.3, the user changes to the =newgames folder.

Elm Aliases: Alias Menu and aliases.text

In Elm you can create alias names for a group of mail addresses. You can then use that alias in place of the addresses to send messages to those users. You can create an alias using either the Elm alias menu, or by entering alias definitions into a special Elm initialization file called **aliases.text** located in the **.elm** directory in your home directory. All Elm aliases are defined in the aliases.text file. You can enter them by editing this file with a text editor, or use the Elm alias menu to add them to it.

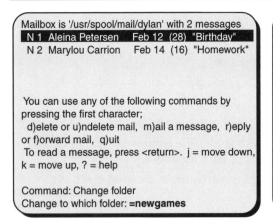

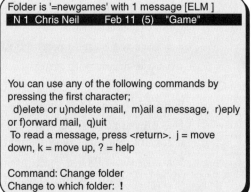

You can change to another mailbox by hitting the c command. You are then prompted for a mailbox file which is called a folder in Elm. In this case, the user changes to the mailbox file called =newgames

The name of the mailbox file that you have changed to is displayed at the top of the screen, along with the list of messages it contains.
   You return to the incoming mailbox with the c command and the !.

Figure 4.3. Changing to other folders (mailbox files) using the c command.

Elm Aliases: Alias Menu

To bring up the Elm alias menu, enter the a command. This alias menu lets you enter commands to create an alias, delete an alias, and list all aliases or particular aliases. You can delete an alias with the d command. Elm will prompt for the alias name and then delete the alias from the **aliases.text** file. You can also list aliases with the l command or list a particular alias with its name and address using the p command. To create a new alias, select the new alias option by pressing the n key. Elm then prompts you for the alias name, user name, and the user's address. It then automatically installs and adds the alias to the **aliases.text** file.

```
    Aliases [ELM 2.4 PL20]

    You can use any of the following commands by
pressing the first character;
    a)lias current message, n)ew alias, d)elete or
    u)ndelete an alias,
    m)ail to alias, or r)eturn to main menu. To view an
alias, press <return>.
    j = move down, k = move up, ? = help

Alias: n
Add a new alias to database.
Enter alias name: mark
```

The prompts are displayed on the same line, one after the other. After entering the name of the alias, that prompt and name are replaced by a prompt for the last name of the person for whom you are making the alias. The prompt for the first name then replaces the one for the last name, and so on for the address. Finally, you are asked if you want to accept the new alias. You can either enter y or n. Example of the prompts for an alias are shown here.

```
Enter last name for mark: Petersen
Enter first name for mark: Mark
```

```
Enter optional comment for mark:
Enter address for mark: mark@violet.berkeley.edu
Messages addressed as: mark@violet.berkeley.edu (mark petersen)
New alias: mark is 'Mark Petersen'. Accept new alias? (y/n) y
```

You can also create an alias for the sender of the message referenced by the current message header. In this case you press the a command at the Elm alias menu. Elm will then prompt you for an alias name, but take the user's name and the user's address from the message header. The alias will be automatically installed and added to the **aliases.txt** file. This is helpful if someone's email address is particularly complex. You can create a simple alias to use in place of the address without ever having to type it.

Elm Aliases: .elm and aliases.text

The Elm utility maintains an **.elm** directory in your own home directory with which it configures your use of Elm. Each time you invoke Elm, Elm generates a shell for your own use within which you can define your own aliases and your own variables. In the **.elm** directory there are special initialization files in which you can place alias or variable definitions.

You can add Elm alias definitions to the **aliases.text** file in the **.elm** directory by simply editing the file with with a standard text editor and typing them in. The syntax for an Elm alias is the alias followed by an = sign and the user's name followed by another = sign and the user's address.

alias = user name = user address

In the next example, the user creates an alias for Chris Neil whose address is chris@garnet.berkeley.edu.

```
chris = Chris Neil = chris@garnet.berkeley.edu
```

Elm lets you have more than one alias for the same person. You just list the aliases separated by a colon. In the next example,

the user creates two aliases for Justin Saturn at justin@violet.
eugene.edu.

```
justin, justy = Justin Saturn = justin@violet.eugene.edu
```

Once you have created individual aliases, you can use these aliases
to create group aliases. A group alias operates in the same way as
aliases used in the **.mailrc** file by mailx. When you send a message
to a group alias, the message is sent to every user in that group.
You define a group alias by first specifying the group alias followed by an = sign and the group name followed by another = sign
and then a list of aliases separated by commas. These aliases are
the aliases previously defined and reference individual users.

group alias = group name = alias-list

In the next example, the user creates an alias group using the
aliases `chris` and `justin` defined previously. The alias group is
called `myclass` and the group name is "photography class". If
you were to send a message to `myclass`, then the message would
be sent to `justin@violet.eugene.edu` and to `chris@garnet.`
`berkeley.edu`.

```
myclass = photography class = justin, chris
```

An example of the **alias.text** file follows. The individual aliases are
defined first, followed by the group aliases that make use of them.

alias.text

```
chris = Chris Neil = chris@garnet.berkeley.edu
justin, justy = Justin Saturn = justin@violet.eugene.edu

myclass = photography class = justin, chris
```

Whenever you add new aliases to the **alias.text** file by editing the
file and typing them in, you also have to install them in the Elm
utility. You do this with the `newalias` command. This is a command you enter at your Unix shell prompt.

```
$ newalias
```

Elm Options: .elmrc

Elm has many different options with which you can configure your Elm shell. Some options work like switches you can turn on or off; others work like variables to which you can assign values. Elm options that work like switches are turned on or off using the special values YES and NO or ON and OFF. For example, the assignment alwaysstore = YES will set the option to always store received mail in the received mailbox file. Elm options that work like variables are assigned string values. For example the assignment receivedmail = mybox assigns the string 'mybox' to the receivedmail option. This option holds the file name of the file used as the received mail mailbox file. In this case, received mail will be saved to a file called **mybox**.

You can set Elm options by either entering assignments to the **.elmrc** file in your **.elm** directory, or by using the options menu from within the Elm utility. Within Elm, the command o will bring up the options menu, which displays the more commonly used options. To change an option, you then press the first character of one of the options displayed, and then you are prompted to enter in a new value. See Table 4.IV for a list of Elm options.

Elm Reference

Table 4.V summarizes Elm commands.

`alwaysdelete` = *ON/OFF*	If ON, make yes the default response for delete message prompt.
`alwayskeep` = *ON/OFF*	If ON, make yes the default response for keep unread mail prompt.
`alwaysstore` = *YESNO*	If YES, store received mail in mailbox file.
`arrow` = *ON/OFF*	Use arrow to identify the current message.
`autocopy` = *ON/OFF*	Automatically include replied-to message in a response.
`editor` = *editor*	Specify editor to use to compose and edit messages.
`localsignamture` = *pathname*	Specify signature file with signature text for local mail.
`maildir` = *directory*	Specify directory where mail is saved.
`print` = *command*	Specify utility to use to display messages on your screen.
`receivedmail` = *directory*	Specify directory for received mail.
`remotesignamture` = *pathname*	Specify signature file with signature text for remote mail.
`savename` = *ON/OFF*	Save messages by login name of sender/recipient.
`sortby` = *option*	Specify how messages are to be sorted.

Table 4.IV. Elm Options

Table 4.V. Elm Commands

SENDING MESSAGES

`elm` *login-name*		Send a message using Elm.
	s	Send the message.
	e	Edit the message.
	f	Forget the message; quit and do not send.
	h	Edit the header of the message.

RECEIVING MESSAGES

`elm`		Invoke the Elm utility.
`?`		Help. Press key used for a command to display information about that command.
	?	Display a list of all commands.
	.	Return to Elm index. *(continued)*

Table 4.V. Elm Commands *(continued)*

q	Quit the Elm utility with prompts for saving read and unread messages, and deleting messages marked for deletion.
Q	Quit the Elm utility with no prompts.
x and **Ctrl-q**	Quit the Elm utility leaving your mail as you found it. No deletions are made or messages saved. Messages remain as you found them.
+	Display next index screen if headers take up more than one screen.
-	Display previous index screen if headers take up more than one screen.

SELECTING A MESSAGE

j	Move down to the next message header, making it the current message.
k	Move up to the previous message header, making it the current message.
msge-number **enter**	Make the header whose message number is *msge-number* the current message.
/pattern	Search for the pattern in the subject or address headers, making the first header with a match the current message.
/ /pattern	Search for the pattern in the text of messages, making the first message with a match the current message.
t	Tag the current message. A + sign appears before the message. You can tag several messages and then perform an operation on them all at once.
Ctrl-t	Search address and subject headers for a pattern and tag all messages that match.

OPERATIONS ON MESSAGES

enter	Display the current message.
i	Return to headers (index).
p	Print the current message.
d	Delete the current message. The header is marked with a D and deleted when you exit Elm.
Ctrl-d	Search address and subject headers for a pattern and delete all messages that match.
u	Undelete the current message.
Ctrl-u	Search address and subject headers for a pattern and undelete all messages that match. *(continued)*

r   Reply to the current message. The address and subject are take
                               from the current message's header. You then compose and send
                               your reply as with any other message.

s   Save the current message or tagged messages in a mailbox file. By
                               default, the message is saved to a mailbox file using the address
                               of the user who sent the message. You can specify your own
                               mailbox file by entering the name of the file preceded by an =
                               sign.

                               =mailbox-filename

                               You can also save the message to a received or sent mailbox files
                               using the following commands.

                               >   Save message to received mailbox file.

                               <   Save message to sent mailbox file.

Elm Operations

m   Send a message from within the Elm utility. You compose and
                               send a message.

c   Use Elm to operate on a specific mailbox file. The command
                               switches from incoming mail to any other mailbox file with
                               messages.

a   Manage Elm aliases. Upon pressing the a command, the alias
                               menu is displayed with the following options.

                               a   Create an alias using the name and address of the current
                                     message.

                               m   Create an alias using a name and address that you enter.

                               d   Delete an alias.

                               l   List aliases.

                               p   Display the name and address of a particular aliases.

                               s   Display any system aliases.

                               r   Return to Elm main menu.

MH Mailer

The Mail Handler utility, commonly known as MH, takes a different approach to managing mail than most other mail utilities. MH consists of a set of commands that you execute within your user shell just as you would execute any other Unix command. There is no special mail shell as there is for the mailx or Elm mail utilities. One MH command will send a message, another will display your incoming messages, still another will save a message. The MH commands and their options are listed in summarized in a table at the end of the chapter. All the time you are executing the MH commands, you remain in your user shell, just as you would if you executed standard Unix commands such as cat, ls, or sort. Instead of managing mail with a special utility, you simply use a set of Unix commands from within your user shell. A set of environment variables provides a context for the MH commands that you execute. Such variables keep track of the current message you are operating on or the mail folder that you are currently examining.

To use MH you may need to add the system directory for MH
commands to your PATH variable. Usually the system directory
for MH commands is /usr/bin/mh. You could add this to your
PATH variable in your **.profile, .login, .cshrc,** or **.kshrc** initialization files. In the Bourne shell you use the command
PATH=$PATH:/usr/bin/mh. In the C-shell you use the command
set path = ($path /usr/bin/mh).

As an alternative to using MH command integrated into your Unix
shell, you can use one of several available MH interface programs
such as msh, vsh, or xmh. You can use these to access your mail
using menus and cursor operations, entering MH commands at
specified prompts. vmh provides a screen-based interface like Elm,
and msh uses a shell-based interface like mailx. xmh is an X-
Windows program that you can use with a Unix GUI such as Open-
Look or Motif. All of these interfaces use the same MH commands
as those described here that are integrated into the Unix shell.

Sending a Message Using MH

To send a message using MH, you first need to compose the message using the comp command, and then send the message with
the send command. To compose a message, type in the word comp
on the command line by itself and press **return**. Then you are then
prompted for each header component, beginning with the address
of the recipient of the message. After entering in the address, usually a login name, you are then prompted for a carbon copy list.
You can enter in a list of addresses for those to whom you want a
carbon copy sent. If you do not want any copies sent, you just press
return at the prompt. You are then prompted for a subject. Enter
the subject of the message and press **return.** At this point you are
placed in an input mode. Anything typed in is taken as the contents of the message. Typing a carriage return adds a newline to
the text. When you have finished typing the message, type in a
Ctrl-c on a line of its own. Notice that the message is ended with a
Ctrl-c , not a **Ctrl-d** as in mailx.

Once you have composed a message, you need to dispose of it in some way. Upon pressing **Ctrl-c**, MH will prompt you to execute another MH command that will dispose of the message. You can send the message, edit it, save it to a file, or just quit without sending the message. Entering the command send will send the message. The edit command will edit the message, and the display command will simply display it again. Each one of these command may be abbreviated using its initial letter (d for display, e for edit, etc.).

In the next example, the user composes a message for another user whose address is robert. The subject of the message is 'Birthday.' After typing in the text of the message, the user presses a **Ctrl-c**. MH then prompts the user to dispose of the message by executing one of several listed MH commands. At the What now? prompt the user enters only a **return**. This displays a list of different commands that the user can enter. At the next What now? prompt, the user then enters the send command to send the message.

```
$ comp
To: robert
cc:
Subject: Birthday
- - - - - - - - - -
Your present is in the mail
really.
^C
What now?
Options are:
            display [<switches>]
            edit [<editor> <switches>]
            list [<switches>]
            push [<switches>]
            quit [-delete]
            refile [<switches>] +folder
            send [<switches>]
            whom [<switches>]
What now? send
$
```

See Table 5.I for a summary of the commands just discussed.

CREATE MESSAGES

`comp`	Compose a new message
`anno`	Annotate messages.
`burst`	Break digest into component messages.

SEND MESSAGES

`dist`	Distribute a message to different addresses.
`forw`	Forward a message.
`repl`	Reply to a message
`send`	Resend a message or send a file as a message.
`mhmail`	Send or read mail in batch mode.

MH INTERFACES

`msh`	MH mail shell.
`vmh`	Screen-oriented MH shell.
`xmh`	X-Windows MH interface.

Table 5.I. Creating and Sending Message

Receiving Messages Using MH

To read your mail with MH, you first need to store newly received mail into a designated MH mailbox file. New mail is not automatically placed in the MH incoming mailbox. The incorporate command (`inc`) will place newly received mail in your MH mailbox. Each time you want to read new mail, you need to execute the `inc` command.

The `inc` command will display a list of headers for each mail message in your incoming mailbox. A MH message header consists only of the message number, the month and year, the address of the sender, and the beginning of the message text.

```
$ inc
1+ 02/97 To:valerie   budget<<You are way under
2  02/97 To:aleina    birthday<<Yes, I did remember
3  02/97 To:robert    homework<<Of course I did my
$
```

Notice that the inc command merely outputs the headers to the screen, much like cat will display text of a file. Once output, you are still in the user shell and can execute any other Unix command. If you want to redisplay the headers you need to use another MH command called scan.

```
$ scan
1+ 02/97 To:valerie  budget<<You are way under
2  02/97 To:aleina   birthday<<Yes, I did remember
3  02/97 To:robert   homework<<Of course I did my
$
```

Displaying Messages Using MH

The show, next, and prev commands are used to display a message (Table 5.II). The show command displays the current message. The next command displays the message after the current one. The prev command displays the message before the current one. Initially the current message is the first of the newly received messages. Executing show at this point will display the first of your new messages. The next command will then go on to display the next message, making it the current message. As you display a message, it becomes the current message. Repeated uses of next will sequentially display messages. Repeated uses of prev will sequentially display messages in reverse order. In the next example, the user displays the first message with the show command, and then the second message with the next command.

```
$ show
(Message inbox:2)
Received: by garnet.berkeley.edu (5.64/1.33r)
           id AA13974; Wed, 12 Feb 97 02:51:56 -0700
Date: Wed, 12 Feb 97 10:14:17 -0700
From: valerie (Valerie Fuller)
Message-Id:  <9309150951.AA13974@garnet.berkeley.edu>
To: chris
Subject: budget

You are way under budget
so far.
```

```
        Congratulations
                        Val
$ next
(Message inbox:2)
Received: by garnet.berkeley.edu (5.64/1.33r)
                id AA13962; Wed, 12 Feb 97 10:14:17 -0700
Date: Wed, 12 Feb 97 10:14:17 -0700
From: aleina (Aleina Petersen)
Message-Id: <9309150951.AA13962@garnet.berkeley.edu>
To: chris
Subject: birthday

Yes, I did remember your present
                Aleina
$
```

Referencing MH Messages

Several commands such as show allow you to reference a particular message using a message number or an offset from the current
message (Table 5.III). For example, if you want to display a particular message, you can use the show command with the number of

inc	Place received mail in your incoming mailbox and display message headers.
show *num*	Display current message or specified messages.
next	Display the next message.
prev	Display the previous message
scan	Redisplay message headers.
mhl	Display formatted listing of messages.
ali	List mail aliases.
folders	Lists all mail folders.

MH INTERFACES

msh	MH mail shell.
vmh	Screen-oriented MH shell.

Table 5.II. Receiving and Displaying Messages

first	The first message in the current folder.
last	The last message in the current folder.
cur	The current message in the current folder.
prev	The previous message in the current folder.
next	The next message in the current folder.
num1-num2	Indicates all messages in the range num1 to num2, inclusive. The specified range must contain at least one message.
num:+n	
num:-n	Up to *n* messages beginning with (or ending with) message num. The value of num may be any of the MH message keywords: first, prev, cur, next, or last.
first:*n*	
prev:*n*	
next:*n*	
last:*n*	The first, previous, next, or last *n* messages, if they exist.

Table 5.III. Referencing Messages

the message. show 2 will display message 2. You can also reference several messages at once by listing their message numbers. The command show 1 3 will display messages 1 and 3. You can also designate a range of messages by specifying the first message number in the range, and the last number, separated by a hyphen sign. show 1-3 displays messages 1, 2, and 3. In the next three commands, the user first displays message 2, then message 1 and 3, and then the range 1 through 3.

```
$ show 2
$ show 1 3
$ show 1-3
```

You can also reference a message by specifying an offset from the current message. A + sign and a number will offset forward that many messages from the current message. A - sign and a number will offset backward that many messages from the current message. If the current message is 5, then +2 will reference message 7, and -3 will reference message 2.

You can also use the keywords `first`, `last`, `prev`, and `next` in the place of message numbers to reference particular messages. `first` references the first message in the message list, and `last` references the last message. With the following commands, the user can display the last message and then the first message.

```
$ show first
$ show last
```

`prev` and `next` offset by one backward and forward from the current message, respectively. In the next example, the user first displays the message before the current message, and then displays the next message.

```
$ show prev
$ show next
```

Printing, Saving, and Replying to MH Messages

You print a message by first outputting it with `show` and then piping the output to a printer. The MH commands operate like other Unix commands. Their output can be redirected or piped. In the following commands, the user first prints the current message, and then prints message 3 (see also Table 5.IV).

```
$ show | lp
$ show 3 | lp
```

A message is saved to a text file in much the same way. First output the message using the `show` command, and then redirect that output to a file. With the following command, the user saves the current message to the file **myfile**.

```
$ show > myfile
```

You reply to the current message using the `repl` command. You need to know either the message number or the address and subject of the message in order to reply to it. If you provide `repl` with a message number, then it will display the header for that message and allow you to input your reply. If there is no message header, then `repl` will prompt you for an address and a subject within which it can identify the message you are replying to. Then it will display the remainder of the header and allow you to input your reply. In the next example, the user sends a reply.

```
$ repl 2
To: aleina@garnet.berkeley.edu
cc:
Subject: Re: birthday
In-reply-to: Your message of "Wed, 12 Feb 97 10:14:17 PDT."
             <9309150951.AA13962@garnet.berkeley.edu>
--------
What did you say the present was?
You can tell me.
^C------
What now? send
$
```

Deleting MH Messages: `rmm`

You delete the current message using the `rmm` command. To delete a specific message, use the message number with `rmm`. `rmm 2` will delete the second message.

```
$ rmm 2
```

You can also use `rmm` to delete a sequence of messages. In the next example, the user selects all messages from `aleina` and deletes them.

```
$ rmm `pick -from aleina'
```

repl	Reply to a message.
mesg-ref > filename	Save a message to a file.
mesg-ref | lp	Print a message.
rmm	Remove a message.

Table 5.IV. Save, Delete, Reply, and Print Messages

Selecting MH Messages: `pick`

The `pick` command allows you to search different components of a message for a certain value. If a message matches the value, then it is selected. Selected messages form into a group that can then be operated on by a specified MH command (Table 5.V). In effect, the `pick` command selects specific messages based on a specified criteria. The criteria consist of a keyword that specifies a certain component of a message, followed by the value to be searched for in that component. For example, `-subject` is the criteria for the subject field, and `-from` specifies the address field. The criteria `-from aleina` will instruct `pick` to select those messages with "aleina" in their address field. For example, suppose you want to display the headers for all messages whose subject field deals with Birthdays. You can invoke `scan` with an evaluated `pick` operation, which will first search for and select messages whose subject is about Birthdays, and then `scan` will display the headers for these messages.

```
$ scan `pick -subject Birthday`
2+ 02/97 To:aleina birthday<Yes, I did remember
$
```

The `pick` command is very helpful when selecting messages by sender address. In the next example, the user displays all messages from `aleina`.

```
$ show `pick -from aleina`
(Message inbox:2)
Received: by garnet.berkeley.edu (5.64/1.33r)
          id AA13962; Wed, 12 Feb 97 10:14:17 -0700
Date: Wed, 12 Feb 97 10:14:17 -0700
From: aleina (Aleina Petersen)
Message-Id: <9309150951.AA13962@garnet.berkeley.edu>
To: chris
Subject: birthday

Yes, I did remember your present

        Aleina
$
```

pick	Select message by specified criteria and assign them a sequence.
mark	Add or remove messages to or from a sequence.
sortm	Sort messages.

Table 5.V. Selecting Messages

You can also label selected messages with a specific name. The pick -seq option creates a set of selected messages called a sequence. Following the -seq option you enter a sequence name with which you want to label the collection of messages. You can then reference the sequence of messages using its sequence name. In the next example, the user places all messages about birthdays and budget in sequence called party. The scan command then list the headers of messages in the party sequence.

```
$ pick -subject Birthday -or -subject Budget -seq party
2 presses
$ scan party
1  02/97  To:valerie  budget<You are way under
2+ 02/97  To:aleina   birthday<<Yes, I did remember
$
```

You could then print all messages in a sequence or save all messages in a sequence to a file. In the next example, the user prints all the messages in the party sequence, and then saves those messages to the bigparty file.

```
$ show party | lp
$ show party > bigparty
```

You can obtain a list of all the pick criteria using the command pick -help. You can, of course, print this output for later reference: pick -help | lp. The manual entry for pick will give you a more detailed explanation: man pick.

```
$ pick -help
syntax: pick [+folder] [msgs] [switches]
  switches are:
  -and
```

```
-or
-not
-lbrace
-rbrace
-cc pattern
-date pattern
-from pattern
-search pattern
-subject pattern
-to pattern
—othercomponent pattern
-after date
-before date
-(datef)ield field
-sequence name
-[no]public
-[no]zero
-[no]list
-(help)
```

Using MH Mail Folders: `refile` and `folder`

You can create your own mailbox files for MH using the `folder` command (Table 5.VI). MH mailbox files are commonly referred to as *folders*. To create a new folder, enter the `folder` command followed by the name of your folder preceded by a + sign. The + sign identifies an argument as a folder name. In MH commands that can operate on folders, the `folder` argument is identified with a preceding + sign. In the next example, the user creates a folder called **mybox**.

```
$ folder +mybox
Create folder "/home/chris/Mail/mybox"? y
          mybox+ has no messages.
$
```

Whenever you use the `folder` command, even just to create a new folder, you change to that folder. That folder becomes the folder on which all your MH commands will now operate. The

folder	Change to another mailbox file (folder).
refile	Save messages to other folders.
rmf	Remove a folder.

Table 5.VI. Folder Operations

scan command will list headers in that folder. The show command will display messages only in that folder. Incoming messages are themselves held in a folder called inbox. If you have created a new folder, and then want to change back to the inbox folder, you simply use the folder command with the +inbox argument. In the next example, the user changes back to the inbox folder and again lists the incoming messages.

```
$ folder +inbox
        inbox+ has 3 messages ( 1- 3).
$ scan
1+ 02/97  To:valerie  budget<You are way under
2  02/97  To:aleina   birthday<Yes, I did remember
3  02/97  To:robert   homework<Of course I did my
$
```

Once you have created another folder, you can move messages to it from another folder. The refile command literally copies a message from one mail folder to another, deleting it from the first. You can refile messages in your inbox folder to another folder, in effect, saving your incoming messages to another folder. This is the same kind of operation that mailx performs when saving messages to a mailbox file. In the next example, the user saves the first two incoming messages to the **mybox** file using the refile command. Notice that you can use a range to represent your messages, or just list their message numbers.

```
$ refile 1-2 +mybox
```

The user then changes to the **mybox** folder and lists the newly refiled messages there.

```
$ folder +mybox
              mybox+ has 2 messages ( 1- 2).
$ scan
1+ 02/97  To:valerie  budget<You are way under
2  02/97  To:aleina   birthday<Yes, I did remember
$
```

To see what effect the `refile` operation has had on the inbox file, the user then changes back to inbox and list the messages still held there. Notice that only message 3 remains. The other were moved to the **mybox** folder.

```
$ folder +inbox
              inbox+ has 1 message ( 1- 1).
$ scan
3+ 02/97  To:robert   homework<Of course I did my
$
```

Using MH for Mail Scripts

Because MH commands are regular Unix commands, you can incorporate them into shell scripts, creating new commands that perform mail operations. For example, suppose that you want a script that prints and saves mail about a specified subject. You can place within a script an `inc` command to incorporate received mail, followed by a `pick` command to select messages with a certain subject, and then a `show` command to print the messages, as well as a `refile` command to save the messages in another MH folder. The `getbudget` script shown below performs such operations. The `inc` command reads new mail; the `pick` command selects all messages about budgets and places them in a sequence called `budgetmesgs`. The `show` command then prints these messages, and the `refile` command saves them to a mail folder called `budgetmail`.

getbudget

```
inc
pick -subject budget -seq budgetmsgs
show budgetmsgs | lp
refile budgetmsgs +budgetmail
```

```
$ getbudget
Incorporating new mail into inbox..
1+ 09/15 To:george        budget<Isn't this great
2  09/15 To:marylou       budget<You've got to be
2  presses
$
```

MH Reference

Table 5.VII summarizes the MH commands.

Table 5.VII. MH Commands

DISPLAYING MESSAGES

inc	Place received mail in your incoming mailbox and display message headers.
show *num*	Display current message or specified messages.
next	Display the next message.
prev	Display the previous message
scan	Redisplay message headers.
mhl	Display formatted listing of messages.
ali	List mail aliases.
folders	Lists all mail folders.

REFERENCING MESSAGES

first	The first message in the current folder.
last	The last message in the current folder.
cur	The current message in the current folder.
prev	The previous message in the current folder.
next	The next message in the current folder.
num1-num2	Indicates all messages in the range num1 to num2, inclusive. The specified range must contain at least one message.
num:+n	
num:-n	Up to *n* messages beginning with (or ending with) message num. The value of num may be any of the MH message keywords: first, prev, cur, next or last. *(continued)*

Table 5.VII. MH Commands *(continued)*

`first:`*n*	
`prev:`*n*	
`next:`*n*	
`last:`*n*	The first, previous, next, or last *n* messages, if they exist.

CREATE MESSAGES

`comp`	Compose a new message
`anno`	Annotate messages.
`burst`	Break digest into component messages

SEND MESSAGES

`dist`	Distribute a message to different addresses.
`forw`	Forward a message.
`repl`	Reply to a message
`send`	Resend a message or send a file as a message.
`mhmail`	Send or read mail in batch mode.

SELECTING MESSAGES

`pick`	Select message by specified criteria and assign them a sequence.
`mark`	Add or remove messages to or from a sequence.
`sortm`	Sort messages.

SAVE, DELETE, REPLY, AND PRINT MESSAGES

`rmm`	Remove a message.
`repl`	Reply to a message.
mesg-ref > *filename*	Save a message to a file.
mesg-ref | `lp`	Print a message.

FOLDER OPERATIONS

`folder`	Change to another mailbox file (folder).
`refile`	Save messages to other folders.
`rmf`	Remove a folder.

MH INTERFACES

`msh`	MH mail shell.
`vmh`	Screen-oriented MH shell.
`xmh`	X-Windows MH interface.

6

Pine

Pine is an easy-to-use and very powerful Mail program providing a wide range of built-in features. Pine stands for Program for Internet News and Email. It has its own editor and functions equally as well as a newsreader. Pine also supports Multi-purpose Internet Mail Extensions (MIME) for sending and receiving binaries. With Pine email functions you can easily send messages, documents, and pictures. Pine has an extensive set of options with flexible Internet connection capabilities, letting you receive both mail and Usenet news through an Internet service provider. You can also maintain an address book for commonly used email addresses. Pine also has its own editor called Pico, which it uses for composing and editing messages. You can also use it as a stand-alone editor. It also has its own file manager called Pilot, which allows you to select files easily to import or attach to messages.

Pine was developed by the University of Washington. Its Pine development team develops new releases and maintains current versions. It was originally based on Elm but is now a fully developed application in its own right. You can download current software and documentation from the Pine Web site, the Pine Information Center at **www.washington.edu/pine**. Current versions can be downloaded directly from the Pine ftp site at **ftp.cac.washington. edu/pine**. You can also post questions and check out current discussions on Pine on its newsgroup:**comp.mail.pine**.

```
Pine Information Center:
http://www.washington.edu/pine

Source distribution:
ftp://ftp.cac.washington.edu/pine/

Newsgroup: comp.mail.pine
```

Pine runs from the command line using a simple cursor-based interface. To start Pine you enter the command `pine`. Pine supports full-screen cursor controls. It initially displays a Main menu (Figure 6.1) whose items you can select by moving the cursor with the arrow keys to the entry and pressing **enter**. Each item is labeled with a capital letter. You can also select the item by entering its letter. Although commands are shown in uppercase, they can be executed in lowercase. Pressing the 'i' key will bring up the Folder Index screen, and pressing 'q' will quit Pine.

Each entry will start up a screen for performing that task. The COMPOSE MESSAGE entry displays a screen in which you can compose and send a message. The FOLDER INDEX entry displays a screen for accessing received mail. On these screens, a menu of commands is displayed in the bottom two rows. The commands are listed from left to right, each entry preceded by the command's key with which you execute it. Not all commands for a given screen will fit on the first two rows displayed. In this case, you will

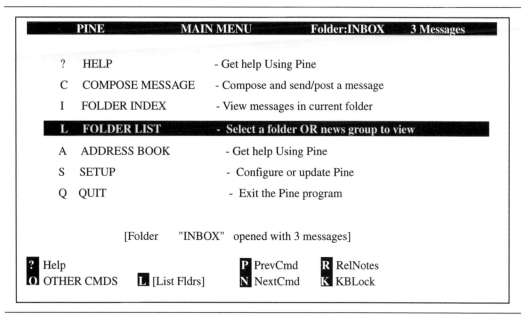

Figure 6.1. Pine Main menu.

see the O command with which you can display the next two rows of commands. Continually pressing the O command will bring you back to the first two rows of commands. Tables 6.I and 6.II show Pine options and global commands, respectively.

The commands shown on the Main menu will display a basic set of screens from which you can perform most Pine functions. In most cases, you can go to a given screen by just entering its command, no matter where you are currently. You do not always have to go through the Main menu. Should you have to go through the Main menu, there will be a M command displayed, labeled as Main menu. For example, if you are finished reading a received message you can jump back to the current list of messages in the Folder Index screen by entering the I command. The Q command will quite Pine regardless of which screen you are working in. You do not have to go back to the Main menu first. This is not the case will all Pine commands. Some are specific to certain tasks such as composing messages and managing folders.

Table 6.I. Pine Options

---

address	Send mail to address. Pine goes directly to the message composition screen.
-c *context-number*	*context-number* is the number corresponding to the folder-collection to which the -f command line argument should be applied. By default the -f argument is applied to the first defined folder-collection.
-d	Debug-level output diagnostic info at debug-level (0–9) to the current **.pine-debug** file. A value of 0 turns debugging off and suppresses the **.pine-debug** file.
-f *folder*	Open folder (in first defined folder-collection) instead of INBOX.
-F *file*	Open named text file and view.
-h	Help, list valid command-line options.
-i	Start up in the Folder Index screen.
-I *keystrokes*	Initial (comma separated list of) keystrokes which Pine should execute on startup.
-k	Use function keys for commands. This is the same as running the command pinef.
-l	Expand all collections in Folder List display.
-n *number*	Start up with current message-number set to number.
-o	Open first folder read-only.
-p *config-file*	Use *config-file* as the personal configuration file instead of the default **.pinerc**.
-P *config-file*	Use *config-file* as the configuration file instead of default system-wide configuration file **pine.conf**.
-r	Use restricted/demo mode. Pine will only send mail to itself and functions like save and export are restricted.
-z	Enable ^Z and SIGTSTP so pine may be suspended.
-conf	Produce a sample/fresh copy of the system-wide configuration file, **pine.conf**, on the standard output.
-create_lu *addrbook sort-order*	Creates auxiliary index (look-up) file for *addrbook* and sorts *addrbook* in *sort-order*, which may be dont-sort, nickname, fullname, nickname-with-lists-last, or fullname-with-lists-last.
-pinerc *file*	Output fresh pinerc configuration to file.

`-sort` *order*	Sort the Folder Index display in one of the following orders: arrival, subject, from, date, size, orderedsubj or reverse. Arrival order is the default. The orderedsubj choice simulates a threaded sort. Any sort may be reversed by adding /reverse to it. Reverse by itself is the same as arrival/reverse.
`-option=`*value*	Assign value to a Pine configuration option.

M	Main menu.
O	Show other commands.
C	Compose a new message or continue a postponed message.
I	Show a folder index.
L	Show a folder list.
G	Go to a folder.
?	Help.
Q	Quit Pine.

Table 6.II. Global Pine Commands

Composing and Sending Messages

If you have started up Pine, to compose and send a message, first select the Compose Message item in the Main menu. Either move the cursor to that item and press **enter**, or simply press the C key. This brings up a screen where you can enter you message using Pine's own built-in editor, Pico. Alternatively, you can specify an address as an argument to pine when you first start it up on the Unix command line. If Pine detects an email address as its argument when starting up, it automatically brings up the Compose Message screen, skipping the Main menu. You can then compose and send your message. In the following example, the user will immediately begin composing a message to the user **aleina@skate. best.com**.

```
$ pine aleina@skate.best.com
```

The Compose Message screen in Pine is divided into two sections, the top one for the header information and the bottom part for the message itself. At the bottom of the screen is a menu of commonly used commands. This menu changes depending on which part of the message you are working on. When you are working on the header information, the menu displays commands for managing header entries. Most of these commands are control keys, and commands for header entries and for editing message text often use the same control keys. For example, the **Ctrl-t** key for the header entries imports an address from your address book, whereas the same key when used for message text starts up the spell checker. Certain commands are displayed on both menus and are executable in either area. The ? command provides help information, **Ctrl-o** command will postpone a message for completion later, the **Ctrl-x** command will send the message, and **Ctrl-c** lets you cancel the message.

Message Header Entries

When the Compose Message screen first appears you are prompted to enter the header entries, beginning with the email address (unless you already specified one). At the following prompts you can enter a carbon copy list, any attachments, and a subject. The carbon copy list is for the addresses of users to whom you want to send a copy of your message. The subject entry can be a sentence-long description if you wish. Figure 6.2 shows the Compose Message screen with the header information shown and the header menu displayed at the bottom of the screen. Table 6.III lists the different header commands. Basic editing operations for deleting characters for clearing an entry are provided by the **Ctrl-d** (Del Char) and **Ctrl-k** (Cut Line) commands.

The attachment entry is used for sending binary files such as pictures like jpeg or gif files, word processing files, database files, or program files. Pine's attachment feature makes it very easy to send binary files by way of email. Unlike uuencode, Pine's encoding and decoding operations are completely automatic and hidden from the user. An attached file will be automatically encoded by Pine using MIME encoding and then decoded by the recipient who also must use Pine or some other mailer capable of decoding

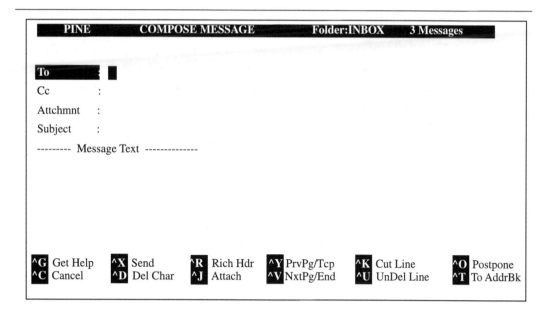

Figure 6.2. Header entries in Compose Message screen with header menu.

MIME-encoded files. You could also send text files this way, though even they will be encoded, ensuring accurate transmission. At the attachment entry you can enter the file name for a file that you want sent attached to the message. Instead of typing in the name of the file, you can use the **Ctrl-j** command followed by the **Ctrl-t** command to start up the Pine File Manager, Pilot, with which you can easily locate and select a file in your file system (see Figure 6.3).

The **Ctrl-r** command brings up a Rich Header menu for additional header entries. Entries for five other header fields are displayed. Lcc (List Carbon Copy) lets you use the names of distribution lists that you have set up as entries in your address book for a carbon copy list. This way you do not have to enter each individual address. A distribution list works like a mail alias, substituting a list of addresses for a specified name. In the Fcc entry (Folder Carbon Copy) you can specify the name of folder in which you want to hold outgoing messages. Bcc is for entering a standard blind carbon copy list. The Newsgroups entry is for posting messages to newsgroups. This is a newsreader function that has been integrated into Pine, letting you use the message composition functions to post messages to newsgroups of your choice.

```
┌──────────────────────────────────────────────────────────────────┐
│  UW PILOT              Dir:/home/dylan/games                       │
├──────────────────────────────────────────────────────────────────┤
│ ..                          (parent dir)                           │
│ soccertimes                     4 KB                               │
│ traininglist                   7.2 KB                              │
│                                                                    │
│                                                                    │
│                                                                    │
│  ? Get Help  Q Quit     L Launch   - PrevPg  D Delete    C Copy    │
│              V [View]   W Where is Spc NextPg R Rename   E Edit     │
└──────────────────────────────────────────────────────────────────┘
```

Figure 6.3. Pine Pilot.

Message Text Editing

After filling in the header entries, you can then type the text of your message in the Message Text section of the Compose Message screen. The menu at the bottom of the screen will display Pico editing commands for editing your text. If your text becomes larger that what will fit on a single screen, a new blank screen is displayed and you can continue entering text. You can move forward and backward screen by screen through your message using the **Ctrl-y** and **Ctrl-v** commands. The **Ctrl-j** command lets you justify your text, using an empty line as the end of a paragraph.

You can perform basic editing operations for copying, deleting, and moving text. You can use the **Ctrl-^** key to mark the text you want to operate on. If you do not mark any text, then the cut or copy commands work on the current line. You can paste or restore text with **Ctrl-u** command. **Ctrl-u** operates both as a paste and an undo command, letting you restore text you may have accidentally cut. For example, to delete the current line you press the **Ctrl-k** command. To move the current line, you first delete with **Ctrl-k**, move to where you want to insert it, and press the **Ctrl-r** key.

The **Ctrl-r** command (Read File) lets you insert a file into your message. It will prompt you to enter in the name of the file, which must be a relative path name starting from your home directory or a full path name. Alternatively, you can enter **Ctrl-t** at this prompt to use the Pilot file browser to select the file. With the **Ctrl-w** command (Where Is) you can search your message for a pattern. **Ctrl-t** brings up the spell checker. Once you have finished composing your message you can send it with the **Ctrl-x** command. Editing commands are listed in Table 6.III. Figure 6.4 shows the Compose Message screen with the editing menu for entering message text.

Pine Address Book

With Pine you can maintain an address book for email addresses. You can automatically read email addresses from your address book into a message address header, or add the address of a message you have received into the address book. You can also easily create lists of addresses for each distribution of a message to several users.

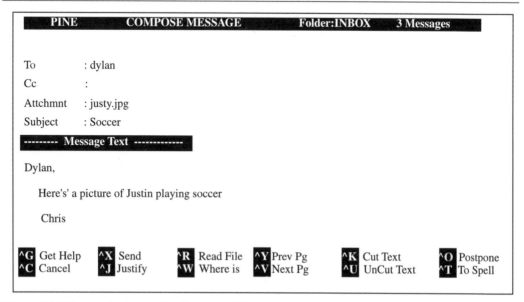

Figure 6.4. Message text entry for Compose Message screen with editing menu.

BASIC COMMANDS

Ctrl-g	Get help.
Ctrl-c	Cancel message.
Ctrl-x	Send message.
Ctrl-o	Postpone a message for completion later. Postponed messages are saved in file **postponed-msgs**.

HEADER COMMANDS

Ctrl-j	Attach files. You can then use **Ctrl-t** to access the Pine file browser (Pilot) to select a file for insert or attachment
Ctrl-t	Select address from address book.
Ctrl-r	Rich header command. Displays four other header fields for entry: Bcc, Fcc, Lcc, Newsgroups (standard header fields are To, Cc, Attchmnt, and Subject). Lcc (List Carbon Copy) uses address book lists. Fcc (Folder Carbon Copy) is name of folder for outgoing messages. Bcc is for a standard blind carbon copy list. Newsgroups is for posting messages to newsgroups.
Ctrl-d	Delete character.
Ctrl-k	Cut line.
Ctrl-u	Undelete line.
Ctrl-y	Move to next page.
Ctrl-v	Move to previous page.

MESSAGE TEXT COMMANDS

Ctrl-j	Justify text. Uses blank line as end of paragraph.
Ctrl-^	Mark text for cut or paste.
Ctrl-k	Cut text. With unmarked text, cut current line.
Ctrl-u	Restore or paste text.
Ctrl-r	Read file, insert a file into a message.
Ctrl-t	Invoke spell checker.
Ctrl-y	Move to next page.
Ctrl-v	Move to previous page.
Ctrl-w	Search for text.

Table 6.III. Pine Message Composition Commands

To create a new address entry, you press the A command (AddNew). You will be prompted for five entries, a nickname for the address, the person's full name, an Fcc list for carbon copies, any comments you may have, and the email address.

You can use the same command to create distribution lists. These function like mail aliases in the mailx and Elm mailers. At the Nickname prompt you enter a name with which to reference the list, then a full name (something more official), any comments, and then at the address prompt you enter a list of email addresses separated by commas. The easiest way to use a distribution list is to select it from your address book with the **Ctrl-t** command while composing your message. You will see the list of addresses that make up the list placed in the address field of your message. You can also just type the nickname for the list at the address prompt when composing a message.

Should you need to modify an address entry, just select it and press the V command, View/Edit. The entries for each field will be displayed and you can change whichever ones you wish. Figure 6.5 shows a sample address book in which the myteam entry is a distribution list of addresses.

The menu at the bottom of the Address Book screen lists commands you can perform on address entries. The O command

PINE	ADDRESS BOOK	Folder:INBOX	Message 1 of 3
chris	**Christopher Neil**	**chris@mygame.hockey.org**	
justin	Justin Saturn	justin@mycar.com	
larisa	Larisa Petersen	larisa@graphic.mag. com	
aleina	Aleina Petersen	aleina@skate.best.com	
myteam	Soccer Team	DISTRIBUTION LIST	
		chris	
		justin	

? Help	**M** Main Menu	**P** PrevEntry	**-** PrevPage	**D** Delete	**C** ComposeTo
O OTHER CMDS	**V** View/EDit	**N** NextEntry	**Spc** NextPage	**A** AddNew	**W** Wheris

Figure 6.5. Pine Address Book.

displays other address book commands. With the `ComposeTo` command you can first select an address then press C to compose a message. The selected address will be automatically inserted in your address field. The `Wheris` command, W, lets you search the address book for a name or pattern.

Receiving Messages: Pine Folders

Pine organizes any messages you receive or send into folders. These are the same as the mailbox files used in mailx. Pine automatically sets up and maintains three folders for you: an **INBOX** folder for mail sent to you, a **saved-mail** folder for mail you have read, and a **sent-mail** folder for messages you have sent to others. To check your mail for any new messages you have to access your **INBOX** folder. There is always a folder that is selected as your current folder. When you first start up Pine, your **INBOX** folder is usually your current folder. You will see the current folder displayed on the top line to the right following the label "Folder:". In Figure 6.6 the current folder is the **INBOX** folder as shown by the display "Folder:INBOX." If you should select another folder as your current folder, such as **sent-mail**, then that display would change to "Folder:sent-mail."

If **INBOX** is your current folder you can select the Folder Index item in the main menu either with the cursor or with the I command to display the messages in it. The Folder Index operation will display a screen with a listing of all the messages in the current folder. For the **INBOX** folder, it will display all the messages that have been sent to you. Figure 6.6 shows a folder index screen listing messages in the user's **INBOX** folder.

The Folder Index screen lists headers of received messages. They have fields similar to those in other mailers. The first field is the status field indicating a new or read message. In front of the status code may be one of several qualifiers, + indicates messages sent directly to you, * indicates important messages, and X indicates selected messages. New messages will have a status code of N and read messages will not have any status code. Messages marked for deletion will have a D status code. Table 6.IV list the possible status

```
┌────────────────────────────────────────────────────────────────────────┐
│ ███ PINE ████████ FOLDER INDEX ███████ Folder:INBOX ███ Message 3 of 3  NEW │
│                                                                          │
│                                                                          │
│  + N  1   May 11   Justin Saturn              (44)      "Car"            │
│    N  2   May 1     Larisa  Petersen          (537)     "Homework"       │
│    N  3   May 15    Chris  Niel               (76)      "Soccer"         │
│                                                                          │
│                                                                          │
│                                                                          │
│  ? Help          M Main Menu   P PrevMsg    - PrevPage  D Delete   R Reply │
│  O OTHER CMDS    V [ViewMsg]   N NextMsg    Spc NextPage U Undelete F Forward │
└────────────────────────────────────────────────────────────────────────┘
```

Figure 6.6. Pine header list.

codes. Following the status field is the message number with which you can reference the message in message operations. After the message number is the date, the name of the sender, the size of the message in bytes, and as much of the subject entry as will fit on the rest of the screen.

MESSAGE STATUS CODES

+	The message was sent directly to you (not a cc: or email list).
A	The message has been answered.
D	The message is marked for deletion.
N	The message is new and unread.
X	The message is selected (for aggregate operations).
*	The message has been flagged as important.

MESSAGE HEADER COMPONENTS

Message number

Date received or sent

Sender (for received messages) or recipient (for sent messages)

Message size: size of the message, plus any attachments, in bytes

Subject

Table 6.IV. Status Codes and Message Headers

The menu at the bottom of the screen will list commands for performing operations on the messages. With the P and N commands you can move up and down the list of headers to the previous message or the next message. The **tab** key moves you to the next new message and the J lets you jump to a specific message using its message number. If the message list takes up more than one screen, you can move to the next screen or back to the previous one with the **space** and **dash** keys. With the V command you can display a specific message. You can delete and undelete messages with the D and U commands. The R command lets you compose and send a reply to a message, and the F command lets you forward it to another address. You can save a message with the S command. Whenever you save a message with the S command or delete a message with the D command, the message is marked for deletion and its status code is changed to D. You can unmark it with the U command. To remove messages marked for deletion, use the X command (eXpunge). Folder Index commands are listed in Table 6.V.

Pine lets you perform aggregate operations on messages in which you can select several messages and then perform an operation on them all at once. You use the ; command (a semicolon) to select messages. For the ; command to work, be sure that the **enable-aggregate-command-set** option switch in the Setup's Config screen is set to on (an X should be displayed in the brackets next to the option; if it is not set, press **enter** or X to toggle it on; see Table 6.VII). You can select messages based on number, status, text, or date. The text entry further lets you select from the contents of the message or from the subject field. For example you could select messages on a certain subject or from a particular user, or just all read messages. If you choose the number criteria, you can list individual message numbers separated by commas or ranges of messages separated by a dash. Selected messages will have an X displayed before the status field.

You can further refine your selection by pressing the ; command again. If a group of messages is already selected, the ; command displays commands to narrow or broaden the number of selected messages using Boolean search terms. You can also unselect specific messages or all selected messages. You can also select messages based on a Where Is command search. The Where Is **Ctrl-x** option will mark messages that result from a search as selection.

Once you have selected your messages, you can the use the Apply command, the A key, to apply an operation to all of them at once. A menu of commands will be displayed including commands to print, save, reply, forward, or delete your selected messages. There is even a command, Take Addresses, that will import the addresses of your selected messages into your address book. The Zoom command, the Z key, will display only the selected messages on your Folder Index screen.

To read a message first make it the current message by selecting its header with the cursor and the pressing the **enter** key. The message header entries and text will be displayed on the Message Text screen (Figure 6.7). Commands for operations on the message will be listed in the menu at the bottom of the screen. If the contents of the message takes up more than one screen you can move back and forth through the message with the **dash** and **space** keys. The V command will let you view any attachment should there be one. You can search for a pattern in the text using the W command (Where Is). The R command lets you compose and send a reply to this message, automatically using the message's header information to determine the subject and address. From this message you can go on directly to display the next message with the N command or go back to the previous message with the P command.

```
  PINE     MESSAGE TEXT        Folder:INBOX              Message 1 of 3  ALL

 Date:Mon, 11 May 1998  11:31:19
 From : Justin Saturn <justin@mycar.com>
 To: Dylan Petersen <dylan@mytrain.com>
 Cc: larisa@graphic.mag.com
 Attchmnt: newcar.jpg
 Subject : Car

   Dylan,

     Here is a picture of my new car.  I will let you drive it tomorrow with Larisa and Aleina.

       Justin
 --------- Message Text -------------


 ? Help            M Main Menu   P PrevMsg    - PrevPage    D Delete     R Reply
 O OTHER CMDS      V ViewAttch   N NextMsg   Spc NextPage   U Undelete   F Forward
```

Figure 6.7. Display received message.

The Message Text screen displays only the basic header information. For full header information you need to switch on the Header Mode with the H command. You can return to the Folder Index screen at any time by pressing I, the folder index command.

The Folder Index screen and the Message Text screen that displays messages share many of the same commands for performing operations on a message (see Table 6.V). With the Y command you can print a message, and the S command lets you save the message in a folder such as the **saved-messages** folder. You can save a message as a plain text file using the E command (export). With the T command you can automatically add the address of the sender to your Pine address book.

Selecting Folders: Pine Folder List

Pine organizes messages into folders that you can select using the Folder List entry on the Main menu. A folder is a Pine-maintained file to which you can save messages, preserving the message header information and allowing Pine to read and manage the messages in it. A folder functions much the same as a mailbox file in other mailers like mailx. Pine automatically sets up three folders: **INBOX** for incoming messages, **saved-messages** for messages you save, and **sent-messages** for messages you have composed and sent. To select a folder you enter the Folder List command, L, to bring up the Folder List screen. The available folders will be displayed. You can move from one to the other using the arrow keys. Folders are displayed across the screen, wrapping around to another row depending on how many there are. Use the left and right arrow keys to move through a row of folder names, and the up and down arrow keys to move from one row to the next. Initially, the three folders defined by Pine will take up only one row, which you can move through with the left and right arrow keys. For example, to see messages you have saved, you can select the **saved-messages** folder. At this point, the **saved-messages** folder will become the current folder. You can then execute the Folder Index command, I, to display the Folder Index screen, which will now show all the headers for saved messages in that **saved-messages** folder.

Moving through the Message List

P	Previous message.
N	Next message.
J	Jump to specific message number.
tab	Next new message.
–	Previous screen.
space	Next screen.
W	(Where Is) Search for a word in the index or go to first/last message.

Operations on Messages: Folder Index Screen

Y	Print a message.
V	View a message.
R	Reply to a message.
F	Forward a message.
B	Bounce (resend) a message with a different address.
D	Mark a message for deletion.
U	Undelete a message marked for deletion.
T	Add address of message to your address book.
S	Save a message in an email folder.
E	Save (export) a message as a text file.
X	Expunge messages marked for deletion (actually erases them).
;	Select a message for aggregate operations (A and Z).
A	Apply command to selected messages.
Z	Show only selected messages.
*	Flag.
|	Pipe contents of a message to a Unix command.
$	Sort messages by subject, date, sender/recipient, etc.

Viewing a Message: Message Text Screen

–	Display previous screen of message text.
space	Display next screen of message text.
W	(Where Is) Search for a word in a message or go to first/last line.
V	View an attachment to a message.
H	Display full header information, Header Mode.

Table 6.V. Folder Index Commands

To return to the **INBOX** folder, select it using the Folder List command, L, once again making it your current folder. Table 6.VI gives the Folder List commands.

You can also create folders of your own and save messages to them. These folders will be displayed on the Folder List screen where you can select them. You create a new folder with the A command, Add. You will be prompted to enter the name of the folder. In Figure 6.8, the Folder List screen shows the three mail folders for your incoming, sent, and saved messages. There is also a folder that was set up by the user called **vacation**.

Folder Collections

Folders are organized into collections. A collection is actually a Unix directory. To say that you are placing folders in a certain collection is the same as saying you are placing folder files in a certain directory. Pine initially creates a collection (directory) called **mail** and in it places the **INBOX**, **saved-messages**, and **sent-messages** folders. If you look in your home directory you will see a directory called **mail** and in it will be the files **INBOX**, **saved-messages**, and **sent-messages** files. You can create collections of your own or you can just add folders to the **mail** collection.

Collections are a way of further organizing your mail folders and their messages. For example, suppose you have messages about different games such as football and baseball. You may also have messages about different projects like oldprojects or newprojects. You could set up a different folder for each of the game and project topics. You could then further separate them into two collections, one for games and one for projects. The games collection would contain the football and baseball folders, and the project collection would contain the newprojects and oldprojects folders. In your home directory you would have a directory called **games** that would contain the **baseball** and **football** folder files, and another directory called **projects** that would have the **newprojects** and **oldprojects** folder files.

Creating a new collection is a two-step process. First, choose a name for your collection and, while in your Unix shell, create a directory with that name. For example, for the games collection you

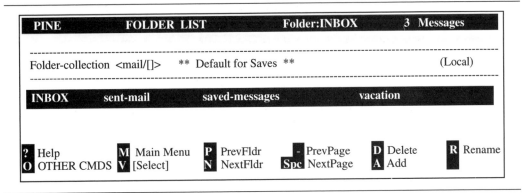

Figure 6.8. Pine Folder list for mail collection.

first have to create a directory called **games** in your home directory. The directory does not have to be in your home directory. You
can place it in any subdirectory or any other directory to which
you have access. When you specify its name in Pine, be sure to include either the relative or full path name:

```
$ mkdir games
```

After creating the directory, start up Pine and go to the Setup screen
using the S command. From there go to the Configuration Screen
using the C command. A list of configuration entries will be displayed, one of which will be "folder collections". Here you can create your own folder collections. Move the cursor to that entry and
press the A command to add a value to that configuration entry. The
name for a collection has a specific format. It is the name followed
by a slash and a set of empty brackets, *name*/[]. The name has to
be the same exact name you gave to the directory when you created
it. For example, the following is the name for the games collection:

```
games/[]
```

You can add several collection names at one time by separating
them with commas. Press **enter** to add the collection names. You
will see each one displayed on a line by itself to the right of the
"folder collections" label. To edit or delete a collection name, move
the cursor to that name and press **enter**. You can then erase the
name or change it as desired.

A new collection is not added until you quit and start up Pine again. When you then go to the Folder List screen, L, a list of collection entries will be displayed. With the games example, there will be a collection entry for **mail** and **games**. **mail** is the collection Pine set up for the **INBOX**, **saved-messages**, and **sent-messages** folders, and **games** is the new collection that you set up. Other collections will be displayed as you add them.

To create a folder in a specific collection, use the up and down arrow keys to move to that collection entry as it is displayed in the Folder List screen. Then use the Add command, A, to add a new folder to that collection. For example, to add **baseball** and **football** folders to the games collection, the user first moves to the **games** collection and then uses the A command to add the **baseball** and **football** folders. There will then be a **baseball** and a **football** folder file in the **games** directory.

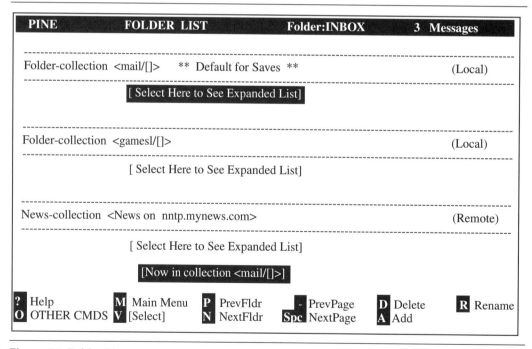

Figure 6.9. Folder List.

The collections in the collection list will not initially display the folders they contain. Instead they will display a single entry with the following message (see Figure 6.9):

```
[Select Here to See Expanded List]
```

To select a folder in a specific collection, move to that collection and then press **enter** on that entry. The folders for that collection will then be displayed and will remain displayed for that Pine session. Use the arrow keys to select the folder you want. The selected folder will become the current folder until you select another one (see Figure 6.10). To again make the **INBOX** folder your current folder, you have to first select the mail collection, expand it to display its list of folders, one of which will be the **INBOX** folder, and then select the **INBOX** folder. In Figure 6.10, the user has selected the **baseball** folder in the **games** collection, which is now displayed as the current folder.

```
  PINE              FOLDER LIST              Folder:baseball      3  Messages

  -----------------------------------------------------------------------------
  Folder-collection <mail/[]>    ** Default for Saves **                (Local)
  -----------------------------------------------------------------------------
  INBOX               saved-messages              sent-messages


  -----------------------------------------------------------------------------
  Folder-collection <games/[]>                                         (Local)
  -----------------------------------------------------------------------------
  baseball                football

  -----------------------------------------------------------------------------
  News-collection <News on  nntp.mynews.com>                          (Remote)
  -----------------------------------------------------------------------------
                   [ Select Here to See Expanded List]

                   [Now in collection <games/[]>]

  ? Help            M Main Menu    P PrevFldr      - PrevPage    D Delete    R Rename
  O OTHER CMDS      V [Select]     N NextFldr    Spc NextPage    A Add
```

Figure 6.10. Folder List.

MOVING THROUGH THE FOLDER LIST

P	Previous folder.
N	Next folder.
-	Previous screen.
space	Next screen.
W	Search for a folder name in the index or go to first/last folder.

OPERATIONS ON THE NEWLY SELECTED FOLDER

V	View.
D	Delete.
R	Rename.

FOLDER LIST COMMANDS

I	Show index of the currently active folder.
Y	Print folder listing.
A	Add new folder.

NEWSGROUP-COLLECTION SPECIFIC COMMANDS

A	Subscribe.
D	Unsubscribe.

Table 6.VI. Folder List Commands

Newsgroups

The Folder List command is also used to access Usenet news servers and their newsgroups. Newsgroups are treated as folders and the articles are managed like messages in that folder. Your news server is considered a collection. In effect, it functions as the place where your news articles are kept.

To set up a news collection you have to first configure Pine to access your newserver. This is usually a remote newserver. First select Pine Setup with the S command. Then select Pine Configuration with the C command. Several entries are listed with various labels. Select the one with the label **nntp-server** and enter the newserver address, such as **nntp.myserver.mydomain.com**. Exit and save the configuration. When you quit and then start up Pine again, the newserver collection will be automatically set up for you. When you go to the Folder list you will see a collection entry for newsgroups. Figure 6.10 shows a news collection entry.

When you expand the news collection, it will list subscribed news-groups instead of folders. You can subscribe to a newsgroup using the Add command, A. To see a newsgroup, select it and a Folder Index screen will display the articles in that newsgroup. You can also post news using Pine, just as you would send a message.

Pine Attachments

Pine attachments are managed so that binary files of different types can be decoded and displayed using their appropriate appli-cations. For example, jpeg picture files can be decoded and dis-played from within Pine using an application like Xview that can display jpeg picture files. In this way, Pine lets you automatically send, receive, and use binary files. Even text files that are attached are encoded to ensure accurate transmission. Files that are attached must be on the same system as Pine. You cannot attach files on a re-mote system unless you first transfer them to your own.

Pine uses the Multipurpose Internet Mail Extensions (MIME) stan-dard for all attachments. MIME was developed for the Internet to provide and easy-to-use method for encoding and decoding binary files. MIME is designed to associate automatically a binary file with a certain application. In this way an appropriate application, such as an image viewer, can be used to display a picture file while the user is still working in the Pine mailer. The View Attachment command in the message text screen performs such an operation.

Applications are associated with binary files by means of a **mailcap** and a **mime.types** file. The **mime.types** file defines different MIME types, associating a MIME type with a certain application. The **mailcap** file then associates each MIME type with a specified application. Your system maintains its own MIME types file, usu-ally in **/etc/mime.types** or **/usr/local/lib/mime.types**. You can also

create your own MIME type file in your home directory, naming it
mime.types.

Entries in a MIME type file associate a MIME type and possible
subtype of an application with a set of possible file extensions used
for files that run on that kind of application. The MIME type is
usually further qualified by a subtype, separated by a slash. For example, a MIME type image can have several subtypes such as jpeg,
gif, or tiff. A sample MIME type entry defining a MIME type for
jpeg files is shown here. The MIME type is image/jpeg and the list
of possible file extensions is jpeg jpg jpe.

```
image/jpeg        jpeg jpg jpe
```

A sample **mime.types** file is shown here.

mime.types

```
application/postscript    ai eps ps
application/rtf           rtf
application/x-tex         tex
application/x-texinfo     texinfo texi
application/x-troff       t tr roff
audio/basic               au snd
audio/x-aiff              aif aiff aifc
audio/x-wav               wav
image/gif                 gif
image/ief                 ief
image/jpeg                jpeg jpg jpe
image/tiff                tiff tif
image/x-xwindowdump       xwd
text/html                 html
text/plain                txt c cc h
video/mpeg                mpeg mpg mpe
video/quicktime           qt mov
video/x-msvideo           avi
video/x-sgi-movie         movie
```

Once MIME types are defined, they can be associated with a specific application. Such associations are made in the **mailcap** file.

The applications specified will depend on those available on your particular system. The MIME type is separated from the application with a semicolon. A sample **mailcap** file is shown here. In many cases X-Windows-based programs are specified. A # symbol at the beginning of a line indicates a comment and is ignored. A * used in a MIME subtype references all subtypes. **image/*** would be used for an application that can run all types of image files. A formatting code, %s, is used to reference the attachment file that will be run on this applications.

mailcap

```
# Audio files --
audio/wav;                    jukebox %s;
audio/mpeg;                   jukebox %s;
audio/x-midi;                 playmidi %s

# Image files --
# These are handled differently under X11 and VGA.
image/*;                      xv %s;
image/*;                      zgv %s;

# Video files --
video/mpeg;                   mpeg_play %s;
video/*;                      xanim %s;

# Web files --
text/html;                    netscape %s;
text/html;                    lynx %s;

# PostScript --
application/postscript;       gv -safer %s;
application/pdf;              xpdf -err %s;

# TeX DVI Files --
application/x-dvi;            xdvi -maketexpk -hush %s; \
```

Pine does not use uuencode or binhex encoding. Instead it uses MIME Base64 encoding. Should you want to send an uuencoded file you would have to include it as part of the message text. Simply insert the file into the message text using the **Ctrl-r** command and send the message as a regular text message with no attachments. The recipient will have to decode it manually using uudecode or a binhex decoder.

Pine Configuration

You can configure Pine with your own personal preferences. Your Pine configuration is kept in a **.pinrc** file in your home directory. The S command on the main menu will display the Setup screen. Here you can configure a printer, create a signature for messages you compose, set up a new password, update Pine from the Pine Web site, or configure Pine using an extensive set of options. The Newpassword command, N , provides an easy interface for changing your Unix password. This is the password that you use to log in to your account. This is really a Unix operating system operation, performing the same task as the Unix passwd command. With the Signature command, S, you can create a standard sign-off for messages you compose. The command places you in a text editor where you type your farewell, usually your full name, title, and email address. It then saves the sign off in a file called **.signature**. You can edit this file later with a standard text editor if desired.

The Configure command, C, displays an extensive list of options (Table 6.VII). To see an explanation of what an entry is for, move the cursor to the entry and press the ? key to display the help screen. Some options are switches that you turn on or off. These will be preceded by brackets, [ ], which will contain an 'x' if they are turned on. To switch such and option from its current setting, you move the cursor to it and press the X key, toggling them on or off. X is the Set/Unset command. Other options will present a choice of two or more possibilities. The possible entries are preceded by a pair of open and closed parentheses, ( ). To select one you move the cursor to it and press the * key.

Many options take values instead. These are followed by an = sign with the current value displayed within <> symbols. If there is no value yet assigned "<No Value Set>" will be displayed. To enter values, you move the cursor to that entry and press the C key, the Change Val command. This is also the default, so you can just press **enter**. A line will open up at the bottom of the screen where you can type the new value. Upon pressing **enter**, the new value will be displayed on the screen next to its option entry. For example, to enter the newserver address, move to the entry with the **nntp-server** label and press enter. A line opens up at the bottom of the screen with that label and you can type in the newserver address. Upon pressing **enter**, you will see the newserver address displayed next to the newserver label. Some options can take multiple values, and for this you would use the Add Value command, the A key. To erase an option's value, you use the Delete Val command, the D key.

Pico and Pilot

Current versions of Pine implement the Pico editor and Pilot file browser as stand-alone applications. You can invoke Pico with the `pico` command and edit text files as you would with Vi or Emacs. With Pilot you can browse files, changing directories, all with a cursor-based screen interface. The Pico editor is shown in Figure 6.11, and the Pilot file browser is shown in Figure 6.3.

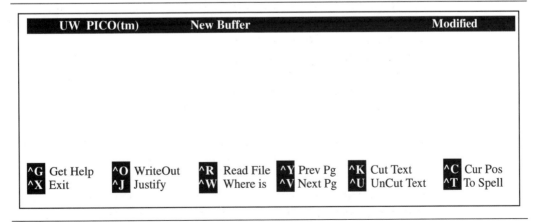

Figure 6.11. Pine Pico Editor.

Table 6.VII. Pine Configuration Options

```
personal-name              = <No Value Set: using "Dylan Petersen">
user-domain                =<No Value Set>
smtp-server                =<No Value Set>
nntp-server                =<No Value Set>
inbox-path                 =<No Value Set: using "inbox">
folder-collections         =<No Value Set: using "mail/[]">
news-collections           =<No Value Set>
incoming-archive-folders   =<No Value Set>
pruned-folders             =<No Value Set>
default-fcc                =<No Value Set: using "sent-mail">
default-saved-msg-folder   =<No Value Set: using "saved-messages">
postponed-folder           =<No Value Set: using "postponed-msgs">
read-message-folder        =<No Value Set>
signature-file             =<No Value Set: using ".signature">
lobal-address-book         =<No Value Set>
address-book               =<No Value Set: using ".addressbook">
feature-list =
               [ ] allow-talk
               [ ] assume-slow-link
               [ ] auto-move-read-msgs
               [ ] auto-open-next-unread
               [ ] auto-zoom-after-select
               [ ] auto-unzoom-after-apply
               [ ] compose-cut-from-cursor
               [ ] compose-maps-delete-key-to-ctrl-d
               [ ] compose-rejects-unqualified-addrs
               [ ] compose-send-offers-first-filter
               [ ] compose-sets-newsgroup-without-confirm
               [ ] delete-skips-deleted
               [ ] disable-keymenu
               [ ] enable-8bit-esmtp-negotiation
               [ ] enable-8bit-nntp-posting
               [X] enable-aggregate-command-set
               [ ] enable-alternate-editor-cmd
```

```
[ ]  enable-alternate-editor-implicitly
[ ]  enable-background-sending
[ ]  enable-bounce-cmd
[ ]  enable-cruise-mode
[ ]  enable-cruise-mode-delete
[ ]  enable-dot-files
[ ]  enable-dot-folders
[ ]  enable-flag-cmd
[ ]  enable-flag-screen-implicitly
[ ]  enable-full-header-cmd
[ ]  enable-goto-in-file-browser
[ ]  enable-incoming-folders
[ ]  enable-jump-shortcut
[ ]  enable-mail-check-cue
[ ]  enable-mouse-in-xterm
[ ]  enable-newmail-in-xterm-icon
[ ]  enable-suspend
[ ]  enable-tab-completion
[ ]  enable-unix-pipe-cmd
[ ]  enable-verbose-smtp-posting
[ ]  expanded-view-of-addressbooks
[ ]  expanded-view-of-distribution-lists
[ ]  expanded-view-of-folders
[ ]  expunge-without-confirm
[ ]  fcc-on-bounce
[ ]  include-attachments-in-reply
[ ]  include-header-in-reply
[ ]  include-text-in-reply
[ ]  news-approximates-new-status
[ ]  news-post-without-validation
[ ]  news-read-in-newsrc-order
[ ]  pass-control-characters-as-is
[ ]  preserve-start-stop-characters
[ ]  print-offers-custom-cmd-prompt
[ ]  print-includes-from-line
```

(continued)

Table 6.VII. Pine Configuration Options *(continued)*

```
                [ ] print-index-enabled
                [ ] print-formfeed-between-messages
                [ ] quell-dead-letter-on-cancel
                [ ] quell-lock-failure-warnings
                [ ] quell-status-message-beeping
                [ ] quell-user-lookup-in-passwd-file
                [ ] quit-without-confirm
                [ ] reply-always-uses-reply-to
                [ ] save-will-quote-leading-forms
                [ ] save-will-not-delete
                [ ] save-will-advance
                [ ] select-without-confirm
                [ ] show-cursor
                [ ] show-selected-in-boldface
                [ ] signature-at-bottom
                [ ] single-column-folder-list
                [ ] tab-visits-next-new-message-only
                [ ] use-current-dir
                [ ] use-sender-not-x-sender
                [ ] use-subshell-for-suspend
initial-keystroke-list    =<No Value Set>
default-composer-hdrs     =<No Value Set>
customized-hdrs           =<No Value Set>
viewer-hdrs               =<No Value Set>
saved-msg-name-rule =
                ( ) by-from
                ( ) by-nick-of-from
                ( ) by-nick-of-from-then-from
                ( ) by-fcc-of-from
                ( ) by-fcc-of-from-then-from
                ( ) by-sender
                ( ) by-nick-of-sender
                ( ) by-nick-of-sender-then-sender
                ( ) by-fcc-of-sender
```

(continued)

```
                ( ) by-fcc-of-sender-then-sender
                ( ) by-recipient
                ( ) by-nick-of-recip
                ( ) by-nick-of-recip-then-recip
                ( ) by-fcc-of-recip
                ( ) by-fcc-of-recip-then-recip
                ( ) last-folder-used
                (*) default-folder
fcc-name-rule =
                (*) default-fcc
                ( ) last-fcc-used [Select]
                ( ) by-recipient
                ( ) by-nickname
                ( ) by-nick-then-recip
                ( ) current-folder
sort-key =
                ( ) Date
                (*) Arrival
                ( ) From
                ( ) Subject
                ( ) OrderedSubj
                ( ) To
                ( ) Cc
                ( ) siZe
                ( ) Reverse Date
                ( ) Reverse Arrival
                ( ) Reverse From
                ( ) Reverse Subject
                ( ) Reverse OrderedSubj
                ( ) Reverse To
                ( ) Reverse Cc
                ( ) Reverse siZe
addrbook-sort-rule =
                (*) fullname-with-lists-last
                ( ) fullname
                ( ) nickname-with-lists-last
```

(continued)

Table 6.VII. Pine Configuration Options *(continued)*

```
                        ( ) nickname
                        ( ) dont-sort
goto-default-rule =
                        (*) inbox-or-folder-in-recent-collection
                        ( ) inbox-or-folder-in-first-collection
                        ( ) most-recent-folder
character-set           =<No Value Set>
editor                  =<No Value Set>
speller                 =<No Value Set>
composer-wrap-column    =<No Value Set: using "74">
reply-indent-string     =<No Value Set: using "> ">
empty-header-message    =<No Value Set: using "Undisclosed
                        recipients">
image-viewer            =<No Value Set>
use-only-domain-name    = No
display-filters         =<No Value Set>
sending-filters         =<No Value Set>
alt-addresses           =<No Value Set>
addressbook-formats     =<No Value Set>
index-format            =<No Value Set>
viewer-overlap          =<No Value Set: using "2">
scroll-margin           =<No Value Set: using "0">
status-message-delay    =<No Value Set: using "0">
mail-check-interval     =<No Value Set: using "150">
newsrc-path             =<No Value Set>
news-active-file-path   =<No Value Set>
news-spool-directory    =<No Value Set>
upload-command          =<No Value Set>
upload-command-prefix   =<No Value Set>
download-command        =<No Value Set>
download-command-prefix =<No Value Set>
mailcap-search-path     =<No Value Set>
mimetype-search-path    =<No Value Set>
download-command-prefix =<No Value Set>
```

Section II

Newsreaders

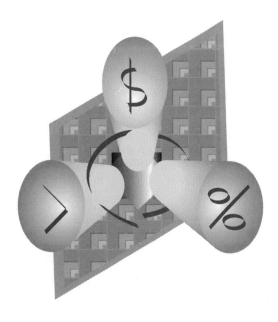

Usenet and Newsreaders:
rn and readnews

Usenet is an open collection of files to which users post news and opinions. It operates like a system-wide mailbox to which any user can read or send messages. Usenet files are distributed throughout the Internet to any system that wishes to receive them. The files contain messages that Internet users have sent in to be incorporated into Usenet files. Each system that receives Usenet files is referred to as a site. Certain sites perform organizational and distribution operations for Usenet, receiving messages from other sites and organizing them into Usenet files that are then broadcast to many other sites. Such sites are called backbone sites and they operate like publishers, receiving articles and organizing them into different groups.

Usenet files were originally designed to function like journals. Messages contained in the files are referred to as articles. With Usenet, a user could write an article, post it in Usenet, and have it immediately distributed to Unix systems around the world. Someone could then read the article on Usenet, instead of waiting for a journal publication. Usenet files themselves were organized as journal publications. Since journals are designed to address specific groups, Usenet files were organized according to groups called newsgroups. When a user posts an article, it is assigned to a specific newsgroup. If another user then wants to read that article, he or she then looks at the articles in that newsgroup. You can think of each newsgroup as a constantly updated magazine. For example, to read articles on computer science, you would access the Usenet newsgroup on computer science. Some Usenet newsgroups are used as a place where people carry on debates. The articles here read more like conversations than journal articles.

Each newsgroup has its own unique name. Names are segmented in order to classify newsgroups. Usually a newsgroup name is divided into three segments: a general topic, subtopic, and specific topic. The segments are delimited by periods. For example, you may have several newsgroups that deal with the general topic `rec`, which stands for recreation. Of those, some newsgroups may deal with only the subtopic of `food`. Of those, there may be a group that discusses only a specific topic such as `recipes`. In this case, the newsgroup name would be `rec.food.recipes`.

Many of the bulletin board groups are designed for discussion only, lacking any journal-like articles. Many of these begin with either `alt` or `talk` as their general topic. For example, `talk.food.chocolate` may contain conversations about how wonderful or awful `chocolate` is thought to be. `alt.food.chocolate` may contain informal speculations about the importance of `chocolate` to the basic structure of civilization as we know it. Here are some examples of Unix newsgroup names:

```
alt.airlines.schedules
comp.lang.pascal
sci.physics.fusion
rec.arts.movies
rec.food.recipes
talk.politics.theory
```

To read Usenet articles you need to use a Usenet newsreader with which you can select a specific newsgroup. A newsreader operates like a user interface, allowing you to browse through and select available articles for reading, saving, or printing. For Unix systems there are several easy-to-use newsreaders that operate from the Unix command-line interface. These are `trn`, `nn`, `tin`, and `pine`. `rn` is an earlier newsreader whose elements have been incorporated in to `trn`. `trn`, `nn`, and, `tin` all provide you with a cursor-based screen interface with menus for easy selection of articles and executing commands. `pine` is a combination mailer and newsreader using the same interface to read articles as is used to read messages. It is discussed in Chapter 6. In addition there is an older newsreader called `readnews` that may still be used on some systems. It is discussed briefly in this chapter. With most of these newsreaders you can compose your own articles and add them to a Usenet newsgroup for others to read. Adding an article to a newsgroup is called posting the article. You can also post an article using a separate application called Pnews.

Posting Articles: `Pnews`

Though several newsreaders let you post articles to a newsgroup, you can use a separate application such as Pnews to post articles directly. Pnews operates like the MH mailer program. It prompts you for certain header information, places you in an editor in which you can type in your article, and then displays a menu with options to send, edit, save, or quit the article.

You start `Pnews` by entering the `Pnews` command at your Unix prompt. Pnews then prompts you to enter in the newsgroup for the article. In Figure 7.1, the user enters the newsgroup `rec.food.recipes`. To see the full list of newsgroups, enter a ? at the `Newgroup(s):` prompt. You can always obtain a listing of newsgroups at any time from the **newsgroups** file located in the news directory on your system.

After selecting your newsgroups, you are then asked to specify distribution. Distribution can be made at ever widening areas. You can post your article for local viewing for users on your own system, or you can post it for worldwide viewing. There are also various intermediate levels of distribution such as North America, the United States, or a specific state or city. Pnews lists possible prefixes, and then you enter in the one you want at the `Distribution ():` prompt. In the Figure 7.1, the user limits distribution to the United States, `usa`.

Enter a subject for the article at the prompt. You are then asked if you really want to post the article. To continue, enter `y`. Pnews then

---

$ Pnews

Newsgroup(s): **rec.food.recipes**

Your local distribution prefixes are:
    Local organization: games
    Organization: Sweets-I-like
    City: ba
    State: ca
    Multi-State Area:
    Country: usa
    Continent: na
    Everywhere: <null> (not "world")

Distribution (): **usa**

Title/Subject: **cookies**

This program posts news to many machines throughout the country. Are you absolutely sure that you want to do this? [ny] y

Prepared file to include [none]: **spcookies**

Your article's newsgroup:
rec.food.recipes   Recipes for interesting food and drink. (Moderated)

Check spelling, Send, Abort, Edit, or List? **s**
$

Figure 7.1. Posting an article using Pnews **and a prepared file.**

asks if you have a prepared file to include in your article. Often it is easier to first write your article and save it to a file using a standard editor. Then, once it is ready, you can post the contents of that file. In Figure 7.1, the user specifies the file **spcookies.** The contents of this file are then read into the article that is being posted. If you do not enter a file name at this point, Pnews will automatically place you in an editor where you can then type your article.

Pnews then displays a menu list, prompting you to either send, abort, edit, or list the article. Enter the first character of a listed command to execute it. For example, if you change your mind and decide not to post the article, enter a at this prompt, quitting Pnews without sending the article. Alternatively, enter e at the prompt to edit the article in case you want to change anything in it. To post the article, enter s for send. The article is then sent to the Usenet manager and posted in the appropriate newsgroup.

Figure 7.2 shows an example of Pnews in which the user makes use of the standard editor to enter the text of the article. When asked for a prepared file to include, the user simply hits **return**. The user is then asked to enter an editor. Within brackets, Pnews will display the default standard editor it uses. In Figure 7.2, the default editor is Vi. In this case the user simply hits **return** to use the default Vi editor. Pnews then places you in the default editor so you can type in your article, correcting any mistakes you might make. Once in the editor, Pnews first displays the header information. You are free to change fields in the header if you want. You could change the subject or even the newsgroup. Use standard editing commands to enter the text of your article. When finished, exit the editor. In the case of the Vi editor, hit ZZ to exit. You then are given the Pnews prompt to send, abort, edit, or list your article. You can, of course, edit your article again by entering e at this prompt. To finally post the article, enter s at the prompt.

The .signature File

Articles are often signed using standard signature information such as the your name, Internet address or addresses, and a polite sign-off. As you write more articles, it is helpful to have your

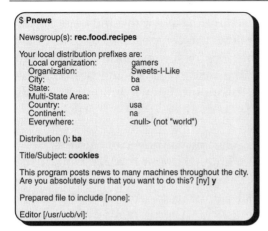

```
$ Pnews

Newsgroup(s): rec.food.recipes

Your local distribution prefixes are:
    Local organization:     gamers
    Organization:           Sweets-I-Like
    City:                   ba
    State:                  ca
    Multi-State Area:
    Country:                usa
    Continent:              na
    Everywhere:             <null> (not "world")

Distribution (): ba

Title/Subject: cookies

This program posts news to many machines throughout the city.
Are you absolutely sure that you want to do this? [ny] y

Prepared file to include [none]:

Editor [/usr/ucb/vi]:
```

The user invokes `Pnews`, entering in the newsgroup, distribution, and subject. There is no prepared file so the user just presses **enter**. At the editor prompt, the user again presses **enter** to use the defualt editor, in this case Vi.

```
Newsgroups: rec.food.recipes
Subject: cookies
Summary:
Followup-To:
Distribution: ba
Organization:  Sweets-I-Like
Keywords:
Cc:


~
~
~
~
~
~
~

"/home/chris/.article" 10 lines, 154 character
```

In the editor, Pnews first displays the article's header.

```
Newsgroups: rec.food.recipes
Subject: cookies
Summary:
Followup-To:
Distribution: ba
Organization:  Sweets-I-Like
Keywords:
Cc:

Does anyone have a recipe for a good chocolate cookie?


~
~
~
~
~
~

"/home/chris/.article" 11 lines, 213 characters
```

Using standard editing commands, the user enters the text of the article. When finished, exit the editor, saving your article. If in the Vi editor, exit and save by hitting Z Z.

```
Your article's newsgroup:
rec.food.recipes       Recipes for interesting food and drink.
(Moderated)

Check spelling, Send, Abort, Edit, or List? l

Newsgroups: rec.food.recipes
Subject: cookies
Summary:
Followup-To:
Distribution: ba
Organization:  Sweets-I-Like
Keywords:
Cc:

    Does anyone have a recipe for a good chocolate cookie?


Check spelling, Send, Abort, Edit, or List? s

$
```

After exiting the editor, Pnews then prompts the user to send, abort, edit, or list the article. The user first lists the article by entering l at the prompt. After listing the article the user is again prompted. At this point the user enters s to send the article, posting it to the Usenet.

Figure 7.2. Posting an article using `Pnews` **and the standard editor.**

signature information automatically added to your articles. To do so, you need to create a file called .**signature** in your home directory and enter your signature information in it. Pnews and mailers such as `Pine` will read the contents of the .**signature** file and place it at the end of an article you are composing. Any standard editor can be used to create your **.signature** file.

The `rn` **Newsreader**

The `rn` newsreader is one of the earlier Usenet newsreaders. Though it is not used much these days, many of its commands are carried over to other more powerful newsreaders such as `trn`. With `rn` you can scroll through a list of newsgroups, selecting one, and then read the articles in it. The `rn` interface has several other powerful features such as pattern searches for groups of articles.

`rn` operates on two levels, the newsgroup list and the article list. When you first execute `rn` you need to select a newsgroup from a list of newsgroups. There are commands that move you from one newsgroup to another in the list. Once you have found the one you want, you can then select articles to read in that newsgroup. When you have finished reading your articles, you can leave that newsgroup and select another in the newsgroup list. The commands for moving through the newsgroup list and the article list are often the same. Depending on what type of list you are operating on, you will either move through newsgroups or articles. For example, the n command for the newsgroup list moves you to the next newsgroup, whereas the n command for the article list moves you to the next article. The `rn` newsreader commands are listed in Tables 7.I, 7.II, and 7.III.

The `rn` newsreader distinguishes between newsgroups with unread news and those with no unread news. You can use certain `rn` commands to search for and select only those newsgroups with unread news. The term *unread news* refers to articles that you personally have not read in a newsgroup. `rn`, as well as other newsreaders like `trn`, keeps tract of what a user has read or not read by means of a **.newsrc** file placed in the user's account. Each user has his or her own **.newsrc** file. This file consists of a list of all the newsgroups provided by your Usenet server. Each entry is used to keep track of whether there is read or unread news in it.

The `rn` newsreader will list newsgroups to which you have subscribed. Depending on how your Unsenet server access is configured,

when you first use rn, you may automatically subscribe to all newsgroups or to none, in which case you can add the ones you want
individually. If you are subscribed to them all, you can unsubsribe
them and then add ones you want. One way of unsubscribing or sub-
scribing to newsgroups is to edit the **.newsrc** file with a text editor
like Vi or Emacs, and then add or delete those newsgroup entries.

Newsgroup List

Enter the rn newsreader by entering the command rn at your Unix
prompt. rn will initially display a short list of newsgroup headers.
However, before doing so, rn will first check an official list of new
newsgroups with those listed in your **.newsrc** file. If there are any
new newsgroups not yet listed in your **.newsrc** file, rn will ask one
by one if you want to subscribe to them. At each prompt, you can
enter y to add the newsgroup and n not to add it.

If there are many new newsgroups to decide on, you can skip this
initial subscription phase by invoking rn the -q option. With -q,
rn will go directly to displaying the newsgroup headers, skipping
any new newsgroup queries.

```
$ rn -q
```

After the subscription phase, rn checks to see if there are any newsgroups listed in your **.newsrc** file that have unread news in them.
If so, the newsgroup headers for the first few of these are displayed. Each newsgroup header tells how many unread articles remain in a given newsgroup. rn then prompts you as to whether
you want to read articles in the first newsgroup. If not, you can
enter the n command to move to the next newsgroup. The p command moves you back to the previous newsgroup.

To read articles in a newsgroup, enter y at the prompt. The first article in the newsgroup is then displayed. You are then prompted to
read the next article. You can leave the newsgroup and return to
the newsgroup list by entering q at the prompt.

In the next example, the user enters the rn interface and a list of
newsgroup headers is displayed. The user is then prompted for the

first header which the user skips with the n command. At the next header, the user enters a y command to read articles in the alt.3d.misc newsgroup.

```
$ rn
Unread news in 3dfx.game.discussion       314 articles
Unread news in alt.3d.misc                  3 articles
Unread news in alt.agriculture.fruit        1 article
Unread news in alt.airlines.schedules       1 article
Unread news in alt.airports                 3 articles
etc.

====== 314 unread articles in 3dfx.game.discussion − −
read now? [+ynq] n
======   3 unread articles in alt.3d.misc − − read now?
[+ynq] y]
```

rn has a variety of commands for moving through the list of newsgroups. You can move to the first or last newsgroup, the next or previous newsgroup, or the newsgroup whose name has a specific pattern. For example, a $ will place you at the end of the newsgroup list. Many commands are designed to distinguish between read and unread newsgroups. The ^ places you at the first newsgroup with unread news, whereas the number 1 places you at the first newsgroup in the list whether it is read or not. The lowercase n and p commands place you at the next and previous unread newsgroups. To move to the next or previous newsgroup regardless of whether it is read or not, you need to use the uppercase N and P commands.

When you first start using rn, many of your newsgroups will have a vast number of unread articles in them. Instead of reading each one, you could simply start with a clean slate by marking them all as read. The c command entered at the newsgroup prompt will mark all articles in the newsgroup as read. Then, unread-sensitive commands such as n and p cannot select the newsgroup until new articles are posted for it.

If you know the name of the newsgroup you want, you can use pattern searches to move directly to it. The pattern searching commands give rn great versatility in locating newsgroups. To perform a pattern search for a newsgroup, at the prompt enter a / followed by the pattern. The / performs a forward search through the list of newsgroups. The ? performs a backward search. In the next example, the user searches for the newsgroup on food recipes.

```
$ rn
Unread news in 3dfx.game.discussion    314 articles
Unread news in alt.3d.misc               3 articles
Unread news in alt.agriculture.fruit     1 article
Unread news in alt.airlines.schedules    1 article
Unread news in alt.airports              3 articles
etc.
====== 314 unread articles in 3dfx.game.discussion − −
read now? [+ynq] /food.recipes
Searching...
====== 245 unread articles in rec.food.recipes − −
read now? [+ynq] y
```

You can also locate a newsgroup by its full name. The g command followed by a newsgroup's name will locate that newsgroup.

```
====== 314 unread articles in to − − read now? [+ynq]
g rec.food.recipes
Searching...
====== 372 unread articles in rec.food.recipes − −
read now? [+ynq] y
```

The rn list and search commands reference only those newsgroups to which you have subscribed. With the l command you can list or search for unsubscribed newsgroups. The l command by itself lists all newsgroups to which you have not subscribed. Followed by a pattern, the l command searches unsubscribed newsgroups for that pattern, listing those matched. For example, ltrek searches for unsubscribed newsgroups with the pattern "trek" in it.

You can subscribe to a newsgroup with the a command. Enter a followed by the name of the newsgroup you want. You can unsubscribe a newsgroup with the u command. For example u rec.foods.recipes will unsubscribe that newsgroup. If you tried to select it with search commands such as / or g, you would not find it. Of course the l command would locate it; lrec.foods.recipes. To once again subscribe to this newsgroup you would use the command a rec.foods.recipes. Commands for selecting newsgroups are summarized in Table 7.I.

y	Select the current newsgroup.
n	Move to the next newsgroup with unread articles.
N	Move to the next newsgroup.
p	Move to the previous newsgroup with unread articles.
P	Move to the previous newsgroup.
−	Move to the previously selected newsgroup.
^	Move to the first newsgroup with unread articles.
num	Move to newsgroup with that number.
$	Move to the last newsgroup.
g*newsgroup-name*	Move to newsgroup with that name.
/*pattern*	Search forward to the newsgroup with that pattern.
?*pattern*	Search backward to the newsgroup with that pattern.
L	List subscribed newsgroups.
l*pattern*	List unsubscribed newsgroups.
u *newsgroup-name*	Unsubscribe a newsgroup.
a *newsgroup-name*	Subscribe to a newsgroup.
c	Mark articles in a newsgroup as read.

Table 7.I. Selecting Newsgroups with rn

Article List

Once you have located the newsgroup you want, you need to enter the article level and select any articles in that newsgroup of interest. Upon hitting y at the newsgroup prompt, you enter the article level and the header of the first article in the newsgroup is displayed. You can then read the first article or use article level commands to move to another article in the newsgroup. The article level commands are the same as those described earlier for moving through the newsgroup list. To move to the next article, you hit the n command. The p command will move you back an article. The ^ command moves to the first unread article, and the $ command moves to the last article. Commands for selecting articles are summarized in Table 7.II.

You can also move to a particular article by entering its number. Articles in a newsgroup are numbered consecutively. You can obtain a list of unread article titles and their numbers by hitting the = sign. Each line will list the number of the article, its title, and its subject. Entering the number of the article will move you to it.

```
End of article 210 (of 372) − − what next? [npq] 223
rec.food.recipes (moderated) #223                    (1)
From: chris@mygame.com (Chris Neil)


Subject: Spelling Cookies
Followup-To: poster
Organization: Sweets-I-Like
Date: Sat Aug 2 04:48:01 PST 1998
Lines: 43
```

rn also allows you to use pattern searches at the article level to locate an article. The / command, followed by a pattern, searches forward in the article list for an article with that pattern in the subject field of its header. The ? command will search backward. In the next example, the user searches the subject field of articles for the pattern "cookies."

```
End of article 210 (of 372) − − what next? [npq] /cookies
Searching...

rec.food.recipes (moderated) #223                    [1]
From: chris@mygame.com (Chris Niel)
Subject: Spelling Cookies
Followup-To: poster
Organization: Sweets-I-Like
Date: Sat Aug 2 04:48:01 PST 1998
Lines: 43


Spelling Cookies
     INGREDIENTS
     1 cup flour
     2 teaspoon single acting baking powder, or
       1 teaspoon double acting baking powder, or
       1 teaspoon baking soda
     1/2 teaspoon nutmeg
     1/4 teaspoon cinnamon
```

```
3/4 cup butter (or 1 1/2 sticks)
1 cup brown or dark-brown sugar
1/2 cup regular sugar
1 egg
1 teaspoon vanilla extract
1/4 cup milk
```
— —MORE— —(44%)

Using qualifiers with the pattern search, you can specify whether you want to search the text of articles, the entire header, or articles you have already read. The a qualifier searches the entire text of articles for a pattern. The h qualifier searches the entire header, and the r qualifier includes read articles in the search. In the next example, the user searches the headers of articles for the pattern "chris," including any articles that have already been read.

```
End of article 194 (of 372) — what next? [^Nnpq] /chris/hr
Searching...

rec.food.recipes (moderated) #223                    [1]
From: chris@mygame.com (Chris Niel)
Subject: Spelling Cookies
Followup-To: poster
Organization: Sweets-I-Like
Date: Sat Aug 2 04:48:01 PST 1998
Lines: 43

Spelling Cookies
         INGREDIENTS
    1 cup flour
    2 teaspoon single acting baking powder, or
       1 teaspoon double acting baking powder, or
       1 teaspoon baking soda
    1/2 teaspoon nutmeg
    1/4 teaspoon cinnamon
    3/4 cup butter (or 1 1/2 sticks)
    1 cup brown or dark-brown sugar
    1/2 cup regular sugar
    1 egg
    1 teaspoon vanilla extract
    1/4 cup milk
```
— —MORE— —(44%)

Table 7.II. Selecting and Marking Articles with `rn`

SELECTING ARTICLES

y	Display the current article.
n	Move to the next article with unread articles.
N	Move to the next article.
p	Move to the previous article with unread articles.
P	Move to the previous article.
–	Move to the previously selected article.
^	Move to the first article with unread articles.
num	Move to article with that number.
$	Move to the last article.
Ctrl-n	Move to the next article with the same subject as the current one.
Ctrl-p	Move to the previous article with the same subject as the current one.
/*pattern*	Search forward to the article with that pattern in each article's subject field.
	Modifiers
h	Search forward to the article with that pattern in the header.
	/*pattern*/h
a	Search forward to the article with that pattern in either the header or the text.
	/*pattern*/a
r	Include read articles in you search.
	/*pattern*/r
c	Make search case sensitive.
	/*pattern*/c
?*pattern*?	Search backward to the article with that pattern in each article's subject field.
	Modifiers
h	Search backward to the article with that pattern in the header.
	?*pattern*?h

a	Search forward to the article with that pattern in either the header or the text.
	*?pattern?*a
r	Include read articles in you search.
	*?pattern?*r
c	Make search case sensitive.
	*?pattern?*c
/	Repeat previous forward search.
?	Repeat previous backward search.
/pattern:command	Select a group of articles matching the pattern and apply the rn command to all of them.
num,num:command	Select a group of articles referenced by the numbers and apply the rn command to all of them.

MARKING ARTICLES

m	Mark current article as read.
n	Mark current article as read and move to next article.
j	Mark current article as read and display end of article.
c	Mark all articles as read in the current newsgroup.

You can also search for articles that have the same subject. To do so, first locate an article with the subject for which you are looking. To locate the next article with that same subject, you hit a **Ctrl-n**. You then move to that article. Using **Ctrl-n** consecutively will find the next articles with the same subject. A **Ctrl-p** searches backward for the previous article with the same subject.

Displaying Articles

When you select an article, its header is displayed followed by a (more) prompt and the first page of the text. The article will be displayed screen by screen, just as files are displayed screen by screen with the pg and more utilities (Figure 7.3). To continue to

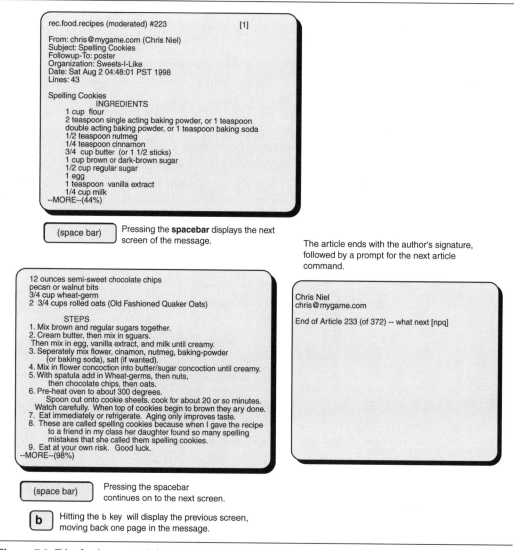

rec.food.recipes (moderated) #223   [1]

From: chris@mygame.com (Chris Niel)
Subject: Spelling Cookies
Followup-To: poster
Organization: Sweets-I-Like
Date: Sat Aug 2 04:48:01 PST 1998
Lines: 43

Spelling Cookies
            INGREDIENTS
    1 cup flour
    2 teaspoon single acting baking powder, or 1 teaspoon
    double acting baking powder, or 1 teaspoon baking soda
    1/2 teaspoon nutmeg
    1/4 teaspoon cinnamon
    3/4 cup butter (or 1 1/2 sticks)
    1 cup brown or dark-brown sugar
    1/2 cup regular sugar
    1 egg
    1 teaspoon vanilla extract
    1/4 cup milk
--MORE--(44%)

(space bar)   Pressing the **spacebar** displays the next
               screen of the message.

The article ends with the author's signature,
followed by a prompt for the next article
command.

12 ounces semi-sweet chocolate chips
pecan or walnut bits
3/4 cup wheat-germ
2 3/4 cups rolled oats (Old Fashioned Quaker Oats)

        STEPS
1. Mix brown and regular sugars together.
2. Cream butter, then mix in sguars.
   Then mix in egg, vanilla extract, and milk until creamy.
3. Seperately mix flower, cinamon, nutmeg, baking-powder
      (or baking soda), salt (if wanted).
4. Mix in flower concoction into butter/sugar concoction until creamy.
5. With spatula add in Wheat-germs, then nuts,
      then chocolate chips, then oats.
6. Pre-heat oven to about 300 degrees.
      Spoon out onto cookie sheets. cook for about 20 or so minutes.
   Watch carefully. When top of cookies begin to brown they ary done.
7. Eat immediately or refrigerate. Aging only improves taste.
8. These are called spelling cookies because when I gave the recipe
      to a friend in my class her daughter found so many spelling
      mistakes that she called them spelling cookies.
9. Eat at your own risk. Good luck.
--MORE--(98%)

Chris Niel
chris@mygame.com

End of Article 233 (of 372) -- what next [npq]

(space bar)   Pressing the spacebar
               continues on to the next screen.

b   Hitting the b key will display the previous screen,
     moving back one page in the message.

Figure 7.3. Displaying an article using rn.

the next screen, hit the **spacebar**. You can move backward a page
of the article by hitting the b key. The q command allows you to
quit before reading the whole article.

You can also search the text of your article for the occurrence of a
pattern. The g command followed by a pattern will locate the first
occurrence of that pattern in the text. You can repeat the search

with the G command. Commands for displaying articles are summarized in Table 7.III.

Saving Articles

You can save any article that you have read. After displaying the
article, enter the s command with a file name. If the file does not
yet exist, you will be asked if you want to use a mailbox file format
for it. If you enter y, the file will be a mailbox file and the article
will be saved as one message in that mailbox. You can then later
use the mailx command with the -f option to read the articles
saved in that file. If, however, you simply hit **return**, the file will
have a standard text file format.

```
rec.food.recipes (moderated) #223                    [1]
From: chris@mygame.com (Chris Niel)
Subject: Spelling Cookies
Followup-To: poster
Organization: Sweets-I-Like
Date: Sat Aug 2 04:48:01 PST 1998
Lines: 43


Spelling Cookies
          INGREDIENTS
    1 cup flour
    2 teaspoon single acting baking powder, or
      1 teaspoon double acting baking powder, or
      1 teaspoon baking soda
    1/2 teaspoon nutmeg
    1/4 teaspoon cinnamon
    3/4 cup butter (or 1 1/2 sticks)
    1 cup brown or dark-brown sugar
    1/2 cup regular sugar
    1 egg
    1 teaspoon vanilla extract
    1/4 cup milk
End of article 223 (of 272) — — what next? [npq] s spellcookies

File /home/dylan/News/spellcookies doesn't exist — —
    use mailbox format? [ynq] y
Saved to mailbox /home/dylan/News/spellcookies

End of article 223 (of 372) — — what next? [npq]
```

DISPLAYING ARTICLES

spacebar	Display the next screen of the article.
return	Scroll to the next line of the article.
d	Scroll to the next half screen of the article.
b	Display the previous screen of the article.
v	Redisplay article from the beginning.
q	Display last screen of the article.
g *pattern*	Search for pattern in the text.
G	Repeat pattern search in the text.

SAVING ARTICLES AND REPLYING TO ARTICLES

s	Save the current article to a mailbox file (includes header).
w	Save the current article to a file, but without its header.
r	Reply to current article.
R	Reply to current article and include article text in the reply.
f	Post a follow-up to the current article.
F	Post a follow-up including the text of the current article.

Table 7.III. Displaying and Saving Articles with rn

Other articles that you save to an already existing file will simply be appended to it. In the case of mailbox files, the added articles will become new messages. When saving several articles in the same file, the mailbox format has several advantages. You can easily access particular articles using `mailx`. You can also mail replies to authors of articles using the R command, or easily incorporate an article in a messages to other users. Commands for saving articles are summarized in Table 7.III.

Marking Articles

Once you have read an article, `rn` will no longer display its header in the article list and you will no longer be able to access it at a later date through `rn`. If, however, you want to come back to the article at a later date, you can mark the article as unread so that `rn` will continue to display its header in the article list. To mark an article as unread, enter the m command when you read it. If you want to read it only during the next session, use the M command.

Article Selections

You can select a group of articles based on pattern searches or on number references. A pattern search followed by a colon and one of the rn commands will apply that command to every article with that pattern, not just to the next article. In effect, a pattern search followed by a colon will select a group of articles on which you can perform operations. For example, if you want to save all articles dealing with the subject "cookies" you could issue the command:

```
/cookies/:s cookfile
```

```
End of article 192 (of 372) − − what next? [npq]
  /cookies/:s cookfile
Searching...
210
File /home/dylan/News/cookfile doesn't exist−
    use mailbox format? [ynq] y
Saved to mailbox /home/dylan/News/cookfile
210 Appended to mailbox /home/dylan/News/cookfile
223 Appended to mailbox /home/dylan/News/cookfile
done
End of article 223 (of 372) − − what next? [npq]
```

The ^ symbol is a special pattern that represents all articles. To save all articles to a file, use the command:

```
    /^/:s myfile
```

When used with the = command, a pattern can provide you with a listing of articles on a certain topic. The = command lists the number and subject of each article. When qualified by a pattern, it only lists articles on that subject. The next example lists the numbers and subjects of all unread articles on cookies: /cookies/:=.

```
End of article 192 (of 372) − − what next? [^Nnpq]
  /cookies/:=
Searching...
210 Oatmeal Cookies
256 Chocolate Chip Cookies
End of article 289 (of 372) − − what next? [^Nnpq]
```

If you want to include all read articles in your list, you need to qualify the pattern with `r`. The next example provides a listing of all articles on cookies, including read ones: `/cookies/r:=`.

```
End of article 192 (of 372) — — what next? [^Nnpq]
  /cookies/r:=
Searching...
110  Oatmeal Cookies
115  REQUEST: Rosettes (Butter Cookies)
161  REQUEST: Sugar Cookies
205  REQUEST: Persimmon Cookies
210  Oatmeal Cookies
223  Spelling Cookies
250  REQUEST: Cookies
266  REQUEST: Oatmeal Cookies
328  Chocolate Chip Cookies
End of article 328 (of 372) — — what next? [^Nnpq]
```

A pattern by default only searches the subject field of an article. When used with the a qualifier a pattern searches throughout the entire text of an article. The next example provides a list of all recipes that use chocolate. The results of this particular query are often too long to print!

```
/chocolate/a:=
```

You can also reference a group of articles by listing their numbers separated by commas. The list ends in a colon followed by a command applied to those articles. Because articles are consecutively numbered, you can include in your list the desired number ranges. A number range consists of the first number in the range followed by a minus sign, and then the last number in the range. 3-5 references articles 3, 4, and 5. To save articles 34, 17, and 9–12 you would use the command:

```
34,17,9-12:s myfile
```

In the next example, the user saves articles 223 and 328 to the file goodcook: `223,328:s goodcook`.

```
End of article 192 (of 372) — — what next? [npq]
  223,328:s goodcook
```

```
223  Appended to mailbox /home/dylan/News/goodcook
328  Appended to mailbox /home/dylan/News/goodcook
End of article 192 (of 372) — what next? [npq]
```

In both pattern and number references, you can append other commands to be applied to the group of articles. Just separate each command with a colon. In the next example, articles 34, 17, and 9–12, are both saved and printed.

```
34,17,9-12:s myfile: | lp
```

Replying to Articles: Follow-Ups and Messages

You can reply to a specific article by either posting a follow-up article of your own, or by sending the author a message by mail (see Figure 7.4). A follow-up article is an article that you post on Usenet in response to another article you have read. If you post a follow-up article, you will be posting an article that anyone on Usenet can read. A mail message, on the other hand, is a private message to that author sent using Unix mail. The f and F commands will post a follow-up article and the r and R commands send a reply message.

Posting Follow-Ups

You post a follow-up article from within the rn newsreader. While you are reading an article, you can post a follow-up to it by entering the f or F commands. These commands then invokes Pnews to actually enter and post your follow-up article. The F command will include in your follow-up the text of the article to which you are responding. The text will be displayed indented with each line preceded by a > sign.

To post a follow-up, first locate the article you want to respond to and hit the f command. You are then placed in the editor with the header for your follow-up article. Enter the text of your article and edit the header fields if you want. Upon exiting the editor, you are prompted to either send, abort, edit, or list the follow-up article. The send command will post the article for you.

```
rec.food.recipes (moderated) #223
From: chris@mygame.com (Chris Niel)

Subject:  Spelling Cookies
Followup-To: poster
Organization: Sweets-I-like
Date: Sat Aug 2 04:48:01 PST 1998
Lines: 44


Spelling Cookies

             INGREDIENTS
    1 cup  flour
    2 teaspoon single acting baking powder, or 1 teaspoon
        double acting baking powder, or 1 teaspoon baking soda
    1/2 teaspoon nutmeg
    1/4 teaspoon cinnamon
    3/4  cup butter  (or 1 1/2 sticks)
    1 cup brown or dark-brown sugar
    1/2 cup regular sugar
    1 egg
    1 teaspoon  vanilla extract
    1/4 cup milk
```

f   While reading an article, you hit the f key to post a follow-up to that article.

```
(Be sure to double-check the attribution against the signature,
and trim the quoted article down as much as possible.)

(leaving cbreak mode; cwd=/h/garnet_d/richpete)
Invoking command: QUOTECHARS='>' Pnews -h
h/garnet_d/richpete/.rnhead


This program posts news to thousands of machines
throughout the entire civilized world.  Your message will cost
the net hundreds if not thousands of dollars to send
everywhere.  Please be sure you know what you are doing.

Are you absolutely sure that you want to do this? [ny] y

Prepared file to include [none]:

Editor [/usr/ucb/vi]:
```

Pnews is automatically invoked and asks you if you really want to post the article. You are then prompted for a prepared file. If none, you are placed in the standard editor to compose your response.

```
To: chris@mygame.com
Subject: Re: Spelling Cookies
Newsgroups: rec.food.recipes
In-Reply-To: <justin@mycar.com>
Organization:  Great-soccer-playters
Cc:
Bcc:


  These are great cookies
~
~
~
~
~
~
~
~
~
~
"/home/justin/.letter" 11 lines, 237 characters
```

Using standard editing commands, you enter in the text of your follow-up article. When finished, exit the editor, saving your article. If using the Vi editor, exit and save by hitting z z.

```
Check spelling, Send, Abort, Edit, or List? s

what  now  [+ynq]
```

After exiting the editor, Pnews then prompts you to send, abort, edit, or list the article. To post your follow-up, enter s. Then the rn newsreader continues with its article prompt.

Figure 7.4. Composing and posting a follow-up to an article.

You can see how follow-ups allow you to carry on discussions about an article in your newsgroup. You cannot only read an article, you can also read what other people think of it by reading follow-up articles posted about the article. You can even post follow-ups to the follow-ups, carrying on discussions with other users about an article. In effect, you are commenting on what other people think of an article. You post a follow-up of a follow-up by locating the follow-up article and then hitting f and posting your response.

When responding to an article, it is often helpful to include the original text in your follow-up (see Figure 7.5). Use the F command to post a follow-up article that includes the text of the article. Each included line of article text is preceded by a > sign. You do not have to keep the entire text of the article in your follow-up. Suppose that you only want to respond to one part of the article. While in the editor, you can delete all but that part of the article to which you want to respond. Your follow-up article will then list only that part of the original article and any comments that you decide to add. You can even use the editor to insert your own comments throughout the included text of the original article, providing a kind of annotated version of it.

The F command is very useful when posting follow-ups to follow-ups because it is often clearer. Instead of painstakingly typing them in yourself, the F command will include the follow-up article text automatically with your own follow-up.

Mailing Replies to Authors

Instead of posting a follow-up for everyone to read, you can simply mail a reply directly to the author of an article (Figure 7.6). You do so with either the r and R commands. First locate the article you want to send a reply for, and hit the r command. The article header is then displayed and the mail program is invoked. You are placed in your editor where you can then enter your message. The header will also be included so that you can change your subject entry or summary line if you want. When you leave the editor, you are asked if you want to send, abort, edit, or list the message. The send command will mail the message to the author of the article.

Should you want to include a copy of the article's text in your message, use the R command. As with the F command, the R command will include the text of article with each line preceded by a > sign. In the editor, you can then delete, copy, or move the text as you wish.

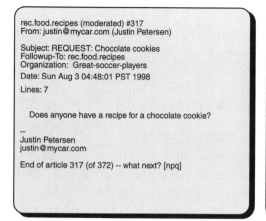

```
rec.food.recipes (moderated) #317
From: justin@mycar.com (Justin Petersen)

Subject: REQUEST: Chocolate cookies
Followup-To: rec.food.recipes
Organization:  Great-soccer-players
Date: Sun Aug 3 04:48:01 PST 1998
Lines: 7


       Does anyone have a recipe for a chocolate cookie?

--
Justin Petersen
justin@mycar.com

End of article 317 (of 372) -- what next? [npq]
```

While reading an article or after reading it, press the F key to post a follow-up to that article and to include the text of the article in your follow-up.

```
(Be sure to double-check the attribution against the signature,
and trim the quoted article down as much as possible.)

(leaving cbreak mode; cwd=/h/garnet_d/richpete)
Invoking command: QUOTECHARS='>' Pnews -h
h/garnet_d/richpete/.rnhead

This program posts news to thousands of machines throughout
the entire civilized world. Your message will cost the net
hundreds if not thousands of dollars to send everywhere.
Please be sure you know what you are doing.

Are you absolutely sure that you want to do this? [ny] y

Prepared file to include [none]:

Editor [/usr/ucb/vi]:
```

Pnews is automatically invoked and displays the header for the article to which you are responding. You are then prompted for a prepared file. If none, you are placed in the standard editor to compose your response.

```
X-ORIGINAL-NEWSGROUPS: rec.food.recipes
Newsgroups: rec.food.recipes
Subject: Re: REQUEST: Chocolate cookies
Summary:
Expires:
References:
Sender:
Followup-To:
Distribution:
Organization: Great-soccer-players
Keywords:
Cc:

In article <2mbj3k$9l6@agate.berkeley.edu>,
Justin Petersen <justin@mycar.com> wrote:
>
>    Does anyone have a recipe for a chocolate cookie?
>
>--
>Justin Petersen
>justing@mycar.com
>

 How  many do you need?

"/home/dylan/.article" 25 lines, 508 characters
```

Using standard editing commands, enter the text of your follow-up article. Notice that the original article's text is included with preceding > signs for each line.

```
Your article's newsgroup:
rec.food.recipes       Recipes for interesting food and drink.
(Moderated)

Check spelling, Send, Abort, Edit, or List? s

what  now  [+ynq]
```

After exiting the editor, Pnews then prompts you to send, abort, edit, or list the article. To post your follow-up, enter s. Then the rn newsreader continues with its article prompt.

Figure 7.5. Including article text in a posted follow-up article.

rn options

A number of options are available with rn, as listed in Table 7.IV. With the -n option you can specify a specific newsgroup or type of

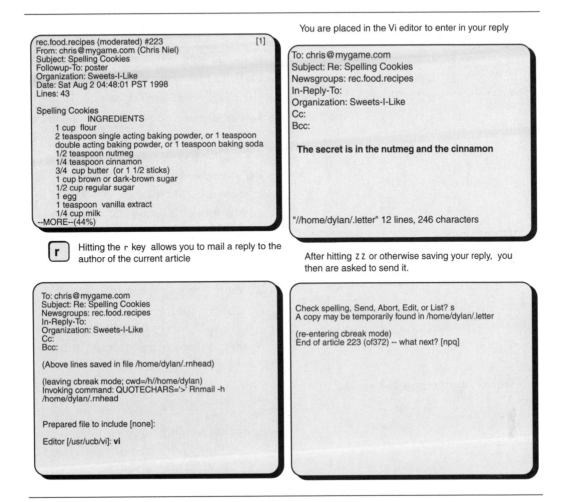

You are placed in the Vi editor to enter in your reply

```
rec.food.recipes (moderated) #223                    [1]
From: chris@mygame.com (Chris Niel)
Subject: Spelling Cookies
Followup-To: poster
Organization: Sweets-I-Like
Date: Sat Aug 2 04:48:01 PST 1998
Lines: 43

Spelling Cookies
            INGREDIENTS
    1 cup  flour
    2 teaspoon single acting baking powder, or 1 teaspoon
    double acting baking powder, or 1 teaspoon baking soda
    1/2 teaspoon nutmeg
    1/4 teaspoon cinnamon
    3/4  cup butter  (or 1 1/2 sticks)
    1 cup brown or dark-brown sugar
    1/2 cup regular sugar
    1 egg
    1 teaspoon  vanilla extract
    1/4 cup milk
--MORE--(44%)
```

```
To: chris@mygame.com
Subject: Re: Spelling Cookies
Newsgroups: rec.food.recipes
In-Reply-To:
Organization: Sweets-I-Like
Cc:
Bcc:

The secret is in the nutmeg and the cinnamon




"//home/dylan/.letter" 12 lines, 246 characters
```

r Hitting the r key allows you to mail a reply to the author of the current article

After hitting z z or otherwise saving your reply, you then are asked to send it.

```
To: chris@mygame.com
Subject: Re: Spelling Cookies
Newsgroups: rec.food.recipes
In-Reply-To:
Organization: Sweets-I-Like
Cc:
Bcc:

(Above lines saved in file /home/dylan/.rnhead)

(leaving cbreak mode; cwd=/h//home/dylan)
Invoking command: QUOTECHARS='>' Rnmail -h
/home/dylan/.rnhead


Prepared file to include [none]:

Editor [/usr/ucb/vi]: vi
```

```
Check spelling, Send, Abort, Edit, or List? s
A copy may be temporarily found in /home/dylan/.letter

(re-entering cbreak mode)
End of article 223 (of372) -- what next? [npq]
```

Figure 7.6. Sending a mail reply to the author of an article.

newsgroup that you want to read. With the -l option you can list just newsgroup headers. In the next example, the user lists the newsgroup headers for the rec.food.recipes newsgroups.

```
$ rn -l -n rec.food.recipes
```

rn also supports several option variables with which you can specify certain header fields, directories, or applications. For example,

OPTIONS

-n *newsgroup,newsgroup*	Select newsgroups.
-t *pattern,pattern*	Select articles that contain the patterns.
-a *date*	Select article posted after the date.
-x	Select all articles including the ones you have read.
-q	Skip subscription of new newsgroups.
-c	Check if any newsgroups are unread.
-l	List only the titles of articles.
-e	List only the titles, but mark the articles as read.
-r	Read articles in reverse order.
-f	Display only original articles.
-h	Display short versions of headers.
-s	Display a user's site.
-p	Output all articles to the standard output, which you can then redirect to a file or pipe to a printer.

OPTION VARIABLES

EDITOR	Editor for composing replies.
MAILPOSTER	Mail utility for sending replies
PAGER	Page utility for reading articles.
SAVEDIR	Directory to which to save articles.
NAME	Your full name to be used for article headers that you post.
ORGANIZATION	Your organization name for article headers that you post.

Table 7.IV. rn **Options**

the MAILPOSTER specifies the mailer to use for sending replies, and the NAME variable is where you can keep the string for your full name as you want it to appear in your article headers. SAVEDIR is the directory where you want your saved articles to be placed.

The readnews **Newsreader**

The readnews newsreader was the first newsreader developed for Usenet. Though it has since been replaced by more powerful news-readers such as rn, some systems may still use it. A brief description is provided here. Many of its commands were carried over to other newsreaders such as rn. The readnews newsreader commands are listed in Table 7.V.

You begin readnews by entering the readnews command on the command line. readnews then displays the header of the first article of the first newsgroup. After the header, you are prompted for a readnews command. You can then perform such actions as read the article, skip the article and go on to the next one, or move to the next newsgroup. The command y will display the current article. A lowercase n will skip to the next article. A uppercase N will move to the next newsgroup. You can also quit readnews by entering the q command. In the next example, the user moves to the next article and displays it.

```
$ readnews

_____
Newsgroup rec.food.recipes
_____
Article 36 of , Sat Aug 2 07:45:05
Subject: cookies
From: chris@mygame.com (Chris Niel)
Newsgroups: rec.food.recipes
( 55 lines) More? [ynq] n

Article 37 of , Fri Aug 1 13:04:48
Subject: cake
From: dylan@train.com
Newsgroups: rec.food.recipes
( 74 lines) More? [ynq] y
```

After you have displayed an article, the header of the next article is displayed. You can then display it or move on. You can move back and forth through the list of articles using the n and p commands. The p command will move back to the previous article.

You can also move from one newsgroup to another using the P and N commands. N moves to the next newsgroup and P moves to the previous newsgroup. In the next example, the user is prompted to act on an article, but, instead, moves to the next newsgroup using the N command.

```
Article 36 of , Sat Aug 2 07:45
Subject: cookies
From: chris@mygame.com (Chris Niel)
Newsgroups: rec.food.recipes
( 55 lines) More? [ynq] N


----------------
Newsgroup rec.food.restaurants
----------------

Article 10 of , Fri Aug 1 07:45:05
Subject: pizza
From: aleina@skate.com
Newsgroups: rec.food.restaurants
( 55 lines) More? [ynq]
```

Replying to Articles

You can reply to a specific article by either posting a follow-up article of your own or by sending the author a message by mail. If you post a follow-up article, you will be posting a article that anyone on Usenet can read. A mail message, on the other hand, is a private message to the article's author sent using Unix mail. The f command will post a follow-up article and the r command sends a reply message.

To post a follow-up article, enter the f command at the prompt. You are then asked to enter a summary of your article and if you want to include a copy of the article you are responding to in your own article. You are then placed in a standard editor where you can then type the text of your article. Upon leaving the editor, you are prompted as to whether you want to send it or perform some other operation on it such as editing it again. The send command will post the article for you. If you quit, the article is not posted.

Table 7.V. readnews **Commands**

DISPLAYING ARTICLES

y	Display the current article.
p	Display the previous article.
D	If an article is encrypted, this command will decrypt it.
d	This command takes a digest of articles and generates the corresponding complete articles.
h	Display expanded header information for an article.
H	Display complete header information for an article.
#	Display number of current article, number of articles in the newsgroup, and the newsgroup name.

QUIT AND HELP

?	List command summary.
q	Quit readnews and register read articles.
x	Quit readnews, but do not register read articles.

MOVING TO ARTICLES

n	Move to the next article, without displaying the current article.
m	Move back to the previous article.
–	Move back to last article displayed.

MOVING TO NEWSGROUPS

N	Move to next newsgroup.
P	Move to previous newsgroup.
U	Unsubscribe to a newsgroup.

SAVING AND MARKING ARTICLES

s	Save the current article to a file.
e	Mark the current article as unread.
+	Skip next article and mark as unread. *(continued)*

Table 7.V. readnews Commands *(continued)*

K	Mark rest of articles in the current newsgroup and move on to the next newsgroup.

POSTING ARTICLES AND REPLIES

f	Post an article.
fd	Post an article without a header.
r	Reply to an article by sending a message to the author.
c	Cancel a posted article.

OPTIONS

-n *newsgroup,newsgroup*	Select newsgroups.
-t *pattern,pattern*	Select articles that contain the patterns.
-a *date*	Select article posted after the date.
-x	Select all articles including the ones you have read.
-l	List only the titles of articles.
-e	List only the titles, but mark the articles as read.
-r	Read articles in reverse order.
-f	Display only original articles.
-h	Display short versions of headers.
-s	Display a user's site.
-p	Output all articles to the standard output, which you can then redirect to a file or pipe to a printer.

To send a reply by mail, enter the r command at the prompt, which places you in the editor, where you can enter a message. The header will also be included so that you can change the subject entry or summary line if you want. Upon saving your text and exiting the editor, your message is automatically sent.

Summary

Usenet can be thought of as an online electronic news service containing journal articles, recent bulletins, and discussions on different topics. Usenet is divided by topic into different newsgroups. You can access a newsgroup and read the articles in it. You can also compose and post articles of your own to a particular newsgroup, or respond to an article either by posting your response in the same newsgroup for everyone to read, or by sending your response as a message directly to the article's author.

To access Usenet articles you can use one of several available newsreader programs. Several of the more popular are rn, trn, and nn. readnews is an older version of rn that may still be used on many systems. rn allows you to search newsgroups and articles using pattern searches, as well as copy articles and post articles of your own. rn also distinguishes between read and unread articles, allowing you to easily access newly posted articles in a newsgroup.

trn Newsreader

With the `trn` newsreader you can display and search articles by subject, article, or threads. The 't' in `trn` stands for threaded. A thread is a connection between articles such as articles that share the same subject or follow-up articles to a previously posted article. `trn` has a special interface called a selector that allows you to move through a threaded set of articles. For example, articles on the same subject are threaded so that if you give an n command to go to the next article, you go to the next article on that subject (in the thread), not to the next sequentially posted article. You can move through a newgroup's articles using different threads, examining articles according to different subjects. The same is true for an article and its follow-up articles. An article and its follow-ups are threaded so that upon reading an article, you can then move to the first follow-up to that article, not to the next sequentially posted article. Using threads, you can then easily read an article and all of its follow-ups, instead of searching separately for each one.

trn works equally well with both a local newserver and a remote one. To use trn with a remote newserver, such as one provided by an ISP, you need to set the NNTPSERVER environment variable to the Internet address of that newserver. Remote servers usually use the NNTP protocol and begin their server addresses with "nntp." This assignment should be placed in a shell initialization file such as **.profile** or **.bashrc**. An example of the NNTPSERVER assignment follows.

```
NNTPSERVER="nntp.myserver.com"
```

The trn **Newsgroup Interface**

trn uses the same line-oriented interface for newsgroups as described for rn in the previous chapter. You enter the trn newsreader by typing trn at your Unix prompt. trn will initially display a short list of newsgroup headers. Upon starting up, trn asks if you want to subscribe to any new newsgroups that have been added to your newserver since your last session. Should you want to skip this initial subscription phase, you can do so by invoking the -q option. After the subscription phase, trn checks to see if there are any newsgroups listed in your **.newsrc** file that have unread news in them. If so, the newsgroup headers for first few of these are displayed. Each newsgroup header tells how many unread articles remains in a given newsgroup.

When trn starts up it prompts you as to whether you want to read articles in the first newsgroup. The prompt contains four of the common responses encases within brackets, [+ynq]. + will select the newsgroup, listing its articles using the trn article selector as described in the next section. y will also select the newsgroup, displaying its first article, instead of using the article selector. n moves on to the next unread newsgroup, and q quits trn. Several other commands are available for moving through the list of newsgroups. p moves you back to the previous unread newsgroup. $ places you at the end of the newsgroup list. The ^ places you at the first newsgroup with unread news, whereas the number 1 places you at the first newsgroup in the list whether it is read or not.

In the next example, the user enters the `trn` interface and a list of newsgroup headers is displayed. The user is then prompted for the first header, which the user skips with the n command. At the next header, the user enters a y command to read articles in the `alt.3d.misc` newsgroup.

```
$ trn
Unread news in 3dfx.game.discussion      314 articles
Unread news in alt.3d.misc                 3 articles
Unread news in alt.agriculture.fruit       1 article
Unread news in alt.airlines.schedules      1 article
Unread news in alt.airports                3 articles
etc.

====== 314 unread articles in 3dfx.game.discussion − −
  read now? [+ynq] n
======    3 unread articles in alt.3d.misc − − read now?
  [+ynq] y
```

Many commands are designed to distinguish between read and unread newsgroups. The ^ places you at the first newsgroup with unread news, whereas the number 1 places you at the first newsgroup in the list whether it is read or not. To move to the next or previous newsgroup regardless of whether it is read or not, you need to use the uppercase N and P commands. If you want to mark all the messages in a newsgroup as read without actually reading them, you use the c command (catchup). Then, unread-sensitive commands such as n and p will skip over the newsgroup until new articles are posted for it.

Often, you will know the name of newsgroup that you want to access. Instead of stepping through newsgroups one at a time with n and p commands to get to the one you want, you can use pattern searches to move directly to it. To perform a pattern search for a newsgroup, at the prompt enter a / followed by the pattern. The / performs a forward search through the list of newsgroups. The ? performs a backward search. In the next example, the user searches for the newsgroup containing the pattern "food.recipes."

```
$ trn
Unread news in 3dfx.game.discussion      314 articles
```

```
Unread news in alt.3d.misc                    3 articles
Unread news in alt.agriculture.fruit          1 article
Unread news in alt.airlines.schedules         1 article
Unread news in alt.airports                   3 articles
etc.

====== 314 unread articles in 3dfx.game.discussion − −
  read now? [+ynq] /food.recipes

Searching...
====== 372 unread articles in rec.food.recipes − −
  read now? [+ynq] y
```

You can also locate a newsgroup by its full name. The g command followed by a newsgroup's name will locate that newsgroup.

```
====== 314 unread articles in to − − read now? [+ynq]
  g rec.food.recipes
Searching...
====== 372 unread articles in rec.food.recipes − −
  read now? [+ynq] y
```

The trn list and search commands reference only those newsgroups to which you have subscribed. With the l command you can list or search for unsubscribed newsgroups. The l command by itself lists all newsgroups to which you have not subscribed. Followed by a pattern, the l command searches unsubscribed newsgroups for that pattern, listing those matched. For example, ltrek searches for unsubscribed newsgroups with the pattern "trek" in it.

You can subscribe to a newsgroup with the a command. Enter a followed by the name of the newsgroup you want. You can unsubscribe a newsgroup with the u command. For example, u rec.food.recipes will unsubscribe that newsgroup. If you tried to select it with search commands such as / or g, you would not find it. Of course, the l command would locate it; lrec.food.recipes. To once again subscribe to this newsgroup you would use the command a rec.food.recipes.

Table 8.I summarizes the trn newsgroup commands.

Table 8.I. trn Newsgroup Commands

ENTERING NEWSGROUPS

+	Enter current newsgroup through the selector.
y	Select the current newsgroup.
=	Enter newsgroup, but list subjects before displaying articles.
space	Enter newsgroup using default, usually + .

MOVING THROUGH NEWSGROUPS

n	Move to the next newsgroup with unread articles.
N	Move to the next newsgroup.
p	Move to the previous newsgroup with unread articles.
P	Move to the previous newsgroup.
–	Move to the previously selected newsgroup.
^	Move to the first newsgroup with unread articles.
num	Move to newsgroup with that number; 1 goes to first newsgroup.
$	Move to the last newsgroup.
g*newsgroup-name*	Move to newsgroup with that name.
/*pattern*	Search forward to the newsgroup with that pattern.
?*pattern*	Search backward to the newsgroup with that pattern.

MANAGING NEWSGROUPS

L	List subscribed newsgroups.
l*pattern*	List unsubscribed newsgroups.
u *newsgroup-name*	Unsubscribe to a newsgroups.
a *newsgroup-name*	Subscribe to a newsgroups.
c	Mark articles in a newsgroup as read..
t	Toggle newsgroup between threaded and unthreaded reading.
A	Abandon changes made to current newsgroup.
o*pattern-list*	Only display newsgroups whose name matches *pattern-list*. The *pattern-list* can be a set of patterns separated by spaces. *(continued)*

Table 8.I. `trn` **Newsgroup Commands** (*continued*)

O*pattern-list*	Same as `o`, but empty newsgroups are automatically excluded.
v	Display `trn` version number.
&	Display current status of the command line.
&&*option-list*	Set new `trn` options.
&&&*keys commands*	Define a macro.
!*command*	Execute a Unix shell command.
QUITTING TRN	
q	Quit `trn`.
x	Quit `trn`, with no changes made to **.newsrc**. Backup copy with any changes for current session is placed in **.newnewsrc**.

The `trn` Selector

The `trn` selector provides you with an easy-to-use interface for accessing threads. To start the selector, enter a + at the `trn` prompt. The selector screen lists a newgroup's articles' authors with their thread count and subject. Follow-up articles are preceded by a > symbol. The articles are grouped according to the threads to which they belong. Preceding each article displayed on the screen is an id. You use this id to select and reference an article. An id is a lower-case alphabetic character or a single digit, beginning with the letter 'a' and continuing in alphabetical order. Figure 8.1 show a sample `trn` selector screen.

When you enter the selector, the first screen of articles for the selected newsgroup is displayed. The first thread has the id 'a' preceding it. To display the next screen of articles, press either the **spacebar** or the > key. To display the previous screen, press the < key. Upon displaying the next screen, threads will again be listed beginning from 'a'. The id preceding a thread is unique to that thread only for that screen. You can think of ids as more of a screen device for referencing threads displayed on the screen at that time.

To read an article, select the thread for that article using its id. Just press the key corresponding to its id. For example, pressing

```
rec.food.recipes                           372 articles (moderated)

        a      Justin Saturn         1    Cookies on the run
        b      Cecelia Petersen      1    Angel Food Cake
        d      Richard Leland        2    Chocolate and Cinnamon
               Larisa@mymag.com
               Aleina Fuller         1    > White Chocolate
               George Gabriel        1    > Chocolate Fudge
               Mark Paul             1    >
               Chris Neil            1    > Chocolate butter
        e      Dylan Petersen        1    Cinnamon Bagels
        f      Marylou Carrion       1    REQUEST: romantic lunches
        g      Valerie Fuller        1    REQUEST: romantic snacks
        i      Carolyn Blacklock     1    REQUEST: Spicy Popcorn
               Bill Bode             1    >
        j      Gloria                1    Lasanga (huge dish)
        l      Maryann               1    Applesauce
        o      Anntoinnete C.        1    REQUEST: Spelling cookies
               augie@napa            3    >
               John Carrion

-- Select threads (date order) -- 32%
```

Figure 8.1. The trn selector.

d selects the thread that has a d at the beginning of its line. When you select a thread, a + symbol appears before its id. Once selected, you can display the articles in a thread by either pressing the **enter** key or the capital Z key. The first article in the thread will be displayed. Pressing the n key moves you on to the next article in the thread.

At any time while viewing articles, you can return to the selector by pressing the + key. Should you no longer want to read articles in a given thread, you need to deselect the thread. You do so by again pressing the key that corresponds to its id. Upon deselecting the thread, the + symbol that appeared when you selected it will now disappear. Sometimes, instead of a + symbol, a * symbol will be displayed before selected threads. A * indicates a thread where not all of its articles are selected.

Instead of ids, you can use cursor commands to select a thread. Upon first displaying the selector screen, the cursor is placed at the 'a' before the first thread. Using the cursor n and p commands or arrow keys, you can move to the next thread or back to the previous thread. The n command moves down to the next thread, and the p command move back to the previous thread. You can also use the up and down arrow keys should you have them. To start displaying articles in a particular thread, simply move the cursor to that thread's id and press **enter** or Z.

If you want to examine several threads, you can mark each thread by pressing the key corresponding to the id displayed before the thread. To select the thread preceded by 'b', just press the b key. Then move on to the next thread you want, and do the same. A + symbol will appear after each thread that you have selected. You can move from one screen to another selecting the threads you want, and then begin displaying articles based on those threads.

Various trn commands can be applied to threads. trn has commands for saving, decoding, and removing articles as well as others. You execute a command on selected articles using the : command followed by the command you want to execute. The : command can also be used for certain operations like posting a new article, :p, or ending a one-by-one extraction process of a multipart file, :E. The :: command, two colons, performs operations on unselected threads. In the following examples, the first command saves (s) selected threads, and the second command removes (j) unselected threads.

```
:s
::j
```

To perform operations on to just the current thread, use the :. or ::. commands. :. will operate on the current thread or, if there are selected articles within it, on just those selected articles. :.s will save selected articles in the current thread. ::. operates on unselected articles in the current thread. ::.j will junk the unselected articles in the current thread.

Table 8.II summarizes the selector commands.

Table 8.II. Selector Commands

SELECTING ARTICLES IN THE SELECTOR

id	Select/unselect an article thread.
id*	Select/unselect articles with the same subject as *id*.
enter	Display and begin reading the current article.
n	Move to the next thread id.
p	Move to the previous thread id.
Z or **tab**	Begin displaying selected articles. Return to newsgroup screen when finished.
X	Mark all unselected articles as read and start reading.
D	Mark all unselected articles on current page as read and start reading if articles are selected.
J	Mark all selected articles as read.
C	Mark all articles as read.
/*pattern*	Search forward for articles with that pattern. Unless qualified, search is carried out on Subject line of article headers.
?*pattern*	Search backward for articles with that pattern. Unless qualified, search is carried out on Subject line of article headers.
.	Toggle current article's selection.
@	Toggle all visible selections.
#	Read the current article only, ignoring other selections.
.	Toggle current article's selection.
m or /	Unmark the current article.

MOVING THROUGH SELECTOR

spacebar	Display the next screen of articles.
>	Display the next screen of threads.
<	Display the previous screen of articles.
$	Display the last screen of articles.
^	Display the first screen of articles.

QUITTING THE NEWSGROUP

escape	Quit selector to basic article reading.	
q	Quit the current newsgroup.	*(continued)*

Table 8.II. Selector Commands (*continued*)

Q	Quit the current newsgroup and return to that newsgroup's prompt.

COMMANDS APPLIED TO SELECTED OR UNSELECTED THREADS

: *command*	Apply command to all selected threads.
: : *command*	Apply command to all unselected threads.
: . *command*	Apply to selected articles in current thread.
: : . *command*	Apply command to unselected articles in the current thread.
p	Post a new article.
+	Select an article.
–	Deselect an article.
=	Print the subject of found articles.
! *cmd*	Execute a Unix shell command.
++	Select a thread.
– –	Deselect a thread.
T+	Auto-select the entire thread.
Tj	Auto-junk the entire thread.
m	Mark as unread.
M	Mark as read until you exit.
t	Display article tree for thread.
j	Mark as read in all groups.
E	End partial uudecode.
s *directory*	Save articles to specified directory using mailbox format.
w *directory*	Save articles to specified directory as plain text file.
e *directory*	Extract articles to specified directory.

Selector Display Modes: Article, Subject, and Thread

The selector has three different display modes: article, subject, and thread (see Table 8.III). The article mode displays individual articles, the subject mode displays articles by subject, and the thread

+	Enter the selector from the `trn` line prompt, or leave the selector and return to the `trn` line prompt.
S	Select selector mode: subject, thread, or article.

> Selector Mode: Threads, Subjects, Articles? [tsa]
>
> s   Subject mode, display articles by subject.
>
> a   Article mode, display individual articles.
>
> t   Thread mode, display articles by threads.

=	Switch between article and subject/thread selector.
O	Sort selector items by date, author, thread count, or subject. User is prompted to enter d, a, n, or s. This command is an uppercase O, not lowercase. The options differ depending on whether you are in the subject or thread modes.

> Subject   Order by Date, Subject, or Count? [dscDSC]
>
> Thread   Order by Date, Subject, Author, subject-date Grops?

L	Set selector item display to short, medium, or long forms.
E	Exclusive mode, display only selected articles.
k or ,	Remove an article or subject from the selector display.
U	Display unread articles.

Table 8.III. Displaying Selector

mode displays articles by threads. You can easily choose the mode you want by pressing the S command and entering either a for article, s for subject, or t for thread. You can also switch back and forth between the different modes by pressing the = key.

You can think of each mode as a kind of thread. When using the subject mode, articles are grouped according to their subject entries. A subject is whatever a user enters into the subject field of an article's header. Articles that have the same subject entry are threaded together. Subject groupings are limited to those articles that share exactly the same subject entries in their header. Articles that have even slightly different subject entries will not be grouped together. When using the thread mode, articles are grouped with any posted follow-ups to them, as well as with articles of the same subject. The follow-up articles are preceded by a > symbol. The thread mode differs from the subject mode in that it will include all follow-up articles, even though such articles may have different subject entries. The article mode does not display threads. Articles are listed individually one by one as they were posted. Each is preceded by its own id.

The selector screen appears differently according to the display mode being used. In the subject mode, the selector displays the author of each article, grouping them into subject categories. Along with the first author in a subject category, the number of articles in the category is displayed, followed by the category's subject. The subject is listed only once, followed by a list of authors, each representing an article. An id is placed only before the first article in the subject category. In the subject mode, an id references a subject, not a particular article. On the screen, ids are placed only at the beginning of different subject groupings. To select a subject just press the key corresponding to its id. For example, pressing d selects the subject that has a 'd' at the beginning of its line. The subject mode provides you with easy access to articles on the same topics. The list of subject headings also provides a quick summary of topics being discussed in the newsgroup.

In Figure 8.2, the selector is in the subject mode. Notice that item d specifies the subject "Chocolate and Cinnamon." There are two articles in this subject category, one by the author Richard Leland and another by the author Larisa@mymag.com. The article count specifies two articles. The same is true for item i, except that the second article is a follow-up article as indicated with a > symbol. Item t specifies a subject category of two articles, both of which are follow-ups.

In the thread mode, the selector displays articles grouped together either by follow-up connection or by subject. Follow-up articles are listed below their original article and preceded by a > sign. Articles related by subject will be in the same thread, along with their own follow-ups. This kind of grouping is referred to as a thread. Using the thread mode, you can easily access an article and all follow-ups posted on it. This lets you check out any discussion or comment on a particular article.

Each thread will have its own id. To select a thread just press the corresponding key for its id. In Figure 8.3, the trn selector is in

```
┌─────────────────────────────────────────────────────────────────┐
│ rec.food.recipes                        372 articles (moderated)  │
│                                                                   │
│     a      Justin Saturn          1    Cookies on the run         │
│     b      Cecelia Petersen       1    Angel Food Cake            │
│     d      Richard Leland         2    Chocolate and Cinnamon     │
│            Larisa@mymag.com                                       │
│     e      Dylan Petersen         1    Cinnamon Bagels            │
│     f      Marylou Carrion        1    REQUEST: romantic lunches  │
│     g      Valerie Fuller         1    REQUEST: romantic snacks   │
│     i      Carolyn Blacklock      1    REQUEST: Spicy Popcorn     │
│            Bill Bode              1    >                          │
│     j      Gloria                 1    Lasanga (huge dish)        │
│     l      Maryann                1    Applesauce                 │
│     o      Anntoinnete C.         2    REQUEST: Spelling cookies  │
│            augie@napa                  >                          │
│     r      George Gabriel         3    REQUEST: Olive Oil Cakes   │
│            Mark Paul                   >                          │
│            Maryann                     >                          │
│     s      Chris Niel             1    Chocolate Chip Donuts      │
│     t      augie@napa             2    >Spelling cookies          │
│            John Carrion                >                          │
│                                                                   │
│ -- Select subjects (date order) -- 32%                            │
│ Selector mode:  Threads, Subjects, Articles? [tsa] s              │
└─────────────────────────────────────────────────────────────────┘
```

Figure 8.2. The `trn` **screen selector in the subject mode.**

the thread mode. Compare how the screen differs from the subject mode example in Figure 8.2. Entry d now includes follow-up articles as well as articles on the same subject. It is a thread consisting of six articles. The first two share the same subject and the remaining four are follow-up articles to them, as indicated by > symbol. Many of these follow-up articles have different subject titles, while two of them, George Gabriel and Mark Paul, are two follow-up articles that have the same subject. Notice that the o item represents a thread beginning with the Anntoinnete C. article and includes its two follow-ups, augie@napa and, John Carrion. The two follow-ups all have the same subject, though it is different from the initial article in the thread in that its subject line does not include the term "REQUEST."

```
 ┌──────────────────────────────────────────────────────────┐
 │  rec.food.recipes                        372 articles (moderated)      │
 │                                                                          │
 │      a      Justin Saturn        1    Cookies on the run                 │
 │      b      Cecelia Petersen     1    Angel Food Cake                    │
 │      d      Richard Leland       2    Chocolate and Cinnamon             │
 │             Larisa@mymag.com                                             │
 │             Aleina Fuller        1    > White Chocolate                  │
 │             George Gabriel       1    > Chocolate Fudge                  │
 │             Mark Paul            1    >                                   │
 │             Chris Neil           1    > Chocolate butter                 │
 │      e      Dylan Petersen       1    Cinnamon Bagels                    │
 │      f      Marylou Carrion      1    REQUEST: romantic lunches          │
 │      g      Valerie Fuller       1    REQUEST: romantic snacks           │
 │      i      Carolyn Blacklock    1    REQUEST: Spicy Popcorn             │
 │             Bill Bode            1    >                                   │
 │      j      Gloria               1    Lasanga (huge dish)                │
 │      l      Maryann              1    Applesauce                         │
 │      o      Anntoinnete C.       1    REQUEST: Spelling cookies          │
 │             augie@napa           2    > Spelling cookies                 │
 │             John Carrion                                                 │
 │                                                                          │
 │  -- Select threads (date order) -- 32%                                   │
 │  Selector mode:  Threads, Subjects, Articles? [tsa] t                    │
 └──────────────────────────────────────────────────────────┘
```

Figure 8.3. The `trn` screen selector in the thread mode.

In the article mode, articles are simply displayed in the order in
which they were posted, with no indication of any subject or thread
grouping. In Figure 8.4, the articles are simply arranged by posted
order, each article having its own id. No threads are active in the
article mode. Articles and their follow-ups are scattered throughout the display. For example, though the article `augie@napa` is a
follow-up to `Anntoinnete C.`, each has its own id in different
parts of the display, w and y. Entries d and e have the same subject,
but each has its own separate id.

Searching Articles

You can also select articles based on a pattern search. The / opens
a line at the bottom of the screen where you can enter a pattern.

```
rec.food.recipes                        372 articles (moderated)


         a     Justin Saturn          Cookies on the run
         b     Cecelia Petersen       Angel Food Cake
         d     Richard Leland         Chocolate  and  Cinnamon
         e     Larisa@mymag.com       Chocolate  and  Cinnamon
         f     Aleina Fuller          > White Chocolate
         g     George Gabriel         > Chocolate Fudge
         i     Chris Neil             > Chocolate butter
         j     Mark Paul              > Chocolate Fudge
         l     Dylan Petersen         Cinnamon Bagels
         o     Marylou Carrion        REQUEST: romantic lunches
         r     Valerie Fuller         REQUEST: romantic snacks
         s     Carolyn Blacklock      REQUEST: Spicy  Popcorn
         t     kenny@myboat.com       Candied sushi
         u     Gloria                 Lasanga (huge dish)
         v     Maryann                Christmas cookies
         w     Anntoinnete C.         REQUEST: Spelling  cookies
         x     maryann@sebast         Applesause
         y     augie@napa             REQUEST: Spelling  cookies



 -- Select subjects (date order) -- 32%
 Selector mode:  Threads, Subjects, Articles? [tsa] a
```

Figure 8.4. The `trn` screen selector in the article mode.

The search is carried out on the Subject line of article headers. A /
command searches forward from the current article, and a ?
searches backward. You can repeat the search by pressing the **escape** key. The searches are applied to unread articles unless qualified to include read articles.

You can further modify the search using codes to designate specific
components of a message to be searched. The modifier codes are
placed after the pattern following a /. A pattern followed by an h
will only search the headers of articles, whereas an a will search
both header and text. To include read articles in your search, use
the r modifier. For example, the following entry searches only
headers for articles with the pattern "romantic" in their headers.

```
/romantic/h
```

Table 8.IV. Article Searches

/pattern	Search forward for articles with that pattern. Unless qualified, search is carried out on Subject line of article headers.
?*pattern*	Search backward for articles with that pattern. Unless qualified, search is carried out on Subject line of article headers.

MODIFIERS

/pattern/modifier-list

a	Search forward to the article with that pattern in either the header or the text. */pattern/* a
b	Search forward to the article with that pattern in the body of the message, but not the signature. */pattern/* b
B	Search forward to the article with that pattern in the body of the message. */pattern/* B
c	Make search case sensitive. */pattern/* c
h	Search forward to the article with that pattern in the header. */pattern/* h
r	Include read articles in you search. */pattern/* r
t	Start the search from the first article in the newsgroup instead of current article. */pattern/* t
I	Force search to ignore THRU lies when executed as a memorized command. */pattern/* I
i	Force search not to ignore THRU lies when executed as a memorized command. */pattern/* i

COMMANDS

/pattern/modifier-list : *command-list*

+	Select the article.

–	Deselect the article.
=	Print the subject of found articles.
!*cmd*	Execute a Unix shell command.
++	Select the associated thread.
– –	Deselect the associated thread .
T+	Auto-select the entire thread.
Tj	Auto-junk the entire thread.
m	Mark as unread.
M	Mark as read until you exit.
x	Mark as read in this group.
j	Mark as read in all groups.
C	Cancel.
s *directory*	Save articles to specified directory.
e *directory*	Extract articles to specified directory.

A b modifier will search the text of an article, but not its signature, whereas a B will search only the text of an article. Articles are searched starting from the current article. If you want to search the entire set of articles in the newsgroup, you can qualify your search with t. This forces a search to begin from the top, the first article in the newsgroup.

You can further qualify your search by adding a command or series of commands to whatever articles are found by the search. The commands are placed after the modifiers and separated by colons. You could mark the found articles as read by placing an x command after any modifiers. The following example marks as read all articles with the pattern "homework" in the body of the article.

```
/homework/b:x
```

You can use the feature to easily select or unselect articles on a given topic using the + or - commands. The following example selects all read and unread articles with the pattern "vacation" in either the header or the text.

```
/vacation/ar:+
```

Table 8.IV summarizes the search commands.

Displaying Articles

When an article is displayed, its header is shown at the top of the screen, followed by the contents of the article (Figure 8.5). If the article takes up more that one page, then a (more) prompt is

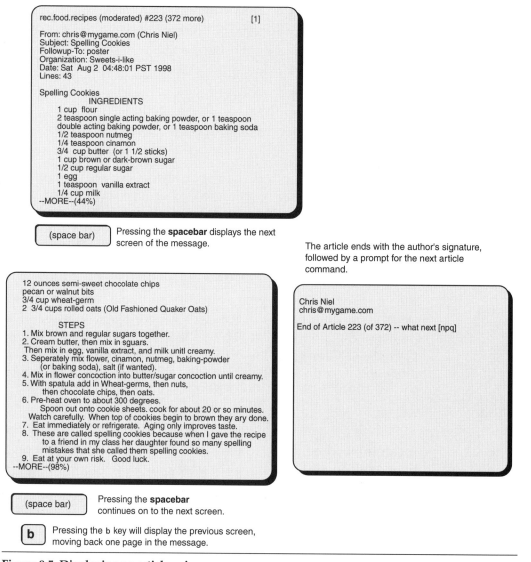

Figure 8.5. Displaying an article using rn.

displayed at the bottom of the screen. Next to the more prompt will be a percentage indicating the amount of the message text that has been displayed so far. To see the next page, press the **spacebar**. Pressing the **spacebar** moves you through the article a page at a time. To move back to the previous page, press the b key. If you want to search for a pattern in the message, press the g key followed by that pattern. The page text with the next occurrence of the pattern will be displayed. Use the uppercase G key to repeat the pattern, locating its next instance in the message.

After displaying the message, you will be prompted for your next action. The prompt ends with commonly executed commands enclosed within brackets, [npq]. The n command displays the next article, the p command displays the previous article, and the q command returns to the newsgroup list. To return the article selector screen, enter the + command.

The commands for displaying articles are summarized in Table 8.V.

Marking Articles

You can mark articles as read or unread in various ways (Table 8.VI). By default, when you enter a newsgroup, only unread articles are displayed. These are usually new articles. Though you can use the U command to display them, an article marked as read effectively removes it from your attention. If there are articles you know you do not want to read, you can simply mark them as read using the j command. This is sometimes referred to as "junking" an article.

On the other hand, if there is an article you have read and want to come back to it in another session, you can mark it as unread with the m command. Still another command, M , lets you mark an article as read for this session only, and will treat it as unread the next session. In this way, you don't have it displayed as unread in your current session, but will see it displayed in your next session. You can undo this kind of marking with the Y command. The Y command will yank all articles marked as read for this session only and select them.

Table 8.V. Article Display Commands

LOCATION COMMANDS

n	Go to the next unread article.
N	Go to the next article.
p or -	Go to the previous unread article.
P	Go to the previous article.
Ctrl-p	Go to previous article with same subject.
^	Go to the first unread article.
$	Go to the last unread article.
num	Go to article with that number.
q	Quit newsgroup.

TREE COMMANDS

t	Display entire article tree.
<	Go to the next selected or unread article.
>	Go to the previous selected or unread article.
[	Move left in the article tree.
]	Move right in the article tree.
{	Go to root of the article tree.
}	Go to a leaf in the article tree.
(	Go to the previous sibling in a thread.
)	Go to the next sibling in a thread.

COMMANDS

space	Display next page.
b	Display previous page.
d	Display next half page.
Ctrl-e	Display last page.
Ctrl-r	Redisplay the current article.
v	Redisplay the current article with the header.
Ctrl-l	Refresh the screen.
c	Mark all articles as read.
/pattern	Search forward for articles with that pattern. Unless qualified, search is carried out on Subject line of article headers.

?*pattern*	Search backward for articles with that pattern. Unless qualified, search is carried out on Subject line of article headers.
gpattern	Search for pattern within current article.
G	Repeat search.

To simply mark all the articles in a newsgroup as read, use the c command. c stands for catchup. It is helpful for newsgroups that you have not accessed in a while to which a large number of articles have been posted. You could mark all of the articles as read with c, and then use m to mark as unread the ones you want to still look at later.

Responding to Articles

You can respond to a selected article by sending a mail message directly to the article's author, or by posting a follow-up article of your own that will be added to the newsgroup (Table 8.VI). You can even forward the article to another user just as you would forward a mail message. With the r and R commands you can send a message directly to an article's author. Both commands send their replies using a designated mailer, taking the author's email address from the article header as well as the Subject line. The r command will not include the body of the article, whereas the R command does. The mailer used is specified in the MAILPOSTER environment variable. The **Ctrl-f** command will forward the selected article, letting you choose which users you want to send it to.

To post a follow-up article to the newsgroup, use the f or F commands. The F command will include the contents of the current article and an attribution line telling who the author is. The attribution line is take from the From: line in the article header. The poster program used is specified in NEWSPOSTER. The f command differs in that it does not include the contents of the article.

Saving Articles

You can save the article after reading it by entering the s command with a file name (Table 8.VI). If the file does not yet exist, you will be asked if you want to use a mailbox file format for it. If you enter y, the file will be a mailbox file and the article will be saved as one message in that mailbox. If, however, you simply press **enter**, the file will have a standard text file format.

```
End of article 223 (of 372) − − what next? [+npq] s spellcookies

File /home/dylan/News/spellcookies doesn't exist − −
     use mailbox format? [ynq] y
Saved to mailbox /home/dylan/News/spellcookies

End of article 223 (of 372) − − what next? [+npq]
```

Articles that you save to an already existing file will simply be appended to it. In the case of mailbox files, the added articles will become new messages in that mailbox. You can then easily access particular articles using a mailer on that file. To save articles in plain text format, use the w command. Such articles are saved without the article header.

Several newsgroups are used to post binary files. These newsgroups usually have the term "binaries" in their name. For example, alt.binaries.pictures is a newsgroup whose articles are usually binary picture files such as jpeg or gif files. Binary files cannot be posted to newsgroups in binary form. Instead they must be encoded into a character equivalent and then posted as regular text articles. You can then save such an encoded article and decode it. The encoding process is much the same as that used for sending binary files as mail messages. Many binary articles are encoded in uuencode format. You can save them and use uudecode to decode them.

In trn, you can use the e (extract) command to both save and decode a uuencoded article. Sometimes a large binary file is cut up into several encoded articles. You can select the articles making up the uuencoded file and use the e command to automatically save, decode, and combine them into the single binary file. The e command takes as its argument the directory where you want the

MARKING ARTICLES

c	Mark all articles in a newsgroup as read.
u	Unsubscribe from the current newsgroup.
m	Mark the current article as unread.
j	Mark the current article as read (junked).
M	Mark current article as read for current session only.
Y	Select articles marked as read for current session only.

REPLIES AND FOLLOW-UPS

r	Send a mail reply directly to the author of the current article.
R	Send a mail reply directly to the author of the current article and include the contents of the article.
Ctrl-f	Forward the article as a mail message to any user.
f	Post a follow-up article for the article to the newsgroup.
F	Post a follow-up article for the article to the newsgroup and include the article contents and attribution line.

SAVING AND EXTRACTING ARTICLES

w	Save selected article.
s	Save selected article to a mailbox file.
e	Extract selected encoded articles to save directory. Decodes uuencoded binaries.
e *directory*	Extract selected encoded articles to specified directory. Decodes uuencoded binaries.
e *directory* | *command*	Extract selected encoded articles and uses the specified command to decode the encoded articles.
E	If extracting selected encoded articles one by one, this cancels the process removing incomplete binary.

Table 8.VI. Display Commands

decoded binary file to be saved. If no directory argument is supplied, the default save directory is used. You can also extract articles in a multipart binary one by one. However, should you wish to cancel you can use the E command to stop the extraction process and remove the incomplete binary file. Should you need to use a different decoding application, you can specify it by placing its command after a pipe following the e command, e *dir* \| *command*.

`trn` **Thread Trees**

When you display an article, you will notice that in the upper right-hand corner there is a thread tree displayed. A thread tree represents the connections between articles in a thread. Each unread article is represented by a number starting from 1 with each enclosed in brackets. Lines connect the different article numbers. The number representing the article you are currently displaying is highlighted in the thread tree. Once you read an article and move on to another, the read article's number is enclosed in parentheses and the next article's number is highlighted.

A thread tree shows the relationship between articles. The first article in a thread is located in the upper left corner. Branching to the right and down, the next column, are any follow-up articles to that article. Follow-up articles are connected to each other by lines. For example, the follow-up articles for the first article in the thread are arranged as a column of bracketed numbers set to the right of the first articles number. There is a line connecting the article's number to its first follow-up. Any other follow-up articles are arranged in a column below this first follow-up, each connected by a line. The last follow-up article will be connected by a slanted line. Figure 8.6 show such a thread tree.

A follow-up article may, in turn, have its own follow-ups. People may respond to another person's response, carrying on a conversation or debate on a particular point. The follow-up number to a follow-up is positioned to the right of the follow-up's number. That follow-up may, in turn, have its own follow-up whose number will

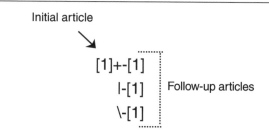

Figure 8.6. A thread tree showing initial article and its follow-up articles.

also be positioned to the right of that follow-up's number. You could have a whole string of sequential follow-ups, arranged in a horizontal line one next to the other. Figure 8.7 shows such a horizontal line of follow-ups.

Any given follow-up could have more than one follow-up of its own. These follow-ups would be arranged in a column, beginning with the first follow-up. In effect, a thread tree can extend horizontally and vertically. Horizontally the thread lists a follow-up that responds to previous follow-ups, and that may, in turn, have a follow-up responding to it. Vertically the thread lists several follow-ups that are responses to a particular follow-up.

Directly below the first article are listed other articles related by subject. These are not connected by lines. In effect, the outer column of article numbers indicates subject groupings, and any articles branching to the right are follow-up articles. As shown in Figure 8.8, articles that share the same subject are arranged in the outer column.

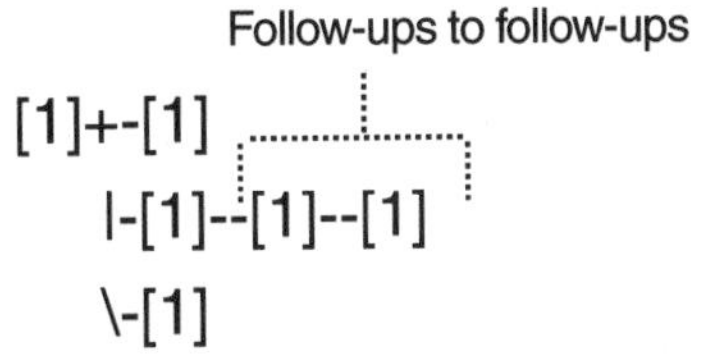

Follow-ups to follow-ups

```
[1]+-[1] ................
 |-[1]--[1]--[1]
 \-[1]
```

Figure 8.7. A thread tree showing articles that are follow-ups to follow-ups.

```
                           [1]+-[1]
                            |-[1]--[1]--[1]
Articles with the           \-[1]
same subject               [1]+-[1]
                           [1]
```

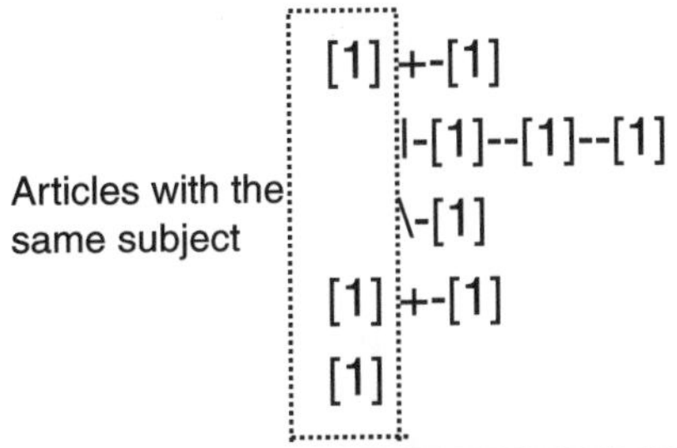

Figure 8.8. trn thread tree showing subject articles.

The numbers used to represent articles in the thread tree indicate whether articles share the same subject. The first article is represented by the number 1, indicating the initial subject of the thread. Articles that share the same subject will have the same number. Those with the number 1 share the same subject as the first article. Many times, however, articles in the same thread may have different subjects. Should an article have a different subject, it will be represented with a different number. Any subsequent articles with that same subject will share that same number. The first article with a different subject will be represented by a number 2. Any other articles with a number 2 will share that same subject. Should there be another article with yet another subject, it will be represented by a number 3. As different subjects in the thread are encountered they are incrementally given a new number. Such a numbering system allows you to identify different subtopics in the thread. It is like detecting different parts of a conversation that veer off into different topics. Also, should part of a thread contain a subject you are not interested in, you can easily identify what articles in the thread to avoid. Figure 8.9 shows a thread tree with different subjects. The first follow-up article is represented by a number 2, indicating that this article has a different subject from that of the first article. Again, the article below it is represented by a number 3, indicating that it has yet another subject.

You can use the thread tree to move from one article to another in the thread. In effect, you can move directly to any article in the thread without having to display any intervening articles. You can even move backward in the thread. Thread trees are a very easy way to move back and forth to different articles in a thread. You use the arrow keys to move up and down and across the thread tree, highlighting different article numbers as you go. For example, if you press a **down arrow** key, you move from the current article number to the one below it, highlighting it. Pressing the **right arrow** key moves you to the article number on the right. Repeatedly pressing the **right arrow** key moves you to article numbers further on the right. The **left arrow** key will move you back to the left, and the **up arrow** will move you up. The article for the number you have currently highlighted will be displayed. As you move through the thread tree, different articles are displayed.

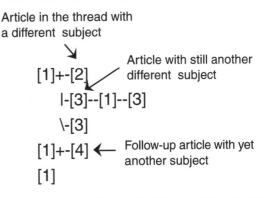

Figure 8.9. trn **thread tree showing articles with different subjects.**

In Figure 8.10, the user selects the thread with the id d and then uses the displayed thread tree to move from one article to the next in the thread. Upon selecting the thread, the first article is displayed along with the thread tree in the upper right-hand corner. The [1] representing the first article is highlighted. Moving the cursor to the right, the user then displays the first follow-up article to the initial article, Aleina Fuller on White Chocolate. Since this article has a different subject title, it bracket representation in the thread tree has the number 2. The user then moves the cursor down the columns of the thread tree to display the next follow-up article, George Gabriel on Chocolate Fudge. This also is a different subject, so it has yet another number, 3. Upon moving the cursor down again, the user displays the next follow-up article, Mark Paul. This article shares the same subject as the previous follow-up article, Chocolate Fudge, and so has the same number, 3. The user then moves to the outside column and down to the next subject article, Larisa@mymag.com. This article shares the same subject as the initial article, and so has the same number, 1. Moving the cursor to the right, the user then displays the follow-up to the Larisa@mymag.com article, Chris Niel on Chocolate butter. This article has yet another subject and so is represented by a new number, 4.

rec.food.recipes   372 articles (moderated)

a	Justin Saturn	1	Cookies on the run
b	Cecelia Petersen	1	Angel Food Cake
+d	Richard Leland	2	Chocolate and Cinnamon
	Larisa@mymag.com		
	Aleina Fuller	1	> White Chocolate
	George Gabriel	1	> Chocolate Fudge
	Mark Paul	1	>
	Chris Neil	1	>Chocolate butter
e	Dylan Petersen	1	Cinnamon Bagels
f	Marylou Carrion	1	REQUEST: romantic lunches
g	Valerie Fuller	1	REQUEST: romantic snacks
i	Carolyn Blacklock	1	REQUEST: Spicy Popcorn
	Bill Bode	1	>
j	Gloria	1	Lasanga (huge dish)
l	Maryann	1	Applesauce
o	Anntoinnete C.	1	REQUEST: Spelling cookies
	augie@napa	3	>

-- Select threads (date order) -- 32%
Selector mode: Threads, Subjects, Articles? [tsa] t

The user selects the thread represented by the id d by pressing d and then **enter**.

---

rec.food.recipes (moderated) #285   **1**--[2]
From: Richard Leland<richp@garnet..berkeley.edu> |-[3]
Subject: Cinnamon and Chocolate   \-[3]
Followup-To: rec.food.recipes
Date: Sat Aug 2 20:18:10 PST 1998   [1]--[4]
Organization: U. C. Berkeley
Lines: 7

I'm looking for chocolate recipes that use cinnamon.
    Does cinnamon always go with chocolate?

Thanks!

-Rich
richp@garnet..berkeley.edu

Upon selecting a thread, the first article is displayed along
with the thread tree in the upper right-hand corner.

---

rec.food.recipes (moderated) #225   (1)+-**2**
From: Aleina Fuller aleinai@myskate.com |-[3]
Subject: White Chocolate   \-[3]
Followup-To: poster
Date: Date: Sat Aug 2 21:14:10 PST 1998   [1]--[4]
Organization: Fast Skates
Lines: 32

n article "Richard Leland" <richp@garnet..berkeley.edu> writes:
    > I'm looking for chocolate recipes that use cinnamon.
    > Does cinnamon always go with chocolate?
    > Thanks!

The following recipe is out of a German cook book, so I had to
transform the amounts from the European system into the
American system of cups, tbsp, etc. You probably have to adjust
slightly the amounts after a first try.

--MORE--(58%)

$\rightarrow$ Hitting the **right arrow** key, the user moves to
the first follow-up article to the first article.

---

rec.food.recipes (moderated) #242   (1)+-(2)
From: George Gabriel<georgeg@sd.myfilm.com> |-**3**
Subject: Chocolate Fudge   \-[3]
Followup-To: poster
Date: Sat Aug 2 23:52:19 PST 1998   [1]--[4]
Organization: The Chocolate Club
Lines: 70

richp@garnet..berkeley.edu (Richard Leland) writes:
    > I'm looking for chocolate recipes that use cinnamon.
    > Does cinnamon always go with chocolate?
    > Thanks!

Chocolate Fudge is the perfect medium for cinnamon
It provides an exotic taste, especially when comibned
with nutmeg

--MORE--(27%)

↓ Pressing the down arrow key, the user moves
to the next follow-up article.

---

rec.food.recipes (moderated) #263   (1)+-(2)
From: Mark Paul <mark@mysound.com> |-(3)
Subject: Chocolate Fudge   \-**3**
Followup: To: poster
Date: Sun Aug 3 12:18:22 PST 1998   [1]--[4]
Organization: sownd & sweet
Lines: 27

<maryann@sd.club> (Maryann Priced) writes:
    > Chocolate Fudge is the perfect medium for cinnamon
    > It provides an exotic taste, especially when comibned
    > with nutmeg

Nutmeg?
    Yuk, you've got to be kidding me.
        fudge is not egg nog.

↓ Pressing the **down arrow** key again, the user
moves to the last follow-up article for the initial
article.

Figure 8.10. Using the `trn` **thread tree to select and display articles in a thread.**   *(continued)*

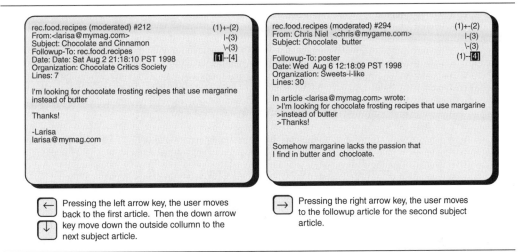

Figure 8.10. *(continued)* **Using the** `trn` **thread tree to select and display articles in a thread.**

The `trn` Options

trn has several startup options that let you skip to some commands. Normally `trn`, like `rn`, will individually ask you if you want to subscribe to each new newsgroup that has been added since your last `trn` session. You can skip this process by starting `trn` with the `-q` option. The `-r` option will start up in a newsgroup you were previously accessing. The `-o` option lets you select the display mode and the sort order for the `trn` article selection. `trn` options are listed in Table 8.VII.

Interpolation Codes

trn has a set of special percent codes the are substituted for specified run-time values when used in string values for environment variables or macros. They are listed in Table 8.VIII. For example, the `ATTRIBUTION` environment variable contains the string that is used to automatically enter an attribution line when you post a follow-up article, F. The default string normally assigned to the Attribution variable will include the `%i` percent code, the "Message-I D" line,

Table 8.VII. `trn` options

`-a`	Thread the unread articles on entering a group, instead of in the background while in a group.
`-b`	Read threads in a breadth-first order, rather than depth-first.
`-B`	Displays a spinner that twirls when `trn` is doing background article processing.
`-c`	Checks for news without reading news. If a list of newsgroups is given on the command line, only those newsgroups will be checked; otherwise all subscribed to newsgroups are checked. A nonzero exit status means that there is unread news in one of the checked newsgroups.
`-C` *number*	Specify how often to checkpoint the **.newsrc** file, in articles read.
`-d` *directory-name*	Specify a news directory. Default is **~/News.** The directory name will be globbed (via csh) if necessary (and if possible).
`-D` *flags*	Enables debugging output. See **common.h** for flag values.
`-e`	Displays each page within an article at the top of the screen, not just the first page.
`-E` *var=val*	Sets the environment variable to the value specified.
`-F`	Avoid various sleep calls used to let you read a message before the screen clears.
`-F` *string*	Specify the prefix string for the F follow-up command to use in prefixing lines of the quote article. The initial default prefix is ">".
`-g` *string*	Specify the line of the screen you want searched for strings to show up on when you search with the g command within an article.
`-G`	Uses "fuzzy" processing on the go command when you don't type in a valid group name. `trn` will attempt to find the group you probably meant to type.
`-h` *string*	Hides header lines beginning with string.
`-i` *=number*	Specifies number of lines displayed in the initial page of an article.
`-I`	Appends all new, unsubscribed groups to the end of the **.newsrc** file.
`-j`	Leaves control characters unchanged in messages.
`-j` *number*	Joins similar subjects into a common thread if they are the same up to the indicated number of characters (the default is 30).
`-k`	Ignore the THRU line when processing selection searches in the memorized commands.
`-K`	Keeps `trn` from checking for new news while you're in the group.

(continued)

Table 8.VII. `trn` **options** *(continued)*

`-l`	Disables the clearing of the screen at the beginning of each article.
`-M`	Use mailbox format for new save files created.
`-n`	Use normal (non-mailbox) format for new save files created. Ordinarily you are asked which format you want.
`-O`*mode sort-order*	Display articles in specified order and thread.
Modes	
`s`	subject mode
`t`	thread mode
`a`	article mode
Sort Order	
`d`	date
`s`	subject
`a`	author
`c`	article count
`g`	subject-date groups
`-q`	Bypasses the automatic check for new newsgroups when starting `trn`.
`-r`	Restart in the last newsgroup read during a previous session with `trn`.
`-s` *num*	Suppress the initial listing of newsgroups with unread news, whether -c is specified or not. With a number, the listing of newsgroups is limited to that number. `-s5` is the default setting.
`-S` *num*	Enter subject search mode automatically when an unthreaded newsgroup starts up that has *num* number of unread articles or more.
`-t`	Terse mode, used for low baud rates.
`-T`	Lets you to type ahead of `trn`.
`-u`	The unbroken-subject-line mode that truncates subjects that are too long.
`-U`	Instruct `trn` not to save the **.newsrc** file after visiting each group.
`-v`	Verification mode for commands, displaying commands typed in.
`-V`	`trn` version number.
`-x` *num list*	Enable the threaded features of `trn` beyond the `rn` compatibility mode. *num* is the maximum number of article-tree lines (from 0 to 11) you want displayed in your header. *list* specifies the thread selector style: 's'hort, 'm'edium, or 'l'ong).

(continued)

Table 8.VII. `trn` **options** *(continued)*

-X *num commands*	Specify the selector command (+) default when a newsgroup is started up with at least *num* unread articles. Also specify commands to be the defaults when using the thread selector. The default is -X1Z>, if just -X is used with no arguments. Makes thread selector the default for newsgroups with one or more unread articles and Z to access the last page, > to access the next page.
-z *num*	Specify minimum number of minutes that must elapse before the active file is refetched to look for new articles. Turned off with +z option.
-Z	Select the style of database for `trn` to access. Use -Zt for thread files, -Zo for overview files, and +Z for none.
-/	By default articles are saved in a subdirectory that has the name of the current newsgroup, with the file name being the article number. The subdirectory will be in your private news directory +/ by default saves articles directly to your private news directory, with the file name being the name of the current newsgroup.

and the %f percent code, the "From:" line in the current article. You can create your own attribution line by assigning a new value to the ATTRIBUTION variable.

There is also a special percent code that operates like a programming if–else control structure, allowing you to implement conditional string selection. For example, for a YOUSAID string (used for mail replies), you could test for a certain newsgroup you are in and then specify one string for that newsgroup and another for all other newsgroups.

%(*test_text=pattern*?*then_text*:*else_text*)

trn also supports file expansion where an initial / is treated as your home directory and *~username* is the login directory of specified user. You can also include escape sequences for special characters such as \n for newlines and \t for tabs. \0*num* where number is an octal value will reference that character. Control sequences are represented by a caret, such as ^i.

Table 8.VIII. `trn` Newsgroup Commands

`%a`	Current article number.
`%A`	Full name of current article (`%P/%c/%a`).
`%b`	Destination directory of last save command.
`%B`	The byte offset to the beginning of the part of the article to be saved, set by the save command. The `s` and `S` commands set it to 0, and the `w` and `W` commands set it to the byte offset of the body of the article.
`%c`	Current newsgroup, directory form.
`%C`	Current newsgroup, dot form.
`%d`	Full name of newsgroup directory (`%P/%c`).
`%D`	"Distribution:" line in the current article.
`%e`	The last command executed to extract data from an article.
`%E`	The last directory where an extracted file went.
`%f`	"From:" line from the current article, or the "Reply-To:" line if there is one. Comments (such as the full name) are not stripped out.
`%F`	"Newsgroups:" line for a new article, constructed from "Newsgroups:" and "Followup-To:" lines of current article.
`%h`	Name of the header file to pass to the mail or news poster, containing all the information that the poster program needs in the form of a message header. It may also contain a copy of the current article. The format of the header file is controlled by the `MAILHEADER` and `NEWSHEADER` environment variables.
`%H`	Your system's host name.
`%i`	"Message-I.D.:" line from the current article.
`%I`	The reference indication mark (see the `-F` switch).
`%l`	The news administrator's login name.
`%L`	Your login name.
`%m`	The current mode of `trn`.
`%M`	The number of articles marked to return via the `M` command.
`%n`	"Newsgroups:" line from the current article.
`%N`	Your full name. *(continued)*

Table 8.VIII. `trn` **Newsgroup Commands** *(continued)*

`%o`	Your organization.
`%O`	Original working directory.
`%p`	Your private news directory, normally **~/News**.
`%P`	System news spool directory (**/usr/spool/news** on systems that don't use NNTP).
`%q`	The value of the last "quoted" input string.
`%r`	Last reference on references line of current article (parent article id).
`%R`	References list for a new article, constructed from the references and article ID of the current article.
`%s`	Subject, with all "Re:" and "(nf)" stripped off.
`%S`	Subject, with one "Re:" stripped off.
`%t`	"To:" line derived from the "From:" and "ReplyTo:" lines of the current article. Returns an Internet format address.
`%T`	"To:" line derived from the "Path:" line of the current article to produce a `uucp` path.
`%u`	Number of unread articles in the current newsgroup.
`%U`	Number of unread articles in the current newsgroup, not counting the current article. If threads are selected, this count reflects only selected articles.
`%v`	The number of unselected articles, not counting the current article if it is unselected.
`%w`	Directory where `mthreads` keeps its **tmp** files.
`%W`	Directory where thread files are placed.
`%x`	News library directory.
`%X`	`trn` library directory.
`%z`	The length of the current article in bytes.
`%Z`	Number of selected threads.
`%~`	Your home directory.
`%.`	The directory containing your dot files, which is your home directory unless the environment variable `DOTDIR` is defined when `trn` is invoked.
`%#`	The current count for a multifile save, starting with 1. This value is incremented by one for each file saved or extracted within a single command.
`%$`	Current process number. *(continued)*

%/   Last search string.

%?   A space unless the current string is >79 characters, at
                which point it turns into a newline.

%%   A percent sign.

%{*name*} or %{*name-default*}   The environment variable *"name"*.

%[*name*]]   The value of header line labeled *"Name:"* from the current
                article. The label is not included. For example *"%D"* and
                "%[distribution]" are equivalent.

%`*command*`   Execute command and use its resulting value, formatted
                as one line with newlines changed to spaces.

%"*prompt*"   Displays prompt on the terminal, then reads user input
                and uses it in one string, and inserts it.

%(*test_text=pattern?then_text:else_text*)

                If *test_text* matches *pattern*, the value *then_text* is used,
                otherwise *else_text* is used. The *:else_text"* is optional, and
                if absent, the null string is used. = can be replaced with !=
                to test for inequality.

The trn Environment Variables

trn supports several environment variables with which you can
specify certain formats, directories, or applications. For example,
the MAILPOSTER specifies the mailer to use for sending replies,
and the NAME variable is where you can keep the string for your
full name as you want it to appear in your article headers.
SAVEDIR is the default directory where you want your saved articles to be placed. NNTPSERVER holds the Internet address of a remote newserver.

Certain environment variables can make extensive use of trn percent codes. A trn percent code contains run-time values such
as header information for the current article or newsgroup information. For example, the ATTRIBUTION variable holds the
ATTRIBUTION string that contains several percent codes with
header information for the current article. The same is true for the
FORWARDHEADER and YOUSAID variables. YOUSAID is used as the
attribution line in mail replies that include the original article text,
R. It contains the %i percent code that will place the "Message-ID"
line from the current article in the string "In article %i you write."

Table 8.IX lists the `trn` environment variables. Those variables with a (%) following the name support only percent code interpolation. Those with (~) support both file name expansion and percent code interpolation.

`trn` **Macros**

`trn` supports the use of custom macros. You can easily create your own macros, mapping keys to `trn` commands. When `trn` starts up, it looks for macro definitions in a `trn` macro file. This file is a standard plain text file that you can edit using a standard text editor such as Vi or Emacs. The default file name of the `trn` macro file is **.trnmac**. You can use a different file as long as you assign its name to the the TRNMACRO `trn` environment variable.

`trn` macros have two fields, separated by a space. The first field is a keystroke sequence, which consists of key designations for the macro. The second field consists of the `trn` commands that you want to be executed. The following example, the first macro, @m, saves an article to the **myarticle** file using the mailbox format, whereas the second macro, @t, saves it to the **mydata** file using the plain text format.

```
@m s myarticle\n
@t w mydata\n
```

You can use any of the `trn` percent codes in the `trn` command field of a macro. For example, the following `trn` macro uses the subject of an article as its file name, `%s`.

```
@m s %s\n
```

You can even use the `trn` percent code test condition. In the following example, the macro tests to see if it is in the selector mode. If it is in the selector mode, then the g key will function only as a g key; otherwise it will function as an export command, decoding an encoded article and placing it in the **gifpic** directory.

```
g %(%m=t?g:e /gifpic)
```

Table 8.IX. trn Environment Variables

ATTRIBUTION (%)	Gives the format of the attribution line in front included by the F command. Default: In article %i,%?%)f <%>f> wrote:
AUTOSUBSCRIBE	A list of newsgroup patterns separated by commas that automatically subscribes to matching new newsgroups, adding them to your **.newsrc** file.
AUTOUNSUBSCRIBE	A list of newsgroup patterns separated by commas that automatically adds matching new newsgroups to the end of your **.newsrc** file as unsubscribed.
CANCEL	The shell command used to cancel an article.
DOTDIR	Location of your dot files, if they aren't in your home directory.
EDITOR	Your standard text editor.
FORWARDHEADER (%)	The format of the header file for forwarding messages.
FORWARDPOSTER (~)	The applications (shell command) used by the forward command (^F) to edit and send the file.
HOME	Your home directory.
KILLGLOBAL (~)	Location of the **Kill** file to apply to every newsgroup.
LOGNAME	Your login name, if User is undefined.
LOCALTIMEFMT	Format for printing the local time.
MAILCALL (~)	Message telling you there is new mail.
MAILFILE (~)	Location of your incoming mailbox.
MAILHEADER (%)	The format of the header file for replies.
MAILPOSTER (~)	The application (shell command) used by the reply commands (r and R) to send replies.
MBOXSAVER (~)	The shell command to save an article in mailbox format. Default: %X/mbox.saver %A %P %c %a %B %C "%b" \ "From %t %`date`".
MODSTRING	The string for the group summary line for a moderated group.
NEWSHEADER (%)	The format of the header file for follow-ups.
NEWSORG	The name of your organization, or the name of a file containing the name of your organization.
NEWSPOSTER (~)	The shell command used by the follow-up commands (f and F) to post a follow-up news article.
NNTPSERVER	Specifies the hostname of your NNTPSERVER.

(continued)

Table 8.IX. trn Environment Variables *(continued)*

NOPOSTRING	The group summary line for a group to which local posting is not allowed.
NORMSAVER (~)	The shell command to save an article in the normal (non-mailbox) format.
ORGANIZATION	The name of your organization, or the name of a file containing the name of your organization.
PIPESAVER (%)	The shell command to save to a pipe (s | command" or w | command).
SAVEDIR (~)	The name of the directory to save to, if the save command does not specify a directory name.
SAVENAME (%)	The name of the file to save to, if the save command contains only a directory name.
SELECTCHARS	The characters used by the thread selector to select the associated thread of discussion. You can specify up to 64 visible characters, including upper- and lowercase letters, numbers, and many punctuation characters.
SUBJLINE (%)	Format of the lines displayed by the = command at the article selection level.
SUPERSEDEHEADER (%)	Format of the header file for a supersede article.
TRNINIT	Default values for switches passed to trn by placing them in the TRNINIT variable. If TRNINIT begins with a '/' it is assumed to be the name of a file containing switches.
TRNMACRO (~)	The name of the file containing macros and key mappings. Default is **.trnmac**.
USER	Your login name.
VISUAL (~)	Your standard editor.
XTERMMOUSE	If set to 'y' (yes), enables use of the xterm mouse in the selector if you are using an xterm. Left-clicking on an item selects it and middle-clicking an item will move to that item. Clicking the top (header) line of the selector it moves up a page, and clicking the bottom (footer) line of the selector goes down a page (middle click). The right mouse button is used to move up or down a page by clicking in the upper half or lower half of the screen.
YOUSAID (%)	Gives the format of the attribution line in front of the quoted article included by an R command. Default: In article %i you write:

Summary

trn is an advanced version of rn that organizes articles into threads, allowing you to easily reference articles by subject or by related follow-up articles. trn makes use of an interface called a selector that lists articles grouped according to threads. You can select the group of articles you want to examine and then move through these related articles. When displaying articles in a thread you can make use of a thread tree that delineates the relationship of follow-up articles. Using the tree you can move from one article to any other article in the thread.

tin and nn Newsreaders

Both tin and nn are newsreaders that provide full-screen interfaces similar to the trn selector. Threads and cursor-based article and group selection are supported. Unlike trn, tin and nn both provide a full-screen interface for newsgroup selection, not just article selection. Both interfaces make much more use of cursor capabilities, letting you to move through and select items more intuitively.

The tin Newsreader

The tin newsreader uses selector screens from both newsgroups and articles. When you start tin, it will display a screen listing your newsgroups. You can then select the newsgroup you want and tin will display a screen listing that newgroup's threads. From this screen you can then display articles. tin is a threaded newsreader and supports subject, reference, and combined subject/reference threading. You can also turn off all threading, displaying just your articles. Articles in a particular thread are displayed in their own screen allowing you easily to select and display different articles in the thread.

Start tin by using the `tin` command. Add any other options you want after the tin command. If you are using a remote news server, you will have to add the `-r` option. A table in a later section lists the tin options.

```
$ tin
```

tin works equally as well with both local and remote news servers. To use trn and tin with a remote news server, such as one provided by an ISP, you need to set the NNTPSERVER environment variable to the Internet address of that news server. Remote servers usually use the NNTP protocol and begin their server addresses with "nntp." This assignment should be placed in a shell initialization file such as **.profile** or **.bashrc**. An example of the NNTPSERVER assignment follows.

```
NNTPSERVER="nntp.myserver.com"
```

You then need to invoke tin using the `-r` option. `-r` instructs tin to use the remote news server specified in NNTPSERVER.

```
$ tin -r
```

The same basic screen movement commands are used for all screens, whether for newsgroup, article lists, or article text. **Ctrl-d**, **Ctrl-f**, and **spacebar** move you forward to the next screen. **Ctrl-u**, **Ctrl-b**, and **b** move you backward to the previous screen. The up arrow and the k key move you up a line on the screen, and the down arrow and j key move you down a line. You use these same commands for newsgroups, threads, or for displaying the text of an article.

You use the q command to quit from your current screen and return to the previous screen. If you are currently viewing a listing of newsgroup articles or threads, pressing q will return you to the listing of newsgroups. You can then select another newsgroup and display its articles. You can quit the tin newsreader entirely at any point by pressing the uppercase Q.

tin Newsgroup Selection Screen

When tin starts up, it displays a screen of newsgroups (Figure 9.1). Each newsgroup entry has its own index number that identifies the newsgroup. These are assigned consecutively beginning from 1. A newsgroup entry begins with its index number and is followed

```
Group Selection                               h=help

    1   3      3dfx.game.discussion
    2   1      alt.3d.misc
    3   7      alt.agriculture.fruit
    4   24     alt.airlines.schedule
    5   32     rec.arts.movies
    6   126    rec.food.recipes




   <n>=set current to n, TAB=next unread, /=search pattern, c)atchup,
 g)oto, j=line down, k=line up, h)elp, m)ove, q)uit, r=toggle all/unread,
     s)ubscribe, S)ub pattern, u)nsubscribe, U)nsub pattern, y)ank in/out

search forwards > rec.food
```

Figure 9.1. The tin newsgroup listing.

by the number of unread articles, and the name of the newsgroup. Certain newsgroup status codes are displayed for new and unsubscribed newsgroups (Table 9.I). u indicates an unsubscribed newsgroup and U refers to new newsgroups. When a newsgroup is no longer in use, it is marked with a D. With the d command, descriptions for newsgroups are also displayed. The i command will display the description of the current newsgroup on the last line of the screen. The title "Group Selection" will be shown at the top of the screen. To its right will be "h=help." Pressing the h key will bring up a Help menu listing newsgroup selection commands. The tin newsgroup selection commands are listed in Table 9.II.

A menu of commonly used commands is displayed at the bottom of the screen. The r command will switch between the display of all subscribed newsgroups and subscribed newsgroups with unread articles. The s command will subscribe to a new newsgroup, and the u command will unsubscribe. You can subscribe or unsubscribe to several newsgroups at once by using a pattern that matches them. With the S command you can enter a pattern that matches on the names of the newsgroups to which you want to subscribe. For example, **alt.binaries.*** will match on all newsgroups that post binary files, and ***unix*** will match on any newsgroup with "unix" in its name. You can use the U command to unsubscribe from a set of newsgroups matching a pattern. With the U command, using the **talk.*** pattern you could unsubscribe from all talk newsgroups.

To select a newsgroup, you must first move to it. You can do this either by moving the cursor, entering its selection number if you know it, or using a pattern search to locate it. Using the cursor, you can use the up and down arrow keys or the j and k keys to move to the article you want. The **tab** key will move you to the next newsgroup with unread news. If the newsgroup is not displayed on the current screen, use **spacebar**, **page-down**, or **Ctrl-f** keys to move to the next screen, and **b**, **page-up**, or **Ctrl-b** to move back. Instead of using the cursor, you can move directly to a newsgroup by entering its selection number if you know it or use the g command and enter its name. To locate a newsgroup with a pattern search, you press the / key and then type a pattern that the newsgroup name contains. Be sure that the pattern uniquely distinguishes the newsgroup from other newsgroup names. You can make it the entire newsgroup name if you want. / performs a forward search from your currently

NEWSGROUP SELECTION SCREEN CODES

u	Unsubscribed newsgroup.
N	New newsgroup created since you last used tin. New newsgroups are unsubscribed and you will need to subscribe to them if you want to access them again.
D	The newsgroup no longer exists. Unsubscribe to remove entry.

NEWSGROUP INDEX STATUS CODES

*num*T	The number of threads in the newsgroup.
*num*A	The number of articles in the newsgroup.
*num*K	The number of killed articles.
*num*H	The number of hot articles.
R	Display unread threads or articles.
M	Moderated newsgroup.

THREAD MODES

U	No threading.
S	Subject threading.
R	Reference threading.
B	Both subject and reference threading.

Table 9.I. Newsgroup Status codes

selected newsgroup. ? performs a backward search. Once you have located the newsgroup you want, press **enter** to access its articles. tin will then display a list of all the articles for that newsgroup using one of several possible threading modes.

You can mark an entire newsgroup as read without reading it by first selecting it and then pressing the z command. The c command will mark all articles in the current newsgroup as read and then move to the next newsgroup whether it is read or not. The C command also marks the current newsgroup as read, but then moves to the next newsgroup with unread news. You can also automatically select articles in newsgroups by moving to its entries and pressing +. A * will appear before the automatically selected entries.

From the newsgroup screen, you can quit tin using either the Q or q commands. q will first ask you to confirm that you really want to quit, and Q will simply quit with no confirmation request.

Table 9.II. Selecting Newsgroups

k up arrow	Move cursor to next newsgroup.
j down arrow	Move cursor to previous newsgroup.
+	Perform autoselection on newsgroup.
num	Select *num* newsgroup.
enter	Read current newsgroup.
tab	View next newsgroup with unread news.
Ctrl-l	Redraw the screen.
Ctrl-r	Reset **.newsrc** file.
&	Toggle use of ANSI color.
c	Mark current newsgroup as read (catchup) and move to next newsgroup.
C	Mark current newsgroup as read (catchup) and move to next unread newsgroup.
d	Toggle between displaying just newsgroup name or newsgroup name with its description.
g	Search for and select a newsgroup using it name. You can also use the position of the newsgroup within the group list. '1' references the first newsgroup and $ references the last.
h	Displays Help screen with selection commands.
H	Toggle on and off the display of the Help menu at the bottom of the screen.
i	Display the description of the current newsgroup on the last line.
I	Toggle inverse video.
m	Move the current group within the group selection list. '1' makes the newsgroup the first displayed, and $ makes it the last. You can enter a number for where you want the newsgroup listed.
M	User-configurable options menu.
q	Quit tin, but ask the user to confirm.
Q	Quit tin without asking the user to confirm.
r	Switch between the display of newsgroups with unread articles and all subscribed newsgroups.
R	Mail a bug report or comment.
s	Subscribe to current newsgroup.

S	Subscribe to newsgroups matching user-specified pattern.
u	Unsubscribe to current newsgroup.
U	Unsubscribe to newsgroups matching user-specified pattern.
v	Print tin version information.
w	Post an article to current newsgroup.
W	List articles posted by user. The date posted, the newsgroup, and the subject are listed.
X	Quit tin without saving any configuration changes.
y	Will read in newsgroups from **$NEWSLIBDIR/active** that are not in your **.newsrc.** You can then subscribe and unsubscribe to them. Pressing y again will read newsgroups from your **.newsrc** file and display only subscribed newsgroups.
Y	Check to see if any new news has arrived by reading the active file.
z	Mark all articles in the current newsgroup as unread.
/	Perform a forward search.
?	Perform a backward search.

Newsgroup Index Screen

Once you have selected a newsgroup, the articles in that newsgroup are displayed using the Newsgroup Index screen (Figure 9.2). The Newsgroup Index screen can display articles according to different threading modes: no threading, threading by subject, threading by references, and threading by subject and references. You use the u command to change the different threading modes. With no threading the individual articles are listed. In the subject mode, articles are organized into subject threads, and in the reference mode articles are organized into follow-up and response threads. With both the subject and reference modes, articles on the same subject with their follow-up and response articles are placed in the same thread. Only the first article in a thread is displayed in the newsgroup index screen. To see a listing of all the articles in a thread, press the l key, displaying a Thread Listing screen for them. You can return to the Newsgroup Index screen by pressing q.

```
rec.food.recipes (250T(B) 372A 0K 0H R M)                        h=help

    1    +         Cookies on the run              Justin Saturn
    2    +         Angel Food Cake                 Cecelia Petersen
    3    +   5     Chocolate and Cinnamon          Richard Leland
    5    +         Cinnamon Bagels                 Dylan Petersen
    6    +         REQUEST: romantic Lunches       Marylou Carrion
    7    +         REQUEST: romantic snacks        Valerie Fuller
    8    +         REQUEST: Spicy Popcorn          Carolyn Blacklock
    9    +         Music cookies                   Bonnie Matoza
   10     +        Passion Fruit                   Gabriel Matoza
   11     + 3      REQUEST: Spelling Cookies       Anntionnete C.
   12     +        REQUEST: Cheese Toast           Pearl
   13     +        REQUEST: Sausage Recipes        Penny Bode
   14     +        Bisket Recipe                   Leslie
   15     +        Oatmeal Cookies                 John Gunther
   16     +        Applesauce                      Maryann
   17     +        Lasanga (huge dish)             Gloria
   18     +        Summer desserts                 Marisa

    <n>=set current to n, TAB=next unread, /=search pattern, ^K)ill/select,
   a)uthor search, c)atchup, j=line down, k=line up, K=mark read, l)ist
thread,
      |=pipe, m)ail, o=print, q)uit, r=toggle all/unread, s)ave, t)ag, w=post
]
```

Figure 9.2. The Newsgroup Index screen.

The number of threads and the current thread mode are displayed
at the top of the Newsgroup Index screen following the newsgroup
name. The thread mode is indicated by a status code that can be
either U, S, R, or B. U represents no threading, S represents subject threading, R is for reference threads, and B indicates both subject
and reference threads. This status code is encased in parentheses
and preceded by a 'T'. The number of threads precedes it. You will
see this number change as you change the thread mode with the u
command. Following the thread count and mode, the total number
of articles, A, the number of killed articles, K, and the number of
selected (hot) articles are displayed, H. After these counts, two other
status codes may be shown, R and M. R appears if only unread
articles are displayed, and M if the newsgroup is moderated. The following example shows a thread count of 250 for both subject and
reference threads, 250T(B). The total number of articles is 372,

372A. There are no killed articles, OK, or hot articles, OH. The newsgroup index currently displays only unread articles, R, and the newsgroup is moderated, M.

```
rec.food.recipes (250T(B) 372A 0K 0H R M)
```

Each thread entry begins with its own ID number, followed by a + indicating unread articles, the number of articles in the thread, the subject of the first article, and possibly the author of the first article. If there is only one article in the thread, then the number of articles will be blank. If you press the d key, the article author will also be shown. Pressing the d key again displays the address instead, and pressing it once more will display both the author name and the address. If there are tagged articles in the thread, the number of tagged articles is shown in place of the + symbol. In effect, you can think of the Newsgroup Index screen as displaying single articles that are not part of a thread and, for a threaded group of articles, just the first article in that group. Other than the first article, articles belonging to a thread are not shown.

The Newsgroup Index uses many of the same commands as the newsgroup selector. The up and down arrow keys move you from one thread to the next. If there is more than one screen of threads, you can move back and forth through them using **Ctrl-f** or **Ctrl-b** or the **page-up** and **page-down** keys. You can also move to a specific thread by typing its ID number. An example of the tin article selector screen follows.

In a thread mode, the Newsgroup Index screen shows only the first article in a thread. When you have selected a thread you can then either display another screen that lists the articles in it by pressing the 1 key or display the first article by just pressing **enter**. The screen of articles in the thread is called a Thread Listing screen. From this screen can select and display the article you want.

When you select a thread in the Newsgroup Index screen, you have the option of either listing the articles in the thread and choosing one to display, or directly displaying the first article in the thread. In other words, you can go directly to the tin Article Viewer and start reading articles in the thread one by one, or go to the Thread Listing screen, which lists all the articles in the thread

and lets you skip to the one you want to display. To start displaying the first article, just press **enter**. To go to the Thread listing
screen you press the l command.

A menu of commonly used commands for accessing articles is displayed at the bottom of the screen. You can search articles for a
specified pattern with the / command. With the a command you
can search for articles by a specified author. To post an article of
your own to the newsgroup, use the w command. Once you have
selected and displayed an article, you will also be able to post
follow-ups and send replies. You can group a set of articles by tagging them using the t command. You can then perform operations
such as printing them or mailing them to another user.

The s command saves an article. If you want to save the article to a
mailbox file, preserving its header information, you precede the
name of the mailbox file with a = sign. To save to your default
mailbox file, just enter = by itself. If you want to save the article to
a directory that has the same name as the article's newsgroup, you
precede the file name with a + sign.

tin distinguishes between read and unread articles. The N command or **tab** key will move to the next thread with unread articles
and the P command moves to the previous unread thread (n and p
simply move to the next or previous article, whether read or unread). With the r command, you can toggle the screen between
showing just unread threads or all threads. To mark an article read
without reading it, use the K command (uppercase). The X command will mark all unselected articles as read. The c command
(catchup) will mark all articles in the newsgroup as read. To mark
a read article as unread, use the z command, and Z will mark as
unread an entire thread.

You can automatically select all the articles in a thread by moving
to its thread entry and pressing +. A * will appear in that thread
entry. With the = command you can perform a search of subjects
that will select threads that match the search pattern. The @ command will reverse selections and . will toggle selections.

Table 9.III lists the Newsgroup Index commands.

Table 9.III. Newsgroup Index Commands

spacebar, Ctrl-f, page-down	Display next page of thread/article entries.
b, Ctrl-b, page-up	Display previous page of thread/article entries.
num	Select article *num*.
$	Move to last thread or article.
Ctrl-l	Redraw page.
enter	Read current article.
tab	View next unread article.
a	Author forward search.
A	Author backward search.
c	Mark all articles as read with confirmation.
C	Mark all articles as read and change to next newsgroup with unread news.
d	Add display of author, address, or author and address to thread entries.
g	Choose a new newsgroup by name.
h	Help screen of newsgroup index commands.
H	Toggle the Help menu display at the bottom of the screen.
i	Display the subject of the first article in the current thread in the last line.
I	Toggle inverse video.
K	Mark current thread or article as read and advance to next unread thread or article.
l	Display articles in a thread using Thread Listing screen.
m	Mail current article or selected or tagged articles to a user.
M	User configurable options menu.
n	Move to next thread/article.
N	Move to next unread thread/article.
o	Print current or selected or tagged articles.
p	Move to previous thread/article.
P	Move to previous unread thread/article.
q	Return to previous level. *(continued)*

Table 9.III. Newsgroup Index Commands *(continued)*

Q	Quit tin.
s	Save articles. Tagged or selected threads are saved with all their articles. Use = to save to a mailbox file and + to use the newsgroup name as a directory.
t	Tag current thread/article or thread. You can mail, print, save, or repost tagged articles.
u	Set the threading mode: no threading, threading by subject, threading by references, threading on subject and references.
U	Untag all threads or articles that were tagged.
v	Print tin version information.
w	Post an article to current group.
W	List articles posted by user.
x	Repost an already posted article to another newsgroup.
X	Mark all unread articles that have not been selected as read. Pressing 'X' again will toggle back to previous state.
z	Mark current article as unread.
Z	Mark current thread as unread.
/	Search forward for specified subject.
?	Search backward for specified subject.
-	Show last message.
|	Pipe current article, thread, selected, or tagged articles into a Unix command for processing by it.
*	Select current thread for later processing.
.	Toggle selection of current thread.
@	Reverse all selections on all articles.
~	Undo all selections on all articles. Undo the effect of the X command.
+	Perform autoselection on current group.
=	Select threads whose subjects match the supplied pattern. "*" matches all subjects.
;	If one unread article in a thread is selected, all unread articles are selected.

tin Thread Listing

When you select a thread in the Newsgroup Index screen, you then have the option of either listing the articles in the thread and choosing one to display, or directly displaying the first article in the thread. In other words, you can go directly to the tin Article Viewer and start reading articles in the thread one by one, or go to the Thread Listing screen, which lists all the articles in the thread and lets you skip to the one you want to display. To start displaying the first article, just press **enter**. To go to the Thread Listing screen, press the 1 command. Figures 9.3 and 9.4 show examples of Thread Listing screens, and Table 9.IV lists the commands.

Think of the Thread Listing screen as a subscreen of the Newsgroup Index screen. The Newsgroup Index screen will show the first article in a thread, and the Thread Listing screen will expand that thread to list all the articles in it. Articles are displayed numbered from 0. An article entry begins with its number followed by its size, the number of lines in the body of the article, and the article subject. Unread articles have a * symbol displayed after the number. Tagged articles have a number. If you press the d key, then

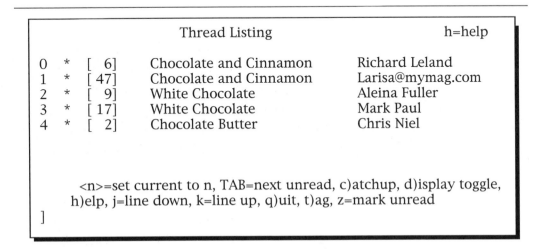

```
                          Thread Listing                          h=help

   0   *   [  6]   Chocolate and Cinnamon      Richard Leland
   1   *   [ 47]   Chocolate and Cinnamon      Larisa@mymag.com
   2   *   [  9]   White Chocolate             Aleina Fuller
   3   *   [ 17]   White Chocolate             Mark Paul
   4   *   [  2]   Chocolate Butter            Chris Niel




      <n>=set current to n, TAB=next unread, c)atchup, d)isplay toggle,
      h)elp, j=line down, k=line up, q)uit, t)ag, z=mark unread
   ]
```

Figure 9.3. Thread Listing screen.

```
                            Thread Listing                              h=help

   0    *    [   2]      REQUEST: Spelling Cookies        Anntionnete C.
   1    *    [  68]      Spelling Cookies                 augie@napa
   2    *    [  19]      Spelling Cookies                 John Carrion




        <n>=set current to n, TAB=next unread, c)atchup, d)isplay toggle,
        h)elp, j=line down, k=line up, q)uit, t)ag, z=mark unread
   ]
```

Figure 9.4. Thread Listing screen.

the article author will also be shown. Pressing the d key again displays the address instead and pressing it once more will display
both the author name and the address.

You select articles just as you would in the Article Listing. You can
use the up and down arrow keys, the j or k keys, or the number of
the article to move to it and select it, making it the current article.
You can then display the selected article by pressing the **enter** key.
This will place you in the Article Viewer, displaying the article for
you to read. When you quit the Article Viewer, you will return to
the Thread Listing screen for the thread you were viewing.

With the z key you can mark a particular article as read, and with
the Z key you can mark all articles as read. The c command will
also mark all articles in the thread a read, but then will quit the
thread listing and return to the Newsgroup Index screen. You can
use the t command to select a group of articles within the thread
which you can then perform an operation on such as mail, print, or
save. The d command will add the author or address to the display
of each article.

You can quit the Thread Listing at any time by entering q. This
will return you to your previous level, usually the Newsgroup
Index screen for the newsgroup you selected the thread from. You
can use T to return back to the Newsgroup Listing screen to select
a different newsgroup.

num	Select article *num* within thread.
Ctrl-l	Redraw page.
enter	Display current article selected in the thread.
tab	View next unread article within thread.
c	Mark all articles in the thread as read and return to previous level.
d	Toggle display to show just the subject or the subject and author.
h	Help for Thread Listing commands.
H	Toggle the display of Help mini menu at the bottom of the screen.
I	Toggle inverse video.
K	Mark thread as read and return to previous level.
q	Return to previous level, usually the Article Listing.
Q	Quit tin.
r	Toggle display to show all articles or only unread articles.
R	Mail a bug report or comment.
t	Tag current article for mailing ('m') / piping ('|') / printing ('o') / saving ('s') / reposting ('x').
T	Return to group index level.
v	Print tin version information.
z	Mark current article in thread as unread.
Z	Mark all articles in thread as unread.

Table 9.IV. Thread Listing Commands

tin Article Viewer

The tin Article Viewer is used to display a newsgroup article (Figure 9.5). Header information such as the date and size is shown at the top of the screen. If the article takes up more than one screen, you can move forward by pressing the **spacebar** and backward by pressing the b key. If the article includes quote text, you can skip it using the : key. The G command will move you to the end of the article, and g will return you to the beginning. The $ key will also move you to the end of the article.

```
Sat, 8 Aug 1998 04:48:o1        rec.food.recipes      Thread  223 of  250
Lines 43                        Spelling Cookies       No responses
chris@mygame.com.         Chris Niel

    Spelling Cookies
              INGREDIENTS
         1 cup  flour
         2 teaspoon single acting baking powder, or 1 teaspoon double
              acting baking powder, or 1 teaspoon baking soda
         1/2 teaspoon nutmeg
         1/4 teaspoon cinnamon
         3/4  cup butter  (or 1 1/2 sticks)
         1 cup brown or dark-brown sugar
         1/2 cup regular sugar
         1 egg
         1 teaspoon  vanilla extract
         1/4 cup milk

 <n>=set current to n, TAB=next unread, /=search pattern, ^K)ill/select,
      a)uthor search, B)ody search, c)atchup, f)ollowup, K=mark read,
        |=pipe, m)ail, o=print, q)uit, r)eply mail, s)ave, t)ag, w=post

    --More--(44%)  [46/100]
```

Figure 9.5. tin Article Viewer screen.

A menu of commands for operations you can perform with this article are displayed at the bottom of the screen and summarized in Table 9.V. With the F command you can post a follow-up to the article, and with the R command you can send a reply message to the author. The r command for replies and f for follow-ups will include a copy of the article. To post an article of your own to the newsgroup at this point, use the w command. You can search an article for a specified pattern with the / command. ? performs the search backward through the article. With the a command you can search for articles by a specified author. With the B command you can search all articles for a specified pattern. Whenever you perform a search, the previous pattern searched is displayed within brackets at the search prompt. To repeat this search, just press **enter**.

Table 9.V. Article Viewer Commands

spacebar, Ctrl-f, page-down	Display next page of article text.
b, Ctrl-b, page-up	Display previous page of article text.
g	Display first page of article text.
G, $	Display last page of article text.
Ctrl-h	Show all of the article's mail header.
Ctrl-k	Kill article(s) via a menu.
0	Read the first article in this thread.
num	Read response *num* in this thread.
Ctrl-l	Redraw page.
enter	Move to first article in next thread.
tab	Move to the next unread article.
a	Author forward search.
A	Author backward search.
c	Mark all articles as read with confirmation and return to newsgroup selection level.
C	Mark current newsgroup as read and next newsgroup with unread articles.
d	Toggle rot-13 decoding for this article.
D	Delete current article. It must have been posted by the same user.
e	Edit the current article.
f	Post a follow-up to the current article, including body of article.
F	Post a follow-up to the current article.
h	List Article Viewer commands.
H	Toggle the Help menu display at the bottom of the screen.
i	Display the subject of the current article in the last line.
I	Toggle inverse video.
k	Mark article as read and move to the next unread article.
K	Mark thread as read and move to the next unread thread.
m	Mail current article or selected or tagged articles to a user.
M	User Global Options menu.
n	Display the next article.
N	Display the next unread article.

(continued)

Table 9.V. Article Viewer Commands *(continued)*

o	Print current or selected or tagged articles.
p	Display the previous article.
P	Display the previous unread article.
q	Return to previous level, either the Newsgroup Index or Thread Listing.
Q	Quit tin.
r	Reply through mail to the author of the current article with a copy of the article included.
R	Reply through mail to the author of the current article.
s	Save articles. Tagged or selected threads are saved with all their articles. Use = to save to a mailbox file and + to use the newsgroup name as a directory.
t	Tag current article or thread. You can mail, print, save, or repost articles.
T	Return to newsgroup selection screen.
v	Print tin version information.
w	Post an article to current group.
W	List articles posted by user.
x	Repost an already posted article to another newsgroup.
z	Mark article as unread.
/	Article forward search.
?	Article backward search.
|	Pipe current article, thread, selected or tagged articles into a Unix command for processing by it.
<	Display the first article in the current thread.
>	Display the last article in the current thread.
*	Select current thread for later processing.
.	Toggle selection of current article.
@	Reverse article selections.
~	Undo all selections on current thread.
:	Skip quoted text.

While remaining within the Articles Viewer, you can directly display all the articles in the current newsgroup or thread. To display the next unread article, press the N or **tab** keys. The P command displays the previous unread article. The n and p commands display the next or previous article, whether read or unread. $ will display the last article in the newsgroup. You can press k at any time to mark the current article as read and go on to display the next unread article. K will skip the rest of the current thread articles, marking it as read, and start you at the next unread thread. z will mark the current article as unread.

To move within a thread of articles you use the 0, >, <, and *num* commands. 0 moves you to the first article in the thread. A number, *num*, will display that article in the sequence of articles in the thread. > will display the last article in the thread, and < will display the first. Pressing **enter** will move you to the first article in the next thread (the next base article), skipping any remaining articles in the current thread.

You use the s command to save articles as you would in the Newsgroup Index screen. To save the article to a mailbox file, preserving its header information, precede the name of the mailbox file with a = sign. To save to your default mailbox file, just enter = by itself. If you want to save the article to a directory that has the same name as the article's newsgroup, precede the file name with a + sign.

To quit the Article Viewer and return to the screen you invoked it from, press the q key. This returns you either to the Newsgroup Index or Thread Listing screen. If you want to return to the Newsgroup listing to move to another newsgroup, press the T key (uppercase). The c command (catchup) will mark all articles in the newsgroup as read and then return you to the Newsgroup listing. The C command will also mark all articles as read, but then move to the next newsgroup with unread articles.

tin Article Filtering

tin has an automatic select and kill capability for selecting or removing articles based on an article's Subject or From line. You can use this feature to mark automatically articles on a certain subject as important. You can also use it to avoid displaying articles posted by certain users or dealing with specified subjects.

The commands for automatically selecting or killing articles are placed in a filter file, **.tin/filter**. To make a kill entry, use the **Ctrl-k** command. This brings up a menu from which you can choose either the Subject or From line. You choose the Subject or From line of the current article selected if you no longer want to read further articles on that subject or from that author, or you can make a Subject or From line entry of your own. You can limit the kill entry to just the current newsgroup or apply it to all newsgroups.

Use the **Ctrl-a** command to autoselect an entry. Like the autokill entry, a menu is displayed for the Subject and From lines. You can use the Subject or From lines from the current article or enter ones of your own. Autoselect entries can be applied to the current newsgroup or all newsgroups.

Kill and select entries are placed in the **.tin/filter** file. You can edit this file directly to add or edit kill or select entries instead of using the **Ctrl-k** menus. When you start up tin, the **.tin/filter** file is read and entries for a newsgroup are applied when you enter it. Articles automatically killed are never displayed in the newsgroup index screen, and articles automatically selected are displayed with a *.

Instead of using the kill and select menus, you can specify autoselect or autokill entries using the [or] commands. These commands make use of defaults set in **tinrc** configuration variables. Using these setting, the [or] commands create an autoselect or autokill entry using either the Subject or From line of the current article as specified by their corresponding configuration variables.

The] command uses the **default_filter_kill_header, default_ filter_kill_global, default_filter_kill_case**, and the **default_ filter_ kill_expire** configuration variables. The **default_filter_kill_ header** is used to specify the line in the header that the kill entry will use, either Subject, From, or ID lines. **default_filter_kill_ global** specifies whether the kill entry will apply to all newsgroups or just to the current one, and **default_filter_kill_expire** indicates whether it will always apply or will expire after the days specified in **default_filter_days**. **default_filter_kill_case** determines if the entry is case sensitive. For example, the] command will create a kill entry using the Subject line of the current article if the **default _filter_kill_header** configuration variable is set to 0. If set to 1,

Ctrl-a	Create an autoselect entry using menu.	
Ctrl-k	Create an autokill entry using menu.	
[	Create autoselect entry using **tinrc** configuration variable defaults.	
	default_filter_days	Default number of filter days. Default is 28.
	default_filter_select_header	Defaults for quick (1 key) autoselection filter header. 0=Subject: 1=From: 2=Message-Id:. Default is 0.
	default_filter_select_case	Defaults for quick (1 key) autoselection filter case. ON=filter case sensitive OFF=ignore case. Default is OFF.
	default_filter_select_expire	Defaults for quick (1 key) autoselection filter expire. ON=limit to default_filter_days OFF=don't ever expire. Default is OFF.
	default_filter_select_global	Defaults for quick (1 key) autoselection filter global. ON=apply to all groups OFF=apply to current group. Default is ON.
]	Create autokill entry using **tinrc** configuration variable defaults.	
	default_filter_kill_expire	Defaults for quick (1 key) kill filter expire. ON=limit to default_filter_days OFF=don't ever expire. Default is OFF.
	default_filter_kill_global	Defaults for quick (1 key) kill filter global. ON=apply to all groups OFF=apply to current group. Default is ON.
	default_filter_kill_header	Defaults for quick (1 key) kill filter header. 0=Subject: 1=From: 2=Message-Id:. Default is 0.
	default_filter_kill_case	Defaults for quick (1 key) kill filter case. ON=filter case sensitive OFF=ignore case. Default is OFF.

Table 9.VI. tin Auto Select and Kill Commands

then the From line is used. If the **default_filter_kill_global** is set to ON, then the kill entry is applied to all newsgroups.

The same process works for the [autoselect command using different **tinrc** configuration variables. **default_filter_select_header** specifies the line in the header used for the select entry (0=Subject,

1=From, and 2=MessageId). **default_filter_select_global** determines whether it is applied to all newsgroups or just the current one, and **default_filter_select_expire** indicates whether it will always apply or will expire after the days specified in **default_filter_days**. **default_filter_select_case** determines whether the entry is case sensitive or not. These commands are summarized in Table 9.VI.

tin Command Line Editing and History

tin has built-in command line editing capabilities that let you easily modify commands you have entered before executing them, as well as a history feature with which you can edit and execute previous commands. If you make a spelling mistake when entering a command, rather than reentering the entire command, you can use the editing operations to correct the mistake before executing the command. This is particularly helpful for commands that use arguments with lengthy path names. You can find a listing of tin editing and history commands in Table 9.VII.

The command line editing operations are a subset of the Emacs editing commands. You can use **Ctrl-f** or the right arrow key to move forward a character; **Ctrl-b** or the left arrow key to move back a character. **Ctrl-a** will move to the beginning of the line, and **Ctrl-e** will move to the end. **Ctrl-r** or **Ctrl-l** will redraw a line. Use **escape** to cancel a command.

Ctrl-d will delete the character the cursor is on. **delete** and **Ctrl-h** will delete the character to left of the character the cursor is on. **Ctrl-k** will delete the remainder of the line. To add text, move the cursor to where you want to insert text and type in the new characters. At any time, you can press **enter** to execute the command.

The tin command line history feature keeps a list of the most recent commands you have executed and lets you select, edit, and execute them. History is a kind of short-term memory, keeping track of the most recent commands executed. You can reference a former command, placing the it on your command line and allowing you to edit or execute it. Use the **Ctrl-p** or the up arrow and **Ctrl-n** or

Ctrl-a	Move to beginning of line.
Ctrl-e	Move to end of line.
Ctrl-f, right arrow	Move forward one character location.
Ctrl-b, left arrow	Move back one character.
Ctrl-d	Delete the character currently under the cursor, or send EOF if no characters in the buffer.
Ctrl-h, **delete**	Delete character to left of cursor.
Ctrl-k	Delete from cursor to end of line.
Ctrl-p, **up-arrow**	Move to previous history entry.
Ctrl-n, **down-arrow**	Move to next history entry.
Ctrl-l, **Ctrl-r**	Redraw the current line.
enter	Add current line to history list.
escape	Cancel the present editing operation.

Table 9.VII. tin Command Line Editing and History

the down arrow keys to move backward through a list of previous commands, displaying them as the current command, one by one. For, example pressing **Ctrl-p** or the up arrow once places the previous command on your command line. Pressing it again displays the next previously executed command. Pressing **Ctrl-n** or the down arrow moves forward through this list of the next command. Once the command is displayed on your command line, you can edit it using editing commands or press **enter** to execute it.

The tin Configuration

Each user can configure tin for his or her own particular use. You can set options on the command line with the tin command when you start up tin. You can also place a sequence of default options in the **TINRC** environment variable that will be used automatically each time you start tin. Tin maintains its own configuration file called **tinrc** located in the **.tin** directory in which an extensive set of configuration variables can be set. Instead of manually editing this file and entering variable assignments, you can use the tin Global Configuration menu to make entries. Simply select an entry on the screen using your cursor and set the appropriate value. In addition, there are environment variables that you can set in any of the initialization files such as **.profile**. You can also set attributes that can be used to configure individual newsgroups. Attributes are set in the **.tin/attributes** file.

tin Files

For each user, tin creates a **.tin** directory in each user's home directory. Note that the directory name begins with a period, **.tin**. The **.tin** directory contains configuration files and directories. The **tinrc** file in this directory is used to hold various configuration information and setting. tin also uses the **.newsrc** file located in your home directory that is used by other newsreaders such as rn and trn. This file will contain a listing of the user's subscribed newsgroups. Notice that the **tinrc** file does not begin with a period, whereas the **.newsrc** file does.

Several directories are used for tin index files. tin provides index files for older news servers that cannot maintain them. **.news**, **.mail**, and **.save** will hold index files for newsgroups, mail, and saved newsgroups. The tin files are listed in Table 9.VIII.

tin Options

tin provides an extensive set of command line options that you can use to configure your newsreader when you start it up (Table 9.IX). For example, the -q command (as with trn), will skip the check for new newsgroups when you start up, going directly to the newsgroup selection screen. As noted previously, if you are using a remote NNTP newserver such as one accessed through an ISP, you need to use the -r option. With this option, tin will look for the NNTP news server address in either the NNTPSERVER environment variable or the system's **/etc/nntpserver file**.

Several options let you streamline certain tasks. The -w option lets access tin to just post an article and then quit, avoiding length startup operations for newsgroup displays. The -z option will first check to

.tin	tin configuration directory, located in user's home directory.
.newsrc	tin **newsrc** file holding newsgroup subscription list.
.tin/tinrc	tin file holding configuration variables.
.tin/.news	tin directory holding news index files.
.tin/.mail	tin directory holding mail index files.
.tin/.save	tin directory holding saved newsgroup index files.
.tin/headers	Holds extra header lines to be added to posted articles.
.tin/bug_address	Address for tin bug reports.
.tin/attributes	Specify the threading types for certain newsgroups.
.newsauth	"nntpserver password [user]" pairs for NNTP servers that require authorization.
.tin/active.mail	Active file of user's mailgroups.
.tin/active.save	Active file of user's saved newsgroups.
.tin/add_address	Address to add to when replying through mail.
.tin/filter	Filtering file for article killing and autoselection.
.tin/group.times	List of last time all groups were updated (used only by tind index demon).
.tin/posted	History of articles posted by user.
.tin/newsrctable	"nntpserver newsrc shortname" pairs to use with -g command-line switch.
.signature	Signature.
.Sig	Signature.
.sigfixed	Fixed part of a randomly generated signature.

Table 9.VIII. tin Files

see if there is any new or unread news in your newsgroups and will start tin only if such news is found. The -z option will also check for new or unread news, but will not start up tin. Instead it return a status value indicating whether there is any new or unread news. This option is helpful if you want to check for news in a Unix script. 0 indicates no news and 3 indicates that there is new or unread news. 1 detects an error and 2 detects an error from an NNTP newserver. With the -f option you can specify an alternative file of subscribed newsgroups, other than your **.newsrc** file. This can be helpful if you

-a	Use ANSI color.
-c	Create or update index files for every group in **$HOME/.newsrc** or file specified by the -f option and mark all articles as read.
-C	Count articles for each subscribed group at startup.
-d	Select index files for each group before indexing article.
-f *file*	Specify user's own file of subscribed to newsgroups in place of **$HOME/.newsrc**.
-g *server*	Use the **$HOME/.tin/newsrctable** specified server and **newsrc**.
-h	Help, lists command-line options.
-H	Detailed help with short introduction to tin.
-I*dir*	Directory in which to store newsgroup index files. Default is **$HOME/.tin/.news**.
-m*dir*	Mailbox directory. Default is **$HOME/Mail**.
-M *user*	Mail unread articles to specified user for later reading.
-n	Load subscribed newsgroups specified in user's **.newsrc**.
-q	Do not check for new newsgroups when starting up.
-P	Remove group index files of articles that no longer exist. Checks every article in each group accessed.
-r	Access remote NNTP news server as specified in the environment variable NNTPSERVER or contained in the file **/etc/nntpserver**.
-R	Read news saved by the -S option.
-s *dir*	Save articles to directory. Default is **$HOME/News**.
-S	Save unread articles for later reading by the -R option.
-u	Create or update index files for every group in **$HOME/.newsrc** or file specified by the -f option. Disabled for an NNTP news server.
-U	Start tin in the background to update index files while reading news in the foreground. Disabled for an NNTP news server.
-v	Verbose mode for -c, -M, -S, -u, and -Z options.
-w	Post an article and then exit.
-z	Check for any new or unread news and start up only if found.
-Z	Check for any new/unread news and exit with appropriate status. With the -v option, the number of unread articles in each group is displayed. A status code 0 indicates no news, 1 that an error occurred, 2 that an nntp error occurred and 3 that new/unread news exists.

Table 9.IX. tin Options

only want to check a few of your subscribed newsgroups. You could create a smaller file that contains just those newsgroup entries and specify it with the -f option when you start up tin.

Like trn, tin supports threads. Usually when you select and enter newsgroups, an index file is created that generates the threads for all the articles in that newsgroup. A previously read newsgroup already has a thread index file that is updated each time you access the newsgroup. For newsgroups with a great many articles this can cause a time delay, forcing you to wait until the indexing for the threads is finished. The -u and -U options help you avoid this wait to some extent. With the -u option you can have tin create or update thread index files for all the subscribed newsgroups in your **.newsrc** file. If you combine it with the -f option, then only the newsgroups in the specified file are indexed. With the -U option you can instruct tin to perform the thread indexing in the background, letting you browse newsgroup listings as the threading is accomplished. The -c option also creates and updates the thread index files, but then marks all their articles as read. -c is a catchup operation that can be applied to all your newsgroups or to just those in a file specified by the -f option.

tin Configuration Variables: tinrc

You can configure different tin features by setting tin configuration and environment variables. tin makes a distinction between configuration variables, which set features of your tin interface, and environment variables, which set more basic items such as the default editor or mail directory. A configuration variable can be set either by entering an assignment for that variable in your **.tin/tinrc** file or by using the tin Global Options menu (Table 9.X).

You can bring the Global Options menu up at any time by pressing M. For each option you select and set, the appropriate assignment entry is placed in your **tinrc** file located in the .tin directory in your home directory. Some environment options you set to on or off; others need values entered. Move the cursor to the option you want to set and press the **spacebar** to toggle it on or off. For entries

Table 9.X. Global Options Menu

Auto save	Save articles or threads using "Archive-name:" line in article header. If process type is not set to None, then postprocess them.
Editor offset	Set ON if the editor used can position the cursor at a specified line in a file.
Mark saved read	Automatically mark saved articles as read.
Confirm command	Allows certain commands that require user confirmation to be executed immediately if set OFF.
Draw arrow	If set ON, newsgroups or articles are selected by an arrow '->', if set OFF, they are selected by a highlighted bar.
Print header	Allows the complete mail header or only the "Subject:" and "From:" fields to be output when displaying articles.
Goto 1st unread	Places the cursor at the first unread article upon entering a newsgroup with unread news.
Scroll full page	If set ON, scrolls newsgroups or articles a full page at a time. If set OFF, scrolls half a page at a time.
Catchup on quit	Asks the user when quitting if all groups read during the current session should be marked read.
Thread articles	Specify how articles are to be threaded (sets the **thread_arts** attribute). 0=none, 1=subject, 2=references.
Show only unread	If set ON, show only new or unread articles. If set OFF, show all articles.
Show description	Show a short descriptive text for each displayed newsgroup. Description taken from the **$NEWSLIBDIR/newsgroups file**.
Show Author	Choose from several options. If 'None', only the "Subject:" line is displayed. If 'Addr', "Subject:" line and address part of the "From:" line are displayed. If 'Name', "Subject:" line and the author's full name are displayed. If 'Both', "Subject:" line and all of the "From:" line are displayed.

Process type	Specify the default type of postprocessing to perform on saved articles. The types are as follows:
	– –None.
	– –Unpacking multi-part shell archives.
	– –Unpacking multi-part uuencoded files.
	– –Unpacking multi-part uuencoded files, which produce a *.zoo archive.
	– –Unpacking multi-part uuencoded files, which produce a *.zoo archive whose contents is extracted.
	– –Unpacking multi-part uuencoded files, which produce a *.zip archive.
	– –Unpacking of multi-part uuencoded files, which produce a *.zip archive whose contents is extracted.
Sort articles by	Specifies how articles should be sorted. The sort types are as follows:
	– –Don't sort articles (default).
	– –Sort articles by "Subject:" field (ascending/descending).
	– –Sort articles by "From:" field (ascending/descending).
	– –Sort articles by "Date:" field (ascending/descending).
Save directory	Directory where articles and threads are saved. Default is **$HOME/News**.
Mail directory	Directory where articles and threads are saved in mailbox format.
Printer	Printer command with options to be used to print articles. Default is `lpr` for BSD machines and `lp` for System V machines.

that require you to enter a value, move the cursor to the entry and press the **enter** key. You will be prompted to enter the value. For example, to have only new or unread articles displayed for a newsgroup, set the **Show only unread** choice to on. If you turn it off, then all articles, read and unread, will be displayed. To enter a different save directory, you select the **Save directory** entry and then type the path name for the directory where you want your saved articles placed. Some entries will display submenus for further options. If you select the **Sort by** entry, you are then given a list of sort options. You can choose what header field to sort by, like the Subject or From fields.

To set a configuration variable directly, you can edit your **.tin/tinrc** file and type an assignment for it. Unlike environment variables, tin configuration variables are lowercase and can be set only in the **.tin/tinrc** file. The **tinrc** file can be edited using any standard text editor such as Vi or Emacs. Configuration variables that are set on or off are assigned values "ON" or "OFF." Those that take values are assigned strings. For example, to show only subscribed newsgroups with unread articles, you would set the **show_only_unread_groups** environment variable on, as follows:

```
show_only_unread_groups="ON"
```

To specify a different default directory for articles you save, you would assign the path name for that directory to the variables, as shown here:

```
default_savedir="$HOME/mydir"
```

Configuration variables are shown in Table 9.XI.

Environment Variables

Unlike configuration variables, tin environment variables can be set in any initialization file such as your **.profile** or **.bashrc** file, as well as your **.tin/tinrc** file. The environment variables are also in uppercase. Several of the environment variables that tin uses are also used by other applications. For example, NNTPSERVER holds the Internet address of a remote newserver and EDITOR holds the Editor command for default editor. tin specific environment variables begin with the pattern TIN. **TINRC** holds the tin default options. These are options that are set each time you start up. **TIN_HOMDIR** can hold a directory location for your **.tin** directory. The **.tin** directory will be placed there instead of in your **HOME** directory.

Table 9.XI. Configuration Variables

`art_marked_deleted`	Status symbol indicating that an article is deleted. Default is `D`.
`art_marked_inrange`	Status symbol indicating that an article is within a range. Default is #.
`art_marked_return`	Status symbol indicating that an article will return. Default is '-'.
`art_marked_selected`	Status symbol indicating that an article/thread is autoselected (hot). Default is *.
`art_marked_unread`	Status symbol indicating that an article is unread. Default is '+'.
`ask_for_metamail`	Ask before using metamail to display MIME messages. `use_metamail` must also be ON. Default is ON.
`auto_cc`	Automatically place your name in the Cc: field when mailing an article. Default is OFF.
`auto_list_thread`	Automatically list thread when entering it using right arrow key. Default is ON.
`auto_save`	Articles/threads that are automatically saved and have Archive-name: in the mail header, are saved with the Archive-name and part/patch no. Default is OFF.
`batch_save`	With the `-S` or `-M` option, articles/threads are saved in batch mode. Default is OFF.
`beginner_level`	A mini menu of the most useful commands is displayed at the bottom of the screen for each level. Default is ON.
`catchup_read_groups`	Ask user on exit if read groups should all be marked read. Default is OFF.
`confirm_action`	Confirm certain commands with y/n before executing. Default is ON.
`confirm_quit`	Ask for confirmation with y/n prompt before quitting. Default is ON.
`default_editor_format`	Specify the format string used to create the editor start command with parameters. Default is '%E +%N %F' .
`default_filter_days`	Default number of filter days. Default is 28.

(continued)

Table 9.XI. Configuration Variables *(continued)*

`default_filter_kill_case`	Defaults for quick (1 key) kill filter case. ON=filter case sensitive OFF=ignore case. Default is OFF.
`default_filter_kill_expire`	Defaults for quick (1 key) kill filter expire. ON=limit to default_filter_days OFF=don't ever expire. Default is OFF.
`default_filter_kill_global`	Defaults for quick (1 key) kill filter global. ON=apply to all groups OFF=apply to current group. Default is ON.
`default_filter_kill_header`	Defaults for quick (1 key) kill filter header. 0=Subject: 1=From: 2=Message-Id:. Default is 0.
`default_filter_select_case`	Defaults for quick (1 key) autoselection filter case. ON=filter case sensitive OFF=ignore case. Default is OFF.
`default_filter_select_expire`	Defaults for quick (1 key) autoselection filter expire. ON=limit to default_filter_days OFF=don't ever expire. Default is OFF.
`default_filter_select_global`	Defaults for quick (1 key) autoselection filter global. ON=apply to all groups OFF=apply to current group. Default is ON.
`default_filter_select_header`	Defaults for quick (1 key) autoselection filter header. 0=Subject: 1=From: 2=Message-Id:. Default is 0.
`default_maildir`	Directory where articles/threads are saved in mailbox format. Default is **$HOME/Mail**.
`default_mailer_format`	The format string used to create the mailer command with parameters that is used for mailing articles to other people. Default is '%M "%T" < %F', which works with mailx. It redirects the composed article kept in **.article** (%F) to the user (%T). You can use this string to add mail options for whatever mailer you choose to use such as elm or pine. `-s %S` inserted to the string adds a subject entry.
`default_printer`	Print command with parameters used to print articles/threads.
`default_savedir`	Directory where articles/threads are saved. Default is **$HOME/News**. *(continued)*

Table 9.XI. Configuration Variables *(continued)*

default_sigfile	Path name for the signature file used when posting articles, follow-ups, or replies. Default is **$HOME/.Sig**.
draw_arrow	Use -> or highlighted bar for selection. Default is OFF.
force_screen_redraw	Specifies whether a screen redraw should always be done after certain external commands. Default is OFF.
full_page_scroll	Scroll full page of groups/articles (ON) or half a page (OFF). Default is ON.
group_catchup_on_exit	Catchup group when leaving with the left arrow key. Default is ON
groupname_max_length	Maximum number of characters of newsgroup names that can be displayed. Default is 32.
highlight_xcommentto	The X-Comment-To name is displayed in the upper-right corner or below the Summary-header. Default is OFF
inverse_okay	Use inverse video for page headers at different levels. Default is ON.
keep_dead_articles	Keep all failed article postings in **$HOME/dead.articles**. Last failed posting is kept in **$HOME/dead.article**. Default is ON.
mail_8bit_header	Permit 8bit characters unencoded in the header of mail message. Default is OFF. Turning it ON is effective only if mail_mime_encoding is also set to 8bit.
mail_mime_encoding	MIME encoding used in the body in mail message, if necessary (8bit, base64, quoted-printable, 7bit). Default is 8bit.
mm_charset	Locally supported character set.
keep_posted_articles	Keep copies of all posted articles in **$HOME/Mail/posted**. Default is ON.
mail_quote_format	Format for quote line (attribution) used in mail replies that insert the referenced article text. Default is "In article %M you wrote:"
mark_saved_read	Mark articles that are saved as read. Default is ON. *(continued)*

Table 9.XI. Configuration Variables *(continued)*

news_quote_format	Format for quote line (attribution) used in articles and follow-ups that insert the referenced article text. (%A=Address, %D=Date, %F=Addr+Name, %G=Groupname, %M=MessageId, %N=Name). Default is "%F wrote:"
no_advertising	Do NOT display advertising in header (X-Newsreader/X-Mailer). Default is OFF.
pos_first_unread	Put cursor at first unread article in group or at last article. Default is ON.
post_8bit_header	Allows 8bit characters unencoded in the header of news article. Default is OFF. post_mime_encoding must also be set to 8bit.
post_mime_encoding	Specify MIME encoding of the body in news message, if needed. (8bit, base64, quoted-printable, 7bit). Default is 8bit, which leads to no encoding.
post_process_type	Type of postprocessing to perform after saving articles. 0=(none) 1=(unshar) 2=(uudecode) 3=(uudecode & list zoo archive) 4=(uudecode & extract zoo archive) 5=(uudecode & list zip archive) 6=(uudecode & extract zip).
post_process_command	Command (with full path name) to be run after uudecoding an article.
print_header	If ON, display complete mail header. If OFF display just Subject: and From: lines. Default is OFF.
process_only_unread	Perform operations (save, print, mail, or pipe) only on unread articles. Default is ON.
quote_chars	Symbol used to indicate included text to article follow-ups and mail replies. The '_' symbol represents a blank character, a ' '. Default is ':_'.
reread_active_file_secs	Interval in which the news active file is reread to check if any new news has arrived. Default is 1200.
save_to_mmdf_mailbox	Allows articles to be saved to a MMDF style mailbox instead of mbox format. Default is OFF.
show_author	Part of From: field to display 0) none, 1) full name, 2) network address, 3) both. Default is 2.

(continued)

Table 9.XI. Configuration Variables *(continued)*

`show_description`	Display newsgroup description after newsgroup name. Default is ON.
`show_last_line_prev_page`	The last line of the previous page is displayed as the first line of next page. Default is OFF.
`show_only_unread`	If ON, show only new or unread articles, otherwise show all articles. Default is ON.
`show_only_unread_groups`	Show only subscribed groups that contain unread articles. Default is OFF.
`show_xcommentto`	Display the real name in the X-Comment-To header. Default is OFF.
`sigdashes`	Prepend the signature with dashes. Default is ON.
`sort_article_type`	Sort articles. Choose from one of the following. 0=none, 1=subject descending, 2=subject ascending, 3=from descending, 4=from ascending, 5=date descending, 6=date ascending. Default is 6.
`start_editor_offset`	If ON, editor will be started with cursor offset into the file. If OFF, cursor will be positioned at the first line. Default is ON.
`strip_blanks`	Strips the blanks from the end of each line to speed up display. Default is ON.
`strip_bogus`	Manage newsgroups listed in your **.newsrc** file that no longer exist on the news server (bogus news-groups). 0=keep bogus newsgroups, 1=remove bogus newsgroups permanently, 2=display bogus newsgroups with a 'D'. Default is 0.
`strip_newsrc`	Permanently remove any unsubscribed newsgroups from your **.newsrc** file. Default is OFF.
`tab_after_X_selection`	Automatically go to the first unread article after having selected all hot articles and threads with the 'X' command at group index level. Default is OFF.
`tab_goto_next_unread`	Pressing **tab** in the Article Viewer moves to the next unread article, skipping the remainder of the current one. Default is ON.
`thread_articles`	Thread mode. 0=no threading, 1=subject, 2=references, 3=Both. Default is 3, thread by references and subject. *(continued)*

Table 9.XI. Configuration Variables *(continued)*

`thread_catchup_on_exit`	Catchup newsgroup or thread when leaving with the left arrow key. Default is ON.
`unlink_article`	Remove ~/.**article** after posting your article. Default is ON.
`use_builtin_inews`	Enables the built-in NNTP inews. Default is ON (enabled).
`use_metamail`	If ON metamail is used to display MIME articles. Default is ON.
`use_mouse`	Permit mouse key support in an xterm window to be enabled. Default is OFF.
`use_color`	Use ANSI colors. Default is OFF.
`wildcard`	Pattern matching capability. 1=full POSIX regular expressions, 0=wildmat notation. Newsgroup names are always matched using the wildmat notation.

As in trn and rn, the tin AUTOSUBSCRIBE and AUTOUNSUBSCRIBE environment variables can be used to subscribe or unsubscribe you from newsgroups automatically. The AUTOSUBSCRIBE variable holds a list of patterns, separated by commands. The names of new newsgroups are searched for any of these patterns. Newsgroups whose names contain any of the patterns are automatically subscribed to. You use the asterisk to match on the remainder of the name. For example, the following pattern list would subscribe to any new newsgroup that contains the patterns "*recipes," "*baseball*," or "comp.os.*" such as rec.foods.recipes and comp.os.unix. The pattern "*.recipes" would match any newsgroup name ending with "recipes" and the pattern "comp.os.*" would match names beginning with the pattern "comp.os." "*baseball*" would match any newsgroup with the pattern "baseball" anywhere in its name.

```
AUTOSUBSCRIBE=*recipes,comp.os.*,*baseball*
```

You can also specify a negative pattern. In this case, any new newsgroup names that do not match the pattern are subscribed to.

Table 9.XII. Environment Variables

TINRC	Holds command-line options that tin starts with. Note that environment variables that are used to set message header lines can also be set by adding the header name and value to the **$HOME/.tin/headers** file.
TIN_HOMEDIR	Holds directory where **.tin** directory is placed. Default is the user's home directory, **$HOME/.tin**.
TIN_INDEX_NEWSDIR	Holds directory where the **.news** directory is placed. Default is **$HOME/.tin/.news**.
TIN_INDEX_MAILDIR	Holds directory where the **.mail** directory is placed. Default is **$HOME/.tin/.mail**.
TIN_INDEX_SAVEDIR	Holds directory where the **.save** directory is placed. Default is **$HOME/.tin/.save**.
TIN_LIBDIR	Specify new path, overriding the NEWSLIBDIR path that was compiled into the tin binary. NEWSLIBDIR is specified in tin source code Makefile.
TIN_SPOOLDIR	Specify new path, overriding the SPOOLDIR path that was compiled into the tin binary. SPOOLDIR is specified in tin source code Makefile.
TIN_NOVROOTDIR	Specify new path, overriding the NOVROOTDIR path that was compiled into the tin binary. NOVROOTDIR is specified in tin source code Makefile.
TIN_ACTIVEFILE	Specify new path, overriding the NEWSLIBDIR/active path that was compiled into the tin binary. NEWSLIBDIR is specified in tin source code Makefile.
NNTPSERVER	Internet address of remote NNTP news server. Use when the -r command-line option is specified and the **/etc/nntpserver** system file does not exist.
NNTPPORT	The NNTP tcp port from which to read news.
DISTRIBUTION	Specify the article header field ``Distribution:''.
ORGANIZATION	Specify the article header field ``Organization:''.
REPLYTO	Specify the return address used in the article header field ``Reply-To:''.
ADD_ADDRESS	Address to append to the return address when replying directly through mail to user whose mail address is not directly recognized by the local host.
BUG_ADDRESS	Specify the bug report mail address. Overrides the address in the **$HOME/.tin/bug_address** file. *(continued)*

Table 9.XII. Environment Variables *(continued)*

`MAILER`	The mailer used in all tin mailing operations. Overrides default mailer set in tin configuration.
`EDITOR`	The editor that is used in all editing operations within tin. Overrides default editor set in tin configuration.
`AUTOSUBSCRIBE`	Specify list of patterns to be used to match newsgroups that are to be automatically subscribed to. Exclamation performs an inverse match.
`AUTOUNSUBSCRIBE`	Specify list of patterns to be used to match newsgroups that are to be automatically unsubscribed to. Exclamation performs an inverse match.

Negative patterns are prefixed with an exclamation point. The following pattern list will not subscribe to any newsgroup that has the patterns "ball" or "golf" in them such as alt.games.football or talk.scores.baseball.

```
AUTOSUBSCRIBE=*recipes,comp.os.*,!*ball,!*golf"
```

AUTOUNSUBSCRIBE works the same way as AUTOSUBSCRIBE, but will unsubscribe from news groups to which you have already subscribed. This is an easy way to remove a whole range from newsgroups. For example, suppose you want to unsubscribe from all your talk newsgroups. You set AUTOUNSUBSCRIBE in the following way.

```
AUTOUNSUBSCRIBE=talk.*
```

The environment variables are summarized in Table 9.XII.

Newsgroup Attributes

With tin you can set configuration options to configure each newsgroup specified in different ways. Such options are referred to as attributes and are set much like configuration variables.

You set newsgroup attributes in the **.tin/attributes** file. The attributes for a given newsgroup begin with a scope line specifying the newsgroup's name. Attributes are then listed and assigned a value, either a string or an ON or OFF value. Each newsgroup you configure this way will have its own listing of attributes and their assignments. Attributes are listed in Table 9.XIII and correspond to configuration and environment variables.

You can set global attributes that apply to several newsgroups by using tin's pattern matching capability. The * when used in a pattern will match on any set of characters. For example, to select all newsgroups beginning with **alt** you would use **alt.***. The following shows a sample attribute setting for a newsgroup, beginning with the scope entry. Notice that comment lines are preceded by a #. The attributes **savedir** and **mailder** correspond to the configuration variables **default_savedir** or **default_maildir**.

```
# in *binaries* set postprocess type to uudecode,
# remove tmp files and Followup-To: poster
scope=*binaries*
post_proc_type=2
delete_tmp_files=ON
followup_to=poster


# set attributes for rec.food.recipes
scope=rec.food.recipes
maildir=/home/dylan/Mail/recipemail
savedir=/home/dylan/News/food
savefile==myrecipes
organization=Sweets I Like
sigfile=/home/dylan/.foodsig
delete_tmp_files=ON
show_only_unread=OFF
thread_arts=1
show_author=1
sort_arts_type=5
post_proc_type=1
news_quote_format=%M %F wrote about recipe:
x_comment_to=ON
```

Table 9.XIII. `tin` **Attributes**

`scope=` *string*	(i.e., alt.sources or *sources*) [mandatory]
`maildir=` *string*	Directory where articles are saved in mailbox format.
`printer=` *string*	Print command with parameters used to print articles/threads.
`savedir=` *string*	Directory where articles are saved.
`savefile=` *string*	Specify a default save file.
`sigfile=` *string*	Pathname for the signature file used when posting articles, follow-ups or replies.
`show_author=`*NUM*	Part of From: field to display 0) none, 1) full name, 2) network address, 3) both.
`batch_save=` *ON/OFF*	With the `-S` or `-M` option, articles are saved in batch mode.
`auto_list_thread`	Automatically list thread when entering it using right arrow key. Default is ON.
`auto_select=` *ON/OFF*	Automatically select articles in a thread when entering it.
`auto_save==` *ON/OFF*	Articles/threads that are automatically saved and have Archive-name: in the mail header, are saved with the Archive-name & part/patch no.
`auto_save_msg=` *ON/OFF*	Automatically save messages.
`organization=` *string*	Specify the article header field "Organization:".
`followup_to=` *string*	Follow-up entry.
`delete_tmp_files=` *ON/OFF*	Automatically delete temporary files.
`show_only_unread=` *ON/OFF*	If ON, show only new or unread articles, otherwise show all articles.
`sort_art_type=`*NUM*	Sort articles. Choose from one of the following. 0=none, 1=subject descending, 2=subject ascending, 3=from descending, 4=from ascending, 5=date descending, 6=date ascending.
`post_proc_type=`*NUM*	Type of postprocessing to perform after saving articles. 0=(none) 1=(unshar), 2=(uudecode), 3=(uudecode & list zoo archive), 4=(uudecode & extract zoo archive), 5=(uudecode & list zip archive), 6=(uudecode & extract zip).
`thread_arts=`*NUM*	Thread articles. Choose from one of the following. 0=nothing, 1=subject, 2=references, 3=both.

`news_quote_format=` *string*	Format for quote line (attribution) used in articles and follow-ups that insert the referenced article text. (%A=Address, %D=Date, %F=Addr+Name, %G=Groupname, %M=MessageId, %N=Name).
`mailing_list=` *string*	Holds addresses for mail responses.
`x_headers=` *string*	File that holds extra header lines to be added to posted articles.
`x_body=` *string*	File that holds extra text to be added to posted articles.
`quick_kill_case=` *ON/OFF*	Quick (1 key) kill filter case. ON=filter case sensitive, OFF=ignore case.
`quick_kill_expire=` *ON/OFF*	Quick (1 key) kill filter expire. ON=limit to quick_days, OFF=don't ever expire.
`quick_kill_scope=` *string*	Quick (1 key) kill filter scope.
`quick_kill_header=`*NUM*	Quick (1 key) kill filter header. 0=subj (case sensitive), 1=subj (ignore case), 2=from (case sensitive), 3=from (ignore case), 4=msgid, 5=lines. Default is 0.
`quick_select_case=` *ON/OFF*	Quick (1 key) autoselection filter case. ON=filter case sensitive, OFF=ignore case.
`quick_select_expire=` *ON/OFF*	Quick (1 key) autoselection filter expire. ON=limit to quick_days, OFF=don't ever expire.
`quick_select_scope=` *string*	Quick (1 key) autoselection filter for scope.
`quick_select_header=`*NUM*	Quick (1 key) autoselection filter header. 0=subj (case sensitive), 1=subj (ignore case), 2=from (case sensitive), 3=from (ignore case), 4=msgid, 5=lines.
`x_comment_to=`*ON/OFF*	Display the real name in the X-Comment-To header.
`quote_chars=`*string*	Symbol used to inidicate included text to article follow-ups and mail replies. The '_' symbol represents a blank character, a ' '.

The nn Newsreader

The nn newsreader operates using a selector that is much like that used in the trn newsreader. When you enter nn, the selector displays the screen of articles for the first newsgroup. You can move to other newsgroups, in turn, displaying their first screen of articles.

The name of the newsgroup is listed at the top of the selector screen, along with the number of unread articles, total number of articles, and the number of newly posted articles. You can move to the next newsgroup by hitting the uppercase N command. The nn newsreader commands are listed in Table 9.XIV.

To move to a particular newsgroup, use the G command. At the prompt, just enter the name of the newsgroup you want to change to and hit **enter**. You will then be prompted for the type of articles you want to display. You can just hit the **spacebar** to select the default and display the selector screen.

```
Group or Folder (+./~%=sneN) rec.food.recipes
Number of articles (uasne) (a)
```

The selector displays the author and subject of each article in the newsgroup preceded by an id consisting of a single character or number. The number of text lines for each article is placed between its author and subject. Working from the selector, you can choose articles you want to display. Figure 9.6 shows a sample nn selector screen.

nn does group together follow-up articles and articles on the same subject. A follow-up article is preceded by a >. A follow-up to a follow-up is preceded by a >>. An article that shares the same subject as the previous one listed, is represented by a dash, −.

You select an article by hitting the key corresponding to its id. Each article has its own id. To select the article with an id of 'c', you hit the c key. Once selected, an asterisk then appears before the selected article (not a + sign as in trn). Though, when reading, you can automatically move forward through a thread of articles, you cannot, unlike trn, automatically move back and forth through them. If you want to, say, browse through the articles on a given subject, you need to explicitly select each one. You can select all the articles in a thread at once using the asterisk qualifier with an id. To select all the articles in a given subject, you hit the id of the first article, and then an *. For example, if articles in a given subject begin with the id 'b', you hit b* to select all of them. The same is true of follow-up articles. If the article with the id 'e' has several follow-up articles listed after it, you can select them all by hitting e*.

```
┌─────────────────────────────────────────────────────────────────┐
│                                                                   │
│   Newsgroup: rec.food.recipes          Articles 258 of 234/10 NEW │
│                                                                   │
│   a   Justin Saturn            234    Cookies on the run          │
│   b   Cecelia Petersen         110    Angel Food Cake             │
│   d   Richard Leland            43    Chocolate and Cinnamon      │
│   e   Larisa@mymag.com          87    -                           │
│   f   Aleina Fuller            120    >White chocolate            │
│   g   George Gabriel           112    > Chocolate Fudge           │
│   h   Mark Paul                120    >                           │
│   i   Chris Niel                58    >Chocolate butter           │
│   j   Dylan Petersen            97    Cinnamon Bagels             │
│   k   Marylou Carrion           34    REQUEST: romantic lunches   │
│   l   Valerie Fuller            12    REQUEST: romantic snacks    │
│   m   Carolyn Blacklock        345    REQUEST: Spicy Popcorn      │
│   n   Bill Bode                 17    >                           │
│   o   Gloria                   214    Lasanga (huge dish)         │
│   p   Maryann                  135    Applesause                  │
│   q   Anntoionnete C.          467    REQUEST: Spelling cookies   │
│   r   augie@napa                26    >                           │
│   s   John Carrion              19    >                           │
│                                                                   │
│   -- 12:34 -- SELECT -- help:? -----Top 3%                        │
│                                                                   │
└─────────────────────────────────────────────────────────────────┘
```

Figure 9.6. The nn newsreader selector.

You can also use the cursor to select articles. To move from one article to another, you can use the the arrow keys or the comma and slash keys, **, /**. The comma moves the cursor down to the next article and the slash moves it up to the previous article. Once you have positioned the cursor at the article you want, you can select it by hitting the period key, **.**. Notice that the comma, period, and slash are located next to each other in the lower right-hand corner of your keyboard.

To begin reading the selected articles, enter the uppercase Z command. Articles are displayed using much the same commands as those used in rn and trn. The n command will then move you to the next selected article, and the p command will move you back to the previously selected article. The * will move to the next article with the same thread such as the same subject or follow-ups.

Once you have read your articles, you can return to the selector with the = command.

To post an article using the nn newsreader, use the command nnpost. Within the nn selector, use the command :post. Posting an article in the nn newsreader is much the same as in the rn newsreader. You are prompted for header information, after which you enter the text of the message. As in the rn newsreader, the f and F commands within the selector will post a follow-up to an article.

Table 9.XIV. nn Commands

DISPLAYING THE NEWSGROUP ARTICLE LIST

N	Move to next newsgroup.
G	Move to particular newsgroup.
spacebar *or* >	Display the next screen of articles.
<	Display the previous screen of articles.
$	Display the last screen of articles.
^	Display the first screen of articles.
\\	Change display layout.
Z	Begin displaying selected articles. Return to newsgroup screen when finished.
X	Begin displaying selected articles, but move to the next newsgroup when finished.

SELECTING ARTICLES FROM THE NEWSGROUP ARTICLE LIST

id	Select/unselect an article.
id*	Select/unselect articles with the same thread as *id*.
\`	Move to the next article heading.
/	Move to the previous article heading.
.	Select the current article.

MOVING TO ARTICLES WHEN READING

n	Move to the next selected article.
p	Move to the previous selected article.
*	Move to next article in the thread such as same subject.
k	Mark as read the current article, skipping it.
=	Return to selector screen.

DISPLAYING ARTICLES

spacebar	Display the next screen of the article.
return	Scroll to the next line of the article.
d	Scroll to the next half screen of the article.
b	Display the previous screen of the article.
^	Display first screen of the article.
$	Display last screen of the article.
/ *pattern*	Search for pattern in the text.
.	Repeat pattern search in the text.

POSTING AND REPLYING TO ARTICLES

r	Reply to current article.
f	Post a follow-up to the current article.
m	Send a copy of the article to another user.
:post	Post a new article.
nnpost	Post a new article. Seperate utility.

Section III
Network and Internet Tools

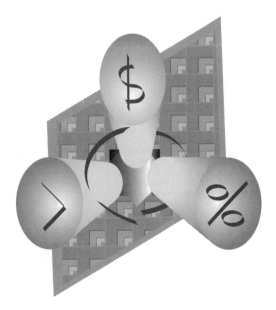

Network Connections: TCP/IP

Different Unix systems can be connected by a network. A network is a communications line connecting several computers. It can connect a few computers or many. It may connect computers in a localized area or across global distances. In the case of networked Unix systems, each computer usually has its own Unix system. The different Unix systems then communicate across a network connecting the different computers. Using a network, you can send messages to users on other Unix systems, transfer files from one system to another, post news and discussion items that can be read by users on other systems, and locate information such as programs and articles on another system and transfer it to your own.

The following chapters 11 to 15 will examine these capabilities and the tools you need to performs such tasks. This chapter discusses how network addressing is implemented on a Unix-based network using the TCP/IP protocols. Unix systems may use either the TCP/IP or UUCP protocols. The TCP/IP protocols are used on most Unix-based networks. UUCP is an older protocol discussed in Chapter 17.

TCP/IP Protocols

A network connects the systems on it by means of communication Protocols. Most Unix systems are configured to connect to networks that use TCP/IP. These are the same protocols that the Internet, as well as many local networks, use. The protocols were designed in the 1970s as a special DARPA project to enhance communications between universities and research centers. They were originally developed on Unix systems with much of the research carried out at the University of California, Berkeley.

TCP/IP consists of different protocols, each designed for a specific task in a TCP/IP network. The two basic protocols are the Transmission Control Protocol (TCP), which handles receiving and sending communications, and the Internet Protocol (IP), which handles transmitting communications. Other protocols provide various network services. The Domain Name Service (DNS) provides address resolution. The File Transmission Protocol (Ftp) provides file transmission, and Network File Systems (NFS) provides access to remote file systems. Table 10.I contains a partial listing of the different TCP/IP protocols.

TCP/IP protocols are not limited to Unix systems. They are designed to operate with any kind of operating system, whether it is a minicomputer running VMS, a mainframe running an IBM system, or a personal computer running Windows. This is one reason the Internet uses the TCP/IP protocols. However, the TCP/IP protocols were first developed on Unix systems and are used for most Unix networks.

Table 10.I. TCP/IP Protocols

TRANSPORT

TCP	Transmission Control Protocol; connect two networked systems.
UDP	User Datagram Protocol; request/reply connection between systems.

NETWORKING

IP	Internet Protocol; transmit data across networks.
ICMP	Internet Control Message Protocol; send routing control messages.
IGMP	Internet Group Management Protocol; transmit data to selected groups.

ROUTING

RIP	Routing Information Protocol; determine routing.
OSPF	Open Shortest Path First; determine routing.
BGP	Border Gateway Protocol; transmit routing information across network.
EGP	Exterior Gateway Protocol; provide routing information for external networks.
GGP	Gateway-to-Gateway Protocol; provide routing between Internet gateways.
IGP	Interior Gateway Protocol; provide routing for internal networks.

NETWORK ADDRESSES

ARP	Address Resolution Protocol; determine unique IP address of systems.
DNS	Domain Name Service; translate hostnames into IP addresses.
RARP	Reverse Address Resolution Protocol; match IP addresses to local system network addresses.

APPLICATIONS

FTP	File Transfer Protocol; transmit files from one system to another.
TFTP	Trivial File Transfer Protocol; simplified version of Ftp.
TELNET	remote login to another system on the network.

(continued)

Table 10.I. TCP/IP Protocols (*continued*)

SMTP	Simple Mail Transfer Protocol; transfer email between systems.
HTML	HyperText Markup Language; compose HyperText documents.
HTTP	HyperText Transfer Protocol; transfers HyperText documents.
MIME	Multi-purpose Internet Mail Extensions; Transmit multiple attached files of varying kinds as electronic mail messages.
WWW	World Wide Web; graphical HyperText browsing service.

NETWORK SERVICES

NFS	Network File Systems; allows shared mounting of file systems on remote systems.
NIS	Network Information Service; maintain user accounts across a network.
RPC	Remote Procedure Call; allows programs on remote systems to communicate.
BOOTP	Boot Protocol; start system using boot information on a remote server.
DHCP	Dynamic Host Configuration; remotely boot and configure system.
SNMP	Single Network Management Protocol; manage networked devices.
NTP	Network Time Protocol; synchronize system clocks on a network.
PPP	Point-to-Point Protocol; direct connection between system and network.
SLIP	Serial Line Internet Protocol; serial connection between system and network.

Domain Name Addresses

In a Unix network, each computer connected to a network has its own Unix systems. A particular Unix system communicates with other Unix systems by means of the network. Systems connected to a network are called hosts. They can operate as a 'host' allowing other systems on the network to connect to them. The term *host* actually applies to any computer connected on a network using TCP/IP, ones with Unix systems or otherwise.

Each system in a network has been given a name by the network manager. This is referred to as its host name. Within a local network, this host name functions as its address, just as a login name is the address of a user. Combining the host name with the login name of a user forms a user address you can use for email operations.

login-name@host-name

Though the host name is usually sufficient to identify a system on a local network, it is not enough to identify one on a different network. To reference systems on different networks you need to use a domain name. A domain name is the name of the network itself. To further qualify a network, an extension is added to its domain name. The extension can indicate the country in which the network is located or the type of network, such as educational or commercial. The domains used for the United States usually have extensions that identify the type of host. For example, **.edu** is used for educational institutions and **.com** is used for businesses. International domains usually have extensions that indicate the country in which they are located, such as **.du** for Germany or **.au** for Australia. Tables 10.II and 10.III list the different extensions. The extension is placed after the domain name separated by a period. For example, a network with the domain name **trek** and the extension **com** would be written as **trek.com**. In some cases, the network may have several domain names instead of just one. These are separated by periods.

domain-name.extension

The domain name combined with a host name constitutes a unique address by which other systems on different networks can identify it. Taken together, these components form what is called a system's fully qualified domain name. The fully qualified domain name is made up of the host name (the name for your system), the domain name (the name that identifies your network), and an extension that identifies the type of network. Each component is separated by a period.

host-name.domain-name.extension

com	Commercial
edu	Educational Institution
gov	Government
int	International
mil	Military
net	Networking organization
org	Nonprofit organization

Table 10.II. Internet United States Domain codes

For example, the fully qualified domain name for the **turtle** system on the **trek** network that is a commercial network would have the host name **turtle**, the domain name **trek**, and the extension **com**.

```
turtle.trek.com
```

The login of a user on a particular system combined with the fully qualified domain name forms the complete email address that can be used on TCP/IP networks such as the Internet. The format of an Internet mail address follows. For example, to send a message to `chris` on the `turtle` system, you simply add the domain name for that system's network, **trek**, and that network's extension, **com**: `chris@turtle.trek.com`.

login-name@host-name.domain-name.extension

The fully qualified domain name can be used as an address to uniquely identify the system. For this reason it is often referred to as the host or host address. The host address for the **turtle** system on the trek commercial network is **turtle.trek.com**. The fully qualified domain name is also used to identify many Internet sites such as Web sites or Ftp sites. A site is simply a host that allows access to its resources by users on other systems connected to the network. An Internet site can be accessed by other users on systems connected to the Internet. For example, the Ftp site for sunsite has a host name **sunsite**, the domain name **unc**, and the extension **edu**.

```
sunsite.unc.edu
```

at	Austria
au	Australia
ca	Canada
ch	Switzerland
cl	Chile
cn	China
de	Germany
dk	Denmark
ec	Ecuador
es	Spain
fi	Finland
fr	France
gr	Greece
ie	Ireland
il	Israel
in	India
it	Italy
jp	Japan
kr	South Korea
nl	Netherlands
nz	New Zealand
pl	Poland
se	Sweden
tw	Taiwan
uk	United Kingdom
us	United States

Table 10.III. Internet International Domain Codes

Often a network will have a system dedicated to a particular service such as Ftp or the World Wide Web. In this case the host name may indicate the type of service, **ftp** for an Ftp site, or **www** for a Web site. For example the fully qualified domain name for a Netscape's Ftp site uses the host name **ftp**, and Netscape's Web site uses the host name **www**.

```
ftp.netscape.com
www.netscape.com
```

Network Tools: Internet and Intranet

TCP/IP networks like the Internet connect computers through which you can access network tools. Many computers on the Internet are configured to operate as servers, providing information to anyone who requests it. The information is contained in files that you can access and copy. Each server, often referred to as a *site,* has its own Internet address by which it can be located. Unix provides a set of network tools that you can use to access systems connected to your network. You can use these tools to connect to sites on the Internet and then locate and download information from them.

The network tools Telnet and Ftp allow you to connect to another system. They are used extensively to connect to Internet sites. Telnet performs a remote login to another computer connected on your network. You could use it to search the Library of Congress on-line catalog, for example. Ftp connects to a site and allows you to perform file transfers both from and to it. You can connect to a site that has Unix software and download software directly to your computer using Ftp.

Finding out what information is available and on what system it is located, as well as where on the system it is stored, can be an overwhelming task. Ordinarily you would need to know the location of the file ahead of time. However, two tools designed for the Internet, Archie and Gopher, allow you to search for files on the network. With Archie you can use patterns to search for the name of a file and retrieve its location on the Internet. Gopher provides you with a series of menus listing different resources. You move from one menu to the other, narrowing your search until you find the information you want. Using Gopher, you can then directly transfer your information without having to resort to Ftp.

In the last few years, the Web Browsers have become the primary tool for accessing information on the Internet. A Web browser relies on underlying Internet tools that actually retrieve and transfer information. Telnet, Ftp, Archie, and Gopher are all tools developed to locate and access Internet sites and to retrieve information from them. Most of the tasks you perform on the Internet may be done easily with a Web browser.

Tools like Web browsers, Gopher, and Archie that were designed for the Internet, work equally as well on any local TCP/IP network that supports sites accessible with these tools. Many local networks, called intranets, support local Internet-like sites that can only be accessed within the local network. Web Browsers will work equally as well on intranets that support their own Web sites, as on the Internet. The same is true for Ftp, Telnet, Archie, and Gopher. An intranet can maintain its own local Ftp sites that are accessible only within that network.

TCP/IP Addresses

TCP/IP stands for Transmission Control Protocol/Internet Protocol. In a TCP/IP network, messages are broken into small components called *packets* which are then transmitted through various interconnected routes and delivered to their destination computers. Once received, the packets are reassembled into the original message. Sending a message broken down into a set of small packets is far more reliable and faster than sending it as a single large transmission. With small packets, if one is lost or damaged, only that packet has to be resent, whereas if any part of a large transmission is corrupted or lost, the entire message has to be resent.

On a TCP/IP network such as the Internet, each computer is given a unique address called an IP address. The IP address is used to identify and locate a particular host, a computer connected to the network. An IP address consists of a set of four segments, each separated by a period. The segments consist of numbers that range from 0 to 255, with certain values reserved for special use. The IP address is divided into two parts, one that identifies the network and the other that identifies a particular host. The number of segments used for each is determined by the class of the network. On the Internet, networks are organized into three classes depending on their size—classes A, B, and C. Class A networks use only the first segment for the IP address and the remaining three for the host, allowing a great many computers to be connected to the same network. Most IP addresses reference smaller, class C, networks. For a class C network, the first three segments are used to identify the network, and the last segment identifies the host.

net.net.net.host

In a class C network, the first three numbers identify the network part of the IP address. This part is divided into three network numbers, each identifying a subnet. Networks on the Internet are organized into subnets beginning with the largest and narrowing to small subnetworks. The last number is used to identify a particular computer, a host. You can think of a large TCP/IP network like the Internet as consisting of a series of networks with subnetworks, and these subnetworks have their own subnetworks. The rightmost number identifies the host computer, and the number preceding it identifies the subnetwork of which the computer is a part. The number to the left of that identifies the network that the subnetwork is part of, and so on. The Internet address 199.35.209.4 references the fourth computer connected to the network identified by the number 209. Network 209 is a subnet to a larger network identified as 35. This larger network is itself a subnet of the network identified as 199. Here's how it breaks down:

199.35.209.4	IP address
199.35.209	Network identification
4	Host identification

IP addresses for computers connected on the Internet are officially provided by the Network Information Center (NIC), which administers the Internet. You can obtain your own Internet IP address from the NIC, or if you are on a network already connected to the Internet, your network administrator can assign you one. If you are using an Internet service provider, the ISP may obtain one for you or, each time you connect, may temporarily assign one from a pool they have on hand.

Certain numbers are reserved. The numbers 127, 0, or 255 cannot be part of an official IP address. The address 127.0.0.0 is the loopback address that allows users on your computer to communicate with each other. The number 255 is a special broadcast identifier that you can use to broadcast messages to all sites on a network. Using 225 for any part of the IP address references all nodes connected at that level. For example, 199.35.255.255 broadcasts a message to all computers on network 199.35, all its subnetworks, and their hosts. The address 199.35.209.255 broadcasts to every computer on the local network. If you use 0 for the network part of the address, the host number will reference a computer within your local network. For example, 0.0.0.5 references the fifth computer in your local network. If you want to broadcast to all computers on your local network, you can use the number 0.0.0.255.

All hosts on a TCP/IP network are identified by their IP addresses. When you send a message to a host on the Internet, you must provide its IP address. However, it can be very easy to make mistakes with a four-number IP address. They are hard to remember and you can easily get one of the numbers wrong. To make it easier to identify a computer on a TCP/IP network, the Domain Name Service (DNS) was implemented. The DNS establishes a fully qualified domain name for a corresponding IP address. As described previously, a fully qualified domain name is used as an address for a particular host on a TCP/IP network. Whenever you use a fully qualified domain name it is automatically converted to an IP address by the Domain Name Service. DNS simply associates a fully qualified domain name with its IP address. This IP address is the address actually used to identify and locate a particular host on the network.

Though you can always use an IP address to connect to a host, fully qualified domain names are far easier to use. A very large TCP/IP network like the Internet makes extensive use of fully qualified domain names to locate hosts. For the Internet, a fully qualified domain name address needs to be registered with the NIC along with its IP address. As noted previously, the fully qualifed domain name consists of the host name, the domain name, and the domain's extension. For example, **sunsite.unc.edu** is a fully qualified domain name that references a computer called **sunsite** on a network named **unc**, that is part of an educational institution, as indicated by the extension **edu**.

host-name.domain-name.extension

The conversion of fully qualified domain names to IP addresses can be performed by each individual host, each computer on the network. For a few frequently used addresses, this is still done.

On very large networks, like the Internet, fully qualified domain name conversion is performed by special servers known as Domain Name Servers or simply nameservers. A nameserver holds a database of fully qualified domain names and their IP addresses. Local networks will sometimes have their own nameservers. If a nameserver does not have the address, then it may call on other nameservers to perform the conversion. When you use a fully qualified domain name to connect to another host, a program on your computer called a resolver will obtain that host's IP address from a nameserver. It submits the fully qualified domain name to the nameserver, which then looks it up in its database of domain names and retrieves the corresponding IP address. The IP address is sent back to your system, which then uses it to make the connection.

With the **whois**, **nslookup**, and **dig** commands, you can obtain information from domain nameservers about different networks and hosts connected to the Internet (see Table 10.IV). Enter **whois** and the domain name address of the host or network, and **whois** will display information about the host, such as the street address and phone number as well as contact persons. The **nslookup** command takes a domain address and finds its corresponding IP address. **dig** is a user-friendly version of **nslookup**.

whois	Display information about the host, such as the street address and phone number as well as contact persons (not lowest level domains).
nslookup	Supplies info of even lowest level domains. Has an interactive mode that you enter by not specifying any domain name. You can then use **nslookup** to search for other kinds of information about a host. For example, the HINFO option will find out what type of operating system a host uses. The **nslookup** man page specifies a list of different options and how to use them.
dig	Like nslookup, but with easy-to-use interface.
host	Converts domain name of a host to its Internet address. With –a options provided detailed information about host.

Table 10.IV. Internet Domain Look-Up

TCP/IP Network Addresses

Other than the IP address (host address), a system uses several other addresses to interact with a network. These are the network, broadcast, gateway, nameserver, and netmask addresses. Table 10.V lists these addresses. You can think of them as network configuration addresses because they configure your system's connection to the network. As explained previously, a system's IP address is organized into four segments consisting of numbers separated by periods. Part of this address is used for the network address, and the other part is used to identify a particular system in that network. The network address identifies the network that a particular host is a part of. Usually the network part of the address takes up the first three segments and the host takes the last segment. For example, in the IP address 203.46.215.31, the network part is 203.46.215 and the host part is 31. The host is a part of a network whose own address is 203.46.215.0. The broadcast address allows a system to send the same message to all systems on your network at once. The broadcast address is just

ADDRESSES

Host address	IP address of your system; it has a network part to identify the network you are on and a host part to identify your own system.
Network address	IP address of your network (network part of your host IP address with host part set to 0).
Broadcast address	IP address for sending messages to all hosts on your network at once (network part of your host IP address with host part set to 255).
Gateway address	IP address of your gateway system if you have one (usually the network part of your host IP address with host part set to 1).
Domain nameserver addresses	IP addresses of domain nameservers used by your network.
Netmask	Network part of your host IP address set to 255s with host part set to 0 (255.255.255.0).

Table 10.V. Network Configuration Addresses

the network address with 255 as the host. For example, the broadcast address for the network 203.46.215 is 203.46.215.255.

Some networks will have a computer designated as the gateway to other networks. Every connection to and from the network to other networks passes through this gateway computer. Gateways are often used to provide security for local networks, checking all traffic in and out to the larger network such as the Internet. The gateway address usually, though not necessarily, has the same network address with 1 added. The gateway address for the network address 203.46.215 could be 203.46.215.1.

Domain nameservers are computers on a network that translate the domain name addresses into IP addresses. With such a translation, you can use domain name addresses to connect to systems, instead of their IP addresses. However, your system needs the IP addresses of the namservers it can access to connect to them initially and ask them to perform such translations.

The netmask is used to determine the address of the network to which you are connected. The network part of the netmask is 255.255.255 and the host part is 0, 255.255.255.0. Other systems can then use this netmask to determine what part of your host address makes up your network address and what those numbers are.

TCP/IP Configuration Files

If you are performing network administration tasks, you will need to maintain certain TCP/IP network configuration files located in your system's **/etc** directory (Table 10.VI). They specify such network information as host names, domain names, and IP addresses. Ordinary users often have read access to these files, so you can examine how network access on your system is configured.

Identifying Host Names: /etc/hosts

When your system connects to another system on your network, it uses that system's IP address to locate it. Systems on a TCP/IP network use IP addresses to identify computers, not host and domain names. Users, however, use host and domain names when referencing other systems in their applications for the simple reason that fully qualified domain names are easier to remember and use. Recall that for each IP address there is a fully qualified domain name. When you use a fully qualified domain name to reference a computer on the network, your system needs to translate it into its associated IP address. Your system can then use the IP address to locate a particular computer on your TCP/IP network. This translation is carried out using a simple list where each entry contains an IP address and its associated domain name address. For example, the following list associates the **chris.mygames.com** fully qualified domain name with the IP address 199.35.209.72. Keep in mind that it is not the address of a particular user that is being mapped here, but the address of an entire system.

```
199.35.209.72 chris.mygames.com
```

In the first TCP/IP networks that were set up, it was the responsibility of every computer on the network to maintain its own list of the host names and their IP addresses. This is still true for small local networks. This list is still kept in a system's **/etc/hosts** file. When you use a fully qualified domain name, your system looks up its IP address in the **/etc/hosts** file. It is the responsibility of the systems administrator to maintain this list. Such a procedure, however, is not practical for very large networks like the Internet. On large networks, the association of domain names and IP addresses is carried out by domain nameservers. Even on large networks, however, your system's **/etc/hosts** file is still used to hold the fully qualified domain names and IP addresses of frequently accessed hosts. In fact, your system will always check its own **/etc/hosts** file for the IP address of a fully qualified domain name before checking a nameserver. It may be convenient for systems on small networks to have simple alias names that users can easily reference.

Entries in the **/etc/hosts** file consist of an IP address followed by its associated fully qualified domain name, separated by a space. After the domain name, aliases for it may be listed. Comments may appear at the end of the entry, on the same line beginning with a # symbol. You will already find an entry in your **/etc/hosts** file for "localhost" with the IP address 127.0.01. Localhost is a special identification used by your computer to enable users on your system to communicate locally with each other. The IP address 127.0.0.1 is a special reserved address called a loopback device used by each system for this purpose. The following example shows a sample **/etc/hosts** file.

/etc/hosts

```
127.0.0.1 turtle.trek.com localhost
199.35.209.4 zebra.trek.com pango
199.35.209.17 minnow.trek.com
202.211.234.1 mygames.soccer.edu
200.111.431.1 mysong.singer.org
```

Network Name: /etc/networks

For a network that is connected to other larger networks, a system also has to associate a network's domain name with that network's address. On very large networks such as the Internet, this is the function of domain nameservers. However, your own system can maintain its own list of network address associations. They are held in the **/etc/networks** file. Depending on the type of network, one, two, or three numbers are used for the IP address. There will also be a localhost network IP address 127.0.0.0 that is used for the loopback device.

Entries in the **/etc/networks** file consist of an IP address followed by the network domain name. Recall that an IP address consists of a network part and a host part. The network part is the network address found in the networks file. There will always be an entry in this file for the network portion of your own system's IP address. This is the network address of the network to which your system is connected.

/etc/networks

```
127.0.0.0 turtle.trek.com localhost
199.35.209.0 trek.com
202.211.234.0 soccer.edu
200.111.431.0 singer.org
```

/etc/hostname

The **/etc/hostname** file holds the host name for your system. Only a system administrator can change the host name. The `hostname` command will display the name in this file.

```
$ hostname
turtle.trek.com
```

Domain Name Service (DNS): /etc/host.conf, /etc/resolv.conf

As previously noted, each system on a TCP/IP network is identified by its IP address. A system's fully qualified domain name has to be translated into its associated IP address, which can then be used by the network to locate it. Before the development of very large TCP/IP networks such as the Internet, it was feasible for each computer on a network to maintain its own **/etc/hosts** file with a list of all the fully qualified domain names and IP addresses of the computers connected on its network. Whenever a domain name was used, it was looked up in this file and the corresponding IP address located. As networks became larger, it became impractical and, in the case of the Internet, impossible for each computer to maintain its own list of all the domain names and IP addresses with which it could possibly connect. To provide the service of translating fully qualified domain names to IP addresses, databases of these names were developed and placed on their own servers called nameservers. This is referred to as a Domain Name Service. To find the IP address of a domain name, a query is sent to a nameserver, which looks up the IP address and sends it back. In a large network, there can be several nameservers covering different parts of the network. If a nameserver cannot find a particular IP address, it will send the query on to another nameserver that is more likely to have it. Nameservers can also provide information such as the company name and street address of a system.

Queries are made to nameserver programs called resolvers. Resolvers are specially designed to obtain addresses from nameservers. The local resolver for your system is configured using two files, **/etc/host.conf** and **/etc/resolv.conf**. The **/etc/host.conf** file lists resolver options. The options tell the resolver what services to use. The order of the list is important. The resolver will begin with the first option listed and move on to the next ones in turn. In particular, the order option will specify the order in which name resolution proceeds, whether it begins with your system's **/etc/hosts** file or moves directly to a nameserver. The hosts option will list files that should be checked for domain name/IP address associations.

The **resolv.conf** file provides a resolver program with the IP addresses of the domain nameservers to which your system has access. Three different types of entries may occur in a **resolv.conf** file beginning with the keyword domain, nameserver, or search. The domain entry lists the domain name of your system. A search entry provides a list of domains to try if only a host name is given in an address, without the domain part of the address. If there is a system that you access frequently, you could enter its domain name in a search entry and then just use its host name as the address. Your resolver will then try to find the host name using the domain name listed in the search entry.

There are nameserver entries for each nameserver to which your system has access. A nameserver's IP address is entered after the nameserver keyword. Nameservers are queried in the order in which they are listed, as shown in the sample **resolv.conf** file given here. The domain of the host computer is **trek.com**. The IP addresses of the nameservers are listed in the nameserver entries. The search entry will allow just the host name for a computer in the **soccer.edu** network to be used as an address. For example, to access **mygames.soccer.edu**, a user would only have to enter the host name **mygames** as an address.

/etc/resolv.conf

```
domain trek.com
search soccer.edu
nameserver 204.199.87.2
nameserver 204.199.77.2
```

/etc/hosts	Associate host names with IP addresses, listing domain names for remote hosts with their IP addresses.
/etc/networks	Associate domain names with network addresses.
/etc/hostname	Hold the name of your system.
/etc/host.conf	List resolver options.
/etc/resolv.conf	List domain nameserver names, IP addresses (nameserver), and domain names where remote hosts may be located (search).
/etc/protocols	List protocols available on your system.
/etc/services	List available network services such as Ftp and Telnet.

Table 10.VI. TCP/IP Configuration Files

Telnet

Telnet is a terminal emulation utility with which you can access another system as if you were using a terminal connected to it. With Telnet you can connect to remote systems on which you already have an account or to systems that support public Telnet access. If you have an account on a remote system, you can use Telnet to log in using that account's login name and password. You can then issue Unix commands as if you were directly connected to that system.

Telnet can connect to any remote system connected to yours on a network. The network can be a local area network or one on the Internet. Many Internet sites provide public Telnet access. You can use Telnet to access many on-line library catalogs, querying collections as if you were using a terminal in the library itself. Such sites allow guest logins, meaning that they do not require any specific login name or password. Anyone can log in. Such sites are specially designed to handle public access, presenting you with menus of options that control your access to the system.

Telnet uses Telnet protocols to connect to any other system on a network using those same protocols. The Telnet protocols are part of TCP/IP, and Telnet can be used to communicate with any other system connected on a TCP/IP network, such as the Internet. This means that Telnet can connect with systems other than Unix systems, as long as they are connected to a network using TCP/IP protocols.

Telnet Connections

Telnet emulates a terminal, letting you log in from your current system as if it were a terminal. If you are logging into a remote account that you have on another system, standard login procedures apply. You will be prompted for a login name, a password, and a terminal type. You invoke the Telnet utility by entering the keyword `telnet` on the command line. You are given a Telnet prompt: `telnet>`. You then enter the Telnet command `open` to connect to another system. The `open` command takes as its argument the system name. In the next example the user establishes a connection to the `mygames` system using Telnet.

```
$ telnet
telnet> open mygames
Connected to mygames
login:
```

Once connected, you follow the login procedure for that system. You can skip the `open` command by specifying the system name as an argument to the Telnet command. In the next example, the `mygames` system is specified on the command line with the keyword `telnet`.

```
$ telnet mygames
Connected to mygames
login:
```

The syntax for the Telnet command follows, showing optional arguments encased in brackets. If you also need to specify a different system port you can add that after the system address.

```
telnet [system-address]     [port]
```

Once connected, you then follow the standard login procedure for that system. You will be prompted for a login name, a password, and a terminal type. Telnet usually emulates a vt100 terminal type, but check with your system administrator for the terminal type used. Once logged in, you will be provided with your login shell prompt, either $, >, or %. You can then issue any Unix commands you want.

You can skip the login prompt by using the -l option to specify the login name for that account. You can use the -l option when invoking Telnet on the command line with a system address, or with the open command at the telnet> prompt. In the following examples, the user is logging into a specific account called dylan on the mytrain.com system.

```
$ telnet mytrain.com -l dylan
telnet> open mytrain.com -l dylan
```

Other Telnet options are listed in Table 11.I. The -a option works if the login name on your remote system is the same as your user name on your current system. The login name is taken from the $USER Telnet variable, which usually holds your current login name. Telnet will use this login name to automatically log in to remote accounts.

When you are finished with your login session, log out from the remote session. You will be returned to the telnet> prompt. If you have trouble logging out, you can use the Telnet escape key, **Ctrl-]**, to return to the Telnet prompt. Close the connection to the remote system by entering the close command. You can then use open to connect to other systems, or issue any other Telnet command. When you are finished using Telnet, quit the utility by entering the quit command. You can skip the close command and exit directly from Telnet by entering quit.

```
telnet> close
telnet> quit
$
```

-8	Request 8-bit operation. Attempts to negotiate the TELNET BINARY option for both input and output.
-E	Disable the escape character, setting the escape character to "no character."
-L	Set 8-bit data path on output, causing the TELNET BINARY option negotiated on output only.
-a	Perform an automatic login using the user name from the Telnet USER variable. By default this is the same as your current login name as specified by your $USER environment variable. The ENVIRON must be supported by the remote system.
-d	Set debug toggle to TRUE.
-r	Emulate rlogin operation. The default escape character is a tilde. An escape character followed by a dot disconnects from the remote system. **Ctrl-z** suspends Telnet, and a ^] escapes to the Telnet command mode. The escape keys can only be entered at the beginning of the line.
-S *tos*	Specify the IP type of service, *tos*.
-e *escapechar*	Specify a new value for the Telnet escape character used to enter the command mode. If no value is specified, no escape character is used.
-l *login-name*	Specify the login name to be used for the remote system. The login name is placed in the Telnet USER variable and requires the remote system to support the TELNET ENVIRON option. This option implies the -a option. You can also use this option with the open command.
-n *tracefile*	Saves recorded trace information in tracefile. See tracefile command.
host	Specify a remote system (*host*) to connect to on your network.
port	Specifiy a port number to use.

Table 11.1. Telnet Options

You do not have to type in the full name of the Telnet command. In most cases the first character will suffice. The following example executes the close command and then the quit command.

```
telnet> c
telnet> q
$
```

Telnet for Public Services

In most cases, when using Telnet to connect to a site that provides public access, you do not need to provide a login name or password. Some sites require a guest login, requesting that you enter `guest` as your login id and your network address as your password. Once connected, access is usually controlled by a series of menus that restricts what you can do on that system. Figure 11.I shows a Telnet session accessing the on-line catalog of the University of California Melvyl on-line library catalog.

Internet access software, such as Gopher or Web browsers, will, when called for, make Telnet connections to public sites automatically. In such cases, you may suddenly find yourself presented with a simple menu of options rather than the detailed graphics interface of a Web browser or page display of a Gopher. At this point, you are remotely logged into another site with Telnet, using that site's interface to obtain controlled access to its resources. Simply follow the menu options, and when you leave the site, you will be returned to your Web browser or Gopher page. Web browsers support a Telnet URL format with which you can use the browser to make a Telnet connection. A Telnet URL begins with the term `telnet//:` as shown here.

telnet://`internet-site-address`

Telnet Commands

The Telnet utility provides you with a command interface in which you can enter Telnet commands for making and configuring connections. The Telnet command interface uses the prompt `telnet>` at which you can enter Telnet commands.

    telnet>

If you start Telnet using just the Telnet command without any system address, you are immediately placed in this interface. You can then use the Telnet `open` command to make a connection to a

```
% telnet melvyl.ucop.edu
Trying 192.35.222.222...
Connected to melvyl.ucop.edu.
Escape character is '^]'.

DLA LINE 5 (TELNET) 01:12:26 08/23/98
(MELVYL.UCOP.EDU)

Please Enter Your Terminal Type Code or Type ? for a List of
Codes.
TERMINAL? vt100

Press RETURN for the MELVYL System ->
```

The user makes use of Telnet to connect to the Melvyl
on-line library catalog.

```
              Welcome to the University of California's

                      MELVYL* LIBRARY SYSTEM

- Catalog of books for UC and California State Library

- Catalog of periodicals titles for UC and for California's

(c)1984. *Registered trademark of The Regents of the University of
California.
=================================================

    To select a database for searching:    press RETURN

    For help getting started:  type HELP and press RETURN

-> cat
```

Once connected, the user begins the session

```
       Welcome to the MELVYL  Catalog Database

  Contents:   As of 8/23/98, approximately 9,587,527 titles
representing14,486,500 holdings for materials in the University of
       California libraries, and the California State Library,

  Coverage:   All publication dates but incomplete for some
libraries.

CAT-> find exact title introductory c

  Search request: FIND EXACT TITLE INTRODUCTORY C #
  Search result: 2 records at all libraries

  Type D to display results, or type HELP.
```

The use searches for a book by author.

```
CAT-> display 1
Search request: FIND EXACT TITLE INTRODUCTORY C #
Search result: 2 records at all libraries
Type HELP for other display options.

1. Petersen, Richard.
     Introductory C : pointers, functions, and files / Richard
Petersen. 2nd
   ed. San Diego, CA : Academic Press, c1997.
     UCSD  S & E    QA76.73.C15 P48 1997
     UCSD  S & E    QA76.73.C15 P48 1997 Circulation Desk
CAT-> logout
ELAPSED TIME = 0:01:35
END OF SESSION
Connection closed by foreign host.
$
```

After displaying the book, the user logs out of Melvyl

Figure 11.1. Telnet session.

remote system. Even during a login session, you can invoke this interface by pressing the Telnet escape character, **Ctrl-]**. With **Ctrl-]** you are prompted to enter a single Telnet command, after the execution of which you automatically continue with your login session. Use **Ctrl-]** again whenever you want to enter a Telnet command during the login session. When you finished a login session and logged out, you will be returned to the Telnet command interface. You can then issue other Telnet commands, even connecting to another system using the open command again. The status command will show the current status of Telnet.

The Telnet help and ? commands will list all Telnet commands that you can use. You can list syntax and options used by specific commands by preceding the command name with the ? . ?mode will display detailed information about the mode command and its extensive set of options. Other than the open and close commands, most Telnet commands are designed to manage difficult connections. Most users will not have to make use of them. Table 11.II provides a list of commonly used Telnet commands, and a comprehensive list is available on your system main pages.

Telnet provides you with special control over the control signals used to manage the command-line interface. Control signals are sent using control keys that implement certain command-line operations such as **Ctrl-h**, which sends an erase control signal to erase a character, or **Ctrl-c**, which sends an interrupt signal to interrupt the current command being executed. Different systems, particularly non-Unix systems, may use different character sets for backspace, erase, and interrupt keys. Telnet, using the Telnet protocols, automatically translates these characters into the remote system's equivalent. Telnet lets you change the keys used send these control signals as well as explicitly send the signals using the Telnet commands. The Telnet protocols are part of TCP/IP, and Telnet can be used to connect to any other system on a TCP/IP network, like the Internet. This means that Telnet can connect to systems other than Unix systems, as long as they are connected to a network using TCP/IP.

You can usually send a control signal just by typing your system's key for that signal. For example, on Unix systems, **Ctrl-c** is the interrupt, **Ctrl-h** is erase, and **Ctrl-d** is an end-of-file key. To send an erase signal to the remote system to erase a character on the command line, just press **Ctrl-h**. Telnet also provides a way to send these control signals from the Telnet command line. With the Telnet send command, you can explicitly send control signals to the remote system. The send command has options for the different control signals. The Telnet send codes are listed in Table 11.III For example, during a Telnet session you could escape to the Telnet command-line interface and use the send command to send an erase control signal, as shown here.

```
telnet> send ec
```

Table 11.II. Telnet Commands

open *host [[-l] user] [-port]*	Open a connection to a remote system (*host*). Optional arguments are a remote login name as specified with the -1 option, or a port number. The host can be a host name or an IP (Internet) address. The default port for the system's Telnet daemon is usually 23. If another port is specified, then Telnet protocols are not implemented. You can force Telnet protocols by placing a - before the port number.
close	Close the connection to the remote system and return to the Telnet command mode.
display *variable...*	Display Telnet variable and toggle values. You can list the variable or toggle values you want displayed.
environ *arguments...*	Exports your shell environment variables across the Telnet link using the TELNET ENVIRON protocol option. By default the DISPLAY and PRINTER variables are exported. The USER variable is sent if the -a or -1 command-line options are used. The remote system may still ask explicitly for variables not marked for export.

ARGUMENTS

define *variable value*	Define a variable with the specified value. The variable is automatically marked for export.
undefine *variable*	Remove definition of variable.
export *variable*	Mark a specified variable for export to the remote system.
unexport *variable*	Specified variable is not marked for export to the remote system.
list	List the current set of environment variables. Those marked with a * will be exported to the remote system.
?	Display environment command help information
logout	Close the Telnet connection (like the close command). Requires that the remote system support the Telnet LOGOUT option.
quit	Close any open session and exit Telnet.
send *code*	Send Telnet special control character sequences to the remote host. The sequences are referenced with Telnet codes. See Table 11.III for the list of send codes.
mode *type*	Sets the mode of operation for the Telnet connection.

MODES

character	Transmit data a character at a time (disables the LINEMODE option).

line	Transmit data a line at a time (enables the LINEMODE option). If remote system cannot use LINEMODE option, then "old line by line" mode is used.
set *variable value*	Assign a value to a Telnet variable or toggle. To assign a value to a toggle, use the values TRUE to turn it on and FALSE to turn it off. Use the display command to list the current values.
unset *variable*	Unset the value of a Telnet variable.
toggle *toggle-list*	Turn a Telnet toggle on or off, toggling between TRUE and FALSE. You can set their values explicitly with the set command.
z	Suspend Telnet.
! *[command]*	Execute a single command in a subshell on the local system. If no command is specified, then an interactive shell is started up.
? *[command]*	Displays a help summary. If a command is specified, Telnet displays the help information for that command.
slc *state*	Set or change the state of the special control characters when the TELNET LINEMODE option has been enabled.

STATES

check	Verify the current settings for the current special control characters. The remote system sends all the current special character settings, and, if there are any discrepancies with the local system, the local system switches to the remote value.
export	Use the local defaults for the special control characters.
import	Use the remote defaults for the special control characters.
status	Show the current status of Telnet. Displays the name of the remote system.

Use the mode, set, and toggle commands to configure your Telnet connections. The mode command determines the mode in which you send data. mode can be set to the character or line options. The character option sends data character by character and the line option sends a line at a time. Line mode speeds up Internet connections because whole lines of data can be sent in the same transmission, instead of transmitting single characters.

```
telnet> mode -line
```

(Send signals with the `send` command.)

abort	TELNET ABORT (Abort Processes) sequence.
ao	TELNET AO (Abort Output) sequence. Causes the remote system to flush all output from the remote system to the user's terminal.
ayt	TELNET AYT (Are You There?) sequence.
brk	TELNET BRK (Break) sequence. Send a break character.
ec	TELNET EC (Erase Character) sequence. Erase the last character entered.
el	TELNET EL (Erase Line) sequence. Erase the current line.
eof	TELNET EOF (End Of File) sequence. Send an end-of-file character, usually a **Ctrl-d**.
eor	TELNET EOR (End of Record) sequence.
escape	The Telnet escape character.
ip	TELNET IP (Interrupt Process) sequence. Send an interrupt character, usually a **Ctrl-c**.
susp	TELNET SUSP (Suspend Process) sequence.
synch	TELNET SYNCH sequence. Discards previously typed input that has not yet been read.
?	Prints help information for the `send` command.

Table 11.III. Telnet Send Codes

When Telnet initially makes a connection, it attempts to enable the TELNET LINEMODE option. If that fails it tries either the character or the "old line by line" modes. In LINEMODE, your local system performs character processing under the control of the remote system. In character mode, most text typed is immediately sent to the remote host for processing. In "old line by line" mode, text is echoed locally and completed lines are sent to the remote host.

With the `set` command you can change the keys used to send control signals to the remote system. Telnet maintains variables to hold the values of the different keys you use to send signals such as kill, erase, end-of-file, and interrupt. The default values of these variables are the keys normally used by your system. The `display` command will list the current keys used for these variables. With the `set` command you can change these keys. For example, the `interrupt` variable holds the interrupt character. On Unix systems this is a **Ctrl-c**. Should you want to use a different key to send an interrupt signal, say, **Ctrl-x**, you could use the set command to change the interrupt variable to that value as shown here. The Telnet variables are listed in Table 11.IV.

```
telnet> set interrupt ^C
```

(Set variable values using the set command and unset them with the unset command.)

ayt	Status character, a TELNET AYT sequence.
echo	Toggles local echoing of entered characters (default is **Ctrl-e**).
eof	End-of-file character.
erase	Erase character, TELNET EC sequence.
escape	Telnet escape character (default is "^["). Causes entry into Telnet command mode.
flushoutput	Flush character, TELNET AO sequence.
forw1	Forward partial lines to the remote systems, based on eol character.
forw2	Forward partial lines to the remote systems, based on eol2 character.
interrupt	Interrupt character, TELNET IP sequence
kill	Kill character, TELNET EL sequence.
lnext	lnext character.
quit	Quit character, Sends a TELNET BRK sequence to the remote system.
reprint	Reprint character.
rlogin	rlogin mode escape character that enables rlogin mode. Same as with the -r Telnet option.
start	Start character; default is your system's kill character.
stop	Stop character.
susp	Suspend character, a TELNET SUSP sequence.
tracefile	File name for tracefile to which netdata or option tracing will write to. If set to "-", then tracing information is written to standard output (the default).
worderase	Word erase character.
?	Displays the set commands.

Table 11.IV. Telnet Variables

Telnet Configuration

Certain variables are used to configure Telnet operations. The `echo` variable holds the character that will echo characters in line mode. The `escape` variable holds the key used as the Telnet escape character. The default escape character is **Ctrl-]**. You can change this by setting a new key value for the `escape` variable.

With the `toggle` command you can turn on and off certain Telnet features (see Table 11.V). `localchars` controls interpretation of control characters that you send. If on, then control characters like interrupt or erase keys are translated into an equivalent Telnet code, which is then translated into the remote system's corresponding control character. For example, say the remote system uses a **Ctrl-b** as its erase key and your Unix system uses a **Ctrl-h**. When you press **Ctrl-h** during a Telnet session, it is translated into the Telnet interrupt code **EC** (erase character) which is then translated by the remote system into its own erase character, **Ctrl-b**.

Toggling the **localchars** feature off will turn off this Telnet translation. Control signals will not be translated into the remote system's equivalent. Instead, they will be sent just as they are, as character data. Pressing **Ctrl-h** would send the **Ctrl-h** key value directly to the remote system.

You can effect a translation of your own by using the `set` command to change the control signal variables to that of the remote system. In this case you could change the `erase` variable to hold a **Ctrl-b** instead of a **Ctrl-h**. Of course you would have to use **Ctrl-b** instead of **Ctrl-h** to erase characters during your Telnet session.

```
telnet> toggle localchars
```

You can use the `crmod` and `crlf` toggles to control the interpretation of newlines. Unix systems use a line-feed character to signal a newline, whereas some systems use only a return character. If `crmod` is on, it will translate a newline character into a line feed and return.

(Use the `toggle` command to toggle features on or off. You can list several features with the same toggle command. You can use the `set` command to turn them on or off by setting their values to TRUE or FALSE)

autoflush	If TRUE, does not display data on the user's system until the remote system acknowledges it has processed `ao` or `quit` sequences sent to it. Default is TRUE unless "`stty noflsh`" is entered.
autologin	Use the user's login name to log in.
autosynch	Flush previously typed input. Default is FALSE.
binary	Enable or disable the TELNET BINARY option on both input and output.
inbinary	Enable or disable the TELNET BINARY option on input.
outbinary	Enable or disable the TELNET BINARY option on output.
crlf	If TRUE, return characters are sent as return and line feed. If FALSE, returns are sent as returns. Default is FALSE.
crmod	Map single return characters received from remote system to return and a line feed. Default is FALSE.
localchars	If TRUE, then Telnet special control characters are recognized locally and translated into TELNET control sequences.
netdata	Display network data (in hexadecimal format). Default is FALSE.
options	Display of internal Telnet protocol processing. Default is FALSE.
prettydump	With `netdata` toggle enabled, `prettydump` outputs `netdata` output in more readable format.
skiprc	If TRUE, the **.telnetrc** file is not read. Default is FALSE.
termdata	Display of terminal data (in hexadecimal format). Default is FALSE.
?	Displays the toggle commands.

Table 11.V. Telnet Toggle Features

Telnet .telnetrc file

You can place Telnet commands such as `mode`, `set`, or `toggle` in your **.telnetrc** file and have then automatically read and executed whenever you start Telnet. In this way you can create your own default configuration for your Telnet sessions. The **.telnetrc** file is located in your home directory. You can edit it using any standard Unix text editor. You can enter comments by beginning comment lines with a #. Blank lines are ignored. Commands have to be indented with a whitespace, a **space** or **tab**. Enter a **tab** or **space** at the beginning of a line before you type the Telnet command.

You can also create configuration profiles for different remote systems. These are commands that are executed whenever you connect to that particular system. These profiles are placed in your **.telnetrc** file. You begin a profile by entering the system address, either the host name or Internet address. A system address is not indented with a whitespace. It must start at the very beginning of a line. Then enter the commands for that system connection, preceding each with a whitespace (**tab** or **space**). Telnet distinguishes between system address and commands in that commands are indented by whitespaces. To start another profile, enter that system's address, followed by the commands you want to be executed whenever you connect to that system.

File Transfer Protocol: Ftp

One very common network operation that users perform is to transfer large files from one system to another. For this purpose Ftp was established as part of TCP/IP. Ftp stands for file transfer protocol and manages speedy transfer of very large files across TCP/IP networks. Ftp along with the TCP/IP, was originally developed on Unix systems, and for years, only Unix systems had Ftp capabilities. Ftp has since been implemented on other operating systems and has become an integrated component of Internet and intranet networks.

The Ftp utility on Unix systems makes use of file transfer protocols to transfer files from one system to another over a network. It operates on systems connected to networks that use TCP/IP, such as the Internet. It can handle both text and binary files. The Ftp utility has its own shell and its own set of commands, allowing you to configure and manage file transfer operations. Ftp works equally well on local networks and on the Internet. You can use Ftp to transfer directly very large files from one system to another on your local network or to transfer files to or from an Internet site. Ftp is often used to download software packages from Internet Ftp sites.

To transfer files with Ftp, you must first log in remotely to another account on another system with which you are connected. Once logged into that other system, you can transfer files to and from it. To log in, you will need to know the login name and password for the account on the remote system. For example, if you have accounts on two different systems on your network, you can use Ftp to transfer files from one to the other. If you have an account on an Internet site, you can use Ftp to upload or download files from it.

Certain Internet sites allow public access using Ftp. Many of these sites serve as depositories for very large files that anyone can access and download. These sites are referred to as Ftp sites. Their Internet address will usually begin with the word "ftp." These Ftp sites allow anonymous Ftp login from any user. For the login name, use the word "anonymous," and for the password use your Internet address. You can then transfer files from that site to your own system.

Ftp Connections

The Ftp utility is invoked with the command `ftp`. Connection to the remote system occurs via the Ftp command `open`. At this point, you are prompted for the name of the remote system with the prompt `(to)`. Upon entering the remote system name, Ftp connects you to the system and then prompts you for a login name. The prompt for the login name will consist of the word `Name` and, within parentheses, the system name and your local login name. Sometimes the login name on the remote system is the same as the login name on your system. Say, for example, you have personal accounts with the same login name on two different systems. If the login names are the same, just press **enter** at the prompt. If they are different, enter the remote system's login name. After entering the login name, you are prompted for the password. In the next example, the user connects to the remote system mygame and logs into the justin account.

```
$ ftp
ftp> open
(to) mygame
Connected to mygame
Name (mygame:chris): justin
password required
Password:
user justin logged in
ftp>
```

To save a step, you can directly specify the remote system on the command line when you invoke ftp. This connects you directly to that system without the need of the open command. The login procedure then begins.

```
$ ftp mygame
Connected to mygame
Name (mygame:chris): justin
```

This method is often used for connecting to an Internet site. Whenever Ftp detects an Internet address as its argument, it will connect directly to that site. In the following example the user specifies the Internet site ftp8.netscape.com.

```
$ ftp ftp8.netscape.com
Connected to ftp.netscape.com.
220 ftp23 FTP server (Version wu-2.4(23) Mon May 20 17:00:27
   PDT 1996) ready.
Name (ftp8.netscape.com:chris):
```

With either connection method you can include any Ftp options you want. Ftp options are listed in Table 12.I. Ftp options for features such as auto-login and interactive prompting are discussed in later sections. Once you have finished Ftp operations with a remote system, you end your connection to the system with the close command. You can then open up a connection to another system if you wish. To end the Ftp application, use the quit or bye command. Either command returns you to the Unix prompt.

-v	Verbose; displays all responses from the remote system and reports data transfer statistics.
-n	Do not perform "auto-login" upon connecting to a remote system. Otherwise, if auto-login is enabled, Ftp will check the **.netrc** file in the user's home directory for an entry with the login name on the remote system. If no entry exists, Ftp will prompt for a remote login name and then prompt for a password if needed. The default login name is the user login name on the local system.
-i	Turns off interactive prompting during multiple file transfers. Applies to mget and mput commands, canceling prompts for the transfer of each individual file in an mget or mput operation.
-d	Enables debugging.
-g	Disables file name expansion (globbing). Use of *, ?, and [] for file name matching is disabled.
system-address	You can specify the remote system to connect to immediately, skipping an open command for that connection.

Table 12.I. FTP Options

```
ftp> close
ftp> quit
Goodbye
$
```

You can check the current status of Ftp using the status command. status will display connection information and whether different Ftp features are on or off. It will also list whatever macros are defined.

Ftp Directory and File Commands

Once logged in, you can execute Unix commands on either the remote system or your local system. To execute a command on your local system, precede it with an exclamation point. Any Unix commands without an exclamation point are executed on the remote system. In the next example, the first command lists files in the remote system and the second command list files in the local system.

```
ftp> ls
ftp> !ls
```

The cd operation on your local system is an exception to this rule. You can use the cd command to change directories on the remote system, but you cannot use !cd to change directories on your local system. Instead a special Ftp command called lcd is used. lcd stands for local cd. In the next example, the first command changes to the **reparchive** directory on the remote system, and the second command changes to the **reports** directory on the local system.

```
ftp> cd reparchive
ftp> lcd reports
```

Ftp supports several commands for accessing directories and files on your and remote system (see Table 12.II). If your remote system permits it, you can use the mkdir and rmdir commands to create or delete directories on the remote system. The mkdir command may be helpful for a system you are uploading files to that you want to place in a directory of their own.

In many cases, the listing of directories on the remote system will be too large to fit on one screen. Many of the directory entries will run off the top. You can list directories a screen at a time by piping them into the more or pg command. Ftp supports command pipes, but there can be no intervening spaces between the '|' and the command, unless you enclose them both with quotes.

```
ftp> ls |more
```

You can save a listing of directories in a file on your local systems by specifying a file name after the ls command.

```
ftp> ls netdirs
```

The dir command performs the same function as ls, listing files and directories, except that it will always use the long form to display files and directories. The long form shows permissions, user

groups, time stamps, and sizes. On some systems `ls` may be set up
to display only the short form, showing only file names.

```
ftp> dir
```

Because of the long form, `dir` often cannot display all file names
on a single screen, and you have to use it in combination with
`|more` to see all the file names. It may also be useful to use it to
save the long file name forms in a file you can view later or to print
them as shown here. If you specify a file name after the `dir` command, then the listing of the current directory will be saved to that
file name on your local system. The second example will save the
list of the current directory on the remote system to the **netdirs** file
on the local system.

```
ftp> dir |more
ftp> dir netdirs
ftp> dir |lpr
```

Ftp supports certain special commands for managing files on the
remote directory. To change to the parent of the remote directory,
use `cdup` instead of `cd ..`. To erase a remote file, use the `delete`
command. The `rename` command is used to rename a file on the
remote directory (instead of `mv`). The `pwd` command prints the
working directory on the remote system.

```
ftp> cdup
ftp> delete rumors
```

If you want to perform operations on more than one directory or
file you will have to use a different Ftp command. The command
is usually the same name with a preceding `m`. To delete several files
or directories, use the `mdelete` command instead of `delete`. To
list the contents of several directories, use the `mdir` or `mls` commands, instead of `dir` or `ls`. To transfer several files at once, use
`mget` and `mput`, instead of `get` and `put`, as described in the next
section.

```
ftp> mdir birthdays reports
ftp> mdelete rumors scoops
```

Table 12.II. FTP Connection and Directory Commands

! [command [args]	Executes a Unix shell command. You can specify arguments for the shell command if needed. With no shell command, the ! places you in an interactive Unix shell where you can issue Unix commands. Enter exit or **Ctrl-d** to return to Ftp.
account [passwd]	Provide a supplemental password after login if the remote system requires one. You can enter the password as an argument to account. If not, you will be prompted for it and entry will not be echoed on your screen.
bye	End and exit the Ftp program. If you are connected to a remote system at the time, the connection will be terminated.
cd remote-directory	Change directory on the remote system to remote-directory, making it your working directory on the remote system.
cdup	Change to the parent directory of the remote system's working directory (like a cd.. operation for remote directories).
chmod mode file-name	Change the permissions of a remote file. The Ftp chmod command works on remote files.
close	Terminate the Ftp session with the remote system, and return to the Ftp command interpreter. Any defined macros are erased.
delete remote-file	Delete a file on the remote system.
debug [debug-level]	Toggle debugging mode. You can set the debug level. In debug mode, Ftp displays commands sent to the remote system, preceding them with `—>'.
dir [remote-directory] [local-file]	List the contents of a remote directory (like ls), using long form. If you do not specify a directory name, the current working remote directory is used. You can specify a local file name to which the directory listing will be saved. If no file name is specified, the local standard output is used, usually displaying the listing on your screen.
disconnect	Same as the close command; terminate a connection to a remote system. *(continued)*

Table 12.II. FTP Connection and Directory Commands (*continued*)

glob	Toggle Unix file name expansion for mdelete, mget and mput. If globbing is turned off with glob, the file name arguments containing expansion characters such as *, ?, and [], are not expanded. These characters are read literally and taken as part of the file name. File name expansion is performed by the remote system and may differ accordingly. You can preview the results using the mls command, mls remote-files -. glob does not enable mget and mput to transfer directory subtrees. You can transfer subtrees using tar archives that are later extracted.
hash	Display hash-signs ("#") during a file transfer. One # is displayed for each data block transferred. The size of a data block is 1024 bytes.
help *[command]*	Display a list of Ftp commands. If command is specified, display help information about that command.
idle *[seconds]*	Display the inactivity timer setting. With a seconds argument, it sets the inactivity timer on the remote server to that number of seconds.
lcd [directory]	Change the working directory on your local system. If you do not specify a directory, your local system's home directory (line cd) is used.
ls *[remote-directory] [local-file]*	List the contents of a remote directory. If you do not specify a directory name, the current working remote directory is used. You can specify a local file name to which the directory listing will be saved. If no file name is specified, the local standard output is used, usually displaying the listing on your screen.
mdelete *[remote-files]*	Delete several *remote-files* on the remote machine.
mdir *remote-files local-file*	Lets you specify several remote files to list as dir does. Instead of specifying a single directory or file you can list several particular files. The last file is take to be the local file where you want to save the listing results. If interactive prompting is on, Ftp will prompt you to verify that the last argument is that local file.
modtime *filename*	Display the last modification time of *filename* on the remote system. (*continued*)

Table 12.II. FTP Connection and Directory Commands *(continued)*

nlist *[remote-directory] [local-file]*	Print a *remote-directory* listing. If *remote-directory* is left unspecified, the current working directory is used. If *local-file* is specified, the listing is saved in that file on your local system. If *local-file* is not specified, the listing is output to standard output, which, by default, is displayed on your screen. If interactive prompting is on, Ftp will prompt you to verify that the last argument is a local file for receiving nlist output.
open *system-address [port]*	Make an Ftp connection to a remote system or Ftp site. You can specify a port number on which to connect to the remote system. With the auto-login option on, Ftp will try to automatically log in the user. auto-login is on by default.
pwd	Display current working directory on the remote system.
quit	Quite Ftp, closing any open connections. Same as bye.
quote *arg1 arg2 ...*	Send the arguments verbatim to the remote system.
remotehelp *[command-name]*	Request help from the remote system. You can specify help for a specific command.
remotestatus *[filename]*	With no arguments, show status of remote system. If *filename* is specified, show status of *filename* on remote system.
rename *[filename] [new-name]*	Rename a file on the remote system.
reset	Clear reply queue. Resynchronizes command/reply sequencing with the remote system. Used if remote system violates Ftp protocol.
rmdir *directory-name*	Delete a directory on the remote system.
site *arg1 arg2 ...*	Send verbatim arguments that are commands to be executed on the remote system.
size *filename*	Obtain the size of a file on remote system.
status	Display the current status of Ftp.
system	Display the type of operating system used on the remote system.
tenex	Set the file transfer type to that needed to talk to TENEX machines.
trace	Toggle packet tracing. *(continued)*

Table 12.II. FTP Connection and Directory Commands (*continued*)

umask [*newmask*]	Set the default umask on the remote server to newmask. With no arguments, the current umask is displayed.
user *user-name [password] [account]*	Identify yourself to the remote system. If the *password* or *account* are required by the remote system, and you do not specify them, Ftp will prompt you to enter them. Unless Ftp is invoked with "auto-login" disabled, this process is done automatically on initial connection to the remote system.
verbose	Toggle verbose mode. If on, all responses from the remote system are displayed. When a file transfer completes, statistics regarding the efficiency of the transfer are reported. verbose is on by default.
? [*command*]	Display help information about a command. Same as help.

In the case of the mdir and mls commands, Ftp will ask you if the last name entered is meant to be local file to which you want to save the directory and file listings. Like dir and ls, you can save directory listings to a local file for viewing later.

File Transfers

Ftp is most often used to transfer files to and from the remote system. The get command is used to send files from the remote system to your local system, and the put command is used to send a file from your local system to the remote system. Your local system *gets* files from the remote system and *puts* files to the remote system. Several other commands are available for managing your Ftp file transfers such as runique or mget. The Ftp commands used in file transfers are listed in Table 12.III. In the next example, the file newsflash is sent from the local system to the remote system using the put command.

```
ftp> put newsflash
PORT command successful.
Opening ASCII mode data connection for newsflash
Transfer complete.
ftp>
```

Ftp can transfer files either in character or binary mode. Many remote systems set the default to binary, but others may have it set to the character mode. The command `ascii` sets the character mode, and the command `binary` sets the binary mode. If you are transferring programs, archives, or compressed files, be sure the binary mode is set. Programs and archived files are binary files and must be transferred in binary mode. Most software packages available at Internet sites are archived and compressed files. These also have to be downloaded in binary mode. However, most Ftp Internet sites already set the transfer mode to binary for you. In the next example the transfer mode is set to binary and the archive file **rumors.tar** is sent from the remote system to your local system using the `get` command.

```
ftp> binary
ftp> get rumors.tar
PORT command successful.
Opening BINARY mode data connection for rumors.tar
Transfer complete.
ftp>
```

If you transfer files as character text using the `ascii` mode, you have to take into consideration one important difference between Unix character files and those on some other operating system. Some operating systems, such as DOS, implement character files using a line feed and a carriage return for each newline. Unix, on the other hand, uses only a line-feed character to implement a newline. You can use the `cr` command to instruct Ftp to strip any carriage returns at the end of the lines in any character files that you download, translating the file into a standard Unix file. The `cr` command is a toggle that will turn this feature on and off.

Normally when Ftp transfers a file, you will see no indication of the transfer's progress. When finished, Ftp will display a notice of

successful transfer followed by the Ftp prompt. This can be discon-
certing when transferring a very large file. With large file transfers
it helps to have an indication that file transfer is progressing. The
hash command will instruct Ftp to display a hash symbol, #, for
each block transferred. When you start a file transfer, you will see
'#' symbols displayed one by one across your screen as each block
of data is transferred. The hash command is a toggle command for
turning this feature on and off. If you are performing other tasks
while downloading a file, if may help to have Ftp beep your computer's bell whenever a transfer is completed. You can turn this
feature on and off with the bell command.

With Ftp you can specify a group of files to transfer at once. You
can use file name matching characters to specify a group of files,
and then transfer them all with one command. For transferring
multiple files at once you use the commands mput and mget. put
and get work on only one file at a time. When you use mput or
mget, you will be prompted for a file name specification. You can
then enter the file specification with file name matching characters.
*.c would specify all the files with a .c extension. * would spec-
ify all files in the current directory. ? will match on any single character and [] can match on specified sets or ranges of characters.
report? will match on **reports**, **report8**, and **reportA**, but not on
reportlate or **report10**. doc[ahs] will match on **doca**, **doch**, and
docs. doc[2-6c-g] will match on **doc3**, **docf**, and **doc6** as well as
any other file name beginning with **doc** and ending in any character from **c** to **g** or number from 2 to 6, inclusive.

In the case of mget, each file will be sent one by one from the remote system to your local system. You will be prompted with the
name of each file being sent. You can enter 'y' to accept the file or
'n' to cancel the transmission for that particular file. The mput
command works in the same way, but sends files from your local
system to the remote system. In the next example all files with a .c
extension are sent to your local system using mget.

```
ftp> mget
(remote-files) news*
mget newsflash? y
PORT command successful
```

```
Opening ASCII mode data connection for newsflash
Transfer complete.
mget newsbreak? y
PORT command successful
Opening ASCII mode data connection for newsbreak
Transfer complete.
ftp>
```

If you do not want to be prompted for each and every file you are downloading, use the prompt command to turn off this interactive prompting. In that case, when you use mget all matched files will be downloaded without prompts. The same it true for mput. This is helpful if there are a large number of files you want to download and you are certain that only those that you want will be selected by your pattern. You can turn interactive prompting back on by executing the prompt command again. prompt is a toggle that turns interactive prompting on and off.

```
ftp> prompt
ftp> mget
(remote-files) news*
mget newsflash
PORT command successful
Opening ASCII mode data connection for newsflash
Transfer complete.
mget newsbreak
PORT command successful
Opening ASCII mode data connection for newsbreak
Transfer complete.
ftp>
```

You can turn off the file expansion feature used for mget and mput with the glob command. This would let you use any of the file expansion symbols as part of a file name, *, ?, [, or]. The glob command is a toggle. To turn file expansion back on, just enter the glob command again. glob also toggles file expansion for other Ftp m commands such as mdelete.

Other file transfer commands let you perform special types of file transfers. If you are interrupted while downloading a file, you can reconnect and use the reget command to continue downloading the same file from the point you left off. When `reget` detects a local file with the same name as the remote file being downloaded, and finds that the local file is smaller than the remote file, it assumes it is a partial download of that remote file. It then resumes the file transfer from the point where the local file ends, adding on to it.

The `newer` command will only download a remote file if its modification time is more recent than that of a specified local file. If you do not specify a local file, then it will look for one that has the same name as that of the remote file. In effect, it downloads only if the remote file is a newer version of the local file.

If there is a file in your current directory that has the same name as the file you are downloading, then, by default, Ftp will overwrite your file, replacing it with the remote file. If, instead, you want to keep the original files with the same name, you can instruct Ftp to generate a new file with an altered name for any remote file names conflicting with a local file. The `runique` command turns this feature on and off. When on, a remote file with the same name as a local file has the extension **.1** added to it. If there is already a local file with the same name and the **.1** extension, then the **.2** extension is used, and so on to **.99**. After that an error is displayed. The `sunique` command performs the same function in the opposite direction. It will rename files that you upload to a remote system with names that conflict with files in the remote current directory. Files are renamed in the same way as `runique`. As with `runique`, `sunique` operates like a toggle, turning the renaming feature on and off as you execute it.

Proxy Ftp

With Ftp you can also transfer files between two remote systems. You connect to the first remote system with the Ftp `open` command, and then you use the `proxy` command to execute an `open` command to connect to the second remote system. A `proxy open` command does not define any new macros for that connection. The macros defined for the first system remain in effect.

The `proxy` command will execute Ftp commands on a second remote system. A `proxy get` command will, in effect, download files from the first system to the second, and a proxy put command will upload files from the second system to the first. You close the connection to the second system with a proxy close command.

```
$ ftp
ftp> open
(to) mygame
Connected to mygame
Name (mygame:chris): justin
password required
Password:
user justin logged in
ftp> ls
rumors newsflash
ftp> proxy open
(to) train.com
Connected to train.com
Name (mygame:chris): george
password required
Password:
user justin logged in
ftp> proxy get schedule1
PORT command successful.
Opening BINARY mode data connection for schedule1
Transfer complete.
ftp> proxy close
ftp> ls
rumors newsfalsh schedule1
ftp> close
```

Anonymous Ftp

Ftp is often used to download freely available data and software from various Internet Ftp sites. Such sites support anonymous Ftp for this purpose. Anonymous Ftp provides a user with a special restricted status. When you log in using Ftp, you use the word anonymous as your login name. Then for the password you enter any set of characters, usually your Internet address. You can then access special public directories and download the files in them. You will usually have to set the transfer mode to binary for software.

The following example connects to the `ftp8.netscapte.site` that contains Unix versions of the Netscape Navigator Web browser and Netscape Communicator, which includes the Web browser, mailer, newsreader, and Web page composer. The user enters anonymous as the login name and his or her email address for the password.

```
$ ftp ftp8.netscape.com
Connected to ftp.netscape.com.
220 ftp23 FTP server (Version wu-2.4(23) Mon May 20 17:00:27
  PDT 1996) ready.
Name (ftp8.netscape.com:root): anonymous
331 Guest login ok, send your complete e-mail address as
  password.
Password: enter-email-address

230-Welcome to the Netscape Communications Corporation FTP
  server.
230-
230-If you have any odd problems, try logging in with a
  minus sign (-)
230-as the first character of your password. This will turn
  off a feature
230-that may be confusing your ftp client program.
230-
230-Please send any questions, comments, or problem reports
  about
230-this server to ftp@netscape.com.
230-
230-
230 Guest login ok, access restrictions apply.
Remote system type is UNIX.
Using binary mode to transfer files.
ftp> cd pub/communicator
250 CWD command successful.
ftp> ls
200 PORT command successful.
150 Opening ASCII mode data connection for /bin/ls.
total 8
drwxr-xr-x 11 888      999       134 Aug 21 20:17 .
drwxr-xr-x 21 888      sys      4096 Aug 22 22:51 ..
drwxr-xr-x  3 888      999        31 Apr 2 22:31 4.0
drwxr-xr-x  3 888      999        26 Jul 17 1997 4.01a
```

```
drwxr-xr-x  4 888      999    46 Jul  3 01:02 4.03
drwxr-xr-x  3 888      999    26 Apr  2 05:54 4.04
drwxr-xr-x  4 888      999    46 Apr  2 04:53 4.05
drwxr-xr-x  4 888      999    73 Aug 21 02:41 4.06
drwxr-xr-x  3 888      999    25 Jul 15 02:51 4.5
drwxr-xr-x  4 888      999    42 Jul  3 01:10 extras
drwxr-xr-x  3 888      999    25 Aug 21 21:04 smartupdate
226 Transfer complete.
ftp> cd 4.05/shipping/english/unix
250 CWD command successful.
ftp> ls
200 PORT command successful.
150 Opening ASCII mode data connection for /bin/ls.
total 8
drwxr-xr-x 14 888      999  4096 Apr  2 05:45 .
drwxr-xr-x  6 888      999    62 Apr  2 06:21 ..
drwxr-xr-x  5 888      999    88 Apr  2 05:04 aix4
drwxr-xr-x  5 888      999    88 Apr  2 05:09 dec_unix
drwxr-xr-x  5 888      999    88 Apr  2 05:11 hpux10
drwxr-xr-x  5 888      999    88 Apr  2 05:17 hpux9
drwxr-xr-x  5 888      999    88 Apr  2 05:21 irix53
drwxr-xr-x  5 888      999    88 Apr  2 05:26 irix62
drwxr-xr-x  5 888      999    88 Apr  2 05:29 linux12
drwxr-xr-x  5 888      999    88 Apr  2 05:34 linux20
drwxr-xr-x  5 888      999    88 Apr  2 05:39 sunos413
drwxr-xr-x  5 888      999    88 Apr  2 05:43 sunos54
drwxr-xr-x  5 888      999    88 Apr  2 05:45 sunos54_x86
drwxr-xr-x  5 888      999    88 Apr  2 05:47 sunos551
226 Transfer complete.
ftp> cd sunos54
250 CWD command successful.
ftp> ls
200 PORT command successful.
150 Opening ASCII mode data connection for /bin/ls.
total 16
drwxr-xr-x  5 888      999    88 Apr  2 05:43 .
drwxr-xr-x 14 888      999  4096 Apr  2 05:45 ..
drwxr-xr-x  2 888      999   133 Apr  2 05:43 base_install
drwxr-xr-x  2 888      999   130 Apr  2 05:43
  navigator_standalone
drwxr-xr-x  2 888      999  4096 May  7 23:16
  professional_edition
226 Transfer complete.
ftp> cd base_install
```

```
250 CWD command successful.
ftp> ls
200 Port command successful.
150 Opening ASCII mode data connection for /bin/ls.
total 14640
drwxr-xr-x  2  888    999    133 Apr 2 05:43 .
drwxr-xr-x  5  888    999    88 Apr 2 05:43 ..
-rw-r—r—    1  888    999    1267 Jul 2 1997 .message
-rw-r—r—    1  888    999    17583 Mar 26 21:28
  README.license.txt
-rw-r—r—    1  888    999    16373 Mar 26 21:30 README.txt
-rw-r—r—    1  888    999    7452463 Mar 27 00:07
  communicator-v405-export.sparc-sun-solaris2.4.tar.gz
226 Transfer complete.
ftp> get communicator-v405-export.sparc-sun-solaris2.4.tar.gz
local: communicator-v405-export.sparc-sun-solaris2.4.tar.gz
  remote: communicator-v405-export.sparc-sun-solaris2.4.tar.gz
200 PORT command successful.
150 Opening BINARY mode data connection for communicator-
  v405-export.sparc-sun-solaris2.4.tar.gz (7452463 bytes).
226 Transfer complete.
7452463 bytes received in 1.33e+03 secs (5.5 Kbytes/sec)
ftp> close
221 Goodbye.
ftp> quit
$ ls
Mail
News
communicator-v405-export.sparc-sun-solaris2.4.tar.gz
$
```

When accessing an Internet Ftp site, you are first placed in the Ftp root directory. This directory usually contains a directory called **pub** along with several maintenance directories. The **pub** directory is the directory that will contain the publicly accessible software. Once in that directory, you can use the `ls` command to see what other directories are available and change to those as needed. If you know the path name of the directory you want, you can change directly to it. In the previous example, the user changes to the **communicator** directory using the path name `pub/communicator` and then again to the **unix** directory using the path name `4.05/shipping/english/unix`.

Table 12.III. FTP File Transfer Commands

append *local-file [remote-file]*	Append a local file to a file on the remote system. If you do not specify a remote file name, then the local file is for that name.
ascii	Set the file transfer type to network ASCII. This is usually the default type (transfer type is changed to binary by many Internet Ftp sites).
bell	Sound bell after a file transfer.
binary	Set the file transfer type to binary.
case	Toggle the remote file name case mapping during mget commands. When case is on, remote file names on the remote system that have letters in uppercase are written in the local directory with the letters mapped to lowercase. Default is off.
cr	Toggle carriage return stripping during ASCII type file transfer. This is used for files such as DOS files that use both a carriage return and line-feed character for a newline, instead of just a line-feed character as Unix does. When on, cr will strip the carriage-return character from ASCII files, making the file conform to the Unix ASCII file using just a line feed for newlines.
form *format*	Set the format for the file transfer form. The default format is "file."
get *remote-file [local-file]*	Transfer a remote file from the remote system to your local system. You can specify a local file name for it; if you don't, the same remote name is used. If there is already a file by that name on your local system, then the file name will be altered. The current settings for type, form, mode, and structure are used for transferring the file.
glob	Toggle Unix file name expansion for mdelete, mget, and mput. If globbing is turned off with glob, the file name arguments containing expansion character such as *, ?, and [], are not expanded. These characters are read literally and taken as part of the file name. File name expansion is performed by the remote system and may differ accordingly. You can preview the results using the mls command, mls remote-files -. glob does not enable mget and mput to transfer directory subtrees. You can transfer subtrees using tar archives that you later extract.

(continued)

Table 12.III. FTP File Transfer Commands *(continued)*

hash	Display hash signs ("#") during a file transfer. One # is displayed for each data block transferred. The size of a data block is 1024 bytes.
mget *remote-files*	Perform any specified file name expansion in *remote-files* on the remote system. Then execute a get operation for each file name generated. File name expansion is performed as indicated by glob. File names are processed according to case, ntrans, and nmap settings.
mput *local-files*	Perform any specified file name expansion in *local-files* on the local system. Then execute a put operation for each file name generated. File name expansion is performed as indicated by glob. File names are processed according to ntrans and nmap settings.
newer *file-name [local-file]*	Perform a get operation to transfer a file from the remote system, only if the modification time of the remote file is more recent that the *local-file* specified on your local system. If no local file is specified, then a file of the same name is used. If the file does not exist on the current system, the remote file is considered newer.
prompt	Toggle interactive prompting for multiple file transfers using mget or mput. Interactive prompting is on by default. If turned off, you are not prompted for individual files. With mput and mget, all matching files are transferred, and with mdelete all matching files are deleted.
proxy *ftp-command*	Allows file transfers between two remote systems. The first proxy operation should be an open command to connect to the second remote system. You can then execute Ftp commands on the second system using the proxy command. Close the connection with a proxy command followed by a close command. Proxy open operation does not define new macros and a proxy close will not erase macros. get and mget transfer files to the second system first. put and mput transfer files from the second system to the first. Execute an Ftp command on a secondary control connection. proxy ? lists help information. Depends on support of the Ftp protocol PASV command by the second system.
put *local-file [remote-file]*	Transfer local file to the remote system. If file name for remote-file is not unspecified, the *local-file* name is used. ntrans or nmap settings may apply. Transfers use the current settings for type, format, mode, and structure.

(continued)

Table 12.III. FTP File Transfer Commands *(continued)*

recv *remote-file [local-file]*	Transfer files from the remote system. Same as get.
reget *remote-file [local-file]*	Transfer files from the remote system, like get. Will also resume transfer of interrupted file transmissions. If the local file exists and is smaller than the remote file, the local file is presumed to be a partially transferred copy of the remote file and the transfer is continued from the apparent point of failure. Useful for transferring large files.
restart *marker*	Restart immediately following get or put at the indicated marker. On UNIX systems, marker is usually a byte offset into the file.
runique	Toggle storing of files on the local system with unique file names. If off (the default) then files transferred with the same name as an existing file will overwrite that file. If off, then a new file name is generated, preserving the existing file. The same name with a **.1** appended to it is used. If the resulting name matches another existing file, a **.2** is appended to the original name. If this process continues beyond **.99**, an error message is printed, and the transfer does not take place.
send *local-file [remote-file]*	Transfer files from your local system to the remote system. Same as put.
sendport	Toggle the use of Port commands. By default, Ftp will attempt to use a Port command when establishing a connection for each data transfer. The use of Port commands can prevent delays when performing multiple file transfers. If the Port command fails, Ftp will use the default data port. When the use of Port commands is disabled, no attempt will be made to use Port commands for each data transfer.
sunique	Toggle storing of files on remote system under unique file names. If off (the default) then files transferred to the remote system with the same name as an existing file will overwrite that file. If off, then a new file name is generated, preserving the exiting file. The same name with a **.1** appended to it is used, and so on.

Once you have reached the directory you want, you can use the ls command to list the software file names. On Internet Ftp sites these are compressed and archived files, ending with a compression extension such as **.Z, .zip,** or **.gz.** Each refers to a different compression program. In this example, the file name ends with a **.gz** extension indicating `gzip` compression. Usually software files are archives containing several files that make up the software application. The method commonly used to archive files is `tar`. `tar` stands for tape archive, and has become a standard archive method for Unix files. A `tar` archive file has the extension **.tar.** An archived file that has been compressed will also have a compression extension, such as **.tar.Z** or **.tar.gz.** You can see that the Netscape Communicator file is both archived and compressed.

```
communicator-v405-export.sparc-sun-solaris2.4.tar.gz
```

Usually the downloaded files are compressed archives. You first have to decompress it with the appropriate decompression command, and then extract its files from the archive using the `archive` command. Software packages located on Internet sites are usually archived with the **tar** command and compressed with the `gzip` command. You can decompress it with the `gunzip` command and then extract the archive with the `tar` command and the `xvf` options. Compression commands and the `tar` archives are discussed in detail in later sections in this chapter. The following example shows the decompression operations using **gunzip,** followed by archive extraction using `tar`. There remainder of the Communicator file is referenced with the * file name expansion character.

```
$ gunzip communicator*
$ ls
communicator-v405-export.sparc-sun-solaris2.4.tar
$ tar xvf communicator-v405*
communicator-v405.sparc-sun-solaris2.4/
communicator-v405.sparc-sun-solaris2.4/README.install
communicator-v405.sparc-sun-solaris2.4/ns-install
communicator-v405.sparc-sun-solaris2.4/vreg
communicator-v405.sparc-sun-solaris2.4/ifc11.jar
communicator-v405.sparc-sun-solaris2.4/iiop10.jar
communicator-v405.sparc-sun-solaris2.4/jae40.jar
communicator-v405.sparc-sun-solaris2.4/java40.jar
communicator-v405.sparc-sun-solaris2.4/jio40.jar
communicator-v405.sparc-sun-solaris2.4/jsd10.jar
communicator-v405.sparc-sun-solaris2.4/ldap10.jar
```

```
communicator-v405.sparc-sun-solaris2.4/scd10.jar
communicator-v405.sparc-sun-solaris2.4/nethelp-v405.nif
communicator-v405.sparc-sun-solaris2.4/netscape-v405.nif
communicator-v405.sparc-sun-solaris2.4/spellchk-v405.nif
$ ls
communicator-v405-export.sparc-sun-solaris2.4.tar
communicator-v405.sparc-sun-solaris2.4
$ ls communicator-v405.sparc*
README.install  java40.jar   nethelp-v405.nif   spellchk-v405.nif
ifc11.jar       jio40.jar    netscape-v405.nif  vreg
iiop10.jar      jsd10.jar    ns-install
jae40.jar       ldap10.jar   scd10.jar
$
```

Automatic Login

For sites and systems with which you transfer files regularly, it is convenient to be able to automatically log in, without having to enter the login name or password each time. You can even automatically log in to public Ftp sites, specifying an anonymous login name and your email address as your password. Ftp has an auto-login capability that reads the login name and password specified for a particular system or Internet site from a **.netrc** file. The **.netrc** file is located in a user's home directory. If you do not have one, you can create one with any standard text editor and place auto-login entries in it. Notice that the **.netrc** file begins with a period.

An entry in the **.netrc** file for automatic login to a particular system begins with the term `machine` followed by the system or Internet site address. On the same line, you enter the term `login` followed by the login name and then the term `password` followed by the password.

```
machine system-address login remote-login-name password password
```

The following example shows an entry for logging into the `richard` account on the `turtle.trek.com` system.

```
machine turtle.trek.com login richard password dylan567
```

In the case of an anonymous Ftp you would enter the word "anonymous" for the login name and your email address for the password, as shown here for `sunsite.unc.edu`.

```
machine sunsite.unc.edu login anonymous password
   chris@mygames.com
```

You can also place default entries in your **.netrc** file that will be read for any system you access. If you are accessing many different Internet Ftp sites with anonymous Ftp, it is helpful to use one default entry for them all, instead of making a separate entry for each one. When Ftp accesses a system, it will first look for a machine entry for it in the **.netrc** file. If there is not one, it will look for a default entry and use that. A default entry begins with the term `default` with no system address. The following example is a default entry for anonymous Ftp.

```
default login anonymous password chris@mygames.com
```

Entries in the **.netrc** file can also contain macro definitions, as described in the following section. Macro definitions will be automatically defined when that connection is made, and erased when the connection is closed. Macros defined in the `default` entry will be defined for each system you automatically log in to, other than the systems that have their own **.netrc** entries.

.netrc

```
machine sunsite.unc.edu login anonymous password
   chris@mygames.com
default login anonymous password chris@mygames.com
```

Ftp Macros

You can streamline operations that you perform on a particular system by defining macros to execute sets of Ftp commands. Macros are very helpful for any repetitive operations you may have to perform on a given remote site. Macros remain defined until you issue a `close` command. In other words, they remain in effect before and during a connection to a remote system. When you close that connection, all currently defined macros are erased and you would have to redefine them to use them again. For this reason, macros are usually defined in your **.netrc** file, placing their definitions in the connection entries for remote systems onto which you want log. When you perform an automatic login using a **.netrc** login entry, any macros you defined in that entry will be automatically defined for you. Any macro definitions that you place in the **.netrc** default entry will be automatically defined for every remote system you connect to other than those with their own auto-login entry.

A macro definition begins with the `macdef` command followed by the name you want to give to this macro. On the following lines you enter the Ftp commands you want executed whenever you invoke this macro. To end the macro definition, enter an empty line. Every command up to the empty line will be read as part of the macro definition.

> ***macdef*** *macro-name*
> *ftp commands*
> *empty-line*

The following macro definition defines a macro called `dirscr` that will execute the `dir` command to display files on the remote current directory and then pipe them to the `pg` command to display them a screen at a time.

```
defmac dirscr
dir *  |more
empty-line
```

The `downet` macro defined next changes to a directory where it then downloads Netscape Communicator. Such a macro assumes that you are connected to a Netscape Ftp site with that directory and file. It would be useful only for that connection.

```
defmac downnet
cd pub/communicator/4.05/shipping/english/unix/sunos54/
  base_install
get communicator-v405-export.sparc-sun-solaris2.4.tar.gz
empty-line
```

Ftp macros can take arguments. Arguments are referenced within the macro with n, where $1 references the first argument, and $2 the second, and so on. If you need to use a '$' character in macro, you have to quote it using the backslash, \$. The $i is a special argument that implements a kind of loop. The entire macro is applied to each argument in turn, with $i referencing the first argument the first time the macro is executed, and then second argument the second time it is executed, and so on. In effect, the macro becomes the body of a for loop in which $i changes its value to the next argument each time through.

When you close a connection, any macros you have defined are erased. To use them when accessing another system, or when you reconnect to the same system, you would have to redefine the macros. However, you can make use of system entries in the **.netrc** file to automatically define macros whenever you connect to a particular system. Instead of defining macros interactively in the Ftp interface, place them in the system entries in the **.netrc** file. For this reason, you would almost always define macros in your **.netrc** file, instead of continuously entering them interactively during Ftp sessions.

Whenever you access a system any macros you have defined for it in the **.netrc** file are automatically defined on the accessed system. You can then execute those macros while you are connected to the system. When you disconnect with a close operation, those macros are erased. Any macros that are placed in the default entry are defined for every system you access other than those for which you have specific system entries. The following example shows a **.netrc** example that defines the downnet macro in the entry for the ftp8.netscape.com site.

```
machine ftp8.netscape.com login anonymous password
  chris@mygames.com
defmac downnet
cd pub/communicator/4.05/shipping/english/unix/sunos54/
  base_install
get communicator-v405-export.sparc-sun-solaris2.4.
  tar.gz
empty-line
```

A sample **.netrc** file follows with macros defined for both specific and default entries. Notice the empty line after a macro definition.

.netrc

```
machine sunsite.unc.edu login anonymous password
  chris@mygames.com
defmac unixdir
cd pub/packages/unix

default login anonymous password
  chris@mygames.com
defmac dirscr
dir * |more
```

File Name Mapping and Translation:
nmap, case, **and** ntrans

If when downloading or uploading files, you do not specify a target file name, then Ftp will generate one. Usually this is the same name as the original file. For example, when uploading a file to a remote system, the file on the remote system will be given the same name as that on the local system, and vice versa. In some cases, you may want to alter the target name that Ftp generates. Remote systems may have different naming conventions, and you may want to map file names to different formats or change certain characters in them. The Ftp nmap command will map file names to different formats, arranging a file name's components differently. The ntrans command will translate specified characters in a file name.

You can specify a file name map using the nmap command with two arguments, an *in-pattern* and an *out-pattern*. File names matching the *in-pattern* are altered to fit the *out-pattern*. During an mput command, local file names that match the *in-pattern* will be changed to fit the out-pattern format. The file name mapping only applies to file names that Ftp generates, not to file names that you specify in a transfer command. You can unset the file name mapping, turning it off, by executing the ntrans command with no arguments.

nmap   *in-pattern*   *out-pattern*

You can copy different segments of a file name from the *in-pattern* for use in the *out-pattern* by using *$n* arguments. These arguments are numbered from 1. A $1 in the *in-pattern* will place that part of the file name it matches in whatever position you have the $1 in the *out-pattern*. For $n to work, they have to be placed in a literal context of specific characters. For example, 1$.dat will match on any name that ends with the characters ".dat". $0 is a special argument that references the entire original file. If you want to use the '$' character you quote with a backslash. For example, to add a **.work** extension to all files, you would use the following mapping.

```
nmap   $0   $0.work
```

The $1.$2 *in-pattern* would specify a file name and its extension, where $2 would reference the file name's extension. For the file name **main.c**, $1 would reference **"main"** and $2 would reference **"c"**. The following example would switch a file name and its extension, changing **main.c** to **c.main**

```
nmap   $1.$2   $2.$1
```

In the *out-pattern* you can specify that two or more *$n* references are to be replaced by only one *$n* reference. These *$n* grouping are encased in brackets. [$1,$2] replaces the references 1$ and 2$ with just $1, effectively cutting out part of the original file name. This is useful for removing extra extensions.

```
nmap   $1.$2.$3   $1.[$2,$3]
```

The replacement takes place provided the first reference is not a null string. For example, with [$2, data], if there is no $2 reference, then data is used. The file name **doc1** would be changed to **doc1.data**, **main.c** would remain **main.c**. In this particular *in-pattern* and *out-pattern*, file names with extensions remain the same and file names without extensions are given the extension **.data**.

```
nmap   $1.$2   $1.[$2,data]
```

If you are connected to a remote system where file names are implemented differently from Unix, you may have to accommodate that system's naming conventions when uploading or downloading files. The file name for a file you are transferring to a remote system may have to be altered so that it can be used by the remote system. For example, Unix systems recognize upper- and lowercase characters in file names, whereas some remote systems may recognize only uppercase characters in file names.

To translate just the case of characters in a file name, use the `case` command. This is useful for systems like mainframes that may only recognize uppercase characters in file names. For more specific translation, use the `ntrans` command. `ntrans` takes as its arguments two sets of characters. The first set of characters are those in the local file names that have to be translated, and the second set are the characters they are to be translated to. If the character's position in the first set is longer than the length of the second set, the character is deleted from the file name. You can unset the file name translation, turning it off, by executing the `ntrans` command with no arguments.

Ftp Transmission Parameters

Ftp is designed to transfer different kinds of files between different operating systems. Certain Ftp commands set transfer parameters for the form, structure, and type of a file, as well as the mode in which it is transferred. Many of these commands currently have only one option, but may implement others in future versions of Ftp. The file type can be either character or binary and is set with the `binary` and `ascii` commands. For binary you can also use `image` command. You can also use the `cr` command to implement carriage return stripping for ASCII files. Ftp also supports a `tenex` file type for TENEX computers. The File transmission parameters are listed in Table 12.IV.

The `from` command applies only to character files (ASCII) and determines if vertical format controls such as the newline or form feed are to be uninterpreted or translated into Telnet or Fortran conventions. Currently only the uninterpreted form, non-print, is supported by Ftp.

The `struct` command is used to determine a file's internal structure and will be able to detect three options: `file`, `record`, and

Table 12.IV. Macros, Map, Help, and Transmission Parameters

$ *macro-name [args]*	Execute the macro *macro-name*. Macros are defined with the `macdef` command. Arguments are passed to the macro unglobbed.
form *format*	Set the format for the file transfer form. The default format is "`file`."
help *[command]*	Display a list of Ftp commands. If command is specified, displays help information about that command.
macdef *macro-name*	Define a macro with the name *macro-name*. Enter Ftp command for the macro on the following lines. End the macro definition with an empty line. There is a limit of 16 macros and 4096 total characters in all defined macros. Macros remain defined until a `close` command is executed. Macros can take arguments that are referenced in the macro definition with a $ and the number of the argument. The $i implements a loop on the macro, repeating it once for each argument entered, with $i referencing each argument in turn. You can quote $ in the macro definition by preceding it with \ to enter the $ character. \\ will enter a backslash character.
nmap *[in-pattern out-pattern]*	With no arguments, turns off file mapping. With *in-pattern* and *out-pattern* arguments, nmap specifies translations to be performed. File names matching the *in-pattern* are translated into the *out-pattern*. Elements of the original pattern name are referenced in the *in-pattern* and *out-pattern* templates using *$num* references. Useful when connecting to non-Unix remote systems with different file naming conventions.
ntrans *[inchars [outchars]]*	With no arguments, the file name character translation mechanism is unset. With arguments, characters in remote file names are translated if there is no specified target file name. Characters in a file name matching a character in *inchars* are replaced with the corresponding character in *outchars*. If the character's position in *inchars* is longer than the length of *outchars*, the character is deleted from the file name. Useful when connecting to non-Unix remote systems with different file naming conventions.
status	Display the current status of Ftp.
struct *[struct-name]*	Set the file transfer structure to *struct-name*. The default is "`stream`."

system	Display the type of operating system used on the remote system.
type *[type-name]*	Set the file transfer type. If no arguments, the current type is displayed. The default type is network ASCII.

page. Currently the `file` option is the only one implemented. `file` is a standard file. `record` refers to a file containing records such as a database file. `page` refers to a file consisting of different pages such as a word processing or man file.

The `mode` command sets the transfer mode. The mode can be `stream`, `block`, or `compressed`. Currently only the `stream` mode is supported. `stream` is a standard file consisting of a sequence of bytes terminating with an end-of-file character. `block` refers to a block file consisting blocks of fixed length bits. `compressed` refers to compressed files.

Archiving Files with `tar`

In most cases, files that you download from Internet Ftp sites to your Unix system are software or data packages that have been archived into a single file for easy transmission. Instead of downloading each separate file for a specific software application, you simply download the single archive that contains all the files making up the application. You can then use the `tar` command to extract the archive's files. In the case of software packages, instructions will be included for installing the application on your Unix system. You can also create your own `tar` archive files for transferring several files at once over the Internet or any Ftp connection.

`tar` is an archive utility that was originally used (and still is) to back up files onto tape. It is more commonly used to store files, directories, and even software into an archive file that can then be transmitted over a network with Ftp. To use `tar` to create an archive file, you have to include the f option with the name of the archive file name. With the f option, the syntax for the `tar` command is the keyword `tar` followed by options ending with the f option and the file name, and then the names of files and directories to be archived. If a directory name is specified, then all its subdirectories will be included in the archive. Notice that the archive file is placed before the directory and file list. By convention, the archive name usually has a **.tar** extension (though this is not required). Table 12.V list the `tar` command options.

$ `tar` *options*f *archive-name* `.tar` *directory-and-file-names*

To create an archive file, use the `c` option together with the `f` option, `cf`. To extract the files from an archive file, use the `x` option with the `f` option, `xf`. In the next example, the directory **mydir** and all its subdirectories are saved in the file **myarch.tar**.

$ **tar cf myarch.tar mydir**

In the next example, the `xf` option directs `tar` to extract all the files and subdirectories from the `tar` file **myarch.tar**.

$ **tar xf myarch.tar**

Extraction is the most common process that you will perform on downloaded `tar` archive files. To have `tar` display the names of files as they are extracted, include the `v` option.

$ **tar xvf myarch.tar**

For archived files that you create, you may, at times, have to make changes such as adding or replacing files. Though you could just recreate the entire archive, `tar` has options that let you add or replace specific files. You use the `r` option to add files to an archive that has already been created. The `r` option will append the files to the archive. In the next example, the user appends the files in the **stories** directory to the **myarch.tar** archive.

$ **tar rf myarch.tar stories**

Should you change any of the files in your directories that you had previously archived, you can use the `u` option to instruct `tar` to update the archive with any modified files. `tar` compares the time of the last update for each archived file with those in the user's directory, and copies into the archive any files that have been

`tar` *options files*	Back up files to tape, device, or archive file.

`tar` **OPTIONS**

c	Create a new archive.
r	Append files to an archive.
u	Update an archive with new and changed files. Add only those files that have been modified since they were archived or files that are not already present in the archive.
w	Wait for a confirmation from the user before archiving each file. Allows you to selectively update an archive.
x	Extracts files from an archive.
m	When extracting a file from an archive, do not give it a new time stamp.
f *archive-name*	Save the tape archive to the file *archive-name* instead of to the default tape device. *archive-name* can be either a file or another device such as a tape or disk. The default device is held in `/etc/default/tar` file.
v	Display each file name as it is archived.
z, - -gzip, - -ungzip	Filter the archive through gzip.
Z, - -compress, - -uncompress	Filter the archive through compress.
- -use-compress-program *prog*	Filter the archive through *prog* (must accept -d option).
d, - -diff, - -compare	Find differences between archive and file system.

Table 12.V. File Backups: `tar`

changed since they were last archived. Any newly created files in these directories will be added to the archive as well. In the next example, the user updates the **myarch.tar** file with any recently modified or newly created files in the **mydir** directory.

```
$ tar uf myarch.tar mydir
```

Compression

Files that are transmitted over a network with Ftp are usually compressed. Compression will both reduce the size of the file as well as better ensure the integrity of the data. Compressed files are less prone to errors in the transmission. Several compression methods are used for Unix files. Each method has its own extension that it appends to the end of the compressed version of a file. The major compression methods in use for Unix files are compress, zip, and gzip. compress uses a **.Z** extension, zip a **.zip** extension, and gzip a **.gz** extension.

compress, uncompress, *and* zcat

compress is a Unix compression method usually included as part of your Unix operating system installation. It uses the Lempel-Ziv coding method. You can use the compress command to compress a file and the uncompress or zcat command to decompress a file. Compressed files will have the extension **.Z**.

compress can operate on several files at once, creating a compressed version for each with a **.Z** extension. It can also work on the standard input, outputting a compressed version to the standard output. With the -c option you can output the compressed version of a specified file to the standard output.

The uncompress command decompresses a file compressed by the compress command. The file must have the **.Z** extension. With the -c option, uncompress will output the decompressed version of the file to the standard output. This is helpful if you want to pipe the output to a filer or program for further processing. If the compressed file is a tar archive file, you can use this option to pipe the decompressed output directly to the tar command for extraction, performing both decompression and extraction on the same command line. Specify the standard output as the file name for the tar command with **-**.

```
$ uncompress -c myarch.tar.Z | tar xv -
```

The zcat command is simply the uncompress command with the -c option. Use zcat whenever you want to pipe the decompressed version of a file directly to another program. You could also use it to effectively rename the decompressed file by redirecting it to another file with a different name.

```
$ zcat myarch.tar.Z | tar xv -
$ zcat mydata.Z > newdata
```

gzip, gunzip, *and* gzcat

gzip is a GNU compression method widely used for Unix system. It uses Lempel-Ziv compression, the same as that used for pkzip. The gzip command compresses a file and the gunzip command decompresses it. gzip compressed files will have a **.gz** extension.

If no file names are listed, gzip will use the standard input and output the compressed version to the standard output. The same is true for gunzip. If you want to decompress a specific file and output it to the standard output, use the gzcat command.

```
$ gzcat myarch.tar.gz | tar xvf -
```

gunzip is capable of decompressing files compressed by either gzip or compress. It will decompress files with extensions **.z**, **.Z**, and **.gz**. The GNU gunzip program also recognizes a **.taz** and **.tgz** extension. These are files that are tar archives that have been compressed with gzip. The **.taz** and **.tgz** extensions are a kind of shorthand for **.tar.gz**. Files exapanded from compressed file with the **.taz** and **.tgz** extensions will automaticaly be given a **.tar** extension.

The GNU version of tar has a -z option that will perform either gzip or gunzip compression operations along with the tar archive operations. This lets you combine both decompression and extraction of a **.tar.gz** file in one tar command, as well as combine archive creation and compression.

```
$ tar czf myarch mydir
myarch.tar.gz
$ tar xzf myarch.tar.gz
mydir
```

zip *and* unzip

zip is a both a compression and archive utility that has been implemented on many different operating systems including Unix, MS-
DOS, OS/2, Linux, and Macintosh. It is designed to work with
pkzip and pkunzip. unzip can decompress any file compressed
by pkzip, and pkunzip and decompress any files compressed by
zip. The zip command compresses a file and the unzip command
decompresses it. Compressed files will have the extension **.Z** or
.zip. With zip you can compress and archive a single file, several
files, or entire directories. If you list a directory then the entire directory tree is archived and compressed. The first argument is the
name of the zip archive and the list of files to be archived follows.
The next example creates a zip archive called **myar** and places the
files **scoop**, **rumors**, and the directory **reports** in that archive

```
$ zip myar scoops rumors reports
```

Unlike other compression applications, zip both compresses and
archives files. A zip file functions as an archive file. This means
that you can remove, add, and change any files stored in a compressed zip file. For example, with the -d option you can delete a
file from the zip file. Table 12.VI lists the zip options.

```
zip -d myar newsflash
```

With the -f option you can update a file in a zip archive, replacing the current one with a new version. Replacement takes place
only if the modification date of the replacement is newer that the
archived version. You can update several files at once and even
whole directories.

```
zip -f myar scoops
zip -f myar *
```

You can use the -u option to add new files and to update files. If a
specified file is not in the archive, then it is added. If an older version is already in the archive, then the newer version will replace it.

```
zip -u myar rumors reports
```

Table 12.VI. Zip Archive and Compression

-A	Adjust self-extracting executable archive.
-b *path*	Use the specified path for the temporary zip archive.
-c	Add one-line comments for each file.
-d	Remove entries from a zip archive.
-D	No entries created for directories in zip archives.
-e	Encrypt the contents of the zip archive using a password that is entered on the terminal in response to a prompt.
-f	Replace (freshen) an existing entry in the zip archive only if it has been modified more recently than the version already in the zip archive. Does not add files new files to the zip archive.
-F	Fix the zip archive. Used if part of the archive is missing.
-g	Grow (append to) the specified zip archive, instead of creating a new one.
-h	Display the zip help information.
-i *files*	Include only the specified files.
-j	Store just the name of a file without the path, and do not store directory names. By default, zip stores the full path (relative to the current path).
-J	Strip any prepended data from the archive.
-k	Attempt to convert the names and paths to conform to MS-DOS.
-l	Translate the Unix end-of-line character line feed into the MS-DOS carriage return and line feed.
-ll	Translate the MS-DOS end of line, carriage return, and line feed into Unix line feed.
-L	Display the zip license.
-m	Move the specified files into the zip archive; actually, this deletes the target directories/files after making the specified zip archive.
-n *suffixes*	Do not compress files named with the given suffixes.
-o	Set the "last modified" time of the zip archive to the latest (oldest) "last modified" time found among the entries in the zip archive.
-q	Quiet mode; eliminate informational messages and comment prompts.
-r	Travel the directory structure recursively.
-t *mmddyy*	Do not operate on files modified prior to the specified date, where *mm* is the month (0–12), *dd* is the day of the month (1–31), and *yy* is the last two digits of the year.
-T	Test the integrity of the new zip file.

(continued)

Table 12.VI. Zip Archive and Compression *(continued)*

-u	Replace (update) an existing entry in the `zip` archive only if it has been modified more recently than the version already in the `zip` archive.
-v	`verbose` mode or print diagnostic version info.
-x *files*	Explicitly exclude the specified *files*.
-X	Do not save extra file attributes (file times on Unix).
-y	Store symbolic links as such in the `zip` archive, instead of compressing and storing the file referred to by the link.
-z	Prompt for a multiline comment for the entire `zip` archive. The comment is ended by an end of file, ^D.
-#	Regulate the speed of compression using the specified digit #, where -0 indicates no compression (store all files), -1 indicates the fastest compression method (less compression), and -9 indicates the slowest compression method (optimal compression, ignores the suffix list). The default compression level is -6.
-@	Take the list of input files from standard input.

The -m option will also add files to a `zip` archive, but will also delete the originals from your system. It is literally a move command, moving files from your directories to the archive. This options should be used with the -T option to test the resulting `zip` archive to make sure it has no errors before the original files are deleted.

Zip has two important options for handling character files that are to be transferred between Unix and MS-DOS systems. The -l options will translate the line feed in Unix files into a carriage return and line feed as used in MS-DOS file, preparing a Unix file for use on a MS-DOS system. The -ll option will translate the carriage return and line feed in an MS-DOS file into a single line feed as used in Unix file. It would prepare an MS-DOS file for use on Unix systems. You can place any default options you want specified in the `ZIPOPT` environment variable, except for -i and -x.

Archie and WAIS

Archie and WAIS are two utilities that help you find out what information is available, on what system it is located, and where on the system it is stored. With these utilities you can search for files on your network and throughout the Internet. Archie operates like searches on an on-line catalog. Just as you can use keywords to search for a title of a book, with Archie you can use patterns to search for the name of a file. WAIS operates like an index. It indexes documents on Ftp, Web, and Gopher sites, making it easier to access them. You can even use WAIS to index documents on any Internet or intranet sites that you maintain.

Archie

A great many sites on the Internet are open to public access. They contain files that anyone can obtain using file transfer programs such as Ftp. Unless you already know where a file is located, finding the ones you want can be very difficult. Archie is designed to search for files and tell you where they can be found. Once you know the site, you can use Ftp to access it and download the file. Think of Archie as an on-line listing of all the files available at different Internet sites.

Archie has a database of file names and their sites that is updated monthly. Copies of this database are located at different Archie sites that operate as Archie servers. You can query these sites, searching for specific file names, and the Archie server will give you the results, listing different files and the sites where they are located.

You can access an Archie server either through an interactive Telnet session or by using an Archie client installed on your own system. An Archie client will automatically access an Archie server for you, perform your query, and retrieve the results. Because of the potential demand on Archie, users are encouraged to use an Archie client if available, instead of interactively logging in. However, if you do not have an Archie client, you will have to log in to an Archie server and perform your queries directly on that server. Because of demand, many Archie servers may limit the number of users that can access it at any one time and may allot a certain amount of time to each user.

Archie Client

If your system has an Archie client, you can send an Archie query by entering the keyword `archie` followed by an option and a pattern. The pattern is then used to search file names. You can include an option to indicate different kinds of searches, though options cannot be combined. Should you do so, only the last option entered will be used. The syntax for the `archie` command follows.

```
$ archie -option pattern
```

If you enter a pattern without an option, then Archie treats the pattern as a full file name. In the next example, the user searches for a file with the file name of games.

$ **archie games**

The following example performs an exact search on the term "games" using the archie client.

$ **archie games**

Host du9ds4.fb9dv.uni-duisburg.de

    Location: /pub/pc
      FILE -r--rw-r-- 35995 Oct 24 1993 games
    Location: /pub/unix/FreeBSD/2.1-960606-SNAP
      FILE -rwxrwxrwx 25 Jun 9 1996 games
    Location: /pub/unix/FreeBSD/2.1.0-RELEASE
     DIRECTORY dr-xrwxr-x 512 Mar 3 1996 games
    Location: /pub/unix/FreeBSD/2.1.0-RELEASE/ports
     DIRECTORY dr-xrwxr-x 512 Nov 24 1995 games
    Location: /pub/unix/FreeBSD/FreeBSD-current/src/games/atc
    Location: /pub/unix/FreeBSD/packages-current
     DIRECTORY dr-xrwxr-x 512 Apr 2 1996 games
    Location: /pub/unix
      FILE -r--rw-r-- 72057 Jun 3 1996 games

Host fsuj01.rz.uni-jena.de
    Location: /pub/.mounts/disk01/linux/MIRROR.sunsite/X11
     DIRECTORY drwxr-xr-x 2048 May 2 1997 games
    Location: /pub/.mounts/disk01/linux/MIRROR.sunsite
     DIRECTORY drwxr-xr-x 1024 May 2 1997 games

Host ftp.uni-stuttgart.de
    Location: /pub/X11
     DIRECTORY drwxrwxr-x 512 Nov 27 1995 games
    Location: /pub/doc/faq/alt
     DIRECTORY dr-xr-xr-x 512 Jul 21 1996 games
    Location: /pub/doc/faq/comp/ai
     DIRECTORY dr-xr-xr-x 512 Jul 21 1996 games

Host ftp.rz.uni-wuerzburg.de
    Location: /pub/FreeBSD/2.1.6-RELEASE/commerce
     DIRECTORY drwxrwxr-x 8192 Feb 21 1997 games
    Location: /pub/FreeBSD/2.1.6-RELEASE

```
   DIRECTORY drwxrwxr-x 8192 Feb 22 1997 games
  Location: /pub/amiga/mpearls4/setattributesdir/pearls/
  game/platform/boulderd
   DIRECTORY dr-xr-xr-x 2048 Oct 22 1996 games
$
```

Different Archie options allow you to create more powerful queries. The options are listed in Table 13.I. The -c option will treat the pattern as an incomplete pattern and search for its occurrence anywhere in a file name. In the next example, the user searches for any file name with the pattern "games" in it. It will match on "games," "cookie_games," and "oldgamess."

$ **archie -c games**

The -s option performs the same kind of pattern search as a -c option, but ignores case sensitivity. It will match either upper- or lower-

---

ARCHIE CLIENT COMMAND

archie *options string*

OPTIONS

-e	Exact pattern match (default).
-c	Search file names for occurrence of pattern.
-s	Search file names ignoring case.
-r	Pattern is a regular expression.
-t	Sort the results by date.
-h *hostname*	Query the host name Archie server.
-m*num*	Limits the maximum number of results (matches).
-N*num*	Estimate number of results of a query (default 0).
-L	Lists the known Archie servers.
-V	Verbose; display messages during long search.
-o*filename*	If specified, place the results of the search in *filename*.

VARIABLES

ARCHIE_HOST	Holds the address of the Archie host to use for Archie client queries, if different for host, compiled in the client.

Table 13.I. Archie Client Options

case versions of a pattern. In the next example, the user will match on file names such as "games," "Games," and "oldGames."

$ **archie -s games**

The -r option allows you to use regular expressions. This means that you can use special characters to match variations on a file name. You can use the * to match any sequence of the preceding character in the name, the ? to match any one character, and the [] to match on classes of characters. However, be sure to quote the regular expression so that it will not be executed by the shell. Suppose, for example, that you want to make an exact search for a file name in which only the first character may or may not be capitalized. The regular expression [Gg]ame searches for file names beginning with either a 'g' or a capital 'G': games or Games. Also, an s* placed at the end will search for file names with or without an ending 's': games or game.

$ **archie -r '[Gg]ames*'**

Other options control Archie's output. The -m option followed by a number limits the number of matched item that are output. If you want to see only the first 10 items, use the -m10 option. The -t option will output items sorted by date, beginning with the most recent.

Archie queues its requests, executing the smaller ones first. If you have a request that you know is going to have a great many results, it is helpful to note that in your query. The -N option which stands for nice, takes as its argument an estimate of how many items will be in your result. Your query is then queued accordingly.

$ **archie -m10 -t -s games**

```
Host fsuj01.rz.uni-jena.de
   Location: /pub/.mounts/disk02/linux/MIRROR.dld/v-5.01
   DIRECTORY drwxr-xr-x 512 Mar 26 1997 xgames1
   Location: /pub/.mounts/disk02/linux/MIRROR.dld/v-
   5.01/xgames1
     FILE -rw-r—r-x 59790 Sep 20 1996 xgames.ger
     FILE -rw-r—r-x 10319 Sep 20 1996 xgames1.ger
     FILE -rw-r—r-x 164963 Sep 20 1996 xgames2.ger
```

```
Host cranach.rz.tu-ilmenau.de

  Location: /pub/unix/linux/distributions/DLD
   DIRECTORY drwxr-xr-x 512 May 6 1996 xgames3
   DIRECTORY drwxr-xr-x 512 May 6 1996 xgames4
   DIRECTORY drwxr-xr-x 512 May 6 1996 xgames1
   DIRECTORY drwxr-xr-x 512 May 6 1996 xgames2
  Location: /pub/unix/linux/distributions/DLD/xgames1
     FILE -rw-r—r— 9201 Nov 26 1995 xgames1.ger
     FILE -rw-r—r— 482647 Nov 20 1995 xgames.ger
$
```

To save your results you can redirect them to a file using the -o option with a file name. In the following example, the results of the
Archie search are placed in a file named gameres.

$ **archie -m50 -t games -o gameres**

The Archie site queried by the archie client will be the one compiled into the Archie client. You can specify another Archie site
using the -h option followed by the site address, or you can use the
environment variable ARCHIE_HOST and assign the site you want
to it. (A list of Archie sites is given later in Table 13.III.) The following example queries the archie.cs.mcgill.ca Archie site.

$ **archie -s games -h archie.cs.mcgill.ca**

Archie Servers

Several Archie public servers are available on the Internet that
you can access and query. With the login name archie, you use
telnet to log in to the Archie server. Table 13.II lists several
Archie public servers to which you can log in. Once logged in, you
will receive an Archie prompt: archie>. At the prompt you can
execute searches or set parameters. Searches are executed with the
command prog followed by the string to search for.

archie> **prog games**

Once you have finished your session, you can then log out using
the quit command.

archie> **quit**

archie.au	139.130.23.2	Australia
archie.univie.ac.at	131.130.1.23	Austria
archie.belnet.be	193.190.198.2	Belgium
archie.bunyip.com	192.77.55.5	Canada
archie.cs.mcgill.ca	132.206.51.250	Canada
archie.funet.fi	128.214.248.46	Finland
archie.cru.fr	129.20.254.2	France
archie.th-darmstadt.de	130.83.22.1	Germany
archie.ac.il	132.65.208.15	Israel
archie.unipi.it	131.114.21.15	Italy
archie.wide.ad.jp	133.4.3.6	Japan
archie.kornet.nm.kr	168.126.63.10	Korea
archie.sogang.ac.kr	163.239.1.11	Korea
archie.nz	140.200.128.20	New Zealand
archie.icm.edu.pl	148.81.209.5	Poland
archie.rediris.es	130.206.1.5	Spain
archie.luth.se	130.240.12.23	Sweden
archie.switch.ch	193.5.24.1	Switzerland
archie.ncu.edu.tw	192.83.166.12	Taiwan
archie.doc.ic.ac.uk	193.63.255.1	UK
archie.hensa.ac.uk	129.12.200.130	UK
archie.unl.edu	129.93.1.14	USA (NE)
archie.internic.net	198.49.45.10	USA (NJ)
archie.internic.net	204.159.111.101	USA (VA)
archie.internic.net	204.179.186.65	USA (NJ)
archie.rutgers.edu	128.6.21.13	USA (NJ)
archie.ans.net	147.225.1.10	USA (NY)

Table 13.II. Archie Server Sites

As with the Archie client, you can qualify your search using regular expressions or a partial pattern match. To do so, set the feature `search` to a specific option using the `set` command. You do not use options as you do for the `archie` client.

```
archie> set search option
```

The `rgex` option searches using a regular expression, and the `sub` option searches with a partial pattern. The `sub` option is the default on many systems. The `exact` option performs an exact search on the pattern provided. In the next example the user searches for file names that contain the pattern "games."

```
archie> set search sub
archie> prog games
```

The following example uses a regular expression to perform a search. The regular expression `[Gg]ames*` searches for file names beginning with either an upper- or lowercase g and ending with or without an `s`: games or Game.

```
archie> set search regex
archie> prog [Gg]ames*
```

The following example is an Archie session on an Archie server. With telnet the user connects to the Archie server and then logs in as `archie`. At the `archie>` prompt the user then enters a search with the `prog` command. The default search type is `sub`, searching for any file name that contains the pattern, in this case, "games." The user then quits with the `quit` command, ending the session and disconnecting from the Archie server.

```
$ telnet archie.mcgill.ca
Trying 192.77.55.2...
Connected to services.bunyip.com.
Escape character is '^]'.

SunOS UNIX (services.bunyip.com)
login: archie

 Note: The 'server' variable no longer has any effect for
   searches. If you want to perform a search on another
   archie server you should login to that server.

# Bunyip Information Systems, Inc., 1993, 1994, 1995

# Terminal type set to 'xterm 24 80'.
# 'erase' character is '^?'.
# 'search' (type string) has the value 'sub'.
archie> prog games
# Search type: sub.
```

working...

```
ftp://ftp.cc.umanitoba.ca/pub/umto0005/stuff/irc-games
          Date: 12:57 9 Sep 1998 Size: 23 bytes

ftp://ftp.cc.umanitoba.ca/pub/umthai01/codegames
          Date: 11:21 9 Sep 1998 Size: 25 bytes

ftp://ftp.risq.qc.ca/pub/ca-domain/registrations-hierarchical/
   qc/sdvideogames
          Date: 02:54 9 Sep 1998 Size: 43 bytes

ftp://ftp.risq.qc.ca/pub/ca-domain/registrations-hierarchical/
   qc/games
          Date: 02:48 9 Sep 1998 Size: 36 bytes

ftp://ftp.risq.qc.ca/pub/ca-domain/registrations-hierarchical/
   on/hamilton/cgames
          Date: 02:40 9 Sep 1998 Size: 49 bytes

ftp://ftp.risq.qc.ca/pub/ca-domain/registrations-hierarchical/
   on/sggames
          Date: 02:37 9 Sep 1998 Size: 38 bytes

ftp://ftp.risq.qc.ca/pub/ca-domain/registrations-hierarchical/
   on/glengarry-games
          Date: 02:31 9 Sep 1998 Size: 46 bytes

ftp://ftp.risq.qc.ca/pub/ca-domain/registrations-hierarchical/
   cgames97
          Date: 00:54 9 Sep 1998 Size: 33 bytes

ftp://ftp.onet.on.ca/pub/usenet/news.answers/games
          Date: 05:02 7 Sep 1998 Size: 1024 bytes

ftp://ftp.risq.qc.ca/pub/ca-domain/registrations-flat/ca.
   dragongames
          Date: 18:33 5 Sep 1998 Size: 933 bytes

ftp://ftp.onet.on.ca/pub/usenet/news.answers/games/board-
   games-faq.gz
          Date: 00:44 2 Sep 1998 Size: 11286 bytes

ftp://ftp.cs.sfu.ca/elibweb/elib-web/statu/LC/indiv_log/www
   .happypuppy.com/games
          Date: 20:00 4 Jul 1997 Size: 96 bytes
```

```
ftp://aupair.cs.athabascau.ca/amiga/games
          Date: 20:00 7 Jul 1991 Size: 512 bytes

archie> quit
# Bye.
Connection closed by foreign host.
$
```

You can control how the results are generated by an Archie query by setting certain Archie variables while connected to the Archie server. For example, you can limit the number of retrieved items by setting the variable maxhits to the maximum number of entries you want. The variable sortby will sort output items on a specified field. You can set a variable using the keyword set followed by the variable name and then the variable value. To set the variable maxhits to 10 you enter the command: set maxhits 10. In the next example, the user limits the items output to 5, and sorts the output by the most recent modification time of the software.

```
archie> set sortby time
archie> set maxhits 5
archie> set search sub
archie> prog games
# Search type: sub.
working...

ftp://ftp.risq.qc.ca/pub/ca-domain/registrations-hierarchical/
  bc/gameslovers
          Date: 01:54 9 Sep 1998 Size: 42 bytes

ftp://ftp.risq.qc.ca/pub/ca-domain/registrations-hierarchical/
  cgames99
          Date: 00:54 9 Sep 1998 Size: 33 bytes

ftp://ftp.risq.qc.ca/pub/ca-domain/registrations-flat/ca.
  cgames99
          Date: 20:00 21 Feb 1998 Size: 1191 bytes

ftp://ftp.risq.qc.ca/pub/ca-domain/registrations-flat/ca.bc.
  gameslovers
          Date: 20:00 4 Sep 1997 Size: 1087 bytes

ftp://ftp.cs.ubc.ca/local/edmonds/anime-fan-works/BGC/Lemon/
  bgc.lemon.no-more-games.gz
          Date: 20:00 26 Aug 1997 Size: 6175 bytes
archie>
```

Archie commands are summarized in Table 13.III.

Table 13.III. Archie Server Commands

ARCHIE PUBLIC SERVER COMMANDS

prog	Search file names for occurence of pattern.
list	Lists the known Archie servers.
site	List files at a particular host.
mail	Mail results of search.
quit	Log out from Archie server.
help	Display help.
set *variable value*	Set Archie variables.
show	Display current values of Archie variables.
unset	Remove a variable.

ARCHIE SERVER VARIABLES

autologout *num*   Number of minutes that Archie waits idle before automatically logging you out of the Archie server. The default is 15 minutes.

```
set autologout 10
```

mailto *address*   Mail address to which results are sent.

```
set mailto chris@mygame.com
```

maxhits *num*   Limit the maximum number of results (matches).

```
set maxhits 10
```

pager   Use the default pager utility such as pg or more to display your results.

```
set pager
unset pager
```

search *option*   Type of search.

```
set search subcase
```

SEARCH OPTIONS

sub   Pattern search within file names.

subcase   Pattern search that distinguishes between upper- and lowercase letters.

exact   Exact pattern match.

regex   Use regular expressions.

sortby *option*   Type of sort for output.

```
set sortby filename
```

(continued)

Table 13.III. Archie Server Commands *(continued)*

Sort Options

none	No sort.
filename	Sort the results alphabetically by file name.
hostname	Sort the results by host name.
time	Sort the results from most recent date.
size	Sort the results from largest size.
rfilename	Reverse alphabetical file name sort.
rhostname	Reverse alphabetical host name sort.
rtime	Sort the results from oldest date.
rsize	Sort the results from smallest size.
status	Issue status reports on searches as they are performed.
set status	
unset status	
term *terminal-id*	Type of terminal you are using.

```
                    set term vt100
```

WAIS

WAIS (Wide Area Information Service) is an information service designed to search available databases on the Internet. Throughout the Internet there are many WAIS databases, which consist of articles covering such diverse topics as movies and programming. A WAIS database is any collection of documents that have been indexed using WAIS indexing software. WAIS servers set up indexes that can be used to search documents.

To search WAIS databases, you use either a WAIS client utility such as waisq, swais, or xwais, a Web browser such as netscape or mosaic, or a Gopher client such as gopher or xgopher. waisq uses a simple command-line interface, whereas swais provides a full-screen interface, and xwais is designed for X-Windows interfaces. The swais commands and options are listed in Table 13.IV. A WAIS client allows you to select a WAIS database and perform

OPTIONS

-s *sourcename*	Select source name for search.
-S *sourcedir*	Specify a source directory. Default is ~/wais-sources.
-C *sourcedir*	Specify a common source directory. Default is /usr/lib/wais-sources.
-h	Help message.

COMMANDS

j, **down-arrow**, ^N	Moves down one source.
k, **up-arrrow**, ^P	Moves up one source.
J, ^V, ^D	Moves down one screen.
K, **escape** v, ^U	Moves up one screen.
#*num*	Position to source number *num*.
/*string*	Searches for source *string*.
spacebar *or* .	Selects current source.
=	Deselects all sources.
v *or* ,	Views current source information.
enter	Performs search.
s	Selects new sources (refresh sources list).
w	Selects new keywords.
X, -	Removes current source permanently.
o	Sets and shows swais options.
h, ?	Shows this help display.
H	Displays program history.
q	Leaves this program.

Table 13.IV. WAIS Commands

searches using complex Boolean queries. The results are then listed and numbered and you can choose the number of the article in this list that you want. This will display the article, and you can save or print it. You can also use your Web browser or Gopher client to access WAIS sites such as www.wais.com. There you can perform searches on many different topics or move to other WAIS sites.

Unlike searches in other information services, WAIS performs full-text searches of database articles and ranks its results. WAIS searches the entire text of each article, not just the article title or a predetermined list of index words. In this respect, the content of each article is examined, providing a more comprehensive search. The results of a WAIS search are ranked from 0 to 1000, beginning with those articles that best respond to the search having the highest scores. You can use these results to further expand or narrow your search.

freeWAIS

WAIS searches a database of documents using keywords and displays the documents it finds with a ranking of their importance. It is a very effective way to make information available throughout a network. WAIS was developed by Thinking Machines and is now managed by WAIS Inc. A free version of WAIS called freeWAIS has been made available by the Clearinghouse for Network Information Discovery and Retrieval (CNIDR). Their Web site at ftp.cnidr.org has Unix versions of freeWAIS already compiled and ready to use. You can also download the source code and compile it yourself. You can also create your own WAIS database using the freeWAIS server software. You can then set up a collection of documents, index them, and make them available for searching by other users on the Internet.

The freeWAIS package includes clients, a server, and an indexer program. The clients are called swais, xwais, and waissearch. They are used to enter requests and display results. The indexer is called waisindex. You can use it to create indexes of keywords for your WAIS documents, providing fast and effective search capabilities. The server is called waisserver. With it you can create your own WAIS site and allow other users to perform searches on your WAIS documents.

The freeWAIS source code package can be configured for different systems. If you download the package of compiled binaries, this directory will hold those binaries. All you have to do is install them in an appropriate directory such as /usr/bin. If you download the source code, however, you have to configure it first before you can create its binaries. Once you are ready to compile `freeWAIS`, issue the `make` command with the term `unix`. This will create your WAIS clients, indexer, and server programs for your Unix system.

WAIS Server

You can use the `freeWAIS` server to index documents on your own system and make them accessible through WAIS index databases either locally or on the Internet. Once you have installed you WAIS server, you can start it up with the `waisserver` command, specifying the location of your WAIS indexes.

```
waisserver -d wais_index-directory
```

To use WAIS you have to create indexes for the documents you want to make available. Indexing is performed by the `waisindex` command. You can index a single file, a group of files, or whole directories and subdirectories of files. The data files together with their index form a WAIS database. You can separately index different files or groups of files, setting up several different WAIS databases on your server. The WAIS databases should be located in the WAIS data directory that was specified when the WAIS server was invoked, for example, `/home/waisindex`.

`waisindex` creates an inverted file index, referencing every word in the designated files. This allows keyword searching on the full text of documents. `waisindex` takes several options followed by the name of the file, group of files, or directory to be indexed as the last argument. With the `-d` option you can specify a name for the index. `waisindex` creates several index files for a document that are used to manage the index. Each will have its own extension indicating its function, but all will have the index name specified by the `-d` option as the prefix. If you do not specify a name, the term "index" will be used as the prefix. Also, if you want to have your database accessible to other users on the Internet, you have to add the `-export` option. Without this option, your database is accessible only to other users on your system. The WAIS index files are listed in Table 13.V.

```
waisindex -d index-file -export file-list
```

.doc	Information about the document, including the size and name.
.dct	Dictionary file with list of each unique word cross-indexed to inverted file.
.fn	List of all files created for the index.
.hl	Table of all headlines; headlines are the titles and are displayed in the retrieved results.
.inv	The inverted file containing a table of words, a ranking of their importance, and their connection to the indexed documents.
.src	A source description file that contains information about the index, what system it is located on, the topic it deals with, who maintains it, etc.
.status	Contains user-defined information.

Table 13.V. WAIS Index Files

If you list more than one file to be indexed then all those files will referenced by the single index. If you want to index all the files in a subdirectory then you use the -r option followed by the directory name.

```
waisindex -d index-file -export -r directory-name
```

To add a file or directory to an existing database, index it with the -a option. Include the -d option with a database name to add the indexing of this file to that database. To add several files at once, just list them. For a directory, be sure to use the -r option followed by the directory name. Other waisindex options are listed in Table 13.VI.

```
waisindex -d index-file -a -export file-list
```

In the next examples, the user first indexes the files **chocolate** and **cheesecake**, creating an index called **recipes** for that group of files. Queries on **recipes** will search both **chocolate** and **cheesecake**. In the next example, the user indexes the **pasta** file and adds it to the **recipes** index. The WAIS **recipes** database now includes the files **chocolate, cheesecake,** and **pasta.** Then the user indexes the **pastry** directory, including all of its files and files in any of its subdirectories. The name of the index is **brunch.** In the last example, indexing is

-a	Appends index to an existing one.
-contents	Indexes the contents of a file (default).
-d *pathname*	Specifies a path name for index files.
-e *logfile*	Redirects error messages to *logfile*.
-export	Adds hostname and TCP port to source description files to allow Internet access.
-l *num*	Sets logging level: 0, 1, 5 and 10. 0, nothing; 1, errors and warnings; 5, Medium priority messages; 10, everything.
-mem	The amount of memory to use during indexing.
-M	Links different types of files.
-nocontents	Indexes only the header and file name, not the contents.
-pairs	Treats capitalized words as one term.
-nopairs	Treats capitalized words as separate terms.
-pos	Include word's position information.
-nopos	Do not include word's position information.
-r	Recursively indexes subdirectories.
-register	Registers indexes with WAIS Directory of Services.
-t	Specifies the type of document file.
-T	Sets the type of document.

Table 13.VI. waisindex Options

carried out again on the **pastry**, but this time the indexing is added to the **recipes** database. The **brunch** database still exists and references the **snacks** directory.

```
# waisindex -d recipes -export chocolate cheesecake
# waisindex -d recipes -export -a    pasta
# waisindex -d brunch  -export -r pastry
# waisindex -d recipes -export -a -r pastry
```

An important waisindex option is the -t option to indicate the type of documents being indexed. You can index images, mailbox files, and even HTML pages, as well as standard text documents. The different document types are listed in Table 13.VII.

```
# waisindex -d index-file -t type documents
```

`filename`	Text type that uses the file name as the headline.
`first_line`	Text type that uses the first line in the file as the headline.
`one_line`	Text type that indexes each sentence.
`text`	Text type that uses the path name as its headline.
`ftp`	Contains Ftp code for accessing other systems.
`GIF`	GIF image file.
`PICT`	PICT image file.
`TIFF`	TIFF image file.
`MPEG`	MPEG file.
`MIDI`	MIDI file.
`HTML`	HTML file (Web page).
`mail_or_rmail`	Mailbox file.
`mail_digest`	Email using the subject as the headline.
`netnews`	Usenet news.
`ps`	Postscript file.

Table 13.VII. Document File Types

For text documents you can refine your indexing by specifying the `one_line` type. If you index by line, WAIS will indicate the line in the document where a keyword is found. In the next example, the user indexes each line of the document **newsflash** and creates the index, called **iflash**.

```
# waisindex -d iflash -t one_line newsflash
```

The `waisindex` command can also associate different types of files with a specified document. For example, if you have image, video, or sound files that you want to associate with a specific text document, you can have `waisindex` link those files. When a user retrieves the text document, the associated image, video, or sound files will also be retrieved. While reading the text, the user can also display a picture or play a sound. Associated files must have the same prefix as the document to which they are linked. For example, if you have a document called `rocket.txt`, you can have a picture of a train in a file called `rocket.gif` and the sound of a rocket in `rocket.midi`. The -M option and a list of file types with the -export option are used to link a set of files to an index.

```
# waisindex -d train -M text, tiff, mpeg, midi -export
/user/waisdata/train/*
```

To make an index available on the Internet you have to register it with the Directory of Servers at cnidr.org or quake.think.com. To do this, use the waisindex command with the -export and -register options followed by the index files. The next example registers the **iflash** index.

```
# waisindex -export -register iflash
```

To integrate WAIS with your Web resources, you need to create WAIS indexes for your Web pages. This will allow users to use Web browsers to access your WAIS resources. It also allows WAIS to search Web HTML documents. The use of waisindex with the -T HTML option specifies that the type of document being indexed is an HTML document. In the next example, the user indexes Web pages located in the /home/httpd directory. The name the user gives to the index is **iweb** and the type is **.html**. The full contents of each Web page are indexed as specified by the -contents option. The -export option will include host name information for easy Internet access. Use the -r option to recursively index any subdirectories.

```
# waisindex -d iweb -T HTML -r -contents -export /home/
httpd/ *.html
```

When you index files, making an accessible database, waisindex will create a source file for the database. This source file is the means by which other users can reach your database. It provides the name of the directory where the database can be found. Some WAIS databases will charge for access, specifying a cost. The source file will show this information. The address of the maintainer is listed to whom you can send comments. The source ends with a short description of the WAIS database. If you specified the -export option when the database was created with waisindex, then fields will be added for Internet address information, one for the Internet address name and another for the IP address. With these entries users on other systems will be able to access the database.

You can edit any of the fields in a source file with a standard text editor. The source entry is enclosed in parentheses, with each field on a line of its own beginning with a colon and the field name. Notice that the description is enclosed in double quotes, with the first quote following the term `description` and the closing quote on a line by itself after the description text. The following example is a source for recipes in a file called **myrecipes.src**.

```
(:source
 :version 3
 :ip-address "192.31.181.1"
 :ip-name "turtle.trek.com"
 :tcp-port 210
 :database-name "/home/wais-index"
 :cost 0.00
 :cost-unit :free
 :maintainer "wais@turtle.trek.com"
 :description "
WAIS index of my favorite recipes database.
 "
)
```

Other users use the source file to access its WAIS database. The source file tells a user what host it is located on and what it is called. You can think of it as a URL for WAIS databases. The remote user must have the source file in order to access the database. You can either send the source file to a user who can then place it in their host's `wais-sources` directory, or you can register the source file with a WAIS server that maintains a Directory of Servers such as `quake.think.com` or `cnidr.org`. Your source will be placed there with other sources. By using a WAIS client such as `swais`, users can access this Directory of Servers and find your WAIS database listed there. Using that source entry, they can select and query your database.

Database-save either registered when you create them by including the `-register` option when indexing the files with `waisindex`, or later with the `waisindex` command, the `-d` option, and the index name followed by the `-register` option.

Gopher

Gopher is a menu-driven utility for accessing network resources, such as files, images, Telnet connections, and Ftp sites. It can work equally as well on the Internet or on a local intranet. Gopher's menu interface is simple and easy to use, reducing the access of Internet resources to the simple task of selecting an item on a menu. You can use it to obtain specific information quickly. Gopher combines the capabilities of Telnet, Ftp, and Archie, allowing you to easily browse through and select different available databases, files, and on-line information services. Gopher provides you with a series of menus listing different items, some of which may be other Gopher menus. You work your way down from one menu to another until you locate the item you want. Gopher provides easy access to information distributed throughout a network. Gopher was created at the University of Minnesota to provide a campus-wide distributed information service connecting different university departments. Each department maintained its own Gopher information server that anyone using a Gopher client could access. This distributed model was quickly adopted for use across the Internet to provide easy access to the numerous information services available on Internet. Many universities maintain Gopher servers that are used both locally within their campuses and can also be accessed across the Internet.

You need to use a Gopher client program to access Gopher servers. A Gopher client provides a menu interface through which you make your requests. The client then carries out your request whether it is to transfer a file or to log in to a remote site. Several Gopher clients are commonly available such as gopher, the cursor-based client that you can run from your command line, and xgopher, an X-Windows-based Gopher client with buttons and drop-down menus for moving through Gopher menus. If they are not already installed on your system, you can download Gopher clients from Unix Ftp sites. The University of Minnesota provides Gopher software at boombox.micro.umn.edu. To start the cursor-based Gopher client, gopher, enter the command gopher.

```
$ gopher
```

When you invoke the Gopher client, you can specify the Gopher server to access. The names of many gopher servers begin with the word "gopher." The following example accesses the gopher.tc.umn.edu Gopher server maintained by the University of Minnesota.

```
$ gopher gopher.tc.umn.edu
```

If you do not specify a Gopher server, the default server will be accessed. In this case merely enter the term gopher on the command line. You can determine the default server by pressing the O command once you have started your Gopher program. This will bring up an options menu from which you can configure your Gopher client. The options menu saves its information in a configuration file called **.gopherrc** that is kept in your home directory.

You can also Telnet to one of several available Gopher public clients such as `gopher.uiuc.edu`. You Telnet to the server's address and log in using the first name of the address, usually "gopher." It is strongly recommended that you use your own Unix system's Gopher client if possible.

Gopher Menus

Your Gopher client will display menus, each of which will consists of a list of menu items. A menu item can reference either a file, a directory, or an Internet resource. A gopher menu is designed to list file and directory names within its directory. On Gopher sites, each directory will usually have its own gopher menu displaying the files and items accessible from it. Accessing another directory will bring up another Gopher menu.

An entry can also be an Internet resource such as an Ftp site or a Telnet connection to a remote site. Each type of item is indicated by a qualifier placed at the end of each menu item entry. Items that are files end with a period qualifier. Directories and other gopher menus end with a slash. Database items end with the symbols `<?>`. The qualifier `<CSO>` indicates a CSO name server used to search for user addresses and information. The `<TEL>` qualifier indicates a Telnet connection. The `<Picture>`, `<Movie>`, and `<)` qualifiers reference images, video, and sound files.

When a Gopher menu is first displayed, an arrow is placed before the first menu item. The arrow indicates the menu item at which you are currently positioned. To select an item, you first have to move the arrow to it. You move the arrow from one menu item to another by using the arrow keys on your keyboard. The **up arrow** key moves the arrow up to the previous item, and the **down arrow** key moves the arrow to the next item.

Figure 14.1 shows a top Gopher menu. Most items have a / qualifier indicating that these are other menus. The tenth item ends in a `<?>` indicating that it is a database. The arrow is currently positioned at the first menu item. Once you have moved the arrow to the menu item you want, you can select and display the item by

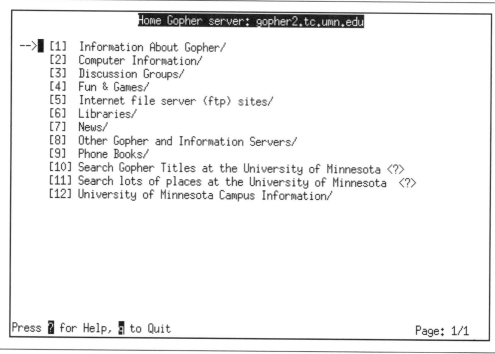

Figure 14.1. Gopher top menu.

pressing the **enter** key. Alternatively, you could also enter the number of the menu item followed by the **enter** key.

You can continue moving from one menu to another until you find the item you want. To move back to a previous menu, press the u key. You can quit Gopher at any point by pressing the q key. If a menu takes up more than one screen, you can move to the next screen by pressing the **spacebar**. The b command will move you back to the previous screen on that same menu (u moves back to the previous menu). The number of the screen you are currently on and the total number of screens in the menu are displayed in the lower right-hand corner. The commands for the gopher client are listed in Table 14.I. The X-Windows-based Gopher clients like xgopher work much the same way. Instead of positioning an arrow, you use your mouse to click on a menu item. You double-click to select an item. Buttons and drop-down menus move you back and forth through the Gopher menus.

The same commands apply to the display of Gopher text files. You can move through a text file with the **spacebar** key or b command. The u command will exit the text file and return to the menu from where you selected it. The percentage of the text displayed thus far is shown in the upper right-hand corner, and the file name is shown on the left. Figure 14.2 shows a display of a Gopher text file, a recipe for chocolate pancakes.

Instead of paging through screens one by one to find an item, you can use Gopher's menu item search capability. Gopher can perform a pattern search on the text of each menu item. This is the text making up the menu entry, not the contents of a file. You press the slash key, /, to perform a search. A box will open up in the middle of the screen, prompting you to enter a search pattern. After you enter the pattern, press the **enter** key to execute the search. The text of each menu item will be searched for the pattern. You can cancel the search at any time with **Ctrl-g**.

Gopher menus can also list services such as on-line library catalogs as menu items. Such a service is usually accessed through a Telnet

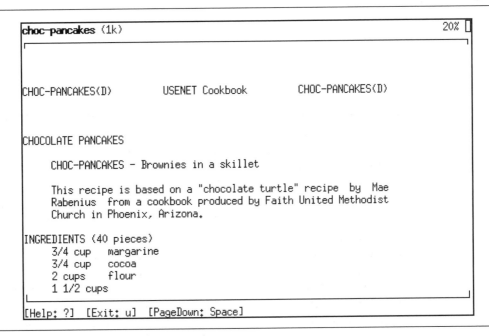

Figure 14.2. Display of a text file in Gopher.

connection. An menu item like this will have a Telnet qualifier at the end, <TEL>. When you choose the item, Gopher will Telnet to the service for you. For example, the Libraries menu will list possible on-line libraries that you can access. You can select Gopher menus until you find the one listing access to the Library of Congress. When you select the item to connect to the Library of Congress on-line catalog, the Gopher client then makes the Telnet connection, warning you that you are now leaving the Internet and Gopher and entering an on-line service.

Once logged into an on-line information service, you are operating according to whatever interface and commands that service provides. In the case of the Library of Congress, you are given a menu and asked to qualify your search. To end the session, you simply log off, ending the Telnet connection and returning to your Gopher menu.

Gopher Bookmarks

If you locate a Gopher menu you want to access again, you can mark and save it for direct access later. You do not have to again access all of the Gopher menus you went through to get to that particular gopher menu. You can go directly to it. A marked and saved Gopher menu is called a *bookmark*. A menu item for it is placed in a special Gopher menu called the Bookmark menu. The items in this menu constitute a bookmark list. You access the bookmark menu with the v command. When you display the Bookmark menu, you will find menu items for any gopher menus you bookmarked. Select the menu item you want to access it again.

You can add either a whole menu or just a menu item to your bookmark list. You use the A and a commands to make bookmark entries. Upon pressing one of these commands, a box opens in the middle of the screen with the menu entry for the item displayed, as shown in Figure 14.3. You can change the menu entry to something else if you wish. Press **enter** to add the item your bookmark list. The A command adds the whole menu you are currently displaying to your bookmark list, whereas the lowercase a command adds only one menu item. Having added the menu or menu item to your bookmark list, you can then access them in your bookmark menu. You can add as many items to your bookmark list as you wish. When you no longer want an item on your bookmark list, you can use the d command to remove it.

The A command is particularly useful in saving the results of searches. The results of a search will display a menu of Gopher items. For example, you can perform Ftp searches with Gopher using Archie. The results will be listed as another Gopher menu. Each menu item is a file located on an anonymous Ftp server. Selecting such a menu item will instruct Gopher to access the Ftp server and transfer the file to your system. The Gopher menu that results from such searches is only temporary. Should you want to save it for further use and reference, you need to place it in your bookmark menu. Simply press the A command when displaying this Gopher menu and it will be added to your bookmark menu. You can then use your bookmark menu to access this menu.

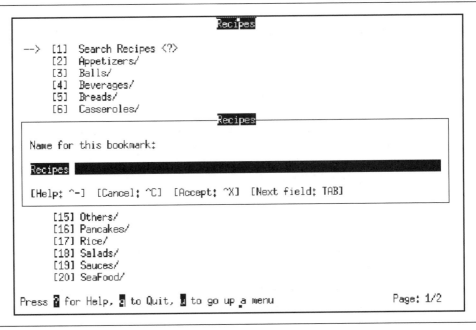

Figure 14.3. Adding a bookmark with the A command.

In Figure 14.4, the user has added "chocolate pancakes" to the bookmark menu. The user first locates the recipe for "choc-pancakes" by
moving through several menus, starting with the Fun & Games
menu. From the Fun & Games menu, the user moves to the Recipes
menu, which lists different kinds of recipes. The user chooses Pancakes and moves to the Pancakes menu, which lists the different
pancake recipes. On that menu, the user moves the arrow to the item
for choc-pancakes. Then the user presses the a key to add the choc-
pancakes menu item to his or her bookmark menu. A box opens in
the middle of the screen with a prompt for the name this menu item
will have in the bookmark menu. The name of the selected menu
item is already displayed as the default name, in this case, choc-
pancakes. The user then modifies it to read "chocolate pancakes."
This is the entry that will be displayed in the bookmark menu. To
find the recipe for chocolate pancakes, the user has only to press the
v key to bring up the bookmark menu and select the menu item
"chocolate pancakes." The user no longer needs to move through
the long series of menus from Fun & Games to Recipes to Pancakes
and finally to choc-pancakes.

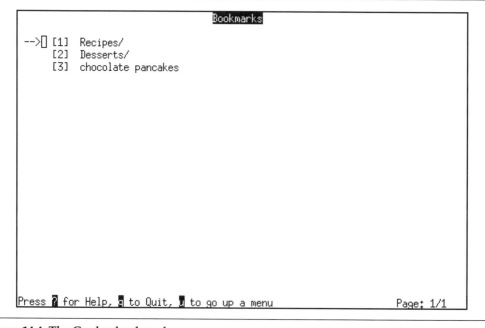

Figure 14.4. The Gopher bookmark menu.

Table 14.I. Gopher Commands

---

gopher [-sb] *options hostname*

OPTIONS

-p *string*	Specifies a specific selector string to send to the root-level server on startup.
-t *string*	Sets the title of the initial screen for the Gopher client.

GOPHER MENU ITEM QUALIFIERS

.	File.
/	Menu (directory).
<CSO>	CSO name server.
<TEL>	Telnet connection.
<?>	Database with keyword search.
<CSO>	CSO name server.
<Picture>	Image file, such as **gif** or **jpeg**.
<Movie>	Video, such as **mov** or **avi**.
<HTML>	Web page (HyperText document).
<Bin>	Binary file.
<PC Bin>	DOS binary file.
<HQX>	Macintosh binhex file.
<MIME>	Multi-purpose Internet Mail Extensions file.
<)	Sound file.

MOVING TO AND SELECTING MENU ITEMS

k	**up-arrow**	Move up to previous menu item.
j	**down-arrow**	Move down to next menu item.
num		Move to *num* item in menu.
l	**right-arrow enter**	Select the current menu item.

SEARCHING A MENU FOR AN ITEM

/*pattern*	Search menu items for pattern and move to first item with that pattern.
n	Repeat previous search of menu items.

OPERATIONS PERFORMED ON MENU ITEMS

=	Display information about a menu item.
s	Save the current item to a file.
S	Save the current list of items to a file.

(continued)

Table 14.I. Gopher Commands (*continued*)

m		Mail the current item to a user.
p		Print the current item.

MOVING THROUGH MENU SCREENS

>	+	**spacebar**	Move to next menu screen.
<	–	b	Move back to previous menu screen.

RETURN TO PREVIOUS MENUS

u	**left-arrow**	Move back to previous menu.
m		Return to top main menu.

BOOKMARK COMMANDS

a	Add selected item to bookmark list.
A	Add current menu to bookmark list.
d	Remove a bookmark from the bookmark list.
v	Display bookmark list.

OPTIONS, QUIT, AND HELP COMMANDS

q	Quit Gopher.
Q	Quit Gopher without prompt.
?	Help.
O	Display and change options for Gopher.

ENVIRONMENT VARIABLES

PAGER	The client will use that to display files to the user.
GOPHER_HTML	The program to display Web pages (HTML).
GOPHER_MAIL	The program to send mail with (must understand -s option).
GOPHER_PLAY	The program to play sound from a pipe.
GOPHER_TELNET	The program to contact Telnet services with.
GOPHER_PRINTER	The program to print from a pipe.

Veronica

Different Gopher sites may hold items on the same topic. To access them, you could access each individual site, locating items after paging through the menus at these sites. In effect, you are searching each Gopher site for items on the same topic. The Veronica utility is a search engine designed to locate such items for you. Veronica displays the results in the form of a Gopher menu. Veronica can search Gopher menus at different sites for menu items using keywords provided by the user. Veronica will then generate a gopher menu consisting of all the menu items it has found. In effect, with Veronica, you can create temporary Gopher menus on specialized topics. You can then select the menu item you want just as you would on any standard Gopher menu.

You access Veronica through the Veronica Gopher menu located on a Gopher site. The Veronica menu lists different Veronica servers that you can use to search Gopher menus. There is a <?> qualifier at the end of each server menu item, indicating a database to be queried by keywords. Select a server and press **enter**. A box will open in the middle of the screen, prompting you to enter keywords for the search. Upon pressing **enter**, Veronica performs the search. The result is a customized Gopher menu consisting of all the menu items Veronica was able to locate. You can then move to the menu item you want and select it. If you find out where a menu item comes from, move to the menu item and press = to display information about it. Though the menus generated by Veronica are temporary, you can save the menu by adding it as an item to your bookmark list using the A command. You can also use the a command to save just particular items in the search results.

Gopher Configuration: .gopherrc

Each user has his or her own **.gopherrc** file located in a home directory that holds personalized configuration information for the use of Gopher clients. In this way a gopher client can be tailored to a particular user's needs. In the gopher client, you can use the O command to enter configuration settings which are then saved to this file. You can also enter settings directly by editing the **.gopherrc** file with a standard editor.

The **.gopherrc** file has three possible entries: map, SearchBolding, and Bookmarks. Comments begins with a pound sign ("#") at the

beginning of a line. The `map` entry will map the content type to
commands for displaying or printing a document. A map entry
tells Gopher what application to use to display or print certain
kinds of files. For example, an image file would be mapped to an
application that can display images such as xv. A `%s` code represents a temporary copy of the file that is passed to the application.
The map entry has three items, separated by a commas: the content-
type such as text/plain or image/gif, a display command, and a
print command.

`map:` *content-type, display-command, print-command*

If the command needs to receive data from the standard input, you
can precede it with a pipe. For example, the `lp` print command
could be entered as `| lp`. If a file such as a text file can be displayed
using the Gopher client's display pager, specify `builtin` as the
display command to use the pager. The first example maps **jpeg**
image files to the xv command for display and has no print command. The second command maps text files to the Gopher pager
for display and to the `lp` command for printing.

```
map:image/jpeg,xv %s,
map: text/plain,builtin,lp %s
```

The `SearchBolding` entry is a feature that you can turn on or off.
It has two possible values, yes and no. If yes, then search words are
displayed in bold letters.

`SearchBolding:` *yes/no*

The `Bookmarks` entry lists link information for each of your bookmark entries. It uses a link format as described in the section on
Gopher servers. The keyword `Bookmarks:` is listed once, followed by different bookmark entries. An bookmark link entry begins with a # and is followed by fields for the type of bookmark
item, name of the bookmark, its host, and its location (path).

```
Bookmarks:
#
Type=num
Name=bookmark-name
Host=gopher-site
```

```
Port=num
Path=path
#
Other-bookmark-entries
```

Types of Gopher files are listed in Table 14.II. The Name is the entry for the item as it appears on the bookmark menu. The Host is the site where the item is located. The Port is the port used to access it. The Path is where it is located on that site. The following example is the bookmark entry for the "chocolate pancakes" bookmark. The 0 type indicates that this is a data file, whereas a 1 indicates a Gopher directory (menu).

```
#
Type=0+
Name=chocolate pancakes
Path=0/fun/Recipes/Pancakes/choc-pancakes
Host=spinaltap.micro.umn.edu
Port=70
```

0	Text file.
1	Gopher directory.
2	CSO phone book server.
3	Error.
4	Binhex Macintosh file, HQX.
5	Binary DOS file.
6	Unix uuencoded file.
7	Full-text index (Gopher menu file).
8	Telnet session, includes the remote host's address.
9	Binary file.
g	GIF image file.
h	HTML file.
I	Graphic image file (other than GIF).
M	MIME multipart mixed message.
P	Adobe PDF file.
s	Sound file.
T	TN3270 Telnet session.

Table 14.II. Gopher File Types

An example of the **.gopherrc** file follows.

.gopherrc

```
RCversion: 1.1
map: Text,builtin,lpr %s
map: text/plain,builtin,lpr %s
map: Image,xv %s,lpr %s
map: Terminal/telnet,telnet %s,
map: text/html,lynx -force_html %s,lynx -
  force_html -dump %s | lpr
map: text/x-troff,nroff %s|more -d,ptroff %s
map: image/gif,xv %s,
map: image/jpeg,xv %s,
map: video/mpeg,,

SearchBolding: yes
bookmarks:
#
Type=1+
Name=Recipes
Path=1/fun/Recipes
Host=spinaltap.micro.umn.edu
Port=70
#
Type=1+
Name=Desserts
Path=1/fun/Recipes/Desserts
Host=spinaltap.micro.umn.edu
Port=70
#
Type=0+
Name=chocolate pancakes
Path=0/fun/Recipes/Pancakes/choc-pancakes
Host=spinaltap.micro.umn.edu
Port=70
```

There is also a global **.gopherrc** file accessible to the system administrator that is the default file used for all users. The **remotegopher.rc** file, similar to **.gopherrc**, is used by the Gopher client when it is invoked with the -r option.

Gopher Server

A Gopher site has its resources organized with Gopher menus. Unlike Ftp, with Gopher you can present users with a menu of items from which they can choose. One menu can lead to another menu or to another Gopher site. In this respect, Gopher is like the Web, allowing you to move from one site to another in search of resources, but it is like Ftp in that only the resources are listed. There is no text or graphics to give you explanations.

Gopher uses a TCP/IP protocol called the Gopher protocol. It provides for the very fast transmission of Gopher menu files. Gopher information is held in these files, which contain lists of items accessible at certain sites. Each item is organized into fields specifying the information about the item and where it can be found.

Gopher was developed at the University of Minnesota where it is currently supported, with new versions continually being developed. You can obtain a copy of the Gopher server software package from the University of Minnesota Gopher ftp site at `boombox.micro.umn.edu` and from most other Unix Ftp sites. The software package includes Gopher clients as well as the server. Another Gopher sever is also available called GN Gopher. It is freely available at Unix Ftp sites. The GN Gopher server has a slightly different implementation than the University of Minnesota Gopher server. The examples in this chapter use the University of Minnesota Gopher server.

Installation of a Gopher server is a task that is carried out by a system's administrator. Once the Gopher server is installed, then Gopher directories and files to be used for the Gopher site can be created. These can be placed in Gopher directories by the system administrator or by users given permission to do so by the administrator.

As a system administrator, you can download Gopher server software and install it on your system. You can download the University of Minnesota Gopher server from `boombox.micro.umn.edu`. Once you download the server software package, you can decompress it and then extract it with the **tar** command. This creates a directory beginning with the term **gopher** with the version number attached. Within this directory are different subdirectories for documentation and the applications. The **gopherd** directory holds your source code for the Gopher server, and the **gopher** directory holds the source code for your Gopher client. The **doc** directory has the documentation, including your man documents.

The University of Minnesota Gopher has a configure utility that automatically detects how your system is configured and creates Makefiles tailored to your specific system. Any system-specific information has to be explicitly set in configuration files. Before you create your Gopher server, you have to configure it using entries in the **gopherd.conf** and **gopherdlocal.conf** files. **gopherd.conf** is designed to configure system-specific features and **gopherdlocal.conf** customizes your Gopher sever such as controlling access by specified remote systems.

After making your configuration entries, enter the configure command to create a customized Makefile. Then enter the `make` command to create the Gopher applications. Use the `make install` command to install them on your system. You will also need to create a special user account for Gopher and a Gopher data directory where you will place your Gopher files. The data directory for your Gopher files should be the same as the home directory for the Gopher user account. After you create the directory, change its ownership to that of the Gopher user with the `chown` command. When you configure your Gopher server software, be sure to specify your Gopher data directory.

Gopher Directories

A Gopher menu is generated using special files contained within a **gopher** directory. Gopher menus are designed to operate by directory, listing the different files available within a directory or referencing another directory. Special Gopher menu configuration files within each directory provide information about the different data files available and how to access them. The University of Minnesota

Gopher server uses **.cap** directories and link files to organize Gopher menus. A GN Gopher server uses **menu** and **.cache** files.

By default any files and subdirectories in a Gopher directory are automatically displayed in a Gopher menu in alphabetical order. Data files are given a type 0, and directories a type 1. The name used for each menu item is the name of the file or directory. You can override this listing by using **.cap** files. Usually a file is described in a Gopher menu using a descriptive sentence. By selecting that menu item, the file associated with that sentence is selected. The association between this descriptive sentence and the Gopher data file is carried out either by special files in a **.cap** directory or by entries in a link file.

Each directory of Gopher data files has its own **.cap** directory, which holds files of the same name as those in the Gopher data directory. If you have a Gopher data file called **bestcookies**, there will be a file in the **.cap** directory also called **bestcookies**. A file in the **.cap** directory contains three entries, beginning with the terms Name, Type, and Numb, respectively. Name is assigned the descriptive sentence used for the menu item that references the Gopher data file. The Type entry specifies the type of gopher resource; 1 is a directory and 0 is a text file. The Numb entry is assigned the number of your Gopher entry in the Gopher menu, for example, Numb=3 indicates that this is the third item in the Gopher menu.

.cap/bestcookies

```
Name= 1. The best cookies on the planet.
Type=0
Numb=1
```

When displayed on the Gopher menu this entry will appear as the first entry. Selecting it will select the **cookies.1** data file.

```
     1. The best cookies on the planet.
```

Though **.cap** files can be used to reference data files in your directory, they do not reference files in other directories or at other Gopher sites. For this you use a link entry in a link file. There is one link file in a directory that has several link entries to different Gopher resources. A link file is any file beginning with a period. A common name for a link file is **.links**.

A **.links** file has five entries instead of three: `Name`, `Type`, `Port`, `Path`, and `Host`. You can also add an entry for the menu order, `Numb`. The `Name` entry is the descriptive sentence used in the menu item. `Port` is the port used to connect to a remote system and is usually set to 70. `Type` is the type of resource that the menu item references. A resource could be a file, but it can also be a Telnet connection, Ftp site, or a graphics file. The code for each type of resource is listed in Table 14.II. `Path` holds the path name for the resource that the menu item references. The path name here is the path starting from the Gopher data directory. The Gopher data directory is the directory on your system where your Gopher site is located, the root directory for your Gopher files and subdirectories. The directory **/home/gopher-data/deserts** would have a path name of **/deserts**, where **/home/gopher-data** is the Gopher data directory. `Host` holds the host name where the resource is to be found. For your own system this will be your own host name. If the resource is located on another system, it will have that system's host name. A + sign for the `Port` and `Host` entries will indicate the current port and host name. For files and directories on your own system, it is best to leave out the `Port` and `Host` entries.

.links

```
Name=The best cookies on the planet
Type=1
Port=70
Path=./cookies
Host=myfood.recipes.com
```

You may also use links to set up ftp or WAIS connections to other systems to access files or information from them. In this case the service you are using and its arguments are specified in the `Path` entry. Both `Host` and `Port` have a + entry. The format for an Ftp link is shown here.

```
Name=ftp-file-or-directory
Type=1
Path=ftp:hostname/path/
Host=+
Port=+
```

For example, to set up an Ftp link to access the file **spelling** on **chris.recipes.com**, you would set the path as shown in the following example. The current port and host name are indicated by + for their entries.

```
Name=Spelling Cookies
Type=0
Port=+
Path=ftp:chris.recipes.com/pub/cookies/spelling
Host=+
```

For a WAIS link you can access WAIS resources on your own system or on a remote system. For your own system you use `waisrc:` followed by the path to the WAIS database. For a remote system you include the hostname after `waisrc:`, for example, **waisrc: chris.recipes.com/usr/wais/data**.

You can also set up a link to execute shell scripts, rather than just accessing a resource. In this case the `Path` variable is set to `exec:` followed by the script arguments and name. The arguments are enclosed in double quotes, and if there are none you just use an empty set of quotes. The argument and script are separated by a colon.

```
Path=exec:"arguments":script
```

Instead of maintaining separate **.cap** files in each directory along with a separate link file, you can use an extended link file to hold both the local file entries and the link entries. A common name for a link file is **.names**. The **.names** file would list each `Name` and `Numb` entry along with a `Path` entry to specify the location of the file. The **.names** file also has an `Abstract` entry that allows you to enter a brief description of the file's contents. In the **.names** file shown next the first entry references a local file in the directory whereas the second entry references a remote gopher site.

.names

```
Path=./cookies
Name=The best cookies on the planet (earth)
Numb=1
Abstract=A discussion of the best chocolate chip cookies
  ever created.
Name=Chocolate Chip
Type=1
Port=70
Path=1/cookieplace
Host=food.desert.com
```

Gopher Indexes

With the `gopherindex` command you can create full-text indexes of your Gopher data documents. Though `gopherindex` is provided as part of the University of Minnesota Gopher software package, it uses **waisindex** to perform its indexing, so you must have WAIS installed to use it. It takes as its arguments several possible options and a Gopher data directory. All the documents in the data directory will be indexed. The `-N` option specifies a description of the index file to be used in a Gopher menu. The following example indexes all the files in **/home/gopher-data/hockey.**

```
gopherindex -v -N "Search Hockey Games" /home/
  gopher-data/hockey
```

Instead of using `gopherindex` you can use `waisindex` directly and then create a link for the index file.

```
waisindex -r /home/gopher-data/hockey
```

You create the link entry for the index file in that directory's link or menu file. Type 7 is a WAIS index type of document.

```
Type=7
Name=Hockey Index
Host=+
Port=+
Path=7/.index/index
```

A Gopher Example

The following example shows the Gopher files used to set up a simple Gopher site with files that hold recipes. The files for each recipe are placed in their own directories. You begin with a Gopher menu in the Gopher data directory. The items in this menu are defined in the **.names** file. Most of the menu items are references to other Gopher directories. One is a file with general introductory information about the Gopher site called **welcome**. In the main Gopher directory there is only this **welcome** file and the **.names** file. The next two items link to local Gopher directories, **deserts** and **pastas**. The last item links to another Gopher site located at world.food.com. Figure 14.5 shows the display of the **.names** file.

.names

```
Path=./welcome
Name=About My Recipe Site
Numb=1
Type=0
Abstract=Critical Recipe Maintenance.

Name=Desert Recipes
Numb=2
Type=1
Port=70
Path=./deserts
Host=turtle.trek.com

Name=Magnificent Pasta
Numb=3
Type=1
Port=70
Path=./pastas
Host=turtle.trek.com

Name=French Pastries
Numb=4
Type=1
Port=70
Path=/home/pastries/France/
Host=world.food.com
```

Figure 14.5. Gopher menu using `.names` **file.**

The Deserts menu item references the **deserts** subdirectory, where the files with desert recipes are located. The **deserts** directory lists two data files, a link file, and a **.cap** directory. In the **.cap** directory there are two files, each having the name of a data file in the **deserts** directory. For the **fudge** and **cheesecake** files in the **deserts** directory, there is also a **fudge** and **cheesecake** file in the .cap directory. These **.cap** directory files are shown here.

fudge

```
Name=Sour Cream Walnut Fudge
Numb=1
Type=0
```

cheesecake

```
Name=New York Strawberry Cheesecake
Numb=2
Type=0
```

In the **deserts** directory, the **.links** file lists an entry to access a file on a remote system. Figure 14.6 shows the display of the Gopher menu using the **fudge, cheesecake**, and **.links** file.

.links

```
Name=The Supreme Chocolate Mousse Cake
Numb=3
Type=0
Port=+
Path=ftp:ftp.cakes.org/pub/cakes/mousse/supreme.tx
t
```

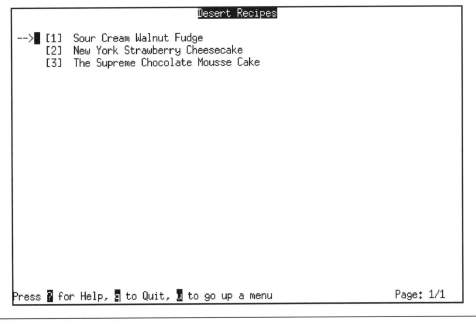

Figure 14.6. Gopher menu using `.cap` files.

Figure 14.7 illustrates the layout of the different files in this example, with their respective directories.

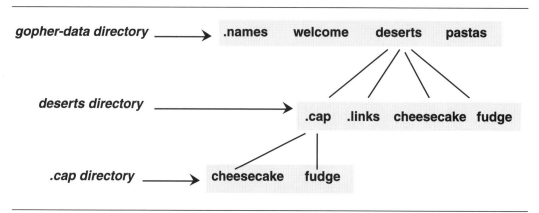

Figure 14.7. Directory structure of Gopher example.

World Wide Web: WWW

The World Wide Web is a network of Internet sites that use a Hyper-Text interface for easily accessing Internet resources throughout the world. The World Wide Web originated in Europe at CERN Research Laboratories (the European Particle Physics Laboratory in Switzerland). It is often referred to as WWW or simply as the Web. A HyperText document can display images, forms, and formatted text on screens known as Web pages. A Web page can contain the Internet addresses of other Internet resources with which they can be accessed. Such embedded addresses are known as links. Using Web pages with links you can access Internet resources such as Ftp or Gopher sites, Telnet connections, or other Web pages. In this respect, Web pages can form an interlocking Web of connections, where accessing one can lead to another, and that one to yet another, and so on. Upon retrieving a Web page, you can use it to retrieve any related items. For example, you could retrieve an article on the New York subways and then use it to retrieve a map of the subways or a picture of a station.

Sites on the World Wide Web are accessed using the HyperText Transfer Protocol (HTTP). The HyperText Transfer Protocol is designed to transfer files that have been formatted for display using HyperText Markup Language (HTML). The HyperText Markup Language consists of tags that, when placed within a file, indicate how its different components are displayed. You can use HTML to display a document with lists, images, and even forms, as well as standard Word-processing features like paragraphs and headings. All Web pages are HTML documents.

Sites on the Internet that support HTTP and provide accessible Web pages are known as Web sites. Web sites usually have an Internet address that begins with www, as in www.netscape.com, the Web site for Netscape. Once connected to a Web site, you can use links to move from one Web page to another. Web sites are not limited to the Internet. Any network that uses TCP/IP can have Web sites. Local networks knows as intranets can maintain their own Web sites accessible only to those with access to that network.

Client programs called Web browsers can access these sites, transfer the Web pages, and then display them on your own system. A Web browser locates a particular Web page using a universal resource locator (URL). URLs function as Web page addresses, allowing you to easily locate and display Web pages on any Web site throughout the Internet. Together, the HyperText Transfer Protocol, the HyperText Markup Language, and universal resource locators support a network of Web sites on the Internet accessible to anyone with a Web browser.

The client program used to access Web sites and display Web pages is called a browser. Browsers are also capable of performing other Internet operations such as downloading files from Ftp sites or accessing Gopher menus. Browsers are available for use on Unix, PCs, and Macs, and many have versions that operate on all such systems. Mosaic and Netscape are two of the most widely used browsers on Unix systems. X-Windows-based browsers like Netscape and Mosaic provide full picture, sound, and video display capabilities. A cursor-based browser such as Lynx, also available for Unix systems, displays only text.

URL Addresses

You access a Web resource using a URL. A URL is designed to easily locate and transfer a resource on the Web. As mentioned, URL combines a transfer protocol with a network address of a particular network site, and a path name indicating where that resource is located on that site. The network address can be either an IP address or a fully qualified domain name that includes the system's host name and its network domain name. The transfer protocol can be any one of several TCP/IP protocols used to connect and transfer information across a TCP/IP network. You can use an Ftp, Web, Gopher, and mail protocols, among others. Table 15.I lists these protocols. In most cases, the transfer protocol is separated from the network address by a colon followed by two forward slashes, ://. The path name starting after the network address begins with a forward slash.

```
transfer-protocol://network-address/path-name
```

The transfer protocol used for Web pages is http, which stands for HyperText Transfer Protocol. gopher is used for the Gopher protocol, ftp for the File Transfer Protocol, and telnet for the Telnet Protocol. The protocol determines what kind of connection takes place. ftp will initiate an Ftp session, usually connecting with an anonymous login. Certain protocols operate on local resources on your own system. The file protocol is used to access a text file on your own system. There is no intervening network address, just the protocol file followed by a colon and the path name on your local system to that file.

The network address is the address of the computer on which a particular site is located. Depending on the transfer protocol used, your browser will look for a Web, Gopher, or Ftp site to access on that computer. You can think of this as the address of the site. The network address of a site usually begins with a term indicating the type of transfer protocol it supports. A Web site will usually have a network address that begins with www. An Ftp site will begin with `ftp`, and a gopher site with `gopher`. In the next examples, the URL locates a Web page called `index.html` on the `www.netscape.com` Web site, an Ftp site at `ftp.netscape.com`, and a gopher site at `gopher.tc.umn.edu`.

```
http://www.netscape.com/index.html
ftp://ftp.netscape.com
gopher://gopher.tc.umn.edu
```

In the case of a Web site, if you do not specify a particular Web page by name, you will automatically access the Web site's home page. This means that to access a Web site you just have to enter its network address. The default name for a Web site's home page is `index.html`, located in the site's main directory. A Web site can override the default and specify a particular file as the home page. In the next example, the user brings up the Sun Corporation home page.

```
http://www.sun.com
```

The path name specifies the directory where the resource can be found on the host system, as well as the name of the resource's file. For example, `/unixworld/index.html` references an HTML document called `index.html` located in the `/unixworld` directory. As you move to other Web pages on a site you may move more deeply into the directory tree. The same is true for Ftp and Gopher sites. You can use the path name to specify a particular directory and file on a Ftp site. In the first of the following examples, the user displays the `index.html` document in the directory `/unixworld/index.html`. In the second, the user transfers the file **README** file located in the `/pub/communicator/4.05` directory.

```
http://www.networkcomputing.com/unixworld/index.html
ftp://ftp.netscape.com/pub/communicator/4.05/README
```

If no particular file is specified, then the default is displayed. For Web sites, the default is a Web page named `index.html` located in that directory. If there is no `index.html` file, then the directory listing is displayed. You can click on an entry to display a file or move to another directory. The first entry will be a special entry for the parent directory. For Ftp and Gopher sites, a directory listing will be displayed if just the directory is specified. In the first example, the `index.html` Web page in the `/unixworld` directory is displayed. In the second example, your browser would display the directory listing for the `/pub` directory.

```
http://www.networkcomputing.com/unixworld/
ftp://ftp.netscape.com/pub
```

You can use a path name with the `file` transfer protocol to access local files, directories, and Web pages on your system. Text files will be displayed as bare text. Web pages will be displayed by the browser in a Web page format, just as it would be on a Web site. If you specify a directory, that directory's listing will be displayed. If the directory contains an `index.html` file, then that file will be displayed as a Web page. Assuming there is an `index.html` file in the `desserts` directory, you need only specify the `desserts` path name to display `index.html` as a Web page.

```
file:./desserts
```

In the case of Web site access, a resource file's extension indicates the type of action to be taken on it. A picture will have a `.gif` or `.jpeg` extension and will be converted for display. A sound file will have a `.au` or `.wav` extension and will be played (see Table 15.II on page 385). The following URL references a jpeg file. Instead of displaying a Web page, your Browser will invoke a graphics viewer to display the picture. Table 15.II provides a list of the different file extensions.

```
http://www.mygames.com/soccer/trophy.jpeg
```

Web browsers are designed to support any one of the transfer protocols. You can enter a URL on your browser and access Web pages, Ftp sites, Gopher menus, and even local files. To access a Web site, you would enter the Web site protocol, `http://`, followed by the network address of the Web site. For a particular Web page you would add the path name for that page. For Web sites on the Internet, you would use the site's Internet address. Once you have entered the URL, on most browsers you simply press **enter**. In the case of a Web site protocol, the browser will connect you to the Web site and display its home page or the Web page you specified. To display a file or Web page located on your own system, use the file protocol followed by a colon, `file:`, and then the path name of the Web page or file you want to display. The `file:` protocol is useful for displaying copies of Web pages you have downloaded to your own system.

With a Web browser you can easily access Ftp and Gopher sites. In most cases, using a Web browser to access an Ftp site is easier than using an Ftp utility like the `ftp` program discussed in Chapter 12. Directories and files are automatically listed, and selecting a file or directory is just a matter of clicking on its name. To access the Ftp site you enter the Ftp transfer protocol, `ftp://`, followed by its network address and the path name for the directory you want if you know it. Ftp sites on the Internet often have network addresses that begin with the name `ftp`, as in `ftp.netscape.com`. The contents of a directory will be displayed, listing files and subdirectories. To move to another directory, click on its name. There will be an entry listed at the top as **..**, which represents the parent directory. You can move down the file structure from one subdirectory to another and move back up one directory at a time by selecting **...** To leave the ftp site just return to your home page or the Web page with the link you used to access the site.

To download a file, you either shift-click ordouble-click on the file name. In the case of the Netscape Navigator browser you hold the **shift** key down while you click on the file name. This will display a box in with the name of the file to be downloaded. You can specify the local directory you want the file downloaded to and then click the OK button to begin downloading. Figure 15.1 shows the Netscape browser being used to download a file.

To use your browser to access a Gopher site, enter `gopher://` followed by the network address of the Gopher site. Your Web browser will display the main Gopher menu for that site. You can then move from one Gopher menu to the next. Most browsers can also connect to your news server to access specified newsgroups or articles. To access your local news server, use the `news` transfer protocol. To access a remote news server, you use the `nntp://` transfer protocol. Some browsers, such as Netscape, have added a newsreader that allows them to access any remote news servers.

`http://`	HyperText Transfer Protocol for Web site access; uses HyperText Transfer and World Wide Web protocols, HTTP and WWW.
`gopher://`	Access Gopher site. Uses Gopher protocol.
`ftp://`	File Transfer Protocol for anonymous Ftp connections; uses File Transfer Protocol, FTP.
`telnet://`	Makes a Telnet connection; uses Telnet protocol, TELNET.
`mailto:`	Send email; uses Simple Mail Transfer Protocol, SMTP.
`wais://`	Access WAIS site.
`nntp://`	Read Usenet news using Net News Transfer Protocol, NNTP.
`news:`	Read Usenet news.
`file:`	Local file.

Table 15.I. URL Protocols

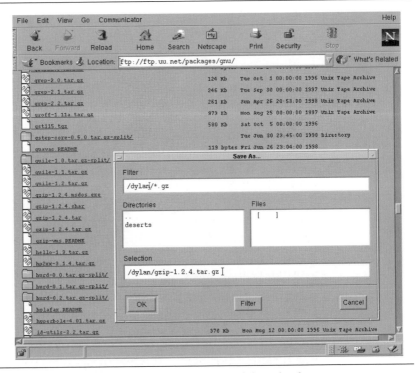

Figure 15.1. Web browser access to Ftp site and download.

Links displayed on a Web page may use any one of these transfer protocols to access resources on the same site or on other sites. A link is simply a URL already entered into the HTML code that makes up a Web page. When you activate a link, usually by clicking on it, you are, in effect, entering a new URL in your browser. Your browser then uses that URL to locate and access the specified resource. A link for a URL with an `ftp` protocol will connect you to an Ftp site and download a particular file for you. A link with a Telnet protocol can connect to a Telnet site and start up a Telnet session, letting you log in to a remote system. A link with a Gopher protocol will connect to a Gopher site and display a Gopher menu for you to work through. Most links on a Web page are for other Web pages. With the HyperText protocol, `http://`, a link can connect you to another Web site and display a Web page on it.

Web Pages

A Web page is a document formatted using the HyperText Markup Language, HTML. Any Web browser can display an HTML document, using HTML commands to format and display it. Using the HyperText Markup Language, Web pages can format text into components such as paragraphs and headings. Graphics of various sizes may be placed anywhere in the page. You can think of a Web page as a word processing document that can display both text and graphics. Within the Web page, links can be embedded that call up other network resources such as an image or an Ftp connection. Such links are also known as *anchors*. Using anchors, a Web page can function as an interface for performing other network operations such as downloading files with Ftp or accessing a Gopher menu.

Throughout the page there will usually be anchor points that you can use to display images, text files, other Web pages, or just another place on the same page. An anchor could be a link that connects you to another Web site, Ftp site, or Telnet session. These anchor points are specially highlighted text or images that usually appear in a different color from the rest of the text. Whereas ordinary text may be black, text used for anchor points may be green, blue, or

| `.html` | Web page document formatted using HTML, the HyperText Markup Language. |

GRAPHICS FILES

| `.gif` | Graphics, using gif compression. |
| `.jpeg` | Graphics, using jpeg compression. |

SOUND FILES

`.au`	Sun (Unix) sound file.
`.wav`	Microsoft Windows sound file.
`.aiff`	Macintosh sound file.

VIDEO FILES

`.QT`	Quicktime video file, multiplatform.
`.mpeg`	Video file.
`.avi`	Microsoft Windows video file.

Table 15.II. Web Resource File Types

red. You select a particular anchor point by moving your mouse pointer to that text or image and then clicking on it. The network resource associated with that anchor point will then be accessed, usually displayed as another Web page on your browser. If the resource is on another Web site, that site will be accessed. If it is another Web page, that Web page will be displayed. Anchors that you have used recently will be displayed in a different color from one that has not been accessed.

You can access other Web pages either by manually entering their URLs or by clicking on links displayed for them on a particular Web page. Through these links you can move from one page to another. As you move from Web page to Web page, using the anchor points or buttons, your Browser will display the URL for the current page. Your browser keeps a list of the different Web pages you have accessed in a given session. Most browsers have buttons that allow you to move back and forth through this list. You can move to the Web page you displayed before the current one, and then move back further to the one before that. You can move forward again to the next page and so on.

On some Web sites, Web pages are meant to be connected in a particular order. These pages usually have buttons displayed within them at the bottom of the page that reference the next and previous pages in the sequence. They may be labeled Next and Previous or may simply display right and left arrow images. The buttons operate as links to the next and previous pages. Clicking on the Next button will display the next Web page in the sequence. Often, there is also a Home button that will return you to the first page for that sequence (not your home page).

To get to a particular page you may have moved through a series of pages, using links in each to finally reach the Web page you want. Keep in mind though, that to access any particular Web page, all you need is its URL address. If you want to access a particular page again, you can enter its URL address and move directly to it, without moving through the intervening pages as you did the first time. Most Web browsers can keep a bookmark list—a list of favorite Web pages you want to access directly. When you are displaying a Web page you want to access later, just instruct your Browser to place it on the bookmark list. The Web page will usually be listed in this list by its title, not its URL. To access that Web page later, select the entry in the bookmark list.

Web Browsers

HyperText databases are designed to access any kind of data, whether it is text, graphics, sound, or even video. Whether you can actually access such data depends to a large extent on the type of browser you use. Several popular browsers are available for Unix such as the Netscape Communicator, Mosaic, and Lynx. Netscape and Mosaic are X-Windows-based Web browsers capable of displaying graphics, video, and sound as well as operating as newsreaders and mailers. Lynx is a command-line-based browser with no graphics capabilities. But in every other respect it is a fully functional Web browser. You can download current versions for each of these browsers from easily accessible Internet sites. All are available free of charge.

These browsers can access different network resources using any one of the URL transfer protocols. There is an input box displayed where you can enter the URL. To access a Web site, enter `http://` followed by the network address of the Web site, and then press **enter**. The browser will connect you to that Web site and display its home page or the page you specified. For an Ftp site you use `ftp://` and the Ftp site's network address.

Netscape Communicator

One of the more popular Web browsers is Netscape Navigator. Netscape Navigator is currently part a larger software application called Netscape Communicator, which includes a newsreader, mailer, address book, and Web page composer. Versions of Netscape operate on different graphical user interfaces such as X-Windows, Microsoft Windows, and the Macintosh. Using X-Windows on a Unix system, the Netscape browser can display graphics, sound, video, and Java-based programs. You can obtain more information about Netscape from its Web site: `www.netscape.com`.

Netscape Communicator is provided free of charge and you can download a current fully functional copy of the application from any Netscape Ftp site or mirror site. The Netscape Ftp site addresses are `ftp2.netscape.com` through `ftp8.netscape.com`. Once you have downloaded the Netscape file, you place it in the directory you want it installed on, such as `/usr/local`. The downloaded file will be a compressed archive that you decompress and then extract with the `tar` command.

Netscape Communicator is an X-Windows application that you operated from an X-Windows interface such as Open-Look or Motif. Find the Netscape icon and double-click on it. Netscape Communicator displays an area at the top of the screen for entering a URL address and a series of buttons for various Web page operations (see Figure 15.2). Drop-down menus at the top provide access to Netscape features. To access a Web site, you enter its address in the URL area labeled "`Location:`" and press **enter**.

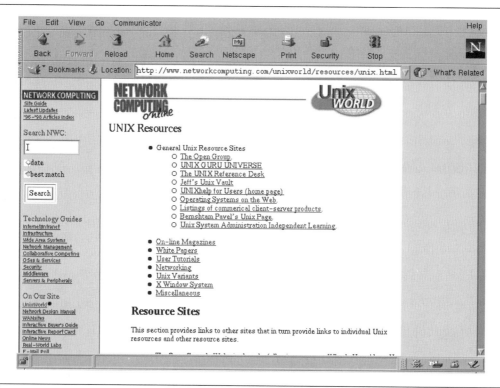

Figure 15.2. Netscape Navigator Web browser.

The icon bar across the top of the browser holds buttons for moving from one page to another and performing other operations. The buttons labeled Back and Forward with back and forward arrow images move you back and forth through the list of Web pages you have already accessed in a given session. The button labeled House with the image of a house will display your home page, in effect exiting from a Web site you are accessing and returning you to your own system. There is also a button labeled Stop with the image of a stop sign that you can use to cancel any Web page requests. It becomes active when you are linking to and displaying a new Web page. Should a Web page take too long to display, you may want to click on the Stop button to stop the process.

Netscape supports both bookmark and history features. You can save the URLs of Web pages you view by adding them to a bookmark list. You can then use this list to directly access any of the pages at a later date. To the right of the Location box for entering URLs, there is a button labeled Bookmarks. Clicking on this button displays a drop-down menu for your booksmarks. The Bookmark item in the Communicator menu also displays this menu. The first entries are commands for managing your bookmarks. To add the URL of the Web page you are currently viewing to your bookmark list, you just click on the Add item in the bookmark menu or press **Ctrl-k**. To display a Web page you have bookmarked, select it on the bookmark menu. To edit your bookmarks, use the **Ctrl-b** command to display them in a separate window with which you can scroll through them. Drop-down menus at the top of this menu have commands for managing and editing your bookmarks. You can also use this list to access bookmarks. The **Ctrl-f** command will search your bookmark entries for a pattern, letting you easily locate a bookmark. If you did not bookmark a page, you could still track it down in the history list. Netscape keeps a list of all the recent Web pages you have accessed. Selecting the History item in the Communicator menu or entering a **Ctrl-h**, will display a list of previous URLs you have accessed.

To save the Web page you are currently viewing, select the Save As entry in the File menu. A dialog box with three boxes is displayed. The bottom box displays the name of the file as it will be saved on your system. You can change this name if you wish. The middle box lists different directories in the current directory. You can click on them to move down to another directory, or click on the .. entry at the top to move to the parent directory. You can move through the directory tree this way until you find the one in which you want to save your file. The top box is a filter. There is button labeled Source that is a drop-down menu with options for the form in which you want to save the page. You can save it as a bare text or as source. Text is the bare text of the page, whereas source includes all the HTML formatting commands.

Web pages will often display links that connect to files on Ftp sites. In Netscape, to download a file referenced by such a link, you need to hold down the **shift** key while you click on it. The same is true for accessing an Ftp site directly. The names of files in a current directory will be listed as highlighted links. To download a file you shift-click on its name. A single click without a shift will only display the contents as text on another Web page. Once you have selected the file you want to download, a window will open up with boxes with the name of the file and the listing of your current local directory (see Figure 15.1). You can use the directory box to move through the directory tree until you find the directory in which you want to save the file. Click OK to begin downloading. As the download progresses, Netscape will display how much of the file has been downloaded and the estimated time remaining.

Netscape Communicator not only provides the Navigator Web browser, but also mail and newsreader clients. With the mail client you can send and receive messages over the Internet just as you would with any other Unix mail client such as `mailx` or Elm (see Figure 15.3). The newreader lets you read and post articles in Usenet newsgroups. On the Communicator menu there are items for the newreader or mailer. You can also use the **Alt-2** key for the mailer and **Alt-3** for the newsreader. **Alt-1** is for the Navigator browser. If you are using a remote mail or news server, you will have to enter their network addresses in the preference boxes accessible through the Edit menu.

If you are on a network that connects to the Internet through a proxy, you will have to supply the IP address of your network's proxy computer. A proxy is a computer that operates as a con-

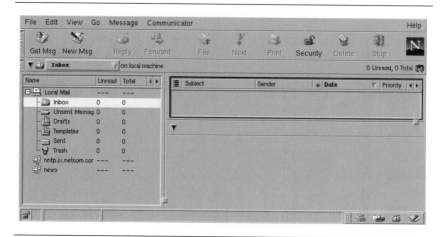

Figure 15.3. Netscape Communicator mailer.

trolled gateway to the Internet for your network. It receives Internet requests from users and then makes those requests on their behalf. There is no direct connection to the Internet. Proxy entries are made in the Preference boxes accessible from the Edit menu.

Mosaic

Mosaic was the first graphics-based browser developed for the Web. Mosaic, like Netscape, is a cross-platform application with versions for Windows, Macintosh, and Unix. It was developed by the National Center for Supercomputing Applications (NCSA) at the University of Illinois at Urbana-Champaign. More information about Mosaic is available at the NCSA Web site: www.ncsa.uiuc.edu. You can download a copy of Mosaic from the Web site or from the Mosaic Ftp site at ftp.ncsa.uiuc.edu.

Like Netscape, Mosaic is an X-Windows application that can only be run from within X-Windows, but may use any window manager or desktop such as Open-Look or Motif. The Mosaic window has two boxes at the top, one for displaying the title of the current Web page, the other for entering URLs. The buttons for managing the Web pages that you access in a given session are located at the bottom of the window. The Back and Forward buttons move you back and forth through a list of Web pages you have accessed. The Home button returns you to your own home page. The Save As button saves the current Web page on your own system.

When you access and start to display a Web page, the globe image in the upper-right corner will spin. Once the Web page is displayed, the globe will stop spinning. The globe functions like a Stop button. Should you decide not to display the Web page while the globe is spinning, you can click on the globe to stop the process.

The drop-down menus across the top of the Mosaic window let you manage your Web searches. With the Navigate menu, you can maintain a bookmark list of favored Web sites. The Options menu has entries for configuring your Mosaic browser. The News menu lets you use your Mosaic browser to access Usenet newsgroups, displaying and saving articles.

Lynx: Line-Mode Browser

Lynx is a line-mode browser that you can use without X-Windows. You can run it from your Unix command line. Lynx uses a cursor-based display much like Elm or Pine. A Web page is displayed as text only. A text page can contain links to other Internet resources, but will not display any graphics, video, or sound. Except for the display limitations, Lynx is a fully functional Web browser. You can use Lynx to download files or make Ftp connections. All information on the Web is still accessible to you. Because Lynx requires much less work than a graphics-based browser, it operates much faster, quickly displaying Web page text. You can download a copy of the Lynx browser for Unix from the Lynx Web site at `lynx.browser.org`. For Unix you download the package of Lynx source files. This is a compressed archive that you decompress and extract, generating a directory containing the source files. Within this directory you use the `continue` command to generate a Makefile tailored to your system. Then the `make` command creates the Lynx browser, which can then be installed on your system.

Whereas a graphic-based Web browser will display a Web page in a scrollable window, Lynx displays a Web page with a series of screens. To move to the next screen of text you can either press the **spacebar** or the **PageDown** key. The **PageUp** key displays the previous screen of text. The down and up arrows will move to the next or previous links in the text, displaying the full screen of text around the link.

Anchors are displayed in bold typeface where they occur in the text of the Web page as shown in Figure 15.4. Instead of using a mouse to click on an anchor, your first have to select it and then press **enter** or the **right arrow** key to activate it. A selected anchor is highlighted in reverse video with a shaded rectangle around the link text. The first anchor displayed on the screen is automatically selected. You can then move sequentially from one anchor to the next by pressing the **down arrow** key. The **up arrow** moves you back to a previous anchor. Be sure to use only the **up** and **down arrow** keys to move from one anchor to the next, not right or left.

Like other Web browsers, Lynx keeps a list of all the Web pages you access in a session. The **left arrow** key moves you back to a

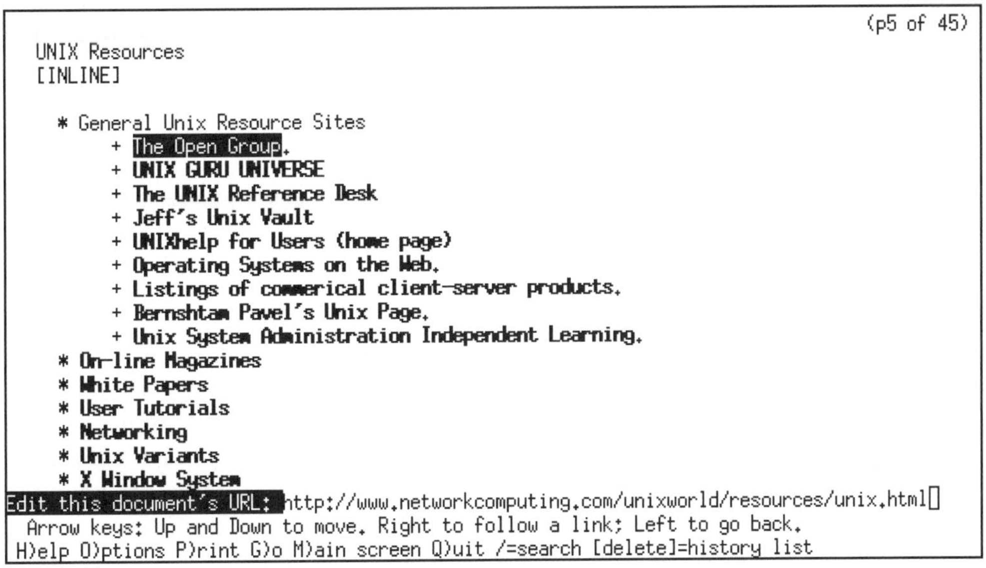

```
                                                                  (p5 of 45)
UNIX Resources
[INLINE]

   * General Unix Resource Sites
        + The Open Group.
        + UNIX GURU UNIVERSE
        + The UNIX Reference Desk
        + Jeff's Unix Vault
        + UNIXhelp for Users (home page)
        + Operating Systems on the Web.
        + Listings of commerical client-server products.
        + Bernshtam Pavel's Unix Page.
        + Unix System Administration Independent Learning.
   * On-line Magazines
   * White Papers
   * User Tutorials
   * Networking
   * Unix Variants
   * X Window System
Edit this document's URL: http://www.networkcomputing.com/unixworld/resources/unix.html
 Arrow keys: Up and Down to move. Right to follow a link; Left to go back.
H)elp O)ptions P)rint G)o M)ain screen Q)uit /=search [delete]=history list
```

Figure 15.4. Lynx Web browser.

previously displayed page, and the **right arrow** key will move you forward to the next page in the list. Pressing the **escape** key displays a history list of the Web pages you have accessed. You can use your **up** and **down arrow** keys on this list to select a particular anchor that is a link to another Web page and then use the **right arrow** or **enter** keys to access that page.

If you want to go to a specific site, press the g key. This opens a line at the bottom of the screen with the prompt "URL to open:". There you can enter the URL for the site you want. Pressing the m key will return you to your home page. Lynx also supports bookmarks. By pressing a you automatically add the current Web page to a bookmark list. Press **v** to display the list of bookmarks. You can use the **up** and **down arrow** keys to select a bookmark link. Pressing either the **right arrow** or **enter** key will move to and display that Web page.

You use one-letter commands to perform certain browser functions such as downloading a file or searching pages. Pressing the ? key displays a list of these commands. To download a file, press the d key. The h key will display a help menu. To search the text of your current Web page you press the / key. This opens up line at the bottom of the screen where you enter your search pattern. Lynx will then highlight the next instance of that pattern in the text. If you press n, Lynx will display the next instance. The \ key will toggle you between a source and rendered version of the current Web page, showing you the HTML tags or the formatted text.

Java

Java is a freely available enhancement to Web browsers that allows you to run programs on a Web site. With Java, you can interact with the information on a Web site. Most browsers such as Netscape include support for Java and can run Java applets. Numerous Java-based products are available for Unix. There are Unix versions of the Java Development Kit (JDK), the HotJava Web browser, and the Java Web server. You can download most of these products through links located at the Sun Web site at www.sun.com.

The Java Development Kit provides tools such as the Java compiler and debugger for creating and debugging your own Java applets as well as support for Java applications such as the HotJava browser. The kit includes demonstration applets with source code. You can obtain detailed documentation on the JDK from the Sun Web site. The JDK package installs the Java applications, libraries, and demos. Java applications include a Java compiler (javac), a Java debugger (jdb), and an applet viewer (appletviewer). The JDK supports several features such as internationalization, signed applets, large math numbers, and database conductivity (JDBC). Detailed descriptions of these features can be found in the JDK documentation.

You can create a Java applet much as you would create a program using a standard programming language. You first use a text editor to create the source code. The source code is saved in a file with a **.java** extension. Then you can use the javac compiler to compile the source code file, generating a Java applet. This applet file will have the extension **.class**. For example, compiling a Java source code file named **Blink.java** will generate a **Blink.class** file. This **Blink.class** applet can then be accessed and run by a Web browser.

An applet is called within a Web page using the <APPLET> HTML tag. This tag can contain several attributes, one of which is required, CODE. You assign to CODE the name of the compiled applet. There are several optional attributes you can use to set features such as the region used to display the applet and its alignment. You can even access applets on a remote Web site. A complete listing of the different applet features can be found in the JDK documentation. In the following example, the applet called **Blink.class** will be displayed in a box on the Web browser that has a height of 100 pixels and a width of 80 pixels and is aligned in the center.

```
<APPLET CODE="Blink.class" WIDTH=80 HEIGHT=100 ALIGN=
    center></APPLET>
```

HyperText Markup Language: HTML

You create Web pages using HTML, the HyperText Markup Language. HTML is a subset of SGML (Standard Generalized Markup Language). Creating an HTML document is a matter of inserting HTML tags in a text file. In this respect, creating a Web page is as simple as using a tag-based word processor. You use the HTML tags to format text for display as a Web page. The Web page itself is a text file that you can create using any text editor, such as Vi. For those familiar with tag-based word processing on Unix systems you will find it conceptually similar to `troff`. HTML tags exist for indicating headings, lists, and paragraphs, as well as to reference Web resources. Table 15.III lists many of the commonly used HTML tags.

Instead of manually creating a Web page you can make use of special Web page creation programs that easily help you create very complex Web pages using an X-Windows interface. One of the components of Netscape Communicator is the Web page composer. You can use the composer to create your own Web pages. With menus and buttons you can create Web page elements such as lists, headings, and links (see Figure 15.5). The Unix version of WordPerfect lets you automatically generate a Web page from a WordPerfect document. You do not have to type any HTML tags. Of course the Web page created will be an HTML document, a text file consisting of text and HTML tags.

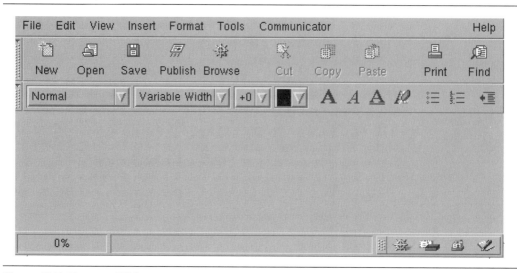

Figure 15.5. Netscape Web page composer.

An HTML tag consists of an HTML code enclosed in angle brackets, <>. For example, the tag for a paragraph is <P>. Tags are usually used in pairs, with the end tag the same as the beginning but with a preceding slash. A paragraph would begin with the <P> tag and end the paragraph with the corresponding </P> tag.

The text of a Web page with its HTML tags has to be enclosed by the <HTML> tag. The first entry in a Web page is the <HTML> tag, and the last entry is the closing </HTML> tag. The Web page can then be divided into sections for the heading and the body. The heading contains the title for a Web page, whereas the body contains the contents. The title is used to identify the Web page to Web browsers. It is the entry that will be used in Web browser bookmarks for that page. The body of the Web page is text that is actually displayed by a browser.

Headings and Lists

HTML tags exist for formatting headings, paragraphs, and different kinds of lists. As you have seen, <P> formats a paragraph, ending the paragraph with a </P> tag. To position components such as pictures or paragraphs at either the top, bottom, or middle of your Web page using the <TOP>, <BOT>, and <MID> tags, respectively. The <CENTER>, <LEFT>, and <RIGHT> tags will place them in the center, left margin, or right margin, respectively, of a page. The <PRE> tag will let you enter unformatted text. The text will appear on the Web page exactly as you enter it.

For headings you use the tag <H*n*>, where *n* refers to the level of the heading. <H1> is a top-level heading, which will be displayed in a large font size. <H2> is the next level with a smaller font size, and so on. Depending on the Browser used, subheadings may be indented or portrayed in a different font. Each heading is terminated with its own ending tag—<H1> with </H1>, and <H2> with </H2>.

A web page can display several kinds of lists: unordered, ordered, or descriptive lists. Each kind of list is enclosed in its own HTML tags. There are also HTML tags for each individual entry in a list. Entries in ordered and unordered lists use the <LI> tag with its closing </LI> tag. An unordered list precedes each entry with a bullet. The HTML tag for a unordered list is <UL>, ending with </UL>. Within these tags you place the list entries, each beginning with its own <LI> tag and ending with a </LI> tag.

An ordered list will number the entries. The first entry will be preceded by a 1., the second by 2., and so on. The tag for an ordered list is <OL>, ending with </OL>. The next example shows the entries for an ordered list.

```
<OL>
<LI>New York Strawberry Cheesecake</li>
<LI>Sour Cream Walnut Fudge</li>
<LI>The Supreme Chocolate Mousse Cake</li>
<LI>Great Pastas</li>
</OL>
```

This list is displayed as shown here, with each entry numbered.

```
1. New York Strawberry Cheesecake
2. Sour Cream Walnut Fudge
3. The Supreme Chocolate Mousse Cake
4. Great Pastas
```

A descriptive list will display a user-specified word or image before a list entry. The tag for a descriptive list is <DL>, ending with </DL>. Unlike the unordered and ordered lists, a descriptive list has its own tags for its entries. The <DT> tag specifies the descriptive text or image to place before the entry. This is in place of numbers in an ordered list and bullets in unordered list. Each entry in a descriptive list will have its own <DT> tag with whatever text or image you choose. Following the <DT> entry, the <DD> tag is used to begin the text of the list entry.

<DT>chris<DD>Best baseball player in the house

The previous example will display the word `chris` followed by the text of the entry and separated from each other by spaces.

```
chris     Best baseball player in the house.
```

An example of a descriptive list follows.

<DL>
<DT>chris<DD>Best baseball player in the house.
<DT>dylan<DD>Fantastic track record.
<DT>justin<DD>Superior soccer skills.
</DL>

The list would be displayed as:

```
chris     Best baseball player in the house.
dylan     Fantastic track record.
justin    Superior soccer skills.
```

The **reclist.html** file shows the code for implementing a simple Web page that displays an ordered list. The entire page is enclosed in <HTML> and </HTML> tags. The title of the page, "My Recipe Site," is defined within the <TITLE> tags, which are placed within the <HEAD> tags. The <BODY> tags mark the text that will be displayed on the Web page. The first object is a heading enclosed within <H1> tags. The ordered list follows, encased in the <OL> and </OL> tags, with entries specified with the <LI> and </LI> tags. Figure 15.6 shows how this page is displayed on a browser. The list entries are numbered sequentially.

reclist.html

```
<HTML>
<HEAD>
<TITLE>My Recipe Site<TITLE>
<HEAD>
<BODY>

<H1>Recipe List<H1>

</OL>
</LI>New York Strawberry Cheesecake</LI>
</LI>Sour Cream Walnut Fudge</LI>
</LI>The Supreme Chocolate Mousse Cake</LI>
</LI>Great Pastas</LI>
</OL>

<BODY>
<HTML>
```

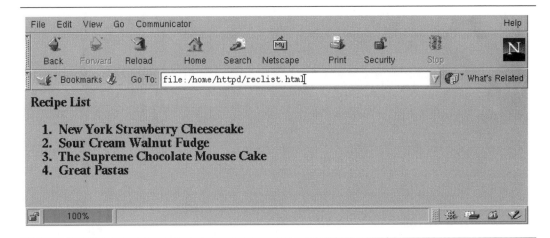

Figure 15.6. Display of reclist.html.

Referencing Internet Resources: HREF

Using the HREF HTML tag, you can designate specified text or pictures in your Web page as links to other Web pages or to items such as pictures or documents. The items can be on your system or at other Web sites. When the user chooses the text referencing a link, that item or Web page will be retrieved. To create a link to a network resource, you associate certain text or pictures in your Web page with a URL for that network resource. This resource can be another Web page, an item such as a picture or file, or even another network tool, such as Ftp or Telnet. It can be located on the Internet, a local network, or on your own system.

An HREF anchor tag is used to create such a link. The HREF anchor tag begins with <A HREF=. The URL is entered following the = sign and is enclosed within double quotes. A closing > ends the opening HREF anchor tag. After the opening HREF tag, you enter the text that is displayed on your Web page to reference this URL. The closing </A> anchor tag ends the text. When the Web page is displayed on a Browser, you will see this text set to a special color to indicate that it references a URL. Instead of text, you could use an image reference, in which case the user can click on the image to reference the URL. You could also use both text and an image reference, in which case the user can click on either the text or image to reference the URL.

<A HREF="URL">text</A>

In the following example, the HREF anchor tag will connect to a Web page on the `www.cakes.org` system. The text "Chocolate Cake" will be displayed in color, usually blue. When the user clicks on that text, the URL `www.cakes.org/cakes/chocolate.html` will be accessed. Because the transfer protocol is HTTP, a Web page is displayed.

<A HREF=http://www.cakes.org/pub/cakes/chocolate.html>Chocolate Cake</A>

HREF entries can also be used to access a Web page on your own system. To do so, you simply enter the path name for the Web page on your system, leaving out the transfer protocol or the host name. The path name can be a relative path name from the directory in which the current Web page is located. In the next example, the Web page `index.html` is located in the subdirectory **desserts** on the site's own system.

<A HREF=./desserts/index.html>Dessert Recipes</A>

The HREF tag is also used to reference text on the same Web page. This involves the use of two HREF entries, one to label the text you want to reference and another to specify the text that performs the referencing. This is often used in pages that have several headings. A table of contents with a list of the headings is used to reference the headings displayed throughout the text of the Web page. Clicking on a headings entry in the table of contents will move you to that heading in the text, displaying it on your browser.

The text to be referenced is referred to as a named element. You use the NAME tag to create a label for the specified text which functions as a name for that text. You can then create HREF anchor entries that can use the name to reference that text. With such an HREF anchor you access this element, jumping to that text. Instead of text, the named element could be an image, letting you jump to that image in the text. To create a named element, use the NAME anchor tag with a name you want to give to that element. The text or image making up the named element then follows the opening NAME tag, and ends with a closing </A> tag. In the next example, the name for the element is `mynewstag` and the text displayed for it is "Recipe Site News." The name `mynewstag` can then be used in HREF anchors to identify this particular HyperText element.

<A NAME="mynewstag"> Recipe Site News</A>

You use the HREF tag with a # qualifier to specify text or images that can reference a named element. You precede the name you specified for the named element with a # sign. In the following HREF anchor, the text "About My Recipe Site" will be displayed on the Web page. When the user clicks on this text, the element on the Web page labeled with the name `mynewstag` will be displayed. The element can be a heading, a picture, or any text segment.

<A NAME="#mynewstag">Recent news</A>

As noted previously, named elements are used to move users to different headings throughout a Web page. For example, a table of contents listing the heading would consist of HREF entries for each named heading in the text. Clicking on the Contents entry will jump to that heading.

<A HREF="#Heading-name">Heading text</A>

The corresponding headings throughout the Web page have to be named using the NAME tag. Be sure the name matches. The following example creates a heading that, when you click on it, will jump to the element named `welcometag`.

<H2><A HREF=#welcometag>About My Recipe Site</A></H2>

The following example shows the HTML entries for the element named `welcometag`. It is a heading that is enclosed within anchor tags with the NAME tag assigned the name of the element, in this case, "welcometag." This is the element that the anchor in the previous example will jump to.

<A NAME="welcometag">
<H2>About My Recipe Site<\H2>
</A>

You can use the ID tag to create named elements. An ID tag can be placed within a heading tag, making for cleaner HTML code.

<Hn ID="name"> Heading text<\Hn>

Web Page Example

With just the few codes discussed so far, you can easily create your own Web page. With a simple text editor you can enter the HTML codes and text. The file can be any name, but must have an **.html** extension. Normally a Web site is made up of many files distributed among several subdirectories. In the following example, there are two Web page files, **recipe.html** and **index.html. recipe.html** is the main file in the Web site's main directory. The **index.html** file is a Web page located in the **desserts** directory, a subdirectory of the Web site's main directory. There is an entry in the **recipe.html** file that calls the **desserts/index.html** file. Usually each subdirectory will have its own **index.html** file that will list links to other Web pages in its own directory or subdirectories.

recipe.html uses several HREF references, accessing local files as well as a Web page on another site. There is even a URL for sending mail messages. The following anchor will display the email address "chris@mygames.com" and when the user clicks on it, will bring up that system's mailer, prompting the user to enter and send a message. The HREF assignment specifies the email address to which the message is sent. The text segment could be any text. It does not have to be an email address. This example could just as easily display "Send Chris a message" for the user to click on, instead of the email address. The address needs only to be specified with the mailto URL in the HREF assignment.

<A>HREF=mailto://chris@mygames.com>chris@mygames.com</A>.

The <H1> tag prints a heading in very large text. <P> tags format the following text into paragraphs. <H2> tags display the smaller subheadings. The <HR> tag draws a line across the page. Anchor tags with URLs are embedded within both paragraphs and headings. The headings in the **recipe.html** file are all anchors, with HREF entries for files on either this site or on another Web site as is the case in the last heading. The anchors are placed within the heading tags, letting the user click anywhere on the heading. Many of the anchors reference local files For example, <A HREF="desserts/index.html"> references the local Web page **index.html** in the subdirectory **desserts**. The last heading references a Web page on remote sites. <A HREF=http://world. food.com/home/pastries/France/index.html>French Pastries </A> references the **index.html** Web page in the **/home/pastries/ France** directory on the **world.food.com** Web site.

The **desserts/index.html** file uses an ordered list instead of headings. Each entry in the list contains an anchor. This has an effect similar to the headings in the **recipe.html** file, but with each entry numbered.

recipe.html

```
<HTML>
<HEAD>
<TITLE>My Recipe Site</TITLE>
</HEAD>
<BODY>

<BR>
<H1>Great Recipes<H1>
<BR>
<P>
The following list features some very edible recipes, or
  so I have been told (sometimes). For comments you can
  reach me at this address <A
HREF=mailto://chris@mygames.com>chris@mygames.com</A>.

<HR>
<H2><A HREF=./welcome>About My Recipe Site</A></H2>
<H2><A HREF=./desserts/index.html>Dessert Recipes</A></H2>
<H2><A HREF=./pastas/index.html>Magnificent Pasta</A></H2>
<H2><A HREF=http://world.food.com/home/pastries/France/
  index.html>French Pastries</A></H2>

<BODY>
</HTML>
```

desserts/index.html

```
<HTML>
<HEAD>
<TILE>Dessert List</TITLE>
</HEAD>
<BODY>

<H1>Desserts<H1>

<OL>
<LI><A HREF=./cheesecake.html>New York Strawberry
  Cheesecake</A></LI>
<LI><A HREF=./fudge.html>Sour Cream Walnut Fudge</A></LI>
<LI><A HREF=ftp://ftp.cakes.org/pub/cakes/mousse/supreme.
```

```
   txt>The Supreme Chocolate Mousse Cake</A></LI>
</OL>

</BODY>
</HTML>
```

Figure 15.7 shows how the **recipe.html** file is displayed on a Web browser. Notice the underline text. In this example, the underlined text indicates an HREF entry, an anchor you can click on to access another Web resource such as another Web page. Figure 15.8 shows how the **desserts/index.html** file is displayed on a Web browser. It uses an ordered list, with each entry numbered. The text for each entry is underlined, indicating an anchor on which you can click.

Images and Sounds

With the IMG tag you can specify images to be displayed on your Web page. The image can be a photograph, figure, or drawing in the form of a gif or jpeg file. The image file is usually in the same directory as the Web page, though not necessarily. Within the

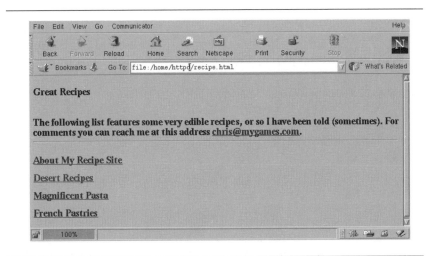

Figure 15.7. Display of recipe.html.

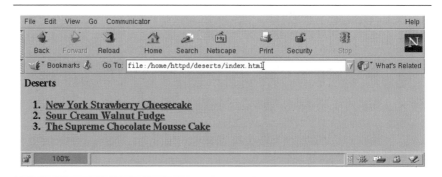

Figure 15.8. Display of desserts/index.html.

IMG tag, the SRC tag is used to specify the file name of the image you want displayed. If the image file is in another directory, use its path name instead of just the file name. The format for an IMG tag is:

    <IMG SRC=filename>

For example, to display a picture called **cakes.gif**, you place it within the IMG tag.

    <IMG SRC="cakes.gif">

The IMG tag displays the picture as part of the Web page. However, if you want to display an image externally using a separate image display program, you use an HREF tag for the image file. In effect you are linking to the image file and the application that displays it.

    <HREF="myphoto.gif">This is a picture of me<\A>

You also use an HREF tag to play sound or video files. These files rely on outside applications to run them. An HREF tag will link to the sound or video file and run its associated application.

    <HREF="munching.au">Satisfaction indicator<\A>

Images are often used as anchors that you can click on to access Web resources. They can be used in place of or with the displayed text for an anchor. You simply enter an IMG entry for the image in the text portion of the HREF entry. The image will be displayed by the Web browser, and users can click on the image to reference the URL specified in the HREF entry. In the next example, an image reference to the **food1.gif** image file will display that image on the Web page. The user can then click on the food1 image to reference the URL, in this case the file **welcome**. The image reference is <IMG SRC="food1.gif">.

<A HREF=./welcome><IMAGE SRC="food1.jpg"></A>

The following example will use both an image, **cake2.jpg**, and text, "Dessert Recipes," as anchors. The user can click on either the displayed text or the image to access the URL, in this case, the **desserts/index.html** file.

<A HREF=./desserts/index.html><IMAGE SRC="cake2.jpg"> Dessert Recipes</A>

The **recpic.html** file is a reworked version of the **recipe.html** file with images added. The BODY tag is qualified with a BACK-GROUND option that specifies an image to be used as the background pattern, in this case, **cloud.gif**. The **food1.jpg** image is then displayed, centered on the page. If the user clicks on it, the contents of the **welcome** file are displayed. The headings, except for the first one, all contain images. These are displayed to the left of the heading text and are part of the anchors. Clicking on one of them will access the Web page specified in its HREF entry. The following example displays as the heading the image **cake2.jpg** followed by the text "Dessert Recipes." Both are anchors for the **desserts/index.html** page.

<H1><A HREF=./desserts/index.html><IMAGE SRC="cake2.jpg"> Dessert Recipes </A></H1>

recpic.html

```
<HTML>
<HEAD>
<TITLE>My Recipe Site</TITLE>

</HEAD>
```

```
<BODY BACKGROUND="cloud.gif">
<BR>
<CENTER>
<A HREF=./welcome><IMAGE SRC="food1.jpg"></A>
<H1>Great Recipes<H1>
<P ALIGN="left">
The following list features some very edible recipe, or so
   I have been told (sometimes). For comments you can send
   a message to me, <A
HREF=mailto://chris@mygames.com>Christopher</A>, and I
will
   reply after dessert.
<A HREF=./welcome><I>About My Recipe Site</I></A>
<H1><A HREF=./desserts/index.html><IMAGE SRC="cake2.jpg">
   Dessert Recipes</A></H1>
<H1><A HREF=./pastas/index.html><IMAGE SRC="food2.jpg">
   Magnificent Pasta</A></H1>
<H1><A HREF=http://world.food.com/home/pastries/France/
   index.html><IMAGE SRC="pastry.jpg"><BR>French Pastries
   </A></H1>

</BODY>
</HTML>
```

Figure 15.9 shows how the **recpic.html** file is displayed on a Web browser. Notice the use of the <BR> tag to start new lines or enter empty lines. In the last heading, the <BR> tag is used to place the image and anchor text on different lines, though they both reference the same HREF entry. Also, the style tag <I> is used to display the first heading in italics.

Forms and Common Gateway Interfaces

Web pages are designed to display text and images. They were not originally meant to perform interactive tasks such as receiving data from a user, processing it, and displaying results. HTML tags perform formatting operations, like a word processor, rather than calculations like a program can. However, Web pages have become

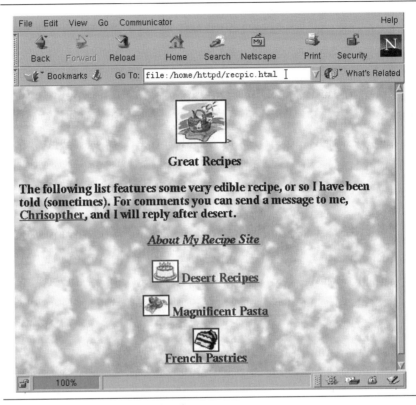

Figure 15.9. Display of recpic.html.

an ideal interface for gathering information from users on the Internet. An example of this is registration procedures or on-line shopping. Still, a Web page cannot perform calculations itself. It is not a program. However, it can gather information from users and pass it on to a program. The program can then process it and pass the results to another Web page that can display it. Programs that interact with Web pages in this way are called common gateway interfaces (CGIs). When using a browser to display a Web page at a particular Web site, the Web page may call up CGI programs to provide you with certain real-time information or to process information received from you. A CGI program can be a Unix shell script or a program. For example, if you want to purchase several items displayed on a Web page, you could click on the items. The Web page sends the information to a program, which then performs the calculations and sends the information to another Web page that displays the total price.

Forms are HTML elements that can receive data from the user and pass it on to a program or another Web page. HTML supports a variety of different kinds of forms. There are simple text boxes where the user can enter a line of text. Radio and check boxes let you choose from several displayed options. Drop-down menus also let you easily choose an option, and they are often used to access other Web pages. Text area boxes operate like small text editors, letting you enter lines of text, edit any of it, and use scrollbars to move through the text.

The simplest forms are input forms. They begin with the tag <INPUT and can then be qualified as to their type. You can have named boxes, radio buttons, and check buttons. You use the TYPE qualifier to specify the type of form: text, check box, radio, submit, or reset. The text type is for a standard text box, a rectangle in which you enter a line of text. You also have to name the input form with the NAME qualifier. This is used to identify a particular form. The following example shows a simple input text form. The name of the form is **cook** and the type is **text**. Following the INPUT tag is the label. The text "Your Name" will be displayed to the left of the input box.

<INPUT NAME=cook TYPE=text>Your Name

The check box displays a check box that you can click on to show a check. Usually you use several check boxes linked together as the same element. You do this by giving each check box the same name. In the following example, there is one Web page element, **favders**, that is made up of four check boxes. There is a separate INPUT tag entry for each checkbox with **checkbox** specified as its TYPE and **favders** as its NAME. The label for a checkbox is placed after the INPUT tag. This example displays four check boxes labeled with "Cake," "Ice Cream," "Pie," and "Rice cakes" (see Figure 15.10).

<INPUT NAME=favders TYPE=checkbox> Cake
<INPUT NAME=favders TYPE=checkbox> Ice Cream
<INPUT NAME=favders TYPE=checkbox> Pie
<INPUT NAME=favders TYPE=checkbox> Rice cakes

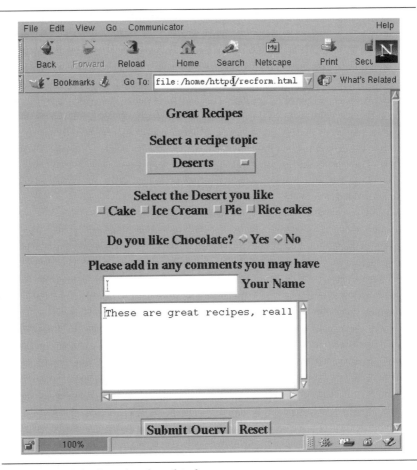

Figure 15.10. Display of recform.html.

A radio button operates the same way, but you can only choose one. Choosing another will turn off the one you chose previously. The TYPE entry is **radio**. The following example shows a simple radio element with two radio buttons. The name of the element is **answ**, as entered in both INPUT tags. The labels are "Yes" and "No" (see Figure 15.10).

<INPUT NAME=answ TYPE=radio> Yes
<INPUT NAME=answ TYPE=radio> No

A drop-down menu is implemented with the SELECT tag, ending with </SELECT>. Entries for the menu are made with the

<OPTION> tag. Within this tag you specify the NAME for the entry. The displayed text on the menu for the entry is placed after the OPTION tag. A SELECT tag has a syntax similar to a list where you have enclosing tags and then entries for each item. The following example implements a drop-down menu of three items, "Desserts," "Pastas," and "French Pastries" (see Figure 15.10).

```
<SELECT>
<OPTION NAME=rec1> Desserts
<OPTION NAME=rec2> Pastas
<OPTION NAME=rec3> French Pastries
</SELECT>
```

A text area form is implemented with the TEXTAREA tag, ending with the </TEXTAREA>. It takes a ROW option that specifies the number of rows on the page it will display, and a COLS option for the number of columns. Following the TEXTAREA tag, you enter the default text. This is text that will be shown in the text area box when the Web page is first displayed. If no changes are made, then the default text is taken as an entry. A button called the Reset button can be displayed that the user can click on to restore the default entries. A text area box has scrollbars, so you are not limited to the displayed area for the amount of text you want to enter. Use the scrollbars to move to different places in your entered text. You have standard editing capabilities for deleting and inserting text, and even for cutting and pasting text. The following example creates a text area box named **com1** with 7 rows and 30 columns. The default text displayed is "These are great recipes, really"

```
<TEXTAREA NAME=com1 ROWS=7 COLS=30>
```

These are great recipes, really

```
</TEXTAREA>
```

The **recform.html** file shows examples of the forms previously discussed. It begins with a drop-down menu, then lists check boxes, followed by radio button. A input box is then placed above a text area box.

recform.html

```
<HTML>
<HEAD>
<TITLE>My Recipe Site</TITLE>
</HEAD>
<BODY>
<BR>
<H1 ALIGN="center">Great Recipes<H1>
<FORM METHOD=post ACTION="myform">
<CENTER>
Select a recipe topic
<BR>

<SELECT>
<OPTION NAME=rec1> Desserts
<OPTION NAME=rec2> Pastas
<OPTION NAME=rec3> French Pastries
</SELECT>

<BR>
<HR>
Select the Dessert you like
<BR>
<INPUT NAME=favders TYPE=checkbox> Cake
<INPUT NAME=favders TYPE=checkbox> Ice Cream
<INPUT NAME=favders TYPE=checkbox> Pie
<INPUT NAME=favders TYPE=checkbox> Rice cakes

<BR>
<BR>
Do you like Chocolate?
<INPUT NAME=answ TYPE=radio> Yes
<INPUT NAME=answ TYPE=radio> No

<BR>
<HR>
Please add in any comments you may have

<BR>
<INPUT NAME=cook TYPE=text> Your Name
<BR>
<TEXTAREA NAME=com1 ROWS=7 COLS=30>              (continued)
```

```
These are great recipes, really
</TEXTAREA>

<BR>
<HR>

<INPUT NAME=sub1 TYPE=submit>
<INPUT NAME=res1 TYPE=reset>

</FORM>
<BODY>
</HTML>
```

Figure 15.10 shows how the **recform.html** file is displayed on a Web browser. Notice the labels and the default text. Submit and Reset buttons are placed at the bottom. Line breaks, BR, and horizontal rules, HR, are used to separate the forms.

Table 15.III. HTML Codes for Web Pages

BASIC TAGS

<HTML>	Web page. Place <HTML> as the first entry in your Web page and </HTML> as the last.
</HTML>	End of Web page.
<HEAD>	Head of Web page. The head segment of a Web page; includes any configuration entries and the title entry.
</HEAD>	End of head.
<TITLE>*title text*</TITLE>	The title of the Web page; this will be used in hotlists to identify the page easily.
<BODY>	Text of Web page. The body of the Web page; this is the material that is displayed as the Web page.
</BODY>	End of Web page body.
<ADDRESS>*Address of creator*<\ADDRESS>	Internet address of Web page creator.
<BASE=*Href "Web page path name"* >	Path name of Web page that serves as base path name for any relative path names on that page. *(continued)*

Table 15.III. HTML Codes for Web Pages *(continued)*

FORMAT

<Hn>Heading title<\Hn>	Headers; *n* is sequential subhead level, as in <H1> for top level, <H2> for subheads, etc.
<P>paragraph text </P>	Paragraphs.
<CENTER>	Center text.
 	Line break.
<PRE>	Preformatted text. Displays the following text as it appears with no formatting.
</PRE>	End of preformatted text.
<HR>	Displays a line across the page.
<CLEAR>	Forces break in text.
<B>bold-text</B>	Bold text.
<I>italic-text</I>	Italic text.
<TT>typwriter-text</TT>	Typewriter text.
<CODE>code-text</CODE>	Code text.
<CITE>citation-text</CITE>	Citation text.
<EM>emphasis-text</EM>	Emphasis text.
<STRONG>emphasis-text</STRONG>	Strong emphasis text.
<KBD>keboard-text</KBD>	Keyboard text.
<VAR>variable-text</VAR>	Variable text.

IMAGES

<IMAGE SRC="file.gif">	Image to be displayed in Web page.
ALIGN="*position*"	Positions images or text on the Web page; position can be bottom, top, left, or right.
WIDTH=	Sets width for display of image.
HEIGHT=	Sets height.

ANCHORS

<AAnchor tag / A>displayed text </A>	Anchor tag associated with displayed text in the Web page.
<A HREF="URL address">displayed text </A>	URL reference; ties the specified text to the URL address. Clicking on specified text in Web page will jump to that URL's Web page. *(continued)*

Table 15.III. HTML Codes for Web Pages (*continued*)

<A HREF=#*Anchor text*>*displayed text*</A>	A named anchor reference. Clicking on displayed text will jump to the NAME anchor defined with the Anchor text following the #. The # is used with NAME to reference NAME anchor entries.
<A NAME=*Anchor text*>*displayed text*</A>	Specifies displayed text as destination for a named anchor reference.
<A NAME=*Anchor text*><H*n*>*Heading* <\H*n*></A>	Makes a heading a destination for a named anchor reference in the Web page.
ID=*Anchor text*	Uses ID instead of NAME to create anchor text in the Web page.
<H*n* ID=*Anchor text*>*Heading text*<\H*n*>	Uses ID to make a heading an anchor text.
<A HREF=*URL address*><IMAGE SRC="*file.gif*">< /A>	URL address tied to the specified image displayed on the page.
<LINK REL=*Relationship* HREF="*URL reference*">	Creates a link to other Web pages making up the Web site; displays buttons at top and bottom of Web page with relationship described by REL.
REL=*Relationship*	Relationship of current Web page to others:
	Previous HRL for previous Web page.
	Next HRL for next Web page.
	Home HRL for home page.
	Banner HRL for banner displayed for all Web pages.

LISTS

<LH>*List header* </LH>	Name for the list.
<LI>*List item text*</LI>	List item entries.
<UL>	Unordered list.
</UL>	End of unordered list.
<OL>	Ordered list, usually numbered.
</OL>	End of ordered list.
<DL>	Definition list; a list of terms and an explanation of each called a definition; a term is a word that you specify.

(continued)

Table 15.III. HTML Codes for Web Pages *(continued)*

</DL>	End of definition list.
<DT>*Definition term* </DT>	Term for a definition list entry.
<DD>*Definition*</DD>	Text associated with a definition term.

TABLES

<TABLE>*Table entries*</TABLE>	Displays a table.
<TC>*Table caption* </TC>	Table caption.
<TR>*Table row* </TR>	A table row entry.
<TH>*Table head* </TH>	Table heading.
<TD>*Table cell* </TD>	A table cell entry.

FORMS

<FORM>
Form entries
</FORM>   Display forms specified.

<INPUT NAME=*name* TYPE=*type* VALUE= *"value"*> *label*

Creates a form for input. NAME is the name of the object that holds the input value. TYPE is the type of input form. VALUE is the initial value displayed in the form.

TYPE=*type*   Type of the input form:

text	Text box.
check box	Check box; use same name object for check boxes used for the same choice.
radio	Radio button; use same name object for radio buttons used for the same choice.
submit	Submit button; used to submit entered data on the page.
reset	Reset button; used to reset forms to initial default values.

<SELECT>
Select options
</SELECT>   Create drop-down menu of possible choices.

<OPTION NAME=*name* > *Option-title*

Creates an entry for a drop-down menu. Used within the SELECT tag to specify option entries for drop down menu.

(continued)

Table 15.III. HTML Codes for Web Pages *(continued)*

<TEXTAREA NAME=*name* ROWS=*num* COLS =*num*>
default-text

</TEXTAREA>	Create text area form to handle free text of several lines that can be edited. The form includes slider bars on the side and bottom. The *default-text* is displayed initially.

CONFIGURATION

BGCOLOR=*rrggbb*	Background color; hexadecimal number representing color; *rr* = red, *gg* = green, *bb* = blue; all 0s = no color (black); all 1s = white, FFFFFF. It is set in the BODY tag. <BODY BGCOLOR=137HF2>.
TEXT=*rrggbb*	Color of text; it is set in the BODY tag.
BACKGOUND=*file.gif*	Picture to use as background for Web page; it is set in the BODY tag.

ENTITIES

&lt	<
&gt	>
&amp	&
&quot	"

Section IV
Remote Access

16. TCP/IP Remote Access Operations
17. Unix to Unix Communications Package: UUCP

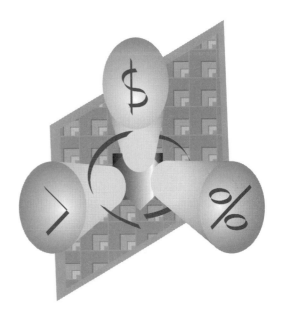

TCP/IP Remote Access Operations

Remote access commands operate across network connections. You can copy files or execute Unix commands, as well as log in remotely to accounts on those systems. Instead of working through an interface, such as Ftp or Gopher, you can execute remote access commands within your own shell that will then perform actions on a remote system.

Unix systems can use two different types of network connections, each with its own protocols, TCP/IP and UUCP. TCP/IP, used with the Internet, can also be used for local networks. Networks using TCP/IP often have dedicated connections, such as Ethernet connections or remote dial-in connections using SLIP or PPP. UUCP is an alternative set of protocols that provides network communication between Unix systems. However, UUCP is an older protocol that was designed to operate between systems that were not already connected on a network. TCP/IP and UUCP each has its own set of remote access commands, reflecting the strengths and weaknesses of each.

The remote access commands for TCP/IP are referred to as remote or simply r commands. Common command names are preceded by an r to indicate that their operations are remote. For example, rcp is the command to copy a file remotely from one system to another. The r commands have the advantage of performing real-time operations. For systems on your network to which you have access, you can copy files and execute commands, and the operations will be carried out immediately. It is very easy, with r commands, to copy whole directories from one system to another. However, you can only access systems connected with TCP/IP protocols.

The TCP/IP network communications package makes use of remote access commands first developed at UC Berkeley for ARPANET. Almost all of these commands begin with an r, indicating a remote operation. They allow you to log in remotely to another account on another system and to copy files from one system to another. You can also obtain information about another system such as who is currently logged on. When a system address is called for, these remote access commands use domain addressing. Domain addressing was originally designed for use on ARPANET as were the TCP/IP remote access commands. The TCP/IP remote access commands are listed in Table 16.I.

Many of the TCP/IP commands have comparable Internet utilities. For example, the TCP/IP command rlogin, which remotely logs into a system, is similar to Telnet. The rcp comamnd that remotely copies files performs much the same function as Ftp. In fact, the TCP/IP commands were precursors of these Internet utilities. The TCP/IP commands differ in the ease of use and control they provide to users. You can easily access other accounts you may have on different Unix systems, and you can control access by other users to your account without having to give out your password. In effect you can provide a kind of group permissions to different users to your account.

TCP/IP Network System Information: `rwho`, `ruptime`, **and** `ping`

Several TCP/IP commands are available for obtaining information about different systems on your network. You can find out who is logged in, or information about a user on another system, or if a system is up and running. For example, the `rwho` command functions in the same way as the `who` command. It displays all the users currently logged into each system in your network.

```
$ rwho
mygame      justin:tty1      Sept 10 10:34
mytrain     chris:tty2       Sept 10 09:22
```

The `ruptime` command displays information about each system on your network. The information shows how each system has been performing. `ruptime` shows whether a system is up or down, how long it has been up or down, the number of users on the system, and the average load on the system for the last 5, 10, and 15 minutes.

```
$ ruptime
mygame      up   11+04:10,    8 users,   load 1.20 1.10    1.00
mytrain     up   11+04:10,   20 users,   load 1.50 1.40    1.30
```

The `ping` command detects whether or not a system is up and running. The `ping` command takes as its argument the name of the system you want to check. The next example checks to see if `mygame` is up and connected to the network.

```
$ ping mygame
mygame is alive
$
```

If the system you want to check is down, you will get a response like that in the next example. In this case, `mytrain` is down and disconnected from the network.

```
$ ping mytrain
no answer from mytrain
$
```

Remote Access Permission: .rhosts

A **.rhosts** file is used to control access to an account by users using TCP/IP commands. The **.rhosts** file is a file that a user creates on his or her own account. It is created and edited with a standard editor such as Vi. It must be located in the user's home directory. In the next example, the user displays the contents of a **.rhosts** file.

```
$ cat .rhosts
mytrain chris
mygame justin
```

The **.rhosts** file is a simple way to allow other people access to your account without giving out your password. To deny access to a user, simply delete a system's name and login name for that user from your **.rhosts** file. If a user's login name and system are in a **.rhosts** file, then that user can directly access that account without having to know the password. This type of access is not necessary for remote login operations to work (you could use a password instead). The **.rhosts** file is required for other remote commands such as remotely copying files or remotely executing Unix commands. If you want to execute such commands on an account in a remote system, that account must have in its **.rhosts** file your login name and system name.

The type of access **.rhosts** provides allows you to use TCP/IP commands to access directly other accounts that you may have on other systems. You do not have to first log in to them. In effect, you can treat your accounts on other systems as extensions of the one you are currentlly logged into. Using the `rcp` command you can copy any files from one directory to another no matter which account they are on. With the `rsh` command you can execute any Unix comand you wish on any of your other accounts.

Remote Login: `rlogin`

You might have accounts on different systems within your network or be permitted to access someone else's account on another system. You can access an account on another system by first logging into your own and then remotely logging in across your network to the account on the other system. You can perform such a remote login using the `rlogin` command. The `rlogin` command takes as its argument a system name. The `rlogin` command will connect you to the other system and begin login procedures.

`rlogin` login procedures differs from regular login procedures in that the user is not prompted for a login name. `rlogin` assumes that the login name on your local system is the same as the login name on the remote system. Upon executing the `rlogin` command you are immediately prompted for a password. Upon entering the password you are logged into the account on the remote system.

`rlogin` assumes the login name is the same because most people use `rlogin` to access accounts they have on other systems also with their own login name. However, the login name on the remote system is often different from the login name on the local system. The `rlogin` command has an option, `-l`, that allows you to enter an different login name for the account on the remote system.

```
$ rlogin system-name -l login-name
```

In the next example, the user logs into a system called `mygame` using the login name `justin`.

```
$ rlogin mygame -l justin
password
$
```

Once logged into a remote system you can execute any command you wish. You can end the connection with the either the commands `exit`, **Ctrl-d**, ~., or `logout` (C-shell).

It is possible for you to log in to a remote system without entering a password. When you remotely log in to an account on another system, a file in the remote account called **.rhosts** is located and read. Remember that **.rhosts** contains the systems and login names of users on other systems that can log in to this account without entering a password. If your own system's name and login name is in an account's **.rhosts** file, you will be logged in without a password.

```
$ rlogin mygame -l justin
$
```

Remote File Copy: `rcp`

You can use the `rcp` command to copy files to and from remote and local systems. `rcp` is a file transfer utility that operates like the `cp` command, but across a network connection to a remote system. The `rcp` command requires that the remote system have your local system and login name in its **.rhosts** file. The `rcp` command begins with the keyword `rcp` and has as its arguments the source file and copy file names. To specify the file on the remote system, you need to place the system name before the file name, separated by a colon.

$ `rcp` *system-name*:*source-file*   *system-name*:*copy-file*

You can either copy a file from the remote system to your own or copy a file from your system to the remote system. When copying to a remote system from your own, the copy file will be a remote file and require the remote system's name. The system name and copy file's name are seperated by a colon. The source file is one on your own system and does not require a system name.

$ `rcp` *source-file*   *remote-system-name:copy-file*

In the next example, the user copies the file **weather** from his or her own system to the remote system `mygame` and renames the file with the name **monday**.

$ **`rcp weather mygame:monday`**

When copying a file on the remote system to your own, the source file is a remote file and will require the remote system's name. The copy file will be a file on your own system and does not require a system name.

$ `rcp` *remote-system-name*:*source-file*   *copy-file*

In the next example, the user copies the file **wednesday** from the remote system `mygame` to his or her own system and renames the file with the name **today**.

$ **`rcp mygame:soccer1  soccerwin`**

You can also use `rcp` to copy whole directories to or from a remote system. The `rcp` command with the `-r` option will copy a directory and all of its subdirectories from one system to another. Like the `cp` command, `rcp` requires a source and copy directory. The directory on the remote system requires the system name and colon placed before the directory name. When you copy a directory from your own system to a remote system, the copy directory will be on the remote system and requires the remote system's name.

$ `rcp -r` *source-directory*   *remote-system-name*:*copy-directory*

In the next example, the user copies the directory **seasonwins** to the directory **oldwins** on the remote system `mygame`.

$ **rcp -r seasonwins mygame:oldwins**

When you copy a directory on a remote system to one on your own system, the source directory is on the remote system and requires the remote system name.

$ `rcp -r` *remote-system-name:source-directory*   *copy-directory*

In the next example, the user copies the directory **birthdays** on the remote system `mygame` to the directory **party** on your own system.

$ **rcp -r mygame:birthdays party**

You may, at times, want to use special characters such as asterisks for file name generation or the dot to reference the current directory. Shell special characters are evaluated by your local system, not by the remote system. If you want a special character to be evaluated by the remote system, you must quote it. To copy all the files with a **.c** extension in the remote system to your own, you will need to use the asterisk special character: ***.c**. You must be careful to quote the asterisk special character. In the next example, the files with a **.c** extension on the `mygame` system are copied to the user's own system. Notice that the asterisk is quoted with a backslash. The dot, indicating the current directory, is not quoted. It will be evaluated to the current directory by the local system.

$ **rcp mygame:*.c .**

The next example copies the directory **reports** from the user's own system to the current directory on the remote system. Notice that the dot is quoted. It will be evaluated by the remote system.

```
$ rcp -r reports mygame:\.
```

Remote Execution: rsh

At times, you may need to execute a single command on a remote system. The rsh command will execute a Unix command on another system and display the results on your own. Your system name and login name must, of course, be in the remote system's **.rhosts** file. The rsh command takes two general arguments, a system name and a Unix command.

```
$ rsh remote-system-name Unix -ommand
```

In the next example, the rsh command executes a ls command on the remote system mygame to list the files in the **/home/justin** directory on the mygame system.

```
$ rsh mygame ls /home/justin
```

Special characters are evaluated by the local system unless quoted. This is particularly true of special characters that control the standard output such as redirection operators or pipes. The next example lists the files on the remote system and sends them to the standard output on the local system. The redirection operator is evaluated by the local system and redirects the output to **myfiles**, which is a file on the local system.

```
$ rsh mygame ls /home/justin > myfiles
```

If you quote a special character, it becomes part of the Unix command evaluated on the remote system. Quoting redirection operators will allow you to perform redirection operations on the remote system. In the next example the redirection operator is quoted. It becomes part of the Unix command, including its argument, the file name **myfiles**. The ls command then generates a list of file names that is redirected on the remote system to a file called **my-files** also located on the remote system.

```
$ rsh mygame ls /home/justin '>' myfiles
```

The same is true for pipes. The first command below prints the list of files on the local system's printer. The standard output is piped to your own line printer. In the second command, the list of files is printed on the remote system's printer. The pipe is quoted and evaluated by the remote system, piping the standard output to the printer on the remote system.

```
$ rsh mygame ls /home/justin | lp
$ rsh mygame ls /home/justin '|' lp
```

rwho	Displays all users logged into systems in your network.
ruptime	Displays information about each system in your network.
ping	Detects whether a system is up and running.

rlogin *system-name*

> Allows you to login remotely to an account on another system. It has an -l option that allows you to specify the login name of the account.
>
> ```
> $ rlogin mygame
> $ rlogin mygame -l justin
> ```

rcp *sys-name*:*file1 sys-name*:*file2*

> Allows you to copy a file from an account on one system to an account on another system. If no system name is given then the current system is assumed.
>
> ```
> $ rcp mydata mygame:newdata
> ```

-r

> The rcp command with the -r option allows you to copy directories instead of just files.
>
> ```
> $ rcp -r newdocs mygame:edition
> ```

rsh *sys-name Unix-command*

> Allows you to execute remotely a command on another system.
>
> ```
> $ rsh mygame ls
> ```

Table 16.I. TCP/IP Remote Access Commands

Unix to Unix Communications
Package: UUCP

Unix provides the ability to access other Unix or Unix systems remotely. You can copy files or execute Unix commands, as well as log in remotely to accounts on those systems. Instead of working through an interface, such as Ftp or Gopher, you can execute remote access commands within your own shell that will then perform actions on a remote system. Unix systems can use two different types of network connections, each with its own protocols. TCP/IP, used with the Internet, can also be used for local networks, as discussed in the previous chapter. UUCP is an alternative set of protocols that provides network communication between Unix systems.

UUCP is an older protocol that was designed to operate between systems that were not already connected on a network. With UUCP, one system can connect to another across phone lines at a predetermined time, sending a batched set of communications all at once. UUCP is very helpful for making a direct connection to a particular system, transferring data, and then cutting the connection. UUCP allows you to set up direct modem-to-modem communication with another system.

With UUCP you can dial across regular phone lines into any system that will permit you access. UUCP operates in batches. Users on a system submit their requests for copying files or executing commands on a remote system. Those requests are then gathered and sent all at once when a connection is made to the remote system. The remote system receives the requests, executes them, and then makes another connection to your system to send back responses. Some requests may be to copy files from the remote system to your own. In this case, those files will be sent by the remote system to yours when it responds. Needless to say, execution of remote operations can be very time consuming with UUCP. A user has to wait for the system to send the request and then continue waiting while the remote system responds.

In previous chapters on electronic mail, you have seen how you can send messages across networks to users on other systems. However, you can also send commands across a network to be executed on another system. For example, you can send a command to copy a file from a directory on one system to a directory on another system. You can also send a command to print files on a given system.

For the System V version of Unix, AT&T developed a network communications package called the Unix to Unix Communications Package (UUCP). UUCP has a set of commands that allows you to perform operations on other systems. For example, the uucp command will copy a file from one system to another. UUCP is part of a standard network package called the Basic Network Utilities (BNU) that has become standard for System V versions of Unix, and is included in some recent versions of BSD Unix. In addition to UUCP commands, BNU also contains the cu utility, which performs remote logins both across a network or from a remote terminal.

UUCP is designed to operate using point-to-point communication. It is as if you were using the mail capabliity of a different system to implement a network. When you issue a UUCP command for a given system, the command is queued and collected with other commands for that same system. The commands are then mailed to that system for execution. Once that system receives the commands and executes them, it mails back any results. The entire process depends on each system in the network sending and receiving commands to and from other systems. In this respect, the network is only as strong as its weakest link. On the other hand, it requires no special structure, only the sending and receiving of mail.

Many of the UUCP commands correspond to the TCP/IP remote access commands. uucp operates much like rcp and uux like rsh. UUCP and TCP/IP are the two major network communications packages currently available on most Unix systems. Early versions of System V used only UUCP, and early versions of BSD Unix used only TCP/IP.

UUCP Addressing

A UUCP network usually uses the path form of addressing. This path form of addressing reflects the UUCP point-to-point form of communication. Systems may be connected to other systems at different locations across the country, which in turn may be connected to other systems in other parts of the world. All of these systems are not directly connected to each other. They are indirectly connected. One system is connected to another system, which in turn is connected to yet another system and so on. You can reach a system on the far end of a network by sending a message that is then passed along by intermediately connected systems. If the mytrain system is connected to the stan system, which in turn is connected to the bell system, then a user on mytrain can reach a user on bell through stan. However, the communication is not made in real time. A message is actually sent as part of a batched collection of messages sent from one system to another.

In the path form of addressing, the system address is placed before the user's login name and separated by an exclamation point. Below is the syntax for path addressing.

system! *login-name*

In the next example, the `mailx` utility sends a message to the user `dylan` on the Unix system called `mytrain`. `dylan`'s address is represented using a path format: `mytrain!dylan`.

```
$ mailx mytrain!dylan < mydata
```

Within the C-shell, the path form of addressing requires that a backslash be placed before the exclamation point. The exclamation point by itself in the C-shell denotes the history command. The backslash will escape the exclamation point treating it as a exclamation point character, not as a history command. The syntax for a C-shell path address follows, as well as an example of the C-shell path used in a `mailx` command.

system\ ! *login-name*
```
% mailx mytrain\!dylan < mydata
```

In a path form of addressing, the address of a user on another system consists of the intermediate systems you have to go through to get to that user's system. Each intermediate system is written in the address sequentially before the user's system and separated by an exclamation point. If you are on `mytrain` and want to send a message to `aleina` on the `bell` system, then you have to specify any intermediate systems through which the message is to be sent. Using the network specified in Figure 17.1, the address would be `stan!bell!aleina`. There may be any number of intermediate systems. If, to send a message to `larisa` at `rose`, you have to go through three intermediate systems, you have to specify those three intermediate systems in the address. In the next examples, messages are sent through an intermediate system to reach a final destination. In the first command a message is sent to the `stan` system, which then passes it on to `bell` where `justin` is located. In the second command, the message is first sent to `lilac`, which

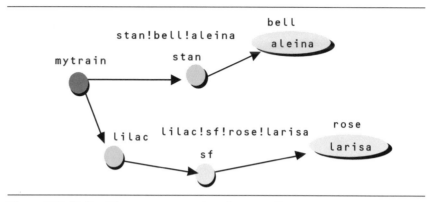

Figure 17.1. Path addresses across network connections.

passes it on to `sf`. `sf` then passes it on to `rose` where `larisa` is located.

```
$ mailx stan!bell!aleina < mydata
$ mailx lilac!sf!rose!larisa < mydata
```

There are often several different intermediate paths of connected systems that you can specify. A network is connected in many different ways. Some connections are shorter than others. Finding a correct sequence of systems with which to address a user can become very complicated very fast. The next two commands show two different paths to the same system using the network described in Figure 17.2. The first example travels through three systems before it arrives at `rose`: `lilac`, `mac`, and `gameplace`. The second example only travels through one systems, `sf`.

```
$ mailx lilac!mac!gameplace!rose!larisa < mydata
$ mailx sf!rose!larisa < mydata
```

Connected Systems: uuname

In a UUCP network you may be connected to many systems. The command uuname will list the systems to which a user can remotely

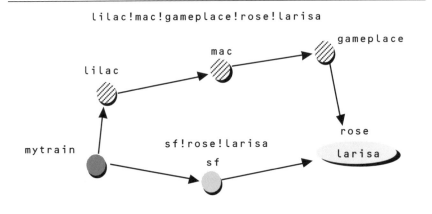

Figure 17.2. Paths of different lengths.

connect and perform remote commands such as uucp. In the next
example, the uuname command lists all connected systems.

```
$ uuname
mytrain
rose
lilac
$
```

The uuname command with the -1 option will display the name of
your own system.

```
$ uuname -1
gameplace
$
```

The uuname command generates a list of system names that are
sent to the standard output. The list of names may be large so you
may want to save it in a file or print it, instead of just displaying it
on the screen. You can redirect this list of system names to a file to
save it, pipe it to a printer to print it, or filter it through a search filter to detect a specific system name. In the next example, the first
command saves the list of system names in a file, the next command prints the list, and the last command uses grep to see if a
specific system name is in the list.

```
$ uuname > syslist
$ uuname | lpr
$ uuname | grep mytrain
mytrain
$
```

To display information about your own system you use uname
(one u).

Making UUCP Connections: uucico and uuxqt

On your Unix system the uucico program handles all your UUCP
communications. uucico stands for UUCP call-incall-out. It is a
daemon that waits for any incoming UUCP transmission, saving it
in the directory **/usr/lib/uucp/uucppublic**. A follow-up program
called uuxqt then interprets and executes the operations specified
in the transmission. Both uucico and uuxqt are system administration operations that are performed only by the root user.

The uucico program also sends transmissions to other systems.
UUCP requests are batched and then sent by uucico to the next
system on its UUCP network. Operations for a specified system
will continue to be transmitted from one system to another in the
UUCP network, until they reach their intended system.

As the root user, you can use uucico to dial into another system
that is waiting for your connection. The program will then make
the connection, transmit any uucp command requests, and then
receive responses and other uucp requests from the other system.
The syntax for using uucico is as follows:

```
uucico -options    remote-name
```

Two helpful options are -r, which suppress an automatic wait
time for redialing, and -x with the number 9, which sets debugging so you can see the actions uucico is taking. In the next example, the root user makes a connection to the rose system.

```
# uucico -r -x 9 rose
```

UUCP Commands

UUCP commands operate on a UUCP network. You can think of UUCP commands as referencing files on other Unix systems through a mail system. Just as you can access files on your own system, you can also access files on other systems. UUCP commands, however, are subject to the same permission restrictions as your own local commands. Protected files and directories cannot be accessed. Only files and directories with the other user permission set can be accessed.

The four major UUCP commands are: uuto, uupick, uucp, and uux. The uuto command mails files to other systems and uupick receives those files. These commands are used for sending and receiving large files. The uucp command copies files from one system to another. The uux command remotely executes a Unix command on another system.

Mail File Transfer: uuto and uupick

UUCP provides a mail facility for sending large files. The command uuto sends files and the command uupick receives files. Together these commands operate much like the mailx command. The uuto command operates in a batch mode. Your request is queued along with other uuto requests on your system. When your request reaches the top of the queue, your file is sent. However, if, in the meantime, you change your file, then that changed file will be sent. The uuto command has an option that allows you to avoid such a conflict. The -p option will immediately copy your file to the system's spool directory and, when the time comes, send that copy. You can then modify the original as much as you wish. The uuto command also has an -m option that notifies you when the file has been sent. The options for uuto are listed in Table 17.I.

```
$ uuto          filename  address    Syntax for uuto command
$ uuto -m -p    filename  address    Options for uuto command
```

In the next example the file **mydata** is sent to address marylou at gameplace.

$ **uuto mydata gameplace!marylou**

You receive files sent to you by the uuto command with the uupick command. To recieve your files, enter the uupick command on the command line without arguments. The files received from other systems sent with the uuto command are then sequentially displayed. You are first prompted with the name of the first file received. The prompt ends with a question mark waiting for you to reply. Enter a reply that specifies how you want to dispose of the received file. One common response is m, which moves the file into your current directory. To move the file to a specific directory, you can specify a directory path after m. Upon hitting the **enter** key you are then prompted with the name of the next file received. You then enter a response and, upon hitting the **enter** key, are prompted with the name of the next file. This continues until you have processed the entire list of files sent to you with the uuto command. If you should just press the **enter** key with no response, then the file remains unreceived and will be prompted for again the next time you execute the uupick command. The different uupick commands are listed in Table 17.I.

In the next example, the uupick command prompts the user for three files received. The first file, **mydata,** is moved to the current directory. The size of the file in blocks is then displayed. The second file, **windata,** is moved to the directory **season**. The file **project** is not disposed of. It will be prompted for again the next time the user executes uupick.

```
$ uupick
from system gameplace: file mydata ? m
10 blocks
from system mytrain: file windata ? m /home/dylan/season
2 blocks
from system gameplace: file project ?
$
```

Table 17.I. Path Mail Addresses

system ! *login-name*	Path mail address for System V (UUCP).
	`rose!mytrain!dylan`
system \ ! *login-name*	Path mail address for C-shell (UUCP). Escape the exclamation point.
	`rose\!mytrain\!dylan`

UUNAME AND UUCICO COMMANDS

uname	Display system name.
−m	Machine type.
−n	Network node hostname.
−r	Operating system release.
−s	Operating system name.
−v	Operating system version.
−a	All information.
uuname	Lists the systems to which yours is connected.
−l	Display local system name.

uucico *options remote-system*

Dials into and connects to a remote system; this is a systems administration action performed only as the root user

```
$ uucico -r -x rose!
```

UUCICO OPTIONS

-r1	Starts in master mode (calls out to a system); implied.
-s	If no system is specified, calls any system for which work is waiting to be done.
-r0	Starts in slave mode; this is the default.
-f	Ignores any required wait for any systems to be called.
-l	Prompts for login name and password using "login:" and "Password:".
-p *port*	Specifies port to call out on or listen to.
-C	Calls named system only if there is work for that system.
-x *type*	Turns on debugging type; the number 9 turns on all types. Types are abnormal, chat, handshake, uucp-proto, proto, port, config, spooldir, execute, incoming, outgoing.
uuxqt	Program called by uucico to execute uux requests.

uuto *filename address*

> Mail command for sending large files to another system.
>
> $ uuto mydata gameplace!larisa

UUTO OPTIONS

-m	Notify sender when file was sent.
-p	Copy file to spool directory and send the copy.
uupick	Mail command that receives files sent to you using uuto. You are sequentially prompted for each file.

UUPICK **COMMANDS**

m *dir*	Move file received to your directory.
a *dir*	Move all files received to your directory.
d	Delete the file received.
p	Display the file received.
enter	Hitting **enter** leaves file waiting.
q	Quit uupick.
*	List uupick commands.
!*cmd*	Execute a Unix command, escaping to your shell.

You may want to check to see if you received any files from someone on a specific system. The uupick -s option followed by a system name will prompt you only for files received from that system. In the next example, uupick will prompt only for those files received from gameplace.

> $ **uupick -s gameplace**

Direct File Copy: uucp **and** uustat

Whereas the uuto command sends files from one account to another, the uucp command copies a file directly from one user's directory to another user's directory. With uucp it is as if the

different accounts are only different directories on other systems, directories to which you have access. Like `cp`, `uucp` takes
two arguments: the name of the source file and the name of the
copy.

> $ uucp *source-file* *copy-file*

You can use `uucp` to copy files from your directory to one on another system, or to copy a file on another system to your own directory. In either instance, the copy name or the source name will
include the name of the other system as well as the full path name
of the file. In the next example, the file **mydata** is copied to the directory **chris** on the `gameplace` system.

> $ **uucp mydata gameplace!/home/chris/mydata**

The `uucp` command operates in a batch mode in the background.
Your `uucp` request is queued and when it reaches the top of the
queue then your file is copied. If you change your file in the meantime, then the current changed version is copied. You can over-
come this conflict with the `-C` option. With the `-C` option the file is
copied to the system spool directory when you issue the `uucp`
command. Then when it is time to actually perform the copy, the
system uses the file version in the spool directory. The different
`uucp` options are listed in Table 17.II. In the next example, the mydata file will be copied to the spool directory and that version used
in the `uucp` operation.

> $ **uucp -C mydata gameplace!/home/chris/mydata**

If you designate in your `uucp` command a directory that does not
actually exist in the remote user's file system, the `uucp` command
will create it. However, the remote user may not want you creating
such a directory in his or her system. In that case you can use the
`-f` option, which will instruct `uucp` not to create a directory if it
does not already exist. In the next example, the user copies a file to
the **season** directory in **chris**'s home directory. In the first `uucp`
command the **season** directory will be created if it does not already
exist. In the second `uucp` command, the **season** directory will not
be created.

```
$ uucp windata gameplace!/home/chris/season/swindata
$ uucp -f windata gameplace!/home/chris/season/swindata
```

There may be times when you only know the user's name, not the user's full path name beginning from the root. Yet, you need to specify the full path name of the file on the other system in order to reference it in a uucp command. You can use the UUCP tilde operator to find the full path name of that user. The tilde, ~, takes as its argument a user name and evaluates to the full path name of that user's home directory. For example, ~**chris** evaluates to **/home/chris**. You can then use the tilde and the user name as part of a path name, to provide you with a full path name for a file. In the next example, the tilde is used to specify a full path name, first for **mydata** and then for **windata**. The second command copies the file windata on the gameplace system to the user's own directory.

```
$ uucp mydata gameplace!~chris/mydata
$ uucp gameplace!~chris/windata windata
```

With uucp, you can also copy files from one remote system to another remote system. The next example copies **mydata** from a directory on gameplace to a directory on mytrain.

```
$ uucp gameplace!~chris/mydata mytrain!~justin/mydata
```

uucp commands are executed in batch mode. They may take some time to perform their task. The command uustat lists information about current uucp operations. With the -u option you can display uucp jobs for a specific user. With the -s option you can display jobs for a specific system. The next example displays the uucp jobs for justin the were directed to the system mytrain.

```
$ uustat -ujustin -smytrain
```

You can also use uustat to kill uucp jobs. uustat will list the job number of each uucp job in progress. uustat with a -k option and the job id will kill the uucp job.

```
$ uustat -k 795
```

Remote Execution: uux

With uux you can remotely execute a command on files on other systems. In a uux command, files and commands are referenced using their paths. gameplace!~justin/filmdata refers to the **filmdata** file in **justin**'s home directory on the gameplace system. Commands and files on your own system are referenced with a preceding exclamation point, !, with no system name. !mydata refers to the **mydata** file on your own system. The same rule is applied to the command to be executed. To execute a command on your own system, you precede it with a single exclamation point. In the next example the file **filmdata** in **justin**'s home directory is displayed on the user's own terminal.

> $ **uux !cat gameplace!~justin/filmdata**

In a uux command, you need to quote special characters such as those used for redirection and pipes (>, <, |) in order to avoid their evaluation by your shell. You can quote them individually or place the entire command within quotes. In the next example, the cat command copies files and pipes them to the your printer.

$**uux `!cat gameplace!~chris/windata mytrain!~justin/food | lp'**

If you want to use a command on a remote system, you need to precede it with its system path. For example, suppose you want to print a file on a remote system's printer instead of your own. You then precede the lp command with the system's path. In the next example, the user prints the file **filmdata** on the remote system's printer.

$ **uux "!cat gameplace!~justin/filmdata | gameplace!lp"**

Like uucp commands, uux commands are not executed right away. They are placed in a queue and executed when they reach the head of the queue. In the meantime you may have changed some of the files your uux command operates on. In that case the changed files are operated on. As in the uucp command, you can avoid this conflict by using the uux command with the -C option. This option makes an immediate copy of the files involved and than operates on those copies when it is time to execute. A list of uux options is provided in Table 17.II.

uucp *sys-name*!*filename*   *sys-name*!*filename*

Copies files from one system to another.

$ uucp mydata gameplace!justin/newdata

UUCP OPTIONS

-m	Notify the user when a uucp job is completed.
-n*user*	Notify the remote user when a uucp job is performed.
-C	Copy file to spool directory and send that copy.
-c	Do not copy file to spool directory (default).
-f	Do not create destination directories.
-g	Specify grade of service (high, medium, low).

uustat   Lists current uucp jobs. With the -k option and the job number, you can delete a uucp job.

$ uustat

UUSTAT OPTIONS

-a	List all jobs for all users.
-u*user*	List all jobs for specific user.
-s*system*	List all jobs for specific system.
-k*jobid*	Kill a uucp job.
-c	The queue time for a job, use with -t .
-t*sys*	The transfer rate for a system.
-q	Display status of jobs.

uux   Remotely execute a command on another system. File names and command name must be preceded with an exclamation point.

$ uux !cat gameplace!mydata

UUX OPTIONS

-z	Notify user the job is successful.
-n	Suppress notification of job's success.
-C	Copy file to spool directory and operate on that copy.
-c	Do not copy file to spool directory (default).
-g	Specify grade of service (high, medium, low).

Table 17.II. uucp, uustat, **and** uux **Commands**

Each particular Unix system will often restrict the commands that can be executed with uux. Commands such as rm that erases files are usually not allowed. The commands that can be executed with uux on a given system are listed in a permissions file. In release 4, that file is **/etc/uucp/Permissions**. In earlier versions it may be **/usr/lib/uucp/Permissions**.

Remote Login: cu **and** ct

The Basic Network Communications package includes the cu command, which allows you to log in remotely to another system. With the cu command you can either dial into a system across a telephone line, or connect across network lines. The cu command also allows you to transfer character files to and from a remote system. Table 17.III summarizes the cu and ct commands.

The cu command (call Unix) allows you to log in remotely to an account on another system. It is very much like the rlogin command used for TCP/IP. To connect to another Unix system, enter the cu command followed by the name of the system. You will then be prompted for a login name and you can then log in to an account on that system. In the next example a user connects to the gameplace system.

```
$ cu gameplace
Connected
login:
```

A list of the systems to which you are connected is kept in the file **/etc/uucp/Systems**. All UUCP remote access commands will reference this file to determine if they are being instructed to access a connected system. If a system is not in the file, the cu command will fail. In the next example the cu command fails because the peach system is not in the **/etc/uucp/Systems** file—it is not registered as a connected system.

```
$ cu peach
Connection failed: SYSTEM NOT IN Systems FILE
$
```

You can also use cu to dial into another system using a telephone number. Many systems allow you to connect to them across telephone lines using a modem. If you use a telephone number as an argument to cu, the cu command will use a modem to dial into another system across a telephone line. In the next example the user dials up a system with cu.

```
$ cu 9999999
```

You can also specify transmission features such as baud rate, duplex, and parity. The next example sets the baud rate to 57600 using the -s option.

```
$ cu -s57600 9999999
```

The ct command (call terminal) allows you to connect to a terminal through a auto-answer modem. In effect, it executes the login process in reverse. Your system initiates and sets up a login connection between your Unix account and the specified terminal. The ct command takes as its argument a telephone number. ct has the same options as cu for specifying transmission features such as baud rate and duplex. In the next example, the system connects to a terminal with the phone number 9999999.

```
$ ct -s57600 9999999
```

Once you have logged into your remote system you can then execute any commands you wish. When you have finished, you then log out from your remote system with the command ~.. When you enter the period, ., the name of the remote system will be displayed within brackets.

```
$ ~[gameplace].
Disconnected
```

Once logged into another system you may want to access your original system. The command sequence ~! generates a shell that allows you to return temporarily to your local system without breaking your login connection. You can then enter commands for your local system. When you are ready to return to your remotely logged in system, end the shell with the exit command. In the next example, the user temporarily returns to the local system and

executes commands to list files and print a file. When the user hits
the exclamation point in the ~! command sequence, the name of
the local system is displayed within the brackets.

```
$ ~[mytrain]!
$ ls
mydata newdocs
$ lp mydata
$ exit
$
```

The ~! command generates a new shell. This is not the same as the
original shell in the local system. Changes in the new shell such as
directory changes or changes to local shell variables, will not be re-
tained when the new shell is exited. If you return to the local system with the !~ command and change directories, then you only
change the working directory for the new shell, not the working
directory for the original shell.

You can affect your local system's original shell with the ~% command. The ~% command effects a command-line escape to the local
system. To change the directory of your local system's original shell,
use the ~% command with the cd command. When you hit the percent sign, the name of the local system will appear within brackets.

```
$ ~[mytrain]% cd letters
```

The cu command also supports simple character file transfers
between systems. The command sequence ~% precedes the commands for sending and receiving files. The command ~% take
sends files from your remote system to the local system. The command ~% put sends files from the local system to the remote system. The commands take as their argument the name of the file
being transferred. If the file is to have a different name from the
one on the other system, you can specify that as the second argument. The syntax for take and put is shown here.

```
$ ~% take remote-file
$ ~% put local-file
```

In the next example, a user sends the file **mydata** from the remote
system, gameplace, to the local system, mytrain, using the take

command. Upon hitting the % sign, the name of the local system is displayed within brackets.

```
$ ~[mytrain]% take mydata
```

In the next example, the file **windata** is sent from the local system, `mytrain`, to the remote system, `gameplace`, with the put command and given a new name, **season**.

```
$ ~[mytrain]% put windata season
```

Table 17.III. cu **and** ct **Commands**

---

cu   Remotely log in to an account on another system (call Unix).

```
$ cu gameplace
```

cu **OPTIONS**

-s	Specify baud rate (transmission speed) such as 300, 1200, 2400, 4800, or 9600.
-c	Select local area network to be used.
-l	Select communications line to be used.
-e	Set even parity.
-o	Set odd parity.
-h	Set half-duplex.
-b*n*	Set byte size to 7 or 8: –b7 or –b8.
-n	Prompt for telephone number instead of entering it on the command line.
-t	Connect to terminal with auto-answer modem like the ct command does.

cu **COMMANDS**

~!   Temporary return to local system

```
$ ~[mytrain]!
```

exit   End use of local system and return to remote.

```
$ ~[mytrain]!
```

~%   A one command escape to local system

```
$ ~[mytrain]% cd newdocs
```

~% take *remote-file*   Copy a file from remote system to local system.

```
$ ~[mytrain]% take mydata
```

(continued)

Table 17.III. cu **and** ct **Commands** *(continued)*

~% put *remote-file*   Copy a file from local system to remote system.

                                  $ ~[mytrain]% put windata

ct   Remotely connect from your system to a terminal through an auto-
                answer modem (connect terminal). The ct command takes as an
                argument a telephone number of the terminal. It has several options for
                specifying transmission features such as baud rate and parity.

                    $ ct 9999999

                    -s   Baud rate

                        $ ct -s57600 9999999

Section V

Unix Reference

18. Unix Glossary
19. Command Reference

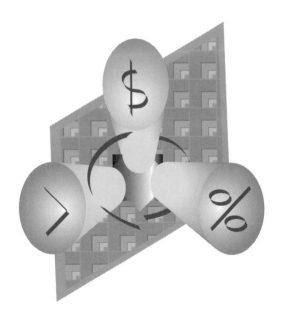

Unix Glossary

absolute pathname   The full path name of a file denoting its place in the file structure. An absolute path name begins with the root, /, and includes all directories from the root to that of the file's.

address   Address of user within a network. You use a user's address to send the user mail.

alias   Another name given to a Unix command. In the Korn and C-shells you use the alias command to give another name to a Unix command.

anchor   Highlighted text or image on a Web page that will connect to a Web resource when selected. Anchors can contain URLs with which to access resources on remote sites as well as access resources on the local system or part of the currently displayed Web page.

anonymous ftp   An Ftp login using any password. Used to provide access to any user by Internet Ftp sites.

append   To add text to the end of a file.

Archie   Search utility for locating and displaying the network address and names of directories and files accessible on Ftp sites on the Internet.

archive   Copying several files into one storage medium that can later be extracted. You can archive to a tape or a file. The `tar` utility is commonly used to create Unix archives.

argument   A value represented by a set of characters that is listed on the command line with a Unix command. An argument can be a string constant, an option, a file name, or an evaluated variable.

ARPANET   A network created by DARPA for corporations and universities engaged in government research. It was the first to use the TCP/IP network protocols and was the precursor of the Internet.

array   An aggregate variable structure consisting of several elements, each of which is its own variable. You reference an element with the array name and the number of the element. Arrays can be defined in the Korn shell, C-shell, and `awk`.

ASCII   A standard character set used widely on computers that run Unix. ASCII stands for American Standard Code for Information Interchange.

back up   To make a copy of files or file systems.

background job   A job executed in the background while the user continues with other processes.

baud rate   Transmission speed, usually applied to a modem or communications line. Rates vary usually from 300 to 56,000 baud. You can calculate the actual number of bytes sent per second by dividing the baud rate by 10; for example, 1200 baud is 120 characters per second.

block   The number of bytes written to disk at any one time. The usual size for a Unix block is 1024, though on some systems it may be 512 or 2048. The Unix file system is organized into blocks that are randomly accessed.

block device   Disk drive or tape on which data are written to and read from in blocks, rather than byte by byte.

Bourne shell   The Unix shell developed at ATT by Steve Bourne for Unix System V versions.

braces   The { and } symbols, sometime called curly brackets.

brackets   The [and] symbols used to denote classes of characters in the shell. Sometimes called a square bracket.

BSD   Berkeley Software Development. This term denotes the Berkeley version of Unix such as BSD 4.2.

byte   Basic memory component of any computer memory. One byte contains 8 bits. One byte can hold one character value.

C programming language   The programming language developed originally for use with Unix and now extensively used on DOS and other systems. The code for the Unix operating system is written in C, as well as many Unix applications software.

character device   A device other than a storage medium for inputting or outputting characters. Keyboards, screens, modems, and printers are all examples of character devices.

client   A user of services and resources on a network.

client/server   A network architecture that divides operations between a client that sends requests to a server that responds to those requests. Instead of all operations being performed with a given system, a client system and request that a server system perform an operation for it and send the results.

client software   Programs designed to access services and resources on a network, such as the Ftp program with which a user can access Ftp sites.

command line   The basic interface for communicating with Unix. The user enters commands and arguments on the command line, ending with a carriage return.

compiler   A program that takes a source code file and generates an executable program.

compression   Generate a version of a file in a reduced size.

control character   A nonprinting character often used to control output. A carriage return and tab are control characters.

control key   A control key is specified on the keyboard by the control key used with another key. Control keys are represented in this text with the term **Ctrl-** and a character; for example, **Ctrl-d** is the control d key.

control structure   Structures used in shell programming to control the execution of Unix commands. A common control structure is a loop, repeating certain Unix commands until a test condition is met.

C-shell   A Unix shell developed for Berkeley Unix by Bill Joy. The C-shell was named for the C programming language with which it shares many of the same programming features.

DARPA   Defense Advanced Research Projects Agency. Military agency that funded research for TCP/IP and was the first to implement it on their network, ARPANET.

delimiters   Selected characters that specify the end of a field or string. The default delimiters for the command line are the space and tab.

device   An input or output component such as a disk drive, printer, or terminal that you can attach to your computer.

device file   All devices in Unix are treated as files.

directory   The organizing component in the Unix file structure. All files are organized into directories. A directory itself is treated as a special type of file that contains a list of files placed within that directory.

domain addressing   A type of addressing for users on different systems in a network using domain names. *user-name@system-name.domain*

domain name   Name given to networks to represent their IP address. Used as part of a fully qualified domain name to provide an address for a system on a network.

Domain Name Service   Service for resolving fully qualified domain names, thus associating them with their IP address. This process is usually carried out by a domain name server on a network.

editor   A utility for creating and modifying text files. Ed, Ex, Vi, and Emacs are the standard Unix editors. Many systems may also have other popular word processors such as WordPerfect and Word.

electronic mail   A utility that allows you to send messages to other users on the system or those connected through a network.

Elm   A mailer for sending and receiving mail on Unix systems. It has an easy-to-use full-screen, cursor-based interface.

environment variable A shell variable used to help configure your user shell.

EOF End of file.

EOT End of transmission.

exit status The status returned by a command when it completes execution. The status is 0 if successful and nonzero if not successful.

file Basic data component of a Unix system. All data are organized into files. Devices and directories are also treated as files.

file name. Name you give to a file.

file name generation The shell can use special characters to generate a list of file names from those in a directory.

file system Files are organized into one overall file structure. This file structure, in turn, can contain several file systems. A file system is a group of files and directories that can be attached to or removed from the file structure.

filter A special Unix utility that can read from the standard input and output data to the standard output. Many filters can also read directly from files. A filter often modifies its output, generating a modified version of the input. The input is never itself modified.

ftp Command to access systems on a network and transfer files to and from them.

FTP File Transfer Protocol, a TCP/IP protocol for transferring files between systems connected on a TCP/IP network such as the Internet.

Fully qualified domain name Address for a system on a network that includes the system name, the domain name used for the network, and its extension. The components are separated by periods. It is used on networks using TCP/IP, such as the Internet. Fully qualified domain names are used extensively as Internet addresses. The fully qualified domain name is associated with an IP address that is actually used to identify a system on the network. This association is usually carried out by the domain name service on the network.

function You can define shell functions in the Bourne and Korn shells to execute several Unix commands.

Gopher   Gopher is a menu-driven utility for accessing network resources, such as files, images, Telnet connections, and Ftp sites. Gopher was created at the University of Minnesota (`gopher.tc.umn.edu.`).

group   A group is a way of organizing users. Users can form a group. You can then send messages to just the members of the group, or restrict access to certain files to just those members.

hard link   Another name for a file. You create a hard link with the `ln` command.

here document   This is a shell script that reads data contained within itself. Part of the script is actually data to be read by a command.

hidden files   Every Unix login has a set of special initialization files that are not normally displayed by the `ls` command. These files begin with a period and are sometimes called dot files. You can list hidden files with `ls` and the `-a` option.

history   A feature of the Korn shell and C-shell for referencing and re-executing previous commands.

home directory   The login directory for a user's account. The path name for a user's home directory is contained in the system variable `HOME`.

host   A system connected to a network that can be accessed by other systems on it and provides services to users on the network.

host name   The name given to a system that is connected to a network. This host name combined with the domain name of its network constitutes a fully qualified domain name.

HTML   HyperText Markup Language, a series of formatting and reference tags used to create Web pages.

HTTP   HyperText Transfer Protocol, the protocol used to transfer and display Web pages and resources on Web sites.

Hypermedia   A method for displaying all forms of media in a document, including sounds and video.

HyperText   A method for linking to and displaying related text and images for a document.

Internet   An open network accessible to all users. It uses TCP/IP, providing a full range of access to the Web, Ftp, Gopher, Telnet, mail, and news clients and servers.

Internet address   An IP address that identifies a system connected to the Internet network. The term also refers to the fully qualified domain name given to the IP address for a system. Most users use the fully qualified domain name.

interrupt   A signal sent to stop a process currently running. A **Ctrl-c** will often interrupt a command currently being executed.

intranet   A local network using TCP/IP with all of the functionality found on the Internet. Local Web, Ftp, and Gopher sites can be set up within an intranet and accessible only within it. Intranets may or may not have access to the Internet.

IP   Internet Protocol, the TCP/IP protocol used to transmit data across a network. Used for the Internet. A transmission is divided into packets that are sent individually and then combined by the receiving system.

IP address   An Internet Protocol address that uniquely identifies a system connected on a TCP/IP network such as the Internet. The IP address consists of four numbers separated by periods. Usually the first three identify the network to which a system is connected, and the last identifies that system.

IP datagram   Internet Protocol datagram, the transmission unit used for the IP protocols (also referred to as a packet).

job   A process being executed by the system. The execution of a command is often referred to as a job if it is queued in some way. For example, a print command or executing a command in the background will queue that command, making it a job.

job shell   The jsh shell the extends the Bourne shell to allow it to control jobs more easily. This shell upgrades the Bourne shell with same job control features found in the Korn and C-shell.

Korn shell   A Unix shell developed by David Korn at AT&T for Unix System V.

link   Another name for a file. There are symbolic and hard links. A hard link is another file name for a file on the disk. A symbolic link is a reference to a file name, through which a file can then be accessed.

links   Term used for anchors on Web pages that connect to other Web resources such as other Web pages, Ftp sites, Gopher sites, or Telnet connections.

log in   The process of gaining access to a Unix system.

login name   The name that identifies a user on the system.

login shell   The type of shell that you use when you log in such as the Bourne, Korn, or C-shell.

log out   The process of terminating a connection to the Unix system.

macro   A word that is replaced by other words or instructions. Macros are used extensively by the `nroff` and `troff` document formatters to represent complex instructions.

mailbox   A special file that holds message received by the `mailx` utility.

mailer   Mail utility that you can use to send and receive mail on Unix systems.

mailx   Mail utility using a simple command-line interface that you can use to send and receive mail on Unix systems.

metacharacter   Another term used for special characters. The *, [], and ? are all examples of metacharacters.

MH   Mail Handler, a mail utility for sending and receiving mail that uses commands that can be executed from your Unix command line rather than a separate interface.

MIME   Multi-purpose Internet Mail Extensions, method for sending nontext files such as image files using email. Such files are coded into a text version that is sent and then decoded when received, restoring it to its original format.

Mosaic   The first widely used Web browser. Available from National Center for Supercomputing Applications (NCSA) at the University of Illinois at Urbana-Champaign. More information about Mosaic is available at the NCSA Web site: `www.ncsa.uiuc.edu`.

mount   Attach a file system to the file structure.

multi-tasking   The process of running more than one job at the same time. In Unix you can place a job in the background and have it running while you are executing other commands in the foreground.

multi-user system   A system that more than one user can use at the same time.

network   A group of computers connected with communication lines and through which users can send information and share data.

network address   The unique identifier for a system on a network.

newsgroup   Usenet news articles are collected into newsgroups, organized by topic.

newsreaders   Application for reading Usenet newsgroup articles. Some of the popular Unix newsreaders are `rn`, `trn`, `tin`, and `nn`. Netscape and Mosaic also provide newsreaders with their Web browser. Pine also has newsreader capabilities.

NNTP   Network News Transfer Protocol, protocol for transferring Usenet news articles across a network. Used by news servers to provide Usenet articles to users on their network.

octal number   A base 8 number.

option   A command argument that qualifies how a command is to be executed. Many commands have a set of predetermined options with which you can vary the way they are executed.

path addressing   A type of addressing for users on different systems in a UUCP network. `system-name!user-name`

path name   A name of a file that includes the path to the file through intervening directories. A path name can be absolute or relative. A relative path name begins from the current working directory to the file. The absolute path name begins from the root.

Pine   Program for Internet news and email, a mailer and newsreader that has its own editor. Pine also supports Multi-purpose Internet Mail Extensions (MIME) for sending and receiving binaries.

pipe   A connection between the standard output of one command with the standard input of another. The output of one command becomes the input of another command.

Pnews   Application for posting Usenet news articles.

process   The execution of a command.

prompt   Symbol displayed by the shell at the beginning of each new command line. The default Bourne and Korn shell prompt is $, and the default C-shell prompt is %.

protocol   A set of rules designed to specify how systems should interact with each other, especially for transmitting information.

quote   Quoting a character removes any special meaning for it. In a shell, certain characters such as > are operators that perform certain shell operations. Quoting the character treats the operator as just another character. You can quote a single character by preceding it with a backslash. You can quote several characters by enclosing them within single or double quotes. Double quotes will not quote a $ character.

rcp   Remote copy command used to copy files between remote systems on a network.

readnews   An early simple newsreader for posting and reading Usenet news articles.

redirection   Process of redirecting the standard output to a file or device, or redirect the standard input from a file or device. By default, the standard input is directed from the keyboard, and the standard output is directed to the screen.

regular expression   A string of characters that includes special characters. A regular expression can match on several strings.

relative path name   The path name of a file beginning from the current working directory.

rn   A newsreader for posting and reading Usenet news articles. It uses a simple line-by-line display of newsgroups and article titles, but has effective search capabilities.

root directory   The first and top directory in the file structure. All other directories are derived from the root.

script   A shell program—an executable file that contains Unix commands. When the file is read by the system, the commands are executed.

server   A system that provides services to users on a network. It receives request from client applications on connected systems and provides the requested service.

shell   A control interface between the user and the operating system. The shell interprets commands received from the user, and sends them to the operating system for execution. There are three major types of shells: Bourne shell, Korn shell, and C-shell.

shell script   See **script**.

SMTP   Simple Mail Transfer Protocol, a protocol for transmitting mail messages across a network.

special character   A set of characters used as operators in the shell and in editors to perform special functions. In the shell, shell special characters are used to generate file names. In editors, edit special characters are used to form regular expressions to match on several possible patterns in the text. Edit special characters are found in all the standard editors as well as the edit filters and in `awk`.

spool   To queue a process or file.

standard error   A special output stream reserved for error messages. This is to ensure that error messages reach the user, even if the standard output is redirected. Default is the screen.

standard input   The input data stream from which a command receives input. Default is the keyboard.

standard output   The output data stream to which the command sends its output. Default is the screen.

string   A set of alphabetic characters. If you want to include spaces, tabs, and special characters in a string, you need to quote the entire string with double or single quotes.

subdirectory   A directory that is located within another directory. All directories, except the root, are subdirectories.

subshell   A shell generated within another shell. When you execute a script, it generates its own shell. Any variable defined within that script will be local to its own shell.

superuser   The system administrator that can control all aspects of the Unix system.

symbolic link   Another name for a file name or directory. A symbolic link is used just like a hard link, except that it can span file systems and be used to reference directories.

system administrator   The person who maintains a Unix system.

System V   The AT&T version of Unix.

TCP   Transmission Control Protocol, the transport protocol for transmitting data on a network. The transport protocol used for TCP/IP networks.

TCP/IP   Transmission Control Protocol/Internet Protocol, communications protocols for transmitting data across a network. A transmission is broken down into packets, sent separately, and then recombined by the receiving system. The term is applied to networks that use the full set of Internet protocols such as HTTP, FTP, SMTP, NNTP, among others.

`telnet`   Command to connect to a remote system using the Telenet protocols, allowing you to log in to a system as if you were using a terminal connected to it.

Telnet   The TCP/IP protocol for connecting to remote systems.

termcap   The **termcap** file contains a list of terminal characteristics used by BSD versions of Unix to identify and interpret signals from your terminal.

terminfo   In System V, the **terminfo** directory contains files that hold terminal characteristics used to identify and interpret signals from your terminal.

`tin`   A newsreader for posting and reading Usenet news articles. It has a full-screen selector for both newsgroups and articles. It uses threads to organize articles by subject, with replies and follow-ups.

`trn`   Thread News Reader, a newsreader for posting and reading Usenet news articles. It has a full-screen selector for accessing articles and uses threads to organize articles by subject, with replies and follow-ups.

`tty`   A command term for 'terminal.' `tty` stands for 'teletypewriter.'

URL   Universal Resource Locator, addressing method use by Web browser to access Web resources. URL includes the protocol to be used for the resource, the network address (usually an Internet address in the form of a fully qualified domain name), and the location (path name) of the resource on that system.

Usenet   A network service for collecting, organizing, and providing news articles.

utility   Standard applications programs included with most Unix systems. The term utility often refers to a complex program that may have its own interface or shell such as the `mailx` utility. However, technically, most commands are utilities.

uucp   Command to perform a remote transfer of files between Unix system using the UUCP protocols.

UUCP   Unix to Unix Communications Package, an older protocol that was designed to operate between Unix systems that were not already connected on a network. Connections are carried out by batched transmissions from one system to another.

variable   An object that holds a value such as a string. You can define variables in the shell and in programs such as awk. There are also special shell variables defined by the system for configuring your user shell.

WAIS   Wide Area Information Service, indexing and search applications for locating resources on a network. Can be used for various types of documents, including Web pages.

Web site   Sites on the Internet that support the HTTP protocols and provide accessible Web pages.

whitespace   Another name for either a space, tab, or carriage return. Whitespaces are the default delimiters for the command-line and input data.

word   A set of characters delimited by a whitespace. Most command-line arguments are words.

working directory   The current default directory. The default directory can be changed using the cd command.

World Wide Web   A network of Internet sites that uses Web browsers for easily accessing Internet resources throughout the world. The World Wide Web originated in Europe at CERN Research Laboratories (the European Particle Physics Laboratory in Switzerland). It is often referred to as WWW or simply as the Web. Web browsers display Web pages created using the HyperText Markup Language (HTML). Web pages are transferred using the HyperText Transfer Protocol (HTTP). Resources on the Web are located using Universal Resource Locators (URLs).

Unix Command
Reference

Unix Command Reference

login-name@ system.domain	Domain mail addresses (Internet)
	`chirs@violet.rose.edu`
system!login-name	Path mail address for System V (UUCP)
	`rose!violet!justin`
system\!login-name	Path mail address for C-Shell (UUCP). Escape the exclamation point.
	`rose\!violet\!justin`

VACATION OPTIONS

`-d`	Append the date to the logfile
`-F` *user*	If mail can't be sent to mailfile, forward mail to specified user.
-l *filename*	Save names of senders who were sent the vacation reply in the specified file (default is **$HOME/.maillog**)
`-m` *mailbox-filename*	Save received messages in specified file (default is **$HOME/.mailfile**)
`-M` *mesg_file*	Use the text in *mesg_file* as vacation's automatic reply message (default is **/usr/lib/mail/std_vac_msg**).

Table 1. Network Mail Addresses: Domain and Path

TILDE COMMANDS FOR MESSAGE HEADER

~h	Prompts the user to enter in addresses, subject, and carbon copy list.
~s *subject*	Enter a new subject.
~t *addresses*	Add addresses to the address list.
~c *addresses*	Add addresses to the carbon copy list.
~b *addresses*	Add addresses to the blind carbon copy list.

TILDE COMMANDS FOR MESSAGE TEXT

~v	Invoke the Vi editor. Changes are saved to the message text.
~p	Redisplay the text of the message.
~x	Quit the message and leave the `mailx` utility.
~w *filename*	Save the message in a file.
~r *filename*	Read the contents of a file into the message text.
~e	Invoke the default text editor.
~|*filter*	Pipe the contents of a message to a filter and replace the message with the ouptut of that filter.
~m *message-list*	When sending messages or replying to received mail, this command inserts the contents of a received message. The contents are indented. Used when receiving messages.
~f *message-list*	When sending messages or replying to received mail, this command inserts the contents of a received message. Unlike ~m, there is no indentation. Used when receiving messages.

GENERAL TILDE COMMANDS

~?	Display a list of all the tilde commands.
~~	Enter a tilde as a character into the text.
~! *command*	Execute a shell command while entering a message.

Table 2. Mailx Tilde Commands for Sending a Message

Table 3. Mailx Commands for Receiving Messages

MAILX COMMAND OPTIONS

-f *mailbox-filename*	Invoke the `mailx` utility to read messages in a mailbox file in your directory rather than your mailbox of waiting messages.
-H	Display only the list of message headers.
-s *subject*	When sending messages, this option specifies the subject.
-F	Save message in a file with the name of the first recipient.

STATUS CODES

N	Newly received messages.
U	Previously unread messages.
R	Read messages in the current session.
P	Preserved messages, read in previous session and kept in incoming mailbox.
D	Deleted messages. Messages marked for deletion.
O	Old messages.
*	Messages that you have saved to another mailbox file.

DISPLAY MESSAGES

h	Redisplay the message headers.
z+ z-	If header list takes up more than one screen you can scroll header list forward and backward with the + and –.
t *msge-list*	Displays a message referenced by the message list. If no message list is used, then the current message is displayed.
p *msge-list*	Displays a message referenced by the message list. If no message list is used, then the current message is displayed.
n	Displays next message.
+	Displays next message.
–	Displays the previous message

(continued)

Table 3. Mailx Commands for Receiving Messages *(continued)*

`top` *message-list*	Displays the top few lines of a message referenced by the message list. If no message list is used, then the current message is displayed.
`=`	Displays the number of the current message

MESSAGE LISTS

message-number	Reference message with message number.
num1-num2	Reference a range of messages beginning with `num1` and ending with `num2`.
`.`	The current message.
`^`	The first message.
`$`	The last message.
`*`	All messages waiting in the mailbox.
/pattern	All messages with *pattern* in the subject field.
address	All messages sent from user with *address*.
`:`*c*	All messages of the type indicated by *c*. Message types are as follows:
`n`	newly received messages
`o`	old messages previously received
`r`	read messages
`u`	unread messages
`d`	deleted messages

DELETING AND RESTORING MESSAGES

`d` *message-list*	Delete a message referenced by the indicated message list from your mailbox.
`u` *message-list*	Undelete a message referenced by the indicated message list that has been previously deleted.
`q`	Quit the `mailx` utility and saves any read messages in the mbox file.
`x`	Quit the `mailx` utility and does *not* erase any messages you deleted. This is equivalent to executing a u command on all deleted messages before quitting.
`pr` *message-list*	Preserve messages in your waiting mailbox even if you have already read them.

(continued)

Table 3. Mailx Commands for Receiving Messages *(continued)*

SENDING AND EDITING MESSAGES

r	Send a reply to all persons who received a message.
R	Send a reply to the person who sent you a message.
m *address*	Send a message to someone while in the `mailx` utility.
v *message-list*	Edit a message with the `vi` editor.

SAVING MESSAGES

s *message-list filename*	Save a message referenced by the message list in a file, including the header of the message.
S *message-list*	Save a message referenced by the message list in a file named for the sender of the message.
w *message-list filename*	Save a message referenced by the message list in a file without the header. Only the text of the message is saved.
c *message-list filename*	Copy a message referenced by the message list to a file without marking it as saved.
folder *mailbox-filename*	Switch to another mailbox file.
%	Represents name of incoming mailbox file. `folder %` Switch to incoming mailbox file.
#	Represents name of previously accessed mailbox file. `folder #` Switch to previous mailbox file.
&	Represents name of mailbox file used to automatically save your read messages, usually called `mbox`. `folder &` Switch to **mbox** file.

GENERAL COMMANDS

?	Display a list of all the mail commands.

(continued)

Table 3. Mailx Commands for Receiving Messages *(continued)*

! *command*	Execute a user shell command from within the mail shell.
alias *name address-list*	Create an alias for a list of addresses.

```
alias myclass chris aleina larisa
$ mailx myclass
```

Table 4. mailx Options

append	Place messages saved in your mailbox at the end, rather than the beginning (disabled by default).
asksub	Prompt for subject. `set asksub`
askcc	Prompt for carbon copy addresses. `set askcc`
autoprint	When deleting messages, shows the next message after the last one deleted (disabled by default).
cmd=*cmd*	Specify default command to use with pip operation should no command be given (disabled by default).
crt=n	For messages that are *n* or more lines, displays them using your PAGER program (disabled by default).
dbug	Debug mode with detailed descriptions of actions taken, but there is no actual delivery of messages (disabled by default).
dot	Allows you to end a message by entering a dot on a line by itself, instead of **Ctrl-d** (disabled by default).
escape=*c*	Specify c as the escape character in the input mode.
flipr	Switch the R and r commands so the R sends a reply to senders of several specified messages and r sends a response to all other recipients of a message you received (disabled by default).
folder=*directory*	Save any mailbox files created by the s or S command to the directory assigned to it. `set folder=$HOME/mail`
header	Show header sumary when starting up (default).
hold	Keep read messages in your incomming mailbox, instead of **mbox** (disabled by default).
ignore	Ignore interrupts when composing messages (disabled by default).
ignoreeof	Disables the use of **Ctrl-d** to end input when composing messages. Should have dot enabled so you can end messages with just a . on a line by itself, or use ~. to end messages (disabled by default).
indentprefix=*string*	Specify string (characters) to be placed at the beginning of each line of a copied message included within a response you are composing (disabled is tab).

(continued)

Table 4. mailx Options *(continued)*

keep	Keep mailbox files when they become empty (disabled by default).
keepsave	When you save a message to a particular mailbox file, also save a copy to your standard mailbox file, usually **mbox** (disabled by default).
metoo	Allows you to send a copy of a message to yourself that you are also sending to others. By default your name would automatically be deleted from a list of addresses (disabled by default).

outfolder	Place record file in folder directory. In the following example, `outbox` will be a file in the directory defined by `folder`.
	
	`set record=outbox`
	
	`set outfolder`

page	When piping several messages through a pipe command, this option inserts a formfeed after each so that each message will start on its own screen (disabled by default).
prompt=*string*	Redefine `mailx` prompt `set prompt="&"`
record=*filename*	Automatically saves a copy of any message that you create and send. Messages are saved in a file specified when you set the record option. `set record=$HOME/outbox`
save	Save incomplete or interrupted messages in your dead letter file (disabled by default).
screen=*n*	Set the number of lines of the header displayed on your screen (default is 5).
sendwait	Wait for background mailer to finish processing before resuming with `mailx`.
showto	For messages shown in the header summary for which you are the sender, shows the recipient's name instead of yours (disabled by default).
sign=*string*	Define string to be inserted by the ~a tilde command into a message that you are inputting (empty by default). `set sign="Justin and Dylan"`
Sign=*string*	Define string to be inserted by the ~A tilde command into a message that you are inputting (empty by default).
toplines=*n*	Specifies how many lines the top command will show of the header summary (default is 5). *(continued)*

Table 4. mailx Options *(continued)*

`quit`	Do not show identification line (disabled by default)

MAILX CONFIGURATION VARIABLES

`MBOX=`*filename*	Holds the name of the **mbox** file to which read messages are automatically saved. By default, **mbox** is placed in your home directory. To put it in the folder directory, place a + sign before the mbox name. `set MBOX=+mbox`
`DEAD=`*filename*	Specifies the dead letter file where incomplete and interrupted messages are placed.
`LISTER=`*cmd*	Specify the command to use to list the contents of the folder directory (default is ls).
`EDITOR=`*cmd*	Specify the editor to use when invoked with the ~e command (default is Ed, a line editor).
`VISUAL=`*cmd*	Specify the editor to use when invoked with the ~v command (default is Vi).
`PAGER=`*cmd*	Specify the pager program to use (default is pg or more).
`sendmail=`*cmd*	Specify the the mail transport agent for your mailer (default is usually sendmail or rmail, include full path names).

Table 5. Elm Commands

SENDING MESSAGES

elm *login-name*	Send a message using Elm.
s	Send the message.
e	Edit the message.
f	Forget the message; quit and do not send.
h	Edit the header of the message.

ELM UTILITY: RECEIVING MESSAGES

elm	Invoke the Elm utility.
?	Help. Press key used for a command to display information about that command.
?	Display a list of all commands.
.	Return to Elm index.
q	Quit the Elm utility with prompts for saving read and unread messages, and deleting messages marked for deletion.
Q	Quit the Elm utility with no prompts.
x and **Ctrl-q**	Quit the Elm utility leaving your mail as you found it. No deletions are made or messages saved. Messages remain as you found them.
+	Display next index screen if headers take up more than one screen.
−	Display previous index screen if headers take up more than one screen.

SELECTING A MESSAGE

j	Move down to the next message header, making it the current message.
k	Move up to the previous message header, making it the current message.
msge -number **enter**	Make the header whose message number is *msge-number* the current message.
/*pattern*	Search for the pattern in the subject or address headers, making the first header with a match the current message.
/ /*pattern*	Search for the pattern in the text of messages, making the first message with a match the current message.
t	Tag the current message. A + sign appears before the message. You can tag several messages and then perform an operation on them all at once.
Ctrl-t	Search address and subject headers for a pattern and tag all messages that match.

OPERATIONS ON MESSAGES

enter   Display the current message.

          i   Return to headers (index).

p   Print the current message.

d   Delete the current message. The header is marked with a D and deleted when you exit Elm.

Ctrl-d   Search address and subject headers for a pattern and delete all messages that match.

u   Undelete the current message.

Ctrl-u   Search address and subject headers for a pattern and undelete all messages that match.

r   Reply to the current message. The address and subject are taken from the current message's header. You then compose and send your reply as with any other message.

s   Save the current message or tagged messages in a mailbox file. By default, the message is saved to a mailbox file using the address of the user who sent the message. You can specify your own mailbox file by entering the name of the file preceded by an = sign.

           =mailbox-filename

         You can also save the message to a received or sent mailbox files using the following commands.

         >   Save message to received mailbox file.

         <   Save message to sent mailbox file.

ELM OPERATIONS

m   Send a message from within the Elm utility. You compose and send a message.

c   Use Elm to operate on a specific mailbox file. The command switches from incoming mail to any other mailbox file with messages.

a   Manage Elm aliases. Upon pressing the a command, the alias menu is displayed with the following options.

         a   Create an alias using the name and address of the current message.

         m   Create an alias using a name and address that you enter.

         d   Delete an alias.

         l   List aliases.

         p   Display the name and address of a particular aliases.

         s   Display any system aliases.

         r   Return to Elm main menu.

`alwaysdelete = ` *ON/OFF*	If ON, make yes the default response for delete message prompt.
`alwayskeep = ` *ON/OFF*	If ON, make yes the default response for keep unread mail prompt.
`alwaysstore = ` *YESNO*	If YES, store received mail in mailbox file.
`arrow = ` *ON/OFF*	Use arrow to identify the current message.
`autocopy = ` *ON/OFF*	Automatically include replied-to message in a response.
`editor = ` *editor*	Specify editor to use to compose and edit messages.
`localsignamture = ` *pathname*	Specify signature file with signature text for local mail.
`maildir = ` *directory*	Specify directory where mail is saved.
`print = ` *command*	Specify utility to use to display messages on your screen.
`receivedmail = ` *directory*	Specify directory for received mail.
`remotesignamture = ` *pathname*	Specify signature file with signature text for remote mail.
`savename = ` *ON/OFF*	Save messages by login name of sender/recipient.
`sortby = ` *option*	Specify how messages are to be sorted.

Table 6. Elm Options

Table 7. MH Commands

DISPLAYING MESSAGES

inc	Place received mail in your incoming mailbox and display message headers.
show *num*	Display current message or specified messages.
next	Display the next message.
prev	Display the previous message
scan	Redisplay message headers.
mhl	Display formatted listing of messages.
ali	List mail aliases.
folders	Lists all mail folders.

REFERENCING MESSAGES

first	The first message in the current folder.
last	The last message in the current folder.
cur	The current message in the current folder.
prev	The previous message in the current folder.
next	The next message in the current folder.
num1-num2	Indicates all messages in the range num1 to num2, inclusive. The specified range must contain at least one message.
num:+n	
num:-n	Up to *n* messages beginning with (or ending with) message num. The value of num may be any of the MH message keywords: first, prev, cur, next, or last.
first:*n*	
prev:*n*	
next:*n*	
last:*n*	The first, previous, next, or last *n* messages, if they exist.

CREATE MESSAGES

comp	Compose a new message
anno	Annotate messages.
burst	Break digest into component messages.

SEND MESSAGES

dist	Distribute a message to different addresses.

(continued)

Table 7. MH Commands *(continued)*

`forw`	Forward a message.
`repl`	Reply to a message
`send`	Resend a message or send a file as a message.
`mhmail`	Send or read mail in batch mode.

SELECTING MESSAGES

`pick`	Select message by specified criteria and assign them a sequence.
`mark`	Add or remove messages to or from a sequence.
`sortm`	Sort messages.

SAVE, DELETE, REPLY, AND PRIINT MEESSAGES

`repl`	Reply to a message.
mesg-ref > *filename*	Save a message to a file.
mesg-ref | `lp`	Print a message.
`rmm`	Remove a message.

FOLDER OPERATIONS

`folder`	Change to another mailbox file (folder).
`refile`	Save messages to other folders.
`rmf`	Remove a folder.

MH INTERFACES

`msh`	MH mail shell.
`vmh`	Screen-oriented MH shell.
`xmh`	X-Windows MH interface.

Table 8. Pine Options

address	Send mail to address. Pine goes directly to the message composition screen.
-c *context-number*	*context-number* is the number corresponding to the folder-collection to which the -f command line argument should be applied. By default the -f argument is applied to the first defined folder-collection.
-d	Debug-level output diagnostic info at debug-level (0–9) to the current **.pine-debug** file. A value of 0 turns debugging off and suppresses the **.pine-debug** file.
-f *folder*	Open folder (in first defined folder-collection) instead of INBOX.
-F *file*	Open named text file and view.
-h	Help, list valid command-line options.
-i	Start up in the Folder Index screen.
-I *keystrokes*	Initial (comma separated list of) keystrokes which Pine should execute on startup.
-k	Use function keys for commands. This is the same as running the command `pinef`.
-l	Expand all collections in Folder List display.
-n *number*	Start up with current message-number set to number.
-o	Open first folder read-only.
-p *config-file*	Use *config-file* as the personal configuration file instead of the default **.pinerc**.
-P *config-file*	Use *config-file* as the configuration file instead of default system-wide configuration file **pine.conf**.
-r	Use restricted/demo mode. Pine will only send mail to itself and functions like save and export are restricted.
-z	Enable ^Z and SIGTSTP so pine may be suspended.
-conf	Produce a sample/fresh copy of the system-wide configuration file, **pine.conf**, on the standard output.
-create_lu *addrbook sort-order*	Creates auxiliary index (look-up) file for *addrbook* and sorts *addrbook* in *sort-order*, which may be dont-sort, nickname, fullname, nickname-with-lists-last, or fullname-with-lists-last.
-pinerc *file*	Output fresh `pinerc` configuration to file.

(continued)

Table 8. Pine Options *(continued)*

-sort *order*	Sort the Folder Index display in one of the following orders: arrival, subject, from, date, size, orderedsubj or reverse. Arrival order is the default. The orderedsubj choice simulates a threaded sort. Any sort may be reversed by adding /reverse to it. Reverse by itself is the same as arrival/reverse.
-option=*value*	Assign value to a Pine configuration option.

Table 9. Pine Commands

GLOBAL PINE COMMANDS

M	Main menu.
O	Show other commands.
C	Compose a new message or continue a postponed message.
I	Show a folder index.
L	Show a folder list.
G	Go to a folder.
?	Help.
Q	Quit Pine.

PINE MESSAGE COMPOSITION COMMANDS

BASIC COMMANDS

Ctrl-g	Get help.
Ctrl-c	Cancel message.
Ctrl-x	Send message.
Ctrl-o	Postpone a message for completion later. Postponed messages are saved in file **postponed-msgs**.

HEADER COMMANDS

Ctrl-j	Attach files. You can then use **Ctrl-t** to access the Pine file browser (Pilot) to select a file for insert or attachment
Ctrl-t	Select address from address book.
Ctrl-r	Rich header command. Displays four other header fields for entry: Bcc, Fcc, Lcc, Newsgroups (standard header fields are To, Cc, Attchmnt, and Subject). Lcc (List Carbon Copy) uses address book lists. Fcc (Folder Carbon Copy) is name of folder for outgoing messages. Bcc is for a standard blind carbon copy list. Newsgroups is for posting messages to newsgroups.
Ctrl-d	Delete character.
Ctrl-k	Cut line.
Ctrl-u	Undelete line.
Ctrl-y	Move to next page.
Ctrl-v	Move to previous page.

MESSAGE TEXT COMMANDS

Ctrl-j	Justify text. Uses blank line as end of paragraph.
Ctrl-^	Mark text for cut or paste.

(continued)

Table 9. Pine Commands *(continued)*

Ctrl-k	Cut text. With unmarked text, cut current line.
Ctrl-u	Restore or paste text.
Ctrl-r	Read file, insert a file into a message.
Ctrl-t	Invoke spell checker.
Ctrl-y	Move to next page.
Ctrl-v	Move to previous page.
Ctrl-w	Search for text.

MESSAGE STATUS CODES

+	The message was sent directly to you (not a cc: or email list).
A	The message has been answered.
D	The message is marked for deletion.
N	The message is new and unread.
X	The message is selected (for aggregate operations).
*	The message has been flagged as important.

MESSAGE HEADER COMPONENTS

Message number

Date received or sent

Sender (for received messages) or recipient (for sent messages)

Message size: size of the message, plus any attachments, in bytes

Subject

FOLDER INDEX COMMANDS

MOVING THROUGH THE MESSAGE LIST

P	Previous message.
N	Next message.
J	Jump to specific message number.
tab	Next new message.
–	Previous screen.
space	Next screen.
W	(Where Is) Search for a word in the index or go to first/last message.

OPERATIONS ON MESSAGES: FOLDER INDEX SCREEN

Y	Print a message.
V	View a message.

(continued)

Table 9. Pine Commands *(continued)*

R	Reply to a message.
F	Forward a message.
B	Bounce (resend) a message with a different address.
D	Mark a message for deletion.
U	Undelete a message marked for deletion.
T	Add address of message to your address book.
S	Save a message in an email folder.
E	Save (export) a message as a text file.
X	Expunge messages marked for deletion (actually erases them).
;	Select a message for aggregate operations (A and Z).
A	Apply command to selected messages.
Z	Show only selected messages.
*	Flag.
|	Pipe contents of a message to a Unix command.
$	Sort messages by subject, date, sender/recipient, etc.

VIEWING A MESSAGE: MESSAGE TEXT SCREEN

–	Display previous screen of message text.
space	Display next screen of message text.
W	(Where Is) Search for a word in a message or go to first/last line.
V	View an attachment to a message.
H	Display full header information, Header Mode.

FOLDER LIST COMMANDS
MOVING THROUGH THE FOLDER LIST

P	Previous folder.
N	Next folder.
–	Previous screen.
space	Next screen.
W	Search for a folder name in the index or go to first/last folder.

OPERATIONS ON THE NEWLY SELECTED FOLDER

V	View.
D	Delete.
R	Rename.

(continued)

Table 9. Pine Commands *(continued)*

FOLDER LIST COMMANDS

I	Show index of the currently active folder.
Y	Print folder listing.
A	Add new folder.

NEWSGROUP-COLLECTION SPECIFIC COMMANDS

A	Subscribe.
D	Unsubscribe.

Table 10. Pine Configuration Options

```
personal-name              = <No Value Set: using "Dylan Petersen">
user-domain                =<No Value Set>
smtp-server                =<No Value Set>
nntp-server                =<No Value Set>
inbox-path                 =<No Value Set: using "inbox">
folder-collections         =<No Value Set: using "mail/[]">
news-collections           =<No Value Set>
incoming-archive-folders   =<No Value Set>
pruned-folders             =<No Value Set>
default-fcc                =<No Value Set: using "sent-mail">
default-saved-msg-folder   =<No Value Set: using "saved-messages">
postponed-folder           =<No Value Set: using "postponed-msgs">
read-message-folder        =<No Value Set>
signature-file             =<No Value Set: using ".signature">
lobal-address-book         =<No Value Set>
address-book               =<No Value Set: using ".addressbook">
feature-list =
              [ ] allow-talk
              [ ] assume-slow-link
              [ ] auto-move-read-msgs
              [ ] auto-open-next-unread
              [ ] auto-zoom-after-select
              [ ] auto-unzoom-after-apply
              [ ] compose-cut-from-cursor
              [ ] compose-maps-delete-key-to-ctrl-d
              [ ] compose-rejects-unqualified-addrs
              [ ] compose-send-offers-first-filter
              [ ] compose-sets-newsgroup-without-confirm
              [ ] delete-skips-deleted
              [ ] disable-keymenu
              [ ] enable-8bit-esmtp-negotiation
              [ ] enable-8bit-nntp-posting
              [X] enable-aggregate-command-set
              [ ] enable-alternate-editor-cmd              (continued)
```

Table 10 Pine Configuration Options *(continued)*

```
[ ] enable-alternate-editor-implicitly
[ ] enable-background-sending
[ ] enable-bounce-cmd
[ ] enable-cruise-mode
[ ] enable-cruise-mode-delete
[ ] enable-dot-files
[ ] enable-dot-folders
[ ] enable-flag-cmd
[ ] enable-flag-screen-implicitly
[ ] enable-full-header-cmd
[ ] enable-goto-in-file-browser
[ ] enable-incoming-folders
[ ] enable-jump-shortcut
[ ] enable-mail-check-cue
[ ] enable-mouse-in-xterm
[ ] enable-newmail-in-xterm-icon
[ ] enable-suspend
[ ] enable-tab-completion
[ ] enable-unix-pipe-cmd
[ ] enable-verbose-smtp-posting
[ ] expanded-view-of-addressbooks
[ ] expanded-view-of-distribution-lists
[ ] expanded-view-of-folders
[ ] expunge-without-confirm
[ ] fcc-on-bounce
[ ] include-attachments-in-reply
[ ] include-header-in-reply
[ ] include-text-in-reply
[ ] news-approximates-new-status
[ ] news-post-without-validation
[ ] news-read-in-newsrc-order
[ ] pass-control-characters-as-is
[ ] preserve-start-stop-characters
[ ] print-offers-custom-cmd-prompt
```
                                                                (continued)

Table 10. Pine Configuration Options *(continued)*

```
                    [ ] print-includes-from-line
                    [ ] print-index-enabled
                    [ ] print-formfeed-between-messages
                    [ ] quell-dead-letter-on-cancel
                    [ ] quell-lock-failure-warnings
                    [ ] quell-status-message-beeping
                    [ ] quell-user-lookup-in-passwd-file
                    [ ] quit-without-confirm
                    [ ] reply-always-uses-reply-to
                    [ ] save-will-quote-leading-forms
                    [ ] save-will-not-delete
                    [ ] save-will-advance
                    [ ] select-without-confirm
                    [ ] show-cursor
                    [ ] show-selected-in-boldface
                    [ ] signature-at-bottom
                    [ ] single-column-folder-list
                    [ ] tab-visits-next-new-message-only
                    [ ] use-current-dir
                    [ ] use-sender-not-x-sender
                    [ ] use-subshell-for-suspend
initial-keystroke-list     =<No Value Set>
default-composer-hdrs      =<No Value Set>
customized-hdrs            =<No Value Set>
viewer-hdrs                =<No Value Set>
saved-msg-name-rule =
                    ( ) by-from
                    ( ) by-nick-of-from
                    ( ) by-nick-of-from-then-from
                    ( ) by-fcc-of-from
                    ( ) by-fcc-of-from-then-from
                    ( ) by-sender
                    ( ) by-nick-of-sender
                    ( ) by-nick-of-sender-then-sender            (continued)
```

Table 10. Pine Configuration Options *(continued)*

```
                    ( ) by-fcc-of-sender
                    ( ) by-fcc-of-sender-then-sender
                    ( ) by-recipient
                    ( ) by-nick-of-recip
                    ( ) by-nick-of-recip-then-recip
                    ( ) by-fcc-of-recip
                    ( ) by-fcc-of-recip-then-recip
                    ( ) last-folder-used
                    (*) default-folder
fcc-name-rule =
                    (*) default-fcc
                    ( ) last-fcc-used [Select]
                    ( ) by-recipient
                    ( ) by-nickname
                    ( ) by-nick-then-recip
                    ( ) current-folder
sort-key =
                    ( ) Date
                    (*) Arrival
                    ( ) From
                    ( ) Subject
                    ( ) OrderedSubj
                    ( ) To
                    ( ) Cc
                    ( ) siZe
                    ( ) Reverse Date
                    ( ) Reverse Arrival
                    ( ) Reverse From
                    ( ) Reverse Subject
                    ( ) Reverse OrderedSubj
                    ( ) Reverse To
                    ( ) Reverse Cc
                    ( ) Reverse siZe                        (continued)
```

Table 10. Pine Configuration Options *(continued)*

```
addrbook-sort-rule =
                (*) fullname-with-lists-last
                ( ) fullname
                ( ) nickname-with-lists-last
                ( ) nickname
                ( ) dont-sort
goto-default-rule =
                (*) inbox-or-folder-in-recent-collection
                ( ) inbox-or-folder-in-first-collection
                ( ) most-recent-folder
character-set               =<No Value Set>
editor                      =<No Value Set>
speller                     =<No Value Set>
composer-wrap-column        =<No Value Set: using "74">
reply-indent-string         =<No Value Set: using "> ">
empty-header-message        =<No Value Set: using "Undisclosed
                            recipients">
image-viewer                =<No Value Set>
use-only-domain-name        = No
display-filters             =<No Value Set>
sending-filters             =<No Value Set>
alt-addresses               =<No Value Set>
addressbook-formats         =<No Value Set>
index-format                =<No Value Set>
viewer-overlap              =<No Value Set: using "2">
scroll-margin               =<No Value Set: using "0">
status-message-delay        =<No Value Set: using "0">
mail-check-interval         =<No Value Set: using "150">
newsrc-path                 =<No Value Set>
news-active-file-path       =<No Value Set>
news-spool-directory        =<No Value Set>
upload-command              =<No Value Set>
upload-command-prefix       =<No Value Set>
```

(continued)

Table 10. Pine Configuration Options *(continued)*

```
download-command        =<No Value Set>
                        =<No Value Set>
mailcap-search-path     =<No Value Set>
mimetype-search-path    =<No Value Set>
download-command-prefix =<No Value Set>
```

Table 11. rn Newsreader Commands

SELECTING NEWSGROUPS WITH RN

y	Select the current newsgroup.
n	Move to the next newsgroup with unread articles.
N	Move to the next newsgroup.
p	Move to the previous newsgroup with unread articles.
P	Move to the previous newsgroup.
-	Move to the previously selected newsgroup.
^	Move to the first newsgroup with unread articles.
num	Move to newsgroup with that number.
$	Move to the last newsgroup.
g*newsgroup-name*	Move to newsgroup with that name.
/*pattern*	Search forward to the newsgroup with that pattern.
?*pattern*	Search backward to the newsgroup with that pattern.
L	List subscribed newsgroups.
l*pattern*	List unsubscribed newsgroups.
u *newsgroup-name*	Unsubscribe a newsgroup.
a *newsgroup-name*	Subscribe to a newsgroup.
c	Mark articles in a newsgroup as read.

SELECTING ARTICLES WITH RN

y	Display the current article.
n	Move to the next article with unread articles.
N	Move to the next article.
p	Move to the previous article with unread articles.
P	Move to the previous article.
-	Move to the previously selected article.
^	Move to the first article with unread articles.
num	Move to article with that number.
$	Move to the last article.
Ctrl-n	Move to the next article with the same subject as the current one. *(continued)*

Table 11. rn Newsreader Commands *(continued)*

Ctrl-p	Move to the previous article with the same subject as the current one.
/pattern	Search forward to the article with that pattern in each article's subject field.
	Modifiers
h	Search forward to the article with that pattern in the header.
	*/pattern/*h
a	Search forward to the article with that pattern in either the header or the text.
	*/pattern/*a
r	Include read articles in you search.
	*/pattern/*r
c	Make search case sensitive.
	*/pattern/*c
?pattern?	Search backward to the article with that pattern in each article's subject field.
	Modifiers
h	Search backward to the article with that pattern in the header.
	*?pattern?*h
a	Search forward to the article with that pattern in either the header or the text.
	*?pattern?*a
r	Include read articles in you search.
	*?pattern?*r
c	Make search case sensitive.
	*?pattern?*c
/	Repeat previous forward search.
?	Repeat previous backward search.
/pattern:command	Select a group of articles matching the pattern and apply the rn command to all of them.
num,num:command	Select a group of articles referenced by the numbers and apply the rn command to all of them.

(continued)

Table 11. rn Newsreader Commands *(continued)*

MARKING ARTICLES

m	Mark current article as read.
n	Mark current article as read and move to next article.
j	Mark current article as read and display end of article.
c	Mark all articles as read in the current newsgroup.

DISPLAYING ARTICLES

spacebar	Display the next screen of the article.
return	Scroll to the next line of the article.
d	Scroll to the next half screen of the article.
b	Display the previous screen of the article.
v	Redisplay article from the beginning.
q	Display last screen of the article.
g *pattern*	Search for pattern in the text.
G	Repeat pattern search in the text.

SAVING ARTICLES AND REPLYING TO ARTICLES

s	Save the current article to a mailbox file (includes header).
w	Save the current article to a file, but without its header.
r	Reply to current article.
R	Reply to current article and include article text in the reply.
f	Post a follow-up to the current article.
F	Post a follow-up including the text of the current article.

RN OPTIONS

-n *newsgroup,newsgroup*	Select newsgroups.
-t *pattern,pattern*	Select articles that contain the patterns.
-a *date*	Select article posted after the date.
-x	Select all articles including the ones you have read.
-q	Skip subscription of new newsgroups.
-c	Check if any newsgroups are unread.
-l	List only the titles of articles.
-e	List only the titles, but mark the articles as read. *(continued)*

Table 11. rn Newsreader Commands *(continued)*

`-r`	Read articles in reverse order.
`-f`	Display only original articles.
`-h`	Display short versions of headers.
`-s`	Display a user's site.
`-p`	Output all articles to the standard output, which you can then redirect to a file or pipe to a printer.

RN OPTION VARIABLES

`EDITOR`	Editor for composing replies.
`MAILPOSTER`	Mail utility for sending replies
`PAGER`	Page utility for reading articles.
`SAVEDIR`	Directory to which to save articles.
`NAME`	Your full name to be used for article headers that you post.
`ORGANIZATION`	Your organization name for article headers that you post.

Table 12. readnews Commands

DISPLAYING ARTICLES

y	Display the current article.
p	Display the previous article.
D	If an article is encrypted, this command will decrypt it.
d	This command takes a digest of articles and generates the corresponding complete articles.
h	Display expanded header information for an article.
H	Display complete header information for an article.
#	Display number of current article, number of articles in the newsgroup, and the newsgroup name.

QUIT AND HELP

?	List command summary.
q	Quit `readnews` and register read articles.
x	Quit `readnews`, but do not register read articles.

MOVING TO ARTICLES

n	Move to the next article, without displaying the current article.
m	Move back to the previous article.
−	Move back to last article displayed.

MOVING TO NEWSGROUPS

N	Move to next newsgroup.
P	Move to previous newsgroup.
U	Unsubscribe to a newsgroup.

SAVING AND MARKING ARTICLES

s	Save the current article to a file.
e	Mark the current article as unread.
+	Skip next article and mark as unread. *(continued)*

Table 12. readnews Commands *(continued)*

K	Mark rest of articles in the current newsgroup and move on to the next newsgroup.

POSTING ARTICLES AND REPLIES

f	Post an article.
fd	Post an article without a header.
r	Reply to an article by sending a message to the author.
c	Cancel a posted article.

OPTIONS

-n *newsgroup,newsgroup*	Select newsgroups.
-t *pattern,pattern*	Select articles that contain the patterns.
-a *date*	Select article posted after the date.
-x	Select all articles including the ones you have read.
-l	List only the titles of articles.
-e	List only the titles, but mark the articles as read.
-r	Read articles in reverse order.
-f	Display only original articles.
-h	Display short versions of headers.
-s	Display a user's site.
-p	Output all articles to the standard output, which you can then redirect to a file or pipe to a printer.

Table 13. `trn` Newsreader Commands

ENTERING NEWSGROUPS

+	Enter current newsgroup through the selector.
y	Select the current newsgroup.
=	Enter newsgroup, but list subjects before displaying articles.
space	Enter newsgroup using default, usually + .

MOVING THROUGH NEWSGROUPS

n	Move to the next newsgroup with unread articles.
N	Move to the next newsgroup.
p	Move to the previous newsgroup with unread articles.
P	Move to the previous newsgroup.
-	Move to the previously selected newsgroup.
^	Move to the first newsgroup with unread articles.
num	Move to newsgroup with that number; 1 goes to first newsgroup.
$	Move to the last newsgroup.
g*newsgroup-name*	Move to newsgroup with that name.
/*pattern*	Search forward to the newsgroup with that pattern.
?*pattern*	Search backward to the newsgroup with that pattern.

MANAGING NEWSGROUPS

L	List subscribed newsgroups.
l*pattern*	List unsubscribed newsgroups.
u *newsgroup-name*	Unsubscribe to a newsgroups.
a *newsgroup-name*	Subscribe to a newsgroups.
c	Mark articles in a newsgroup as read..
t	Toggle newsgroup between threaded and unthreaded reading.
A	Abandon changes made to current newsgroup.
o*pattern-list*	Only display newsgroups whose name matches *pattern-list*. The *pattern-list* can be a set of patterns separated by spaces.
O*pattern-list*	Same as o, but empty newsgroups are automatically excluded. *(continued)*

Table 13. `trn` Newsreader Commands *(continued)*

v	Display `trn` version number.
&	Display current status of the command line.
&&*option-list*	Set new `trn` options.
&&&*keys commands*	Define a macro.
!*command*	Execute a Unix shell command.

QUITTING TRN

q	Quit `trn`.
x	Quit `trn`, with no changes made to **.newsrc**. Backup copy with any changes for current session is placed in **.newnewsrc**.

SELECTING ARTICLES IN THE SELECTOR

id	Select/unselect an article thread.
id*	Select/unselect articles with the same subject as *id*.
enter	Display and begin reading the current article.
n	Move to the next thread id.
p	Move to the previous thread id.
Z or **tab**	Begin displaying selected articles. Return to newsgroup screen when finished.
X	Mark all unselected articles as read and start reading.
D	Mark all unselected articles on current page as read and start reading if articles are selected.
J	Mark all selected articles as read.
c	Mark all articles as read.
/*pattern*	Search forward for articles with that pattern. Unless qualified, search is carried out on Subject line of article headers.
?*pattern*	Search backward for articles with that pattern. Unless qualified, search is carried out on Subject line of article headers.
.	Toggle current article's selection.
@	Toggle all visible selections.
#	Read the current article only, ignoring other selections.
.	Toggle current article's selection.
m or /	Unmark the current article. *(continued)*

Table 13. `trn` Newsreader Commands *(continued)*

MOVING THROUGH SELECTOR

spacebar	Display the next screen of articles.
>	Display the next screen of threads.
<	Display the previous screen of articles.
$	Display the last screen of articles.
^	Display the first screen of articles.

QUITTING THE NEWSGROUP

escape	Quit selector to basic article reading.
q	Quit the current newsgroup.
Q	Quit the current newsgroup and return to that newsgroup's prompt.

COMMANDS APPLIED TO SELECTED OR UNSELECTED THREADS

: *command*	Apply command to all selected threads.
: : *command*	Apply command to all unselected threads.
: . *command*	Apply to selected articles in current thread.
: : . *command*	Apply command to unselected articles in the current thread.
p	Post a new article.
+	Select an article.
–	Deselect an article.
=	Print the subject of found articles.
! *cmd*	Execute a Unix shell command.
++	Select a thread.
– –	Deselect a thread.
T+	Auto-select the entire thread.
Tj	Auto-junk the entire thread.
m	Mark as unread.
M	Mark as read until you exit.
t	Display article tree for thread.
j	Mark as read in all groups.
E	End partial `uudecode`.
s *directory*	Save articles to specified directory using mailbox format.
w *directory*	Save articles to specified directory as plain text file.
e *directory*	Extract articles to specified directory. *(continued)*

Table 13. `trn` **Newsreader Commands** *(continued)*

DISPLAYING SELECTOR

+	Enter the selector from the `trn` line prompt, or leave the selector and return to the `trn` line prompt.
S	Select selector mode: subject, thread, or article.

                     Selector Mode: Threads, Subjects, Articles? [tsa]

                        s   Subject mode, display articles by subject.

                        a   Article mode, display individual articles.

                        t   Thread mode, display articles by threads.

=	Switch between article and subject/thread selector.
O	Sort selector items by date, author, thread count, or subject. User is prompted to enter d, a, n, or s. This command is an uppercase O, not lowercase. The options differ depending on whether you are in the subject or thread modes.

          Subject   Order by Date, Subject, or Count? [dscDSC]

          Thread   Order by Date, Subject, Author, subject-date Grops?

L	Set selector item display to short, medium, or long forms.
E	Exclusive mode, display only selected articles.
k or ,	Remove an article or subject from the selector display.
U	Display unread articles.

ARTICLE SEARCHES

/*pattern*	Search forward for articles with that pattern. Unless qualified, search is carried out on Subject line of article headers.
?*pattern*	Search backward for articles with that pattern. Unless qualified, search is carried out on Subject line of article headers.

MODIFIERS

/*pattern*/*modifier-list*

a	Search forward to the article with that pattern in either the header or the text.

                    /*pattern*/a

b	Search forward to the article with that pattern in the body of the message, but not the signature.

                    /*pattern*/b   *(continued)*

Table 13. `trn` **Newsreader Commands** *(continued)*

B	Search forward to the article with that pattern in the body of the message.
	*/pattern/*B
c	Make search case sensitive.
	*/pattern/*c
h	Search forward to the article with that pattern in the header.
	*/pattern/*h
r	Include read articles in you search.
	*/pattern/*r
t	Start the search from the first article in the newsgroup instead of current article.
	*/pattern/*t
I	Force search to ignore THRU lies when executed as a memorized command.
	*/pattern/*I
i	Force search not to ignore THRU lies when executed as a memorized command.
	*/pattern/*i

COMMANDS

/pattern/modifier-list : command-list

+	Select the article.
–	Deselect the article.
=	Print the subject of found articles.
!*cmd*	Execute a Unix shell command.
++	Select the associated thread.
– –	Deselect the associated thread .
T+	Auto-select the entire thread.
Tj	Auto-junk the entire thread.
m	Mark as unread.
M	Mark as read until you exit.
x	Mark as read in this group.
j	Mark as read in all groups.
C	Cancel. *(continued)*

Table 13. `trn` **Newsreader Commands** *(continued)*

s *directory*	Save articles to specified directory.
e *directory*	Extract articles to specified directory.

LOCATION COMMANDS

n	Go to the next unread article.
N	Go to the next article.
p or –	Go to the previous unread article.
P	Go to the previous article.
Ctrl-p	Go to previous article with same subject.
^	Go to the first unread article.
$	Go to the last unread article.
num	Go to article with that number.
q	Quit newsgroup.

TREE COMMANDS

t	Display entire article tree.
<	Go to the next selected or unread article.
>	Go to the previous selected or unread article.
[	Move left in the article tree.
]	Move right in the article tree.
{	Go to root of the article tree.
}	Go to a leaf in the article tree.
(	Go to the previous sibling in a thread.
)	Go to the next sibling in a thread.

COMMANDS

space	Display next page.
b	Display previous page.
d	Display next half page.
Ctrl-e	Display last page.
Ctrl-r	Redisplay the current article.
v	Redisplay the current article with the header.
Ctrl-l	Refresh the screen.
c	Mark all articles as read. *(continued)*

Table 13. `trn` Newsreader Commands *(continued)*

/pattern	Search forward for articles with that pattern. Unless qualified, search is carried out on Subject line of article headers.
?pattern	Search backward for articles with that pattern. Unless qualified, search is carried out on Subject line of article headers.
gpattern	Search for pattern within current article.
G	Repeat search.

MARKING ARTICLES

c	Mark all articles in a newsgroup as read.
u	Unsubscribe from the current newsgroup.
m	Mark the current article as unread.
j	Mark the current article as read (junked).
M	Mark current article as read for current session only.
Y	Select articles marked as read for current session only.

REPLIES AND FOLLOW-UPS

r	Send a mail reply directly to the author of the current article.
R	Send a mail reply directly to the author of the current article and include the contents of the article.
Ctrl-f	Forward the article as a mail message to any user.
f	Post a follow-up article for the article to the newsgroup.
F	Post a follow-up article for the article to the newsgroup and include the article contents and attribution line.

SAVING AND EXTRACTING ARTICLES

w	Save selected article.
s	Save selected article to a mailbox file.
e	Extract selected encoded articles to save directory. Decodes uuencoded binaries.
e *directory*	Extract selected encoded articles to specified directory. Decodes uuencoded binaries.
e *directory* | *command*	Extract selected encoded articles and uses the specified command to decode the encoded articles.
E	If extracting selected encoded articles one by one, this cancels the process removing incomplete binary.

Table 14. `trn` **Options**

`-a`	Thread the unread articles on entering a group, instead of in the background while in a group.
`-b`	Read threads in a breadth-first order, rather than depth-first.
`-B`	Displays a spinner that twirls when `trn` is doing background article processing.
`-c`	Checks for news without reading news. If a list of newsgroups is given on the command line, only those newsgroups will be checked; otherwise all subscribed to newsgroups are checked. A nonzero exit status means that there is unread news in one of the checked newsgroups.
`-C` *number*	Specify how often to checkpoint the **.newsrc** file, in articles read.
`-d` *directory-name*	Specify a news directory. Default is **~/News.** The directory name will be globbed (via csh) if necessary (and if possible).
`-D` *flags*	Enables debugging output. See **common.h** for flag values.
`-e`	Displays each page within an article at the top of the screen, not just the first page.
`-E` *var=val*	Sets the environment variable to the value specified.
`-F`	Avoid various sleep calls used to let you read a message before the screen clears.
`-F` *string*	Specify the prefix string for the F follow-up command to use in prefixing lines of the quote article. The initial default prefix is ">".
`-g` *string*	Specify the line of the screen you want searched for strings to show up on when you search with the g command within an article.
`-G`	Uses "fuzzy" processing on the go command when you don't type in a valid group name. `trn` will attempt to find the group you probably meant to type.
`-h` *string*	Hides header lines beginning with string.
`-i` *=number*	Specifies number of lines displayed in the initial page of an article.
`-I`	Appends all new, unsubscribed groups to the end of the **.newsrc** file.
`-j`	Leaves control characters unchanged in messages.
`-j` *number*	Joins similar subjects into a common thread if they are the same up to the indicated number of characters (the default is 30).
`-k`	Ignore the THRU line when processing selection searches in the memorized commands.
`-K`	Keeps `trn` from checking for new news while you're in the group.

(continued)

Table 14. `trn` **Options** (*continued*)

`-1`	Disables the clearing of the screen at the beginning of each article.
`-M`	Use mailbox format for new save files created.
`-n`	Use normal (non-mailbox) format for new save files created. Ordinarily you are asked which format you want.
`-O`*mode sort-order*	Display articles in specified order and thread.

Modes

`s`	subject mode
`t`	thread mode
`a`	article mode

Sort Order

`d`	date
`s`	subject
`a`	author
`c`	article count
`g`	subject-date groups
`-q`	Bypasses the automatic check for new newsgroups when starting `trn`.
`-r`	Restart in the last newsgroup read during a previous session with `trn`.
`-s` *num*	Suppress the initial listing of newsgroups with unread news, whether -c is specified or not. With a number, the listing of newsgroups is limited to that number. -s5 is the default setting.
`-S` *num*	Enter subject search mode automatically when an unthreaded newsgroup starts up that has *num* number of unread articles or more.
`-t`	Terse mode, used for low baud rates.
`-T`	Lets you to type ahead of `trn`.
`-u`	The unbroken-subject-line mode that truncates subjects that are too long.
`-U`	Instruct `trn` not to save the **.newsrc** file after visiting each group.
`-v`	Verification mode for commands, displaying commands typed in.
`-V`	trn version number.
`-x` *num list*	Enable the threaded features of `trn` beyond the `rn` compatibility mode. *num* is the maximum number of article-tree lines (from 0 to 11) you want displayed in your header. *list* specifies the thread selector style: 's'hort, 'm'edium, or 'l'ong).

(*continued*)

Table 14. `trn` **Options** (*continued*)

-X *num commands*	Specify the selector command (+) default when a newsgroup is started up with at least *num* unread articles. Also specify commands to be the defaults when using the thread selector. The default is -X1Z>, if just -X is used with no arguments. Makes thread selector the default for newsgroups with one or more unread articles and Z to access the last page, > to access the next page.
-z *num*	Specify minimum number of minutes that must elapse before the active file is refetched to look for new articles. Turned off with +z option.
-Z	Select the style of database for `trn` to access. Use -Zt for thread files, -Zo for overview files, and +Z for none.
-/	By default articles are saved in a subdirectory that has the name of the current newsgroup, with the file name being the article number. The subdirectory will be in your private news directory +/ by default saves articles directly to your private news directory, with the file name being the name of the current newsgroup.

Table 15. `trn` Interpolation Codes

`%a`	Current article number.
`%A`	Full name of current article (`%P/%c/%a`).
`%b`	Destination directory of last save command.
`%B`	The byte offset to the beginning of the part of the article to be saved, set by the save command. The s and S commands set it to 0, and the w and W commands set it to the byte offset of the body of the article.
`%c`	Current newsgroup, directory form.
`%C`	Current newsgroup, dot form.
`%d`	Full name of newsgroup directory (`%P/%c`).
`%D`	"Distribution:" line in the current article.
`%e`	The last command executed to extract data from an article.
`%E`	The last directory where an extracted file went.
`%f`	"From:" line from the current article, or the "Reply-To:" line if there is one. Comments (such as the full name) are not stripped out.
`%F`	"Newsgroups:" line for a new article, constructed from "Newsgroups:" and "Followup-To:" lines of current article.
`%h`	Name of the header file to pass to the mail or news poster, containing all the information that the poster program needs in the form of a message header. It may also contain a copy of the current article. The format of the header file is controlled by the `MAILHEADER` and `NEWSHEADER` environment variables.
`%H`	Your system's host name.
`%i`	"Message-I.D.:" line from the current article.
`%I`	The reference indication mark (see the `-F` switch).
`%l`	The news administrator's login name.
`%L`	Your login name.
`%m`	The current mode of `trn`.
`%M`	The number of articles marked to return via the M command.
`%n`	"Newsgroups:" line from the current article.
`%N`	Your full name. *(continued)*

Table 15. `trn` **Interpolation Codes** *(continued)*

`%o`	Your organization.
`%O`	Original working directory.
`%p`	Your private news directory, normally **~/News**.
`%P`	System news spool directory (**/usr/spool/news** on systems that don't use NNTP).
`%q`	The value of the last "quoted" input string.
`%r`	Last reference on references line of current article (parent article id).
`%R`	References list for a new article, constructed from the references and article ID of the current article.
`%s`	Subject, with all "Re:" and "(nf)" stripped off.
`%S`	Subject, with one "Re:" stripped off.
`%t`	"To:" line derived from the "From:" and "ReplyTo:" lines of the current article. Returns an Internet format address.
`%T`	"To:" line derived from the "Path:" line of the current article to produce a `uucp` path.
`%u`	Number of unread articles in the current newsgroup.
`%U`	Number of unread articles in the current newsgroup, not counting the current article. If threads are selected, this count reflects only selected articles.
`%v`	The number of unselected articles, not counting the current article if it is unselected.
`%w`	Directory where `mthreads` keeps its **tmp** files.
`%W`	Directory where thread files are placed.
`%x`	News library directory.
`%X`	`trn` library directory.
`%z`	The length of the current article in bytes.
`%Z`	Number of selected threads.
`%~`	Your home directory.
`%.`	The directory containing your dot files, which is your home directory unless the environment variable `DOTDIR` is defined when `trn` is invoked.
`%#`	The current count for a multifile save, starting with 1. This value is incremented by one for each file saved or extracted within a single command.
`%$`	Current process number. *(continued)*

%/	Last search string.
%?	A space unless the current string is >79 characters, at which point it turns into a newline.
%%	A percent sign.

%{*name*} or %{*name-default*}   The environment variable "*name*".

%[*name*]]   The value of header line labeled "*Name:*" from the current article. The label is not included. For example "%D" and "%[distribution]" are equivalent.

%`*command*`   Execute command and use its resulting value, formatted as one line with newlines changed to spaces.

%""*prompt*""   Displays prompt on the terminal, then reads user input and uses it in one string, and inserts it.

%(*test_text=pattern?then_text:else_text*)

If *test_text* matches *pattern*, the value *then_text* is used, otherwise *else_text* is used. The *:else_text*" is optional, and if absent, the null string is used. = can be replaced with != to test for inequality.

Table 16. `trn` **Environment Variables**

`ATTRIBUTION (%)`	Gives the format of the attribution line in front included by the `F` command. Default: In article %i,%?%)f <%>f> wrote:
`AUTOSUBSCRIBE`	A list of newsgroup patterns separated by commas that automatically subscribes to matching new newsgroups, adding them to your **.newsrc** file.
`AUTOUNSUBSCRIBE`	A list of newsgroup patterns separated by commas that automatically adds matching new newsgroups to the end of your **.newsrc** file as unsubscribed.
`CANCEL`	The shell command used to cancel an article.
`DOTDIR`	Location of your dot files, if they aren't in your home directory.
`EDITOR`	Your standard text editor.
`FORWARDHEADER (%)`	The format of the header file for forwarding messages.
`FORWARDPOSTER (~)`	The applications (shell command) used by the forward command (`^F`) to edit and send the file.
`HOME`	Your home directory.
`KILLGLOBAL (~)`	Location of the **Kill** file to apply to every newsgroup.
`LOGNAME`	Your login name, if User is undefined.
`LOCALTIMEFMT`	Format for printing the local time.
`MAILCALL (~)`	Message telling you there is new mail.
`MAILFILE (~)`	Location of your incoming mailbox.
`MAILHEADER (%)`	The format of the header file for replies.
`MAILPOSTER (~)`	The application (shell command) used by the reply commands (`r` and `R`) to send replies.
`MBOXSAVER (~)`	The shell command to save an article in mailbox format. Default: %X/mbox.saver %A %P %c %a %B %C "%b" \ "From %t %`date`".
`MODSTRING`	The string for the group summary line for a moderated group.
`NEWSHEADER (%)`	The format of the header file for follow-ups.
`NEWSORG`	The name of your organization, or the name of a file containing the name of your organization.
`NEWSPOSTER (~)`	The shell command used by the follow-up commands (`f` and `F`) to post a follow-up news article.
`NNTPSERVER`	Specifies the hostname of your `NNTPSERVER`.
`NOPOSTRING`	The group summary line for a group to which local posting is not allowed.

NORMSAVER (~)	The shell command to save an article in the normal (non-mailbox) format.
ORGANIZATION	The name of your organization, or the name of a file containing the name of your organization.
PIPESAVER (%)	The shell command to save to a pipe (s | command" or w | command).
SAVEDIR (~)	The name of the directory to save to, if the save command does not specify a directory name.
SAVENAME (%)	The name of the file to save to, if the save command contains only a directory name.
SELECTCHARS	The characters used by the thread selector to select the associated thread of discussion. You can specify up to 64 visible characters, including upper- and lowercase letters, numbers, and many punctuation characters.
SUBJLINE (%)	Format of the lines displayed by the = command at the article selection level.
SUPERSEDEHEADER (%)	Format of the header file for a supersede article.
TRNINIT	Default values for switches passed to trn by placing them in the TRNINIT variable. If TRNINIT begins with a '/' it is assumed to be the name of a file containing switches.
TRNMACRO (~)	The name of the file containing macros and key mappings. Default is **.trnmac**.
USER	Your login name.
VISUAL (~)	Your standard editor.
XTERMMOUSE	If set to 'y' (yes), enables use of the xterm mouse in the selector if you are using an xterm. Left-clicking on an item selects it and middle-clicking an item will move to that item. Clicking the top (header) line of the selector it moves up a page, and clicking the bottom (footer) line of the selector goes down a page (middle click). The right mouse button is used to move up or down a page by clicking in the upper half or lower half of the screen.
YOUSAID (%)	Gives the format of the attribution line in front of the quoted article included by an R command. Default: In article %i you write:

Table 17. `tin` **Newsreader Commands**

SELECTING NEWSGROUPS

`k` up arrow	Move cursor to next newsgroup.
`j` down arrow	Move cursor to previous newsgroup.
`+`	Perform autoselection on newsgroup.
num	Select *num* newsgroup.
enter	Read current newsgroup.
tab	View next newsgroup with unread news.
Ctrl-l	Redraw the screen.
Ctrl-r	Reset **.newsrc** file.
`&`	Toggle use of ANSI color.
`c`	Mark current newsgroup as read (catchup) and move to next newsgroup.
`C`	Mark current newsgroup as read (catchup) and move to next unread newsgroup.
`d`	Toggle between displaying just newsgroup name or newsgroup name with its description.
`g`	Search for and select a newsgroup using it name. You can also use the position of the newsgroup within the group list. '1' references the first newsgroup and $ references the last.
`h`	Displays Help screen with selection commands.
`H`	Toggle on and off the display of the Help menu at the bottom of the screen.
`i`	Display the description of the current newsgroup on the last line.
`I`	Toggle inverse video.
`m`	Move the current group within the group selection list. '1' makes the newsgroup the first displayed, and $ makes it the last. You can enter a number for where you want the newsgroup listed.
`M`	User-configurable options menu.
`q`	Quit tin, but ask the user to confirm.
`Q`	Quit tin without asking the user to confirm.
`r`	Switch between the display of newsgroups with unread articles and all subscribed newsgroups.
`R`	Mail a bug report or comment. *(continued)*

Table 17. `tin` Newsreader Commands *(continued)*

s	Subscribe to current newsgroup.
S	Subscribe to newsgroups matching user-specified pattern.
u	Unsubscribe to current newsgroup.
U	Unsubscribe to newsgroups matching user-specified pattern.
v	Print tin version information.
w	Post an article to current newsgroup.
W	List articles posted by user. The date posted, the newsgroup, and the subject are listed.
X	Quit tin without saving any configuration changes.
y	Will read in newsgroups from **$NEWSLIBDIR/active** that are not in your **.newsrc.** You can then subscribe and unsubscribe to them. Pressing y again will read newsgroups from your **.newsrc** file and display only subscribed newsgroups.
Y	Check to see if any new news has arrived by reading the active file.
z	Mark all articles in the current newsgroup as unread.
/	Perform a forward search.
?	Perform a backward search.

NEWSGROUP STATUS CODES

NEWSGROUP SELECTION SCREEN CODES

u	Unsubscribed newsgroup.
N	New newsgroup created since you last used tin. New newsgroups are unsubscribed and you will need to subscribe to them if you want to access them again.
D	The newsgroup no longer exists. Unsubscribe to remove entry.

NEWSGROUP INDEX STATUS CODES

*num*T	The number of threads in the newsgroup.
*num*A	The number of articles in the newsgroup.
*num*K	The number of killed articles.
*num*H	The number of hot articles.
R	Display unread threads or articles.
M	Moderated newsgroup.

(continued)

Table 17. `tin` **Newsreader Commands** *(continued)*

THREAD MODES

U	No threading.
S	Subject threading.
R	Reference threading.
B	Both subject and reference threading.

NEWSGROUP INDEX COMMANDS

spacebar, Ctrl-f, page-down	Display next page of thread/article entries.
b, Ctrl-b, page-up	Display previous page of thread/article entries.
num	Select article *num*.
$	Move to last thread or article.
Ctrl-l	Redraw page.
enter	Read current article.
tab	View next unread article.
a	Author forward search.
A	Author backward search.
c	Mark all articles as read with confirmation.
C	Mark all articles as read and change to next newsgroup with unread news.
d	Add display of author, address, or author and address to thread entries.
g	Choose a new newsgroup by name.
h	Help screen of newsgroup index commands.
H	Toggle the Help menu display at the bottom of the screen.
i	Display the subject of the first article in the current thread in the last line.
I	Toggle inverse video.
K	Mark current thread or article as read and advance to next unread thread or article.
l	Display articles in a thread using Thread Listing screen.
m	Mail current article or selected or tagged articles to a user.
M	User configurable options menu.
n	Move to next thread/article.
N	Move to next unread thread/article.

(continued)

Table 17. `tin` **Newsreader Commands** *(continued)*

o	Print current or selected or tagged articles.
p	Move to previous thread/article.
P	Move to previous unread thread/article.
q	Return to previous level.
Q	Quit tin.
s	Save articles. Tagged or selected threads are saved with all their articles. Use = to save to a mailbox file and + to use the newsgroup name as a directory.
t	Tag current thread/article or thread. You can mail, print, save, or repost tagged articles.
u	Set the threading mode: no threading, threading by subject, threading by references, threading on subject and references.
U	Untag all threads or articles that were tagged.
v	Print tin version information.
w	Post an article to current group.
W	List articles posted by user.
x	Repost an already posted article to another newsgroup.
X	Mark all unread articles that have not been selected as read. Pressing 'X' again will toggle back to previous state.
z	Mark current article as unread.
Z	Mark current thread as unread.
/	Search forward for specified subject.
?	Search backward for specified subject.
-	Show last message.
|	Pipe current article, thread, selected, or tagged articles into a Unix command for processing by it.
*	Select current thread for later processing.
.	Toggle selection of current thread.
@	Reverse all selections on all articles.
~	Undo all selections on all articles. Undo the effect of the X command.
+	Perform autoselection on current group.
=	Select threads whose subjects match the supplied pattern. "*" matches all subjects. *(continued)*

Table 17. tin **Newsreader Commands** *(continued)*

;	If one unread article in a thread is selected, all unread articles are selected.

THREAD LISTING COMMANDS

num	Select article *num* within thread.
Ctrl-l	Redraw page.
enter	Display current article selected in the thread.
tab	View next unread article within thread.
c	Mark all articles in the thread as read and return to previous level.
d	Toggle display to show just the subject or the subject and author.
h	Help for Thread Listing commands.
H	Toggle the display of Help mini menu at the bottom of the screen.
I	Toggle inverse video.
K	Mark thread as read and return to previous level.
q	Return to previous level, usually the Article Listing.
Q	Quit tin.
r	Toggle display to show all articles or only unread articles.
R	Mail a bug report or comment.
t	Tag current article for mailing ('m') / piping ('|') / printing ('o') / saving ('s') / reposting ('x').
T	Return to group index level.
v	Print tin version information.
z	Mark current article in thread as unread.
Z	Mark all articles in thread as unread.

ARTICLE VIEWER COMMANDS

spacebar, Ctrl-f, page-down	Display next page of article text.
b, Ctrl-b, page-up	Display previous page of article text.
g	Display first page of article text.
G, $	Display last page of article text.
Ctrl-h	Show all of the article's mail header.
Ctrl-k	Kill article(s) via a menu.
0	Read the first article in this thread.
num	Read response *num* in this thread. *(continued)*

Table 17. `tin` **Newsreader Commands** *(continued)*

Ctrl-l	Redraw page.
enter	Move to first article in next thread.
tab	Move to the next unread article.
a	Author forward search.
A	Author backward search.
c	Mark all articles as read with confirmation and return to newsgroup selection level.
C	Mark current newsgroup as read and next newsgroup with unread articles.
d	Toggle rot-13 decoding for this article.
D	Delete current article. It must have been posted by the same user.
e	Edit the current article.
f	Post a follow-up to the current article, including body of article.
F	Post a follow-up to the current article.
h	List Article Viewer commands.
H	Toggle the Help menu display at the bottom of the screen.
i	Display the subject of the current article in the last line.
I	Toggle inverse video.
k	Mark article as read and move to the next unread article.
K	Mark thread as read and move to the next unread thread.
m	Mail current article or selected or tagged articles to a user.
M	User Global Options menu.
n	Display the next article.
N	Display the next unread article.
o	Print current or selected or tagged articles.
p	Display the previous article.
P	Display the previous unread article.
q	Return to previous level, either the Newsgroup Index or Thread Listing.
Q	Quit tin.
r	Reply through mail to the author of the current article with a copy of the article included.　*(continued)*

Table 17. `tin` **Newsreader Commands** *(continued)*

R	Reply through mail to the author of the current article.
s	Save articles. Tagged or selected threads are saved with all their articles. Use = to save to a mailbox file and + to use the newsgroup name as a directory.
t	Tag current article or thread. You can mail, print, save, or repost articles.
T	Return to newsgroup selection screen.
v	Print tin version information.
w	Post an article to current group.
W	List articles posted by user.
x	Repost an already posted article to another newsgroup.
z	Mark article as unread.
/	Article forward search.
?	Article backward search.
|	Pipe current article, thread, selected or tagged articles into a Unix command for processing by it.
<	Display the first article in the current thread.
>	Display the last article in the current thread.
*	Select current thread for later processing.
.	Toggle selection of current article.
@	Reverse article selections.
~	Undo all selections on current thread.
:	Skip quoted text.

TIN AUTO SELECT AND KILL COMMANDS

Ctrl-a	Create an autoselect entry using menu.
Ctrl-k	Create an autokill entry using menu.
[	Create autoselect entry using **tinrc** configuration variable defaults.
default_filter_days	Default number of filter days. Default is 28.
default_filter_select_header	Defaults for quick (1 key) autoselection filter header. 0=Subject: 1=From: 2=Message-Id:. Default is 0.
default_filter_select_case	Defaults for quick (1 key) autoselection filter case. ON=filter case sensitive OFF=ignore case. Default is OFF. *(continued)*

Table 17. `tin` **Newsreader Commands** *(continued)*

default_filter_select_expire	Defaults for quick (1 key) autoselection filter expire. ON=limit to default_filter_ days OFF=don't ever expire. Default is OFF.
default_filter_select_global	Defaults for quick (1 key) autoselection filter global. ON=apply to all groups OFF=apply to current group. Default is ON.
]	Create autokill entry using **tinrc** configuration variable defaults.
default_filter_kill_expire	Defaults for quick (1 key) kill filter expire. ON=limit to default_filter_days OFF=don't ever expire. Default is OFF.
default_filter_kill_global	Defaults for quick (1 key) kill filter global. ON=apply to all groups OFF=apply to current group. Default is ON.
default_filter_kill_header	Defaults for quick (1 key) kill filter header. 0=Subject: 1=From: 2=Message-Id:. Default is 0.
default_filter_kill_case	Defaults for quick (1 key) kill filter case. ON=filter case sensitive OFF=ignore case. Default is OFF.

TIN COMMAND LINE EDITING AND HISTORY

Ctrl-a	Move to beginning of line.
Ctrl-e	Move to end of line.
Ctrl-f, right arrow	Move forward one character location.
Ctrl-b, left arrow	Move back one character.
Ctrl-d	Delete the character currently under the cursor, or send EOF if no characters in the buffer.
Ctrl-h, delete	Delete character to left of cursor.
Ctrl-k	Delete from cursor to end of line.
Ctrl-p, up-arrow	Move to previous history entry.
Ctrl-n, down-arrow	Move to next history entry.
Ctrl-l, Ctrl-r	Redraw the current line.

TIN FILES

enter	Add current line to history list. *(continued)*

Table 17. `tin` **Newsreader Commands** (*continued*)

---

escape	Cancel the present editing operation.
TIN FILES	
.tin	tin configuration directory, located in user's home directory.
.newsrc	tin **newsrc** file holding newsgroup subscription list.
.tin/tinrc	tin file holding configuration variables.
.tin/.news	tin directory holding news index files.
.tin/.mail	tin directory holding mail index files.
.tin/.save	tin directory holding saved newsgroup index files.
.tin/headers	Holds extra header lines to be added to posted articles.
.tin/bug_address	Address for tin bug reports.
.tin/attributes	Specify the threading types for certain newsgroups.
.newsauth	"nntpserver password [user]" pairs for NNTP servers that require authorization.
.tin/active.mail	Active file of user's mailgroups.
.tin/active.save	Active file of user's saved newsgroups.
.tin/add_address	Address to add to when replying through mail.
.tin/filter	Filtering file for article killing and autoselection.
.tin/group.times	List of last time all groups were updated (used only by tind index demon).
.tin/posted	History of articles posted by user.
.tin/newsrctable	"nntpserver newsrc shortname" pairs to use with -g command-line switch.
.signature	Signature.
.Sig	Signature.
.sigfixed	Fixed part of a randomly generated signature.

-a	Use ANSI color.
-c	Create or update index files for every group in **$HOME/.newsrc** or file specified by the -f option and mark all articles as read.
-C	Count articles for each subscribed group at startup.
-d	Select index files for each group before indexing article.
-f *file*	Specify user's own file of subscribed to newsgroups in place of **$HOME/.newsrc**.
-g *server*	Use the **$HOME/.tin/newsrctable** specified server and **newsrc**.
-h	Help, lists command-line options.
-H	Detailed help with short introduction to tin.
-I*dir*	Directory in which to store newsgroup index files. Default is **$HOME/.tin/.news**.
-m*dir*	Mailbox directory. Default is **$HOME/Mail**.
-M *user*	Mail unread articles to specified user for later reading.
-n	Load subscribed newsgroups specified in user's **.newsrc**.
-q	Do not check for new newsgroups when starting up.
-p	Remove group index files of articles that no longer exist. Checks every article in each group accessed.
-r	Access remote NNTP news server as specified in the environment variable NNTPSERVER or contained in the file **/etc/nntpserver**.
-R	Read news saved by the -S option.
-s *dir*	Save articles to directory. Default is **$HOME/News**.
-S	Save unread articles for later reading by the -R option.
-u	Create or update index files for every group in **$HOME/.newsrc** or file specified by the -f option. Disabled for an NNTP news server.
-U	Start tin in the background to update index files while reading news in the foreground. Disabled for an NNTP news server.
-v	Verbose mode for -c, -M, -S, -u, and -Z options.
-w	Post an article and then exit.
-z	Check for any new or unread news and start up only if found.
-Z	Check for any new/unread news and exit with appropriate status. With the -v option, the number of unread articles in each group is displayed. A status code 0 indicates no news, 1 that an error occurred, 2 that an nntp error occurred and 3 that new/unread news exists.

Table 18. tin Options

Table 19. `tin` **Global Options Menu**

Auto save	Save articles or threads using "Archive-name:" line in article header. If process type is not set to None, then postprocess them.
Editor offset	Set ON if the editor used can position the cursor at a specified line in a file.
Mark saved read	Automatically mark saved articles as read.
Confirm command	Allows certain commands that require user confirmation to be executed immediately if set OFF.
Draw arrow	If set ON, newsgroups or articles are selected by an arrow '->', if set OFF, they are selected by a highlighted bar.
Print header	Allows the complete mail header or only the "Subject:" and "From:" fields to be output when displaying articles.
Goto 1st unread	Places the cursor at the first unread article upon entering a newsgroup with unread news.
Scroll full page	If set ON, scrolls newsgroups or articles a full page at a time. If set OFF, scrolls half a page at a time.
Catchup on quit	Asks the user when quitting if all groups read during the current session should be marked read.
Thread articles	Specify how articles are to be threaded (sets the **thread_arts** attribute). 0=none, 1=subject, 2=references.
Show only unread	If set ON, show only new or unread articles. If set OFF, show all articles.
Show description	Show a short descriptive text for each displayed newsgroup. Description taken from the **$NEWSLIBDIR/newsgroups file**.
Show Author	Choose from several options. If 'None', only the "Subject:" line is displayed. If 'Addr', "Subject:" line and address part of the "From:" line are displayed. If 'Name', "Subject:" line and the author's full name are displayed. If 'Both', "Subject:" line and all of the "From:" line are displayed.

Process type	Specify the default type of postprocessing to perform on saved articles. The types are as follows:
	– –None.
	– –Unpacking multi-part shell archives.
	– –Unpacking multi-part uuencoded files.
	– –Unpacking multi-part uuencoded files, which produce a *.zoo archive.
	– –Unpacking multi-part uuencoded files, which produce a *.zoo archive whose contents is extracted.
	– –Unpacking multi-part uuencoded files, which produce a *.zip archive.
	– –Unpacking of multi-part uuencoded files, which produce a *.zip archive whose contents is extracted.
Sort articles by	Specifies how articles should be sorted. The sort types are as follows:
	– –Don't sort articles (default).
	– –Sort articles by "Subject:" field (ascending/descending).
	– –Sort articles by "From:" field (ascending/descending).
	– –Sort articles by "Date:" field (ascending/descending).
Save directory	Directory where articles and threads are saved. Default is **$HOME/News**.
Mail directory	Directory where articles and threads are saved in mailbox format.
Printer	Printer command with options to be used to print articles. Default is `lpr` for BSD machines and `lp` for System V machines.

Table 20. `tin` **Configuration Variables**

`art_marked_deleted`	Status symbol indicating that an article is deleted. Default is `D`.
`art_marked_inrange`	Status symbol indicating that an article is within a range. Default is #.
`art_marked_return`	Status symbol indicating that an article will return. Default is '-'.
`art_marked_selected`	Status symbol indicating that an article/thread is autoselected (hot). Default is *.
`art_marked_unread`	Status symbol indicating that an article is unread. Default is '+'.
`ask_for_metamail`	Ask before using metamail to display MIME messages. `use_metamail` must also be ON. Default is ON.
`auto_cc`	Automatically place your name in the Cc: field when mailing an article. Default is OFF.
`auto_list_thread`	Automatically list thread when entering it using right arrow key. Default is ON.
`auto_save`	Articles/threads that are automatically saved and have Archive-name: in the mail header, are saved with the Archive-name and part/patch no. Default is OFF.
`batch_save`	With the `-S` or `-M` option, articles/threads are saved in batch mode. Default is OFF.
`beginner_level`	A mini menu of the most useful commands is displayed at the bottom of the screen for each level. Default is ON.
`catchup_read_groups`	Ask user on exit if read groups should all be marked read. Default is OFF.
`confirm_action`	Confirm certain commands with y/n before executing. Default is ON.
`confirm_quit`	Ask for confirmation with y/n prompt before quitting. Default is ON.
`default_editor_format`	Specify the format string used to create the editor start command with parameters. Default is '%E +%N %F' .
`default_filter_days`	Default number of filter days. Default is 28.

(continued)

Table 20. `tin` **Configuration Variables** *(continued)*

`default_filter_kill_case`	Defaults for quick (1 key) kill filter case. ON=filter case sensitive OFF=ignore case. Default is OFF.
`default_filter_kill_expire`	Defaults for quick (1 key) kill filter expire. ON=limit to default_filter_days OFF=don't ever expire. Default is OFF.
`default_filter_kill_global`	Defaults for quick (1 key) kill filter global. ON=apply to all groups OFF=apply to current group. Default is ON.
`default_filter_kill_header`	Defaults for quick (1 key) kill filter header. 0=Subject: 1=From: 2=Message-Id:. Default is 0.
`default_filter_select_case`	Defaults for quick (1 key) autoselection filter case. ON=filter case sensitive OFF=ignore case. Default is OFF.
`default_filter_select_expire`	Defaults for quick (1 key) autoselection filter expire. ON=limit to default_filter_days OFF=don't ever expire. Default is OFF.
`default_filter_select_global`	Defaults for quick (1 key) autoselection filter global. ON=apply to all groups OFF=apply to current group. Default is ON.
`default_filter_select_header`	Defaults for quick (1 key) autoselection filter header. 0=Subject: 1=From: 2=Message-Id:. Default is 0.
`default_maildir`	Directory where articles/threads are saved in mailbox format. Default is **$HOME/Mail**.
`default_mailer_format`	The format string used to create the mailer command with parameters that is used for mailing articles to other people. Default is '%M "%T" < %F', which works with mailx. It redirects the composed article kept in **.article** (%F) to the user (%T). You can use this string to add mail options for whatever mailer you choose to use such as elm or pine. `-s %S` inserted to the string adds a subject entry.
`default_printer`	Print command with parameters used to print articles/threads.
`default_savedir`	Directory where articles/threads are saved. Default is **$HOME/News**. *(continued)*

Table 20. `tin` **Configuration Variables** *(continued)*

`default_sigfile`	Path name for the signature file used when posting articles, follow-ups, or replies. Default is **$HOME/.Sig**.
`draw_arrow`	Use -> or highlighted bar for selection. Default is OFF.
`force_screen_redraw`	Specifies whether a screen redraw should always be done after certain external commands. Default is OFF.
`full_page_scroll`	Scroll full page of groups/articles (ON) or half a page (OFF). Default is ON.
`group_catchup_on_exit`	Catchup group when leaving with the left arrow key. Default is ON
`groupname_max_length`	Maximum number of characters of newsgroup names that can be displayed. Default is 32.
`highlight_xcommentto`	The X-Comment-To name is displayed in the upper-right corner or below the Summary-header. Default is OFF
`inverse_okay`	Use inverse video for page headers at different levels. Default is ON.
`keep_dead_articles`	Keep all failed article postings in **$HOME/dead.articles**. Last failed posting is kept in **$HOME/dead.article**. Default is ON.
`mail_8bit_header`	Permit 8bit characters unencoded in the header of mail message. Default is OFF. Turning it ON is effective only if mail_mime_encoding is also set to 8bit.
`mail_mime_encoding`	MIME encoding used in the body in mail message, if necessary (8bit, base64, quoted-printable, 7bit). Default is 8bit.
`mm_charset`	Locally supported character set.
`keep_posted_articles`	Keep copies of all posted articles in **$HOME/Mail/posted**. Default is ON.
`mail_quote_format`	Format for quote line (attribution) used in mail replies that insert the referenced article text. Default is "In article %M you wrote:"
`mark_saved_read`	Mark articles that are saved as read. Default is ON. *(continued)*

Table 20. `tin` **Configuration Variables** *(continued)*

`news_quote_format`	Format for quote line (attribution) used in articles and follow-ups that insert the referenced article text. (%A=Address, %D=Date, %F=Addr+Name, %G=Groupname, %M=MessageId, %N=Name). Default is "%F wrote:"
`no_advertising`	Do NOT display advertising in header (X-Newsreader/X-Mailer). Default is OFF.
`pos_first_unread`	Put cursor at first unread article in group or at last article. Default is ON.
`post_8bit_header`	Allows 8bit characters unencoded in the header of news article. Default is OFF. `post_mime_encoding` must also be set to 8bit.
`post_mime_encoding`	Specify MIME encoding of the body in news message, if needed. (8bit, base64, quoted-printable, 7bit). Default is 8bit, which leads to no encoding.
`post_process_type`	Type of postprocessing to perform after saving articles. 0=(none) 1=(unshar) 2=(uudecode) 3=(uudecode & list zoo archive) 4=(uudecode & extract zoo archive) 5=(uudecode & list zip archive) 6=(uudecode & extract zip).
`post_process_command`	Command (with full path name) to be run after uudecoding an article.
`print_header`	If ON, display complete mail header. If OFF display just Subject: and From: lines. Default is OFF.
`process_only_unread`	Perform operations (save, print, mail, or pipe) only on unread articles. Default is ON.
`quote_chars`	Symbol used to indicate included text to article follow-ups and mail replies. The '_' symbol represents a blank character, a ' '. Default is ':_'.
`reread_active_file_secs`	Interval in which the news active file is reread to check if any new news has arrived. Default is 1200.
`save_to_mmdf_mailbox`	Allows articles to be saved to a MMDF style mailbox instead of mbox format. Default is OFF.
`show_author`	Part of From: field to display 0) none, 1) full name, 2) network address, 3) both. Default is 2.

(continued)

Table 20. `tin` **Configuration Variables** *(continued)*

`show_description`	Display newsgroup description after newsgroup name. Default is ON.
`show_last_line_prev_page`	The last line of the previous page is displayed as the first line of next page. Default is OFF.
`show_only_unread`	If ON, show only new or unread articles, otherwise show all articles. Default is ON.
`show_only_unread_groups`	Show only subscribed groups that contain unread articles. Default is OFF.
`show_xcommentto`	Display the real name in the X-Comment-To header. Default is OFF.
`sigdashes`	Prepend the signature with dashes. Default is ON.
`sort_article_type`	Sort articles. Choose from one of the following. 0=none, 1=subject descending, 2=subject ascending, 3=from descending, 4=from ascending, 5=date descending, 6=date ascending. Default is 6.
`start_editor_offset`	If ON, editor will be started with cursor offset into the file. If OFF, cursor will be positioned at the first line. Default is ON.
`strip_blanks`	Strips the blanks from the end of each line to speed up display. Default is ON.
`strip_bogus`	Manage newsgroups listed in your **.newsrc** file that no longer exist on the news server (bogus newsgroups). 0=keep bogus newsgroups, 1=remove bogus newsgroups permanently, 2=display bogus newsgroups with a 'D'. Default is 0.
`strip_newsrc`	Permanently remove any unsubscribed newsgroups from your **.newsrc** file. Default is OFF.
`tab_after_X_selection`	Automatically go to the first unread article after having selected all hot articles and threads with the 'X' command at group index level. Default is OFF.
`tab_goto_next_unread`	Pressing **tab** in the Article Viewer moves to the next unread article, skipping the remainder of the current one. Default is ON.
`thread_articles`	Thread mode. 0=no threading, 1=subject, 2=references, 3=Both. Default is 3, thread by references and subject. *(continued)*

Table 20. `tin` **Configuration Variables** *(continued)*

`thread_catchup_on_exit`	Catchup newsgroup or thread when leaving with the left arrow key. Default is ON.
`unlink_article`	Remove **~/.article** after posting your article. Default is ON.
`use_builtin_inews`	Enables the built-in NNTP inews. Default is ON (enabled).
`use_metamail`	If ON metamail is used to display MIME articles. Default is ON.
`use_mouse`	Permit mouse key support in an xterm window to be enabled. Default is OFF.
`use_color`	Use ANSI colors. Default is OFF.
`wildcard`	Pattern matching capability. 1=full POSIX regular expressions, 0=wildmat notation. Newsgroup names are always matched using the wildmat notation.

Table 21. `tin` **Environment Variables**

`TINRC`	Holds command-line options that tin starts with. Note that environment variables that are used to set message header lines can also be set by adding the header name and value to the **$HOME/.tin/headers** file.
`TIN_HOMEDIR`	Holds directory where **.tin** directory is placed. Default is the user's home directory, **$HOME/.tin**.
`TIN_INDEX_NEWSDIR`	Holds directory where the **.news** directory is placed. Default is **$HOME/.tin/.news**.
`TIN_INDEX_MAILDIR`	Holds directory where the **.mail** directory is placed. Default is **$HOME/.tin/.mail**.
`TIN_INDEX_SAVEDIR`	Holds directory where the **.save** directory is placed. Default is **$HOME/.tin/.save**.
`TIN_LIBDIR`	Specify new path, overriding the `NEWSLIBDIR` path that was compiled into the tin binary. `NEWSLIBDIR` is specified in tin source code Makefile.
`TIN_SPOOLDIR`	Specify new path, overriding the `SPOOLDIR` path that was compiled into the tin binary. `SPOOLDIR` is specified in tin source code Makefile.
`TIN_NOVROOTDIR`	Specify new path, overriding the `NOVROOTDIR` path that was compiled into the tin binary. `NOVROOTDIR` is specified in tin source code Makefile.
`TIN_ACTIVEFILE`	Specify new path, overriding the `NEWSLIBDIR`/active path that was compiled into the tin binary. `NEWSLIBDIR` is specified in tin source code Makefile.
`NNTPSERVER`	Internet address of remote NNTP news server. Use when the `-r` command-line option is specified and the **/etc/nntpserver** system file does not exist.
`NNTPPORT`	The NNTP tcp port from which to read news.
`DISTRIBUTION`	Specify the article header field ``Distribution:''.
`ORGANIZATION`	Specify the article header field ``Organization:''.
`REPLYTO`	Specify the return address used in the article header field ``Reply-To:''.
`ADD_ADDRESS`	Address to append to the return address when replying directly through mail to user whose mail address is not directly recognized by the local host.
`BUG_ADDRESS`	Specify the bug report mail address. Overrides the address in the **$HOME/.tin/bug_address** file.

MAILER	The mailer used in all tin mailing operations. Overrides default mailer set in tin configuration.
EDITOR	The editor that is used in all editing operations within tin. Overrides default editor set in tin configuration.
AUTOSUBSCRIBE	Specify list of patterns to be used to match newsgroups that are to be automatically subscribed to. Exclamation performs an inverse match.
AUTOUNSUBSCRIBE	Specify list of patterns to be used to match newsgroups that are to be automatically unsubscribed to. Exclamation performs an inverse match.

Table 22. `tin` **Attributes**

`scope=` *string*	(i.e., alt.sources or *sources*) [mandatory]
`maildir=` *string*	Directory where articles are saved in mailbox format.
`printer=` *string*	Print command with parameters used to print articles/threads.
`savedir=` *string*	Directory where articles are saved.
`savefile=` *string*	Specify a default save file.
`sigfile=` *string*	Pathname for the signature file used when posting articles, follow-ups or replies.
`show_author=`*NUM*	Part of From: field to display 0) none, 1) full name, 2) network address, 3) both.
`batch_save=` *ON/OFF*	With the `-S` or `-M` option, articles are saved in batch mode.
`auto_list_thread`	Automatically list thread when entering it using right arrow key. Default is ON.
`auto_select=` *ON/OFF*	Automatically select articles in a thread when entering it.
`auto_save==` *ON/OFF*	Articles/threads that are automatically saved and have Archive-name: in the mail header, are saved with the Archive-name & part/patch no.
`auto_save_msg=` *ON/OFF*	Automatically save messages.
`organization=` *string*	Specify the article header field ``Organization:''.
`followup_to=` *string*	Follow-up entry.
`delete_tmp_files=` *ON/OFF*	Automatically delete temporary files.
`show_only_unread=` *ON/OFF*	If ON, show only new or unread articles, otherwise show all articles.
`sort_art_type=`*NUM*	Sort articles. Choose from one of the following. 0=none, 1=subject descending, 2=subject ascending, 3=from descending, 4=from ascending, 5=date descending, 6=date ascending.
`post_proc_type=`*NUM*	Type of postprocessing to perform after saving articles. 0=(none) 1=(unshar), 2=(uudecode), 3=(uudecode & list zoo archive), 4=(uudecode & extract zoo archive), 5=(uudecode & list zip archive), 6=(uudecode & extract zip).
`thread_arts=`*NUM*	Thread articles. Choose from one of the following. 0=nothing, 1=subject, 2=references, 3=both.

news_quote_format= *string*	Format for quote line (attribution) used in articles and follow-ups that insert the referenced article text. (%A=Address, %D=Date, %F=Addr+Name, %G=Groupname, %M=MessageId, %N=Name).
mailing_list= *string*	Holds addresses for mail responses.
x_headers= *string*	File that holds extra header lines to be added to posted articles.
x_body= *string*	File that holds extra text to be added to posted articles.
quick_kill_case= *ON/OFF*	Quick (1 key) kill filter case. ON=filter case sensitive, OFF=ignore case.
quick_kill_expire= *ON/OFF*	Quick (1 key) kill filter expire. ON=limit to quick_days, OFF=don't ever expire.
quick_kill_scope= *string*	Quick (1 key) kill filter scope.
quick_kill_header =*NUM*	Quick (1 key) kill filter header. 0=subj (case sensitive), 1=subj (ignore case), 2=from (case sensitive), 3=from (ignore case), 4=msgid, 5=lines. Default is 0.
quick_select_case= *ON/OFF*	Quick (1 key) autoselection filter case. ON=filter case sensitive, OFF=ignore case.
quick_select_expire= *ON/OFF*	Quick (1 key) autoselection filter expire. ON=limit to quick_days, OFF=don't ever expire.
quick_select_scope= *string*	Quick (1 key) autoselection filter for scope.
quick_select_header =*NUM*	Quick (1 key) autoselection filter header. 0=subj (case sensitive), 1=subj (ignore case), 2=from (case sensitive), 3=from (ignore case), 4=msgid, 5=lines.
x_comment_to=*ON/OFF*	Display the real name in the X-Comment-To header.
quote_chars=*string*	Symbol used to inidicate included text to article follow-ups and mail replies. The '_' symbol represents a blank character, a ' '.

Table 23. nn **Commands**

DISPLAYING THE NEWSGROUP ARTICLE LIST

N	Move to next newsgroup.
G	Move to particular newsgroup.
spacebar *or* >	Display the next screen of articles.
<	Display the previous screen of articles.
$	Display the last screen of articles.
^	Display the first screen of articles.
"	Change display layout.
Z	Begin displaying selected articles. Return to newsgroup screen when finished.
X	Begin displaying selected articles, but move to the next newsgroup when finished.

SELECTING ARTICLES FROM THE NEWSGROUP ARTICLE LIST

id	Select/unselect an article.
id*	Select/unselect articles with the same thread as *id*.
`	Move to the next article heading.
/	Move to the previous article heading.
.	Select the current article.

MOVING TO ARTICLES WHEN READING

n	Move to the next selected article.
p	Move to the previous selected article.
*	Move to next article in the thread such as same subject.
k	Mark as read the current article, skipping it.
=	Return to selector screen.

DISPLAYING ARTICLES

spacebar	Display the next screen of the article.
return	Scroll to the next line of the article.
d	Scroll to the next half screen of the article.
b	Display the previous screen of the article.
^	Display first screen of the article.
$	Display last screen of the article.

| / *pattern* | Search for pattern in the text. |
| . | Repeat pattern search in the text. |

POSTING AND REPLYING TO ARTICLES

r	Reply to current article.
f	Post a follow-up to the current article.
m	Send a copy of the article to another user.
:post	Post a new article.
nnpost	Post a new article. Seperate utility.

Table 24. TCP/IP Protocols

TRANSPORT

TCP	Transmission Control Protocol; connect two networked systems.
UDP	User Datagram Protocol; request/reply connection between systems.

NETWORKING

IP	Internet Protocol; transmit data across networks.
ICMP	Internet Control Message Protocol; send routing control messages.
IGMP	Internet Group Management Protocol; transmit data to selected groups.

ROUTING

RIP	Routing Information Protocol; determine routing.
OSPF	Open Shortest Path First; determine routing.
BGP	Border Gateway Protocol; transmit routing information across network.
EGP	Exterior Gateway Protocol; provide routing information for external networks.
GGP	Gateway-to-Gateway Protocol; provide routing between Internet gateways.
IGP	Interior Gateway Protocol; provide routing for internal networks.

NETWORK ADDRESSES

ARP	Address Resolution Protocol; determine unique IP address of systems.
DNS	Domain Name Service; translate hostnames into IP addresses.
RARP	Reverse Address Resolution Protocol; match IP addresses to local system network addresses.

APPLICATIONS

FTP	File Transfer Protocol; transmit files from one system to another.
TFTP	Trivial File Transfer Protocol; simplified version of Ftp.
TELNET	remote login to another system on the network.

SMTP	Simple Mail Transfer Protocol; transfer email between systems.
HTML	HyperText Markup Language; compose HyperText documents.
HTTP	HyperText Transfer Protocol; transfers HyperText documents.
MIME	Multi-purpose Internet Mail Extensions; Transmit multiple attached files of varying kinds as electronic mail messages.
WWW	World Wide Web; graphical HyperText browsing service.

NETWORK SERVICES

NFS	Network File Systems; allows shared mounting of file systems on remote systems.
NIS	Network Information Service; maintain user accounts across a network.
RPC	Remote Procedure Call; allows programs on remote systems to communicate.
BOOTP	Boot Protocol; start system using boot information on a remote server.
DHCP	Dynamic Host Configuration; remotely boot and configure system.
SNMP	Single Network Management Protocol; manage networked devices.
NTP	Network Time Protocol; synchronize system clocks on a network.
PPP	Point-to-Point Protocol; direct connection between system and network.
SLIP	Serial Line Internet Protocol; serial connection between system and network.

INTERNET UNITED STATES DOMAIN CODES

com	Commercial	mil	Military
edu	Educational Institution	net	Networking organization
gov	Government		
int	International		
org	Nonprofit organization		

INTERNET INTERNATIONAL DOMAIN CODES

at	Austria
au	Australia
ca	Canada
ch	Switzerland
cl	Chile
cn	China
de	Germany
dk	Denmark
ec	Ecuador
es	Spain
fi	Finland
fr	France
gr	Greece
ie	Ireland
il	Israel
in	India
it	Italy
jp	Japan
kr	South Korea
nl	Netherlands
nz	New Zealand
pl	Poland
se	Sweden
tw	Taiwan
uk	United Kingdom
us	United States

Table 25. Internet Domain Codes

Table 26. Network Configuration and Look-Up

INTERNET DOMAIN LOOKUP

whois
Display information about the host, such as the street address and phone number as well as contact persons (not lowest level domains).

nslookup
Supplies info of even lowest level domains. Has an interactive mode that you enter by not specifying any domain name. You can then use **nslookup** to search for other kinds of information about a host. For example, the HINFO option will find out what type of operating system a host uses. The **nslookup** man page specifies a list of different options and how to use them.

dig
Like nslookup, but with easy-to-use interface.

host
Converts domain name of a host to its Internet address. With -a options provided detailed information about host.

NETWORK CONFIGURATION ADDRESSES

ADDRESSES

Host address
IP address of your system; it has a network part to identify the network you are on and a host part to identify your own system.

Network address
IP address of your network (network part of your host IP address with host part set to 0).

Broadcast address
IP address for sending messages to all hosts on your network at once (network part of your host IP address with host part set to 255).

Gateway address
IP address of your gateway system if you have one (usually the network part of your host IP address with host part set to 1).

Domain nameserver addresses   IP addresses of domain nameservers used by your network.

Netmask
Network part of your host IP address set to 255s with host part set to 0 (255.255.255.0).

TCP/IP CONFIGURATION FILES

/etc/hosts
Associate host names with IP addresses, listing domain names for remote hosts with their IP addresses.   *(continued)*

Table 26. Network Configuration and Look-Up *(continued)*

/etc/networks	Associate domain names with network addresses.
/etc/hostname	Hold the name of your system.
/etc/host.conf	List resolver options.
/etc/resolv.conf	List domain nameserver names, IP addresses (nameserver), and domain names where remote hosts may be located (search).
/etc/protocols	List protocols available on your system.
/etc/services	List available network services such as Ftp and Telnet.

-8	Request 8-bit operation. Attempts to negotiate the TELNET BINARY option for both input and output.
-E	Disable the escape character, setting the escape character to "no character."
-L	Set 8-bit data path on output, causing the TELNET BINARY option negotiated on output only.
-a	Perform an automatic login using the user name from the Telnet USER variable. By default this is the same as your current login name as specified by your $USER environment variable. The ENVIRON must be supported by the remote system.
-d	Set debug toggle to TRUE.
-r	Emulate rlogin operation. The default escape character is a tilde. An escape character followed by a dot disconnects from the remote system. **Ctrl-z** suspends Telnet, and a **^]** escapes to the Telnet command mode. The escape keys can only be entered at the beginning of the line.
-S *tos*	Specify the IP type of service, *tos*.
-e *escapechar*	Specify a new value for the Telnet escape character used to enter the command mode. If no value is specified, no escape character is used.
-l *login-name*	Specify the login name to be used for the remote system. The login name is placed in the Telnet USER variable and requires the remote system to support the TELNET ENVIRON option. This option implies the -a option. You can also use this option with the open command.
-n *tracefile*	Saves recorded trace information in tracefile. See tracefile command.
host	Specify a remote system (*host*) to connect to on your network.
port	Specifiy a port number to use.

Table 27. Telnet Options

Table 28. Telnet Commands

open *host [[-l] user] [-port]*	Open a connection to a remote system (*host*). Optional arguments are a remote login name as specified with the -1 option, or a port number. The host can be a host name or an IP (Internet) address. The default port for the system's Telnet daemon is usually 23. If another port is specified, then Telnet protocols are not implemented. You can force Telnet protocols by placing a - before the port number.
close	Close the connection to the remote system and return to the Telnet command mode.
display *variable...*	Display Telnet variable and toggle values. You can list the variable or toggle values you want displayed.
environ *arguments...*	Exports your shell environment variables across the Telnet link using the TELNET ENVIRON protocol option. By default the DISPLAY and PRINTER variables are exported. The USER variable is sent if the -a or -1 command-line options are used. The remote system may still ask explicitly for variables not marked for export.

ARGUMENTS

define *variable value*	Define a variable with the specified value. The variable is automatically marked for export.
undefine *variable*	Remove definition of variable.
export *variable*	Mark a specified variable for export to the remote system.
unexport *variable*	Specified variable is not marked for export to the remote system.
list	List the current set of environment variables. Those marked with a * will be exported to the remote system.
?	Display environment command help information
logout	Close the Telnet connection (like the close command). Requires that the remote system support the Telnet LOGOUT option.
quit	Close any open session and exit Telnet.
send *code*	Send Telnet special control character sequences to the remote host. The sequences are referenced with Telnet codes. See Table 11.III for the list of send codes.
mode *type*	Sets the mode of operation for the Telnet connection.

MODES

character	Transmit data a character at a time (disables the LINEMODE option).

`line`	Transmit data a line at a time (enables the LINEMODE option). If remote system cannot use LINEMODE option, then "old line by line" mode is used.
`set` *variable value*	Assign a value to a Telnet variable or toggle. To assign a value to a toggle, use the values TRUE to turn it on and FALSE to turn it off. Use the `display` command to list the current values.
`unset` *variable*	Unset the value of a Telnet variable.
`toggle` *toggle-list*	Turn a Telnet toggle on or off, toggling between TRUE and FALSE. You can set their values explicitly with the `set` command.
`z`	Suspend Telnet.
`!` *[command]*	Execute a single command in a subshell on the local system. If no command is specified, then an interactive shell is started up.
`?` *[command]*	Displays a help summary. If a command is specified, Telnet displays the help information for that command.
`slc` *state*	Set or change the state of the special control characters when the TELNET LINEMODE option has been enabled.

STATES

`check`	Verify the current settings for the current special control characters. The remote system sends all the current special character settings, and, if there are any discrepancies with the local system, the local system switches to the remote value.
`export`	Use the local defaults for the special control characters.
`import`	Use the remote defaults for the special control characters.
`status`	Show the current status of Telnet. Displays the name of the remote system.

(Send signals with the `send` command.)

`abort`	TELNET ABORT (Abort Processes) sequence.
`ao`	TELNET AO (Abort Output) sequence. Causes the remote system to flush all output from the remote system to the user's terminal.
`ayt`	TELNET AYT (Are You There?) sequence.
`brk`	TELNET BRK (Break) sequence. Send a break character.
`ec`	TELNET EC (Erase Character) sequence. Erase the last character entered.
`el`	TELNET EL (Erase Line) sequence. Erase the current line.
`eof`	TELNET EOF (End Of File) sequence. Send an end-of-file character, usually a **Ctrl-d**.
`eor`	TELNET EOR (End of Record) sequence.
`escape`	The Telnet escape character.
`ip`	TELNET IP (Interrupt Process) sequence. Send an interrupt character, usually a **Ctrl-c**.
`susp`	TELNET SUSP (Suspend Process) sequence.
`synch`	TELNET SYNCH sequence. Discards previously typed input that has not yet been read.
`?`	Prints help information for the `send` command.

Table 29. Telnet Send Codes

Table 30. Telnet Variables and Features

Telnet Variables

(Set variable values using the set command and unset them with the unset command.)

`ayt`	Status character, a TELNET AYT sequence.
`echo`	Toggles local echoing of entered characters (default is **Ctrl-e**).
`eof`	End-of-file character.
`erase`	Erase character, TELNET EC sequence.
`escape`	Telnet escape character (default is "^["). Causes entry into Telnet command mode.
`flushoutput`	Flush character, TELNET AO sequence.
`forw1`	Forward partial lines to the remote systems, based on `eol` character.
`forw2`	Forward partial lines to the remote systems, based on `eol2` character.
`interrupt`	Interrupt character, TELNET IP sequence
`kill`	Kill character, TELNET EL sequence.
`lnext`	`lnext` character.
`quit`	Quit character, Sends a TELNET BRK sequence to the remote system.
`reprint`	Reprint character.
`rlogin`	`rlogin` mode escape character that enables `rlogin` mode. Same as with the `-r` Telnet option.
`start`	Start character; default is your system's kill character.
`stop`	Stop character.
`susp`	Suspend character, a TELNET SUSP sequence.
`tracefile`	File name for `tracefile` to which `netdata` or option tracing will write to. If set to "-", then tracing information is written to standard output (the default).
`worderase`	Word erase character.
`?`	Displays the `set` commands.

Telnet Toggle Features

(Use the `toggle` command to toggle features on or off. You can list several features with the same toggle command. You can use the `set` command to turn them on or off by setting their values to TRUE or FALSE) *(continued)*

Table 30. Telnet Variables and Features *(continued)*

`autoflush`	If TRUE, does not display data on the user's system until the remote system acknowledges it has processed `ao` or `quit` sequences sent to it. Default is TRUE unless "stty noflsh" is entered.
`autologin`	Use the user's login name to log in.
`autosynch`	Flush previously typed input. Default is FALSE.
`binary`	Enable or disable the TELNET BINARY option on both input and output.
`inbinary`	Enable or disable the TELNET BINARY option on input.
`outbinary`	Enable or disable the TELNET BINARY option on output.
`crlf`	If TRUE, return characters are sent as return and line feed. If FALSE, returns are sent as returns. Default is FALSE.
`crmod`	Map single return characters received from remote system to return and a line feed. Default is FALSE.
`localchars`	If TRUE, then Telnet special control characters are recognized locally and translated into TELNET control sequences.
`netdata`	Display network data (in hexadecimal format). Default is FALSE.
`options`	Display of internal Telnet protocol processing. Default is FALSE.
`prettydump`	With `netdata` toggle enabled, `prettydump` outputs `netdata` output in more readable format.
`skiprc`	If TRUE, the **.telnetrc** file is not read. Default is FALSE.
`termdata`	Display of terminal data (in hexadecimal format). Default is FALSE.
`?`	Displays the toggle commands.

Table 31. FTP Options and Commands

FTP OPTIONS

-v	Verbose; displays all responses from the remote system and reports data transfer statistics.
-n	Do not perform "auto-login" upon connecting to a remote system. Otherwise, if auto-login is enabled, Ftp will check the **.netrc** file in the user's home directory for an entry with the login name on the remote system. If no entry exists, Ftp will prompt for a remote login name and then prompt for a password if needed. The default login name is the user login name on the local system.
-i	Turns off interactive prompting during multiple file transfers. Applies to mget and mput commands, canceling prompts for the transfer of each individual file in an mget or mput operation.
-d	Enables debugging.
-g	Disables file name expansion (globbing). Use of *, ?, and [] for file name matching is disabled.
system-address	You can specify the remote system to connect to immediately, skipping an open command for that connection.

FTP CONNECTION AND DIRECTORY COMMANDS

! *[command [args]*	Executes a Unix shell command. You can specify arguments for the shell command if needed. With no shell command, the ! places you in an interactive Unix shell where you can issue Unix commands. Enter exit or **Ctrl-d** to return to Ftp.
account *[passwd]*	Provide a supplemental password after login if the remote system requires one. You can enter the password as an argument to account. If not, you will be prompted for it and entry will not be echoed on your screen.
bye	End and exit the Ftp program. If you are connected to a remote system at the time, the connection will be terminated.
cd *remote-directory*	Change directory on the remote system to *remote-directory*, making it your working directory on the remote system.
cdup	Change to the parent directory of the remote system's working directory (like a cd.. operation for remote directories).
chmod *mode file-name*	Change the permissions of a remote file. The Ftp chmod command works on remote files.
close	Terminate the Ftp session with the remote system, and return to the Ftp command interpreter. Any defined macros are erased.

(continued)

Table 31. FTP Options and Commands *(continued)*

delete *remote-file*   Delete a file on the remote system.

debug *[debug-level]*   Toggle debugging mode. You can set the debug level. In debug mode, Ftp displays commands sent to the remote system, preceding them with `—>'.

dir *[remote-directory] [local-file]*

List the contents of a remote directory (like ls), using long form. If you do not specify a directory name, the current working remote directory is used. You can specify a local file name to which the directory listing will be saved. If no file name is specified, the local standard output is used, usually displaying the listing on your screen.

disconnect   Same as the close command; terminate a connection to a remote system.

glob   Toggle Unix file name expansion for mdelete, mget and mput. If globbing is turned off with glob, the file name arguments containing expansion characters such as *, ?, and [], are not expanded. These characters are read literally and taken as part of the file name. File name expansion is performed by the remote system and may differ accordingly. You can preview the results using the mls command, mls remote-files -. glob does not enable mget and mput to transfer directory subtrees. You can transfer subtrees using tar archives that are later extracted.

hash   Display hash-signs ("#") during a file transfer. One # is displayed for each data block transferred. The size of a data block is 1024 bytes. *(continued)*

help *[command]*   Display a list of Ftp commands. If command is specified, display help information about that command.

idle *[seconds]*   Display the inactivity timer setting. With a seconds argument, it sets the inactivity timer on the remote server to that number of seconds.

lcd [directory]   Change the working directory on your local system. If you do not specify a directory, your local system's home directory (line cd) is used.

ls *[remote-directory] [local-file]*

List the contents of a remote directory. If you do not specify a directory name, the current working remote directory is used. You can specify a local file name to which the directory listing will be saved. If no file name is specified, the local standard output is used, usually displaying the listing on your screen.

mdelete *[remote-files]*   Delete several *remote-files* on the remote machine.   *(continued)*

Table 31. FTP Options and Commands *(continued)*

`mdir` *remote-files local-file*	Lets you specify several remote files to list as `dir` does. Instead of specifying a single directory or file you can list several particular files. The last file is take to be the local file where you want to save the listing results. If interactive prompting is on, Ftp will prompt you to verify that the last argument is that local file.
`modtime` *filename*	Display the last modification time of *filename* on the remote system.
`nlist` *[remote-directory] [local-file]*	
	Print a *remote-directory* listing. If *remote-directory* is left unspecified, the current working directory is used. If *local-file* is specified, the listing is saved in that file on your local system. If *local-file* is not specified, the listing is output to standard output, which, by default, is displayed on your screen. If interactive prompting is on, Ftp will prompt you to verify that the last argument is a local file for receiving `nlist` output.
`open` *system-address [port]*	Make an Ftp connection to a remote system or Ftp site. You can specify a port number on which to connect to the remote system. With the auto-login option on, Ftp will try to automatically log in the user. auto-login is on by default.
`pwd`	Display current working directory on the remote system.
`quit`	Quite Ftp, closing any open connections. Same as bye.
`quote` *arg1 arg2 ...*	Send the arguments verbatim to the remote system.
`remotehelp` *[command-name]*	Request help from the remote system. You can specify help for a specific command.
`remotestatus` *[filename]*	With no arguments, show status of remote system. If *filename* is specified, show status of *filename* on remote system.
`rename` *[filename] [new-name]*	Rename a file on the remote system.
`reset`	Clear reply queue. Resynchronizes command/reply sequencing with the remote system. Used if remote system violates Ftp protocol.
`rmdir` *directory-name*	Delete a directory on the remote system.
`site` *arg1 arg2 ...*	Send verbatim arguments that are commands to be executed on the remote system.
`size` *filename*	Obtain the size of a file on remote system.
`status`	Display the current status of Ftp. *(continued)*

Table 31. FTP Options and Commands *(continued)*

`system`	Display the type of operating system used on the remote system.
`tenex`	Set the file transfer type to that needed to talk to TENEX machines.
`trace`	Toggle packet tracing.
`umask` *[newmask]*	Set the default `umask` on the remote server to `newmask`. With no arguments, the current `umask` is displayed.
`user` *user-name [password] [account]*	
	Identify yourself to the remote system. If the *password* or *account* are required by the remote system, and you do not specify them, Ftp will prompt you to enter them. Unless Ftp is invoked with "auto-login" disabled, this process is done automatically on initial connection to the remote system.
`verbose`	Toggle `verbose` mode. If on, all responses from the remote system are displayed. When a file transfer completes, statistics regarding the efficiency of the transfer are reported. `verbose` is on by default.
`?` *[command]*	Display help information about a command. Same as `help`.

FTP FILE TRANSFER COMMANDS

`append` *local-file [remote-file]*	
	Append a local file to a file on the remote system. If you do not specify a remote file name, then the local file is for that name.
`ascii`	Set the file transfer type to network ASCII. This is usually the default type (transfer type is changed to binary by many Internet Ftp sites).
`bell`	Sound bell after a file transfer.
`binary`	Set the file transfer type to binary.
`case`	Toggle the remote file name case mapping during `mget` commands. When `case` is on, remote file names on the remote system that have letters in uppercase are written in the local directory with the letters mapped to lowercase. Default is off.
`cr`	Toggle carriage return stripping during ASCII type file transfer. This is used for files such as DOS files that use both a carriage return and line-feed character for a newline, instead of just a line-feed character as Unix does. When on, `cr` will strip the carriage-return character from ASCII files, making the file conform to the Unix ASCII file using just a line feed for newlines. *(continued)*

Table 31. FTP Options and Commands *(continued)*

form *format*	Set the format for the file transfer form. The default format is "file."
get *remote-file [local-file]*	Transfer a remote file from the remote system to your local system. You can specify a local file name for it; if you don't, the same remote name is used. If there is already a file by that name on your local system, then the file name will be altered. The current settings for type, form, mode, and structure are used for transferring the file.
glob	Toggle Unix file name expansion for mdelete, mget, and mput. If globbing is turned off with glob, the file name arguments containing expansion character such as *, ?, and [], are not expanded. These characters are read literally and taken as part of the file name. File name expansion is performed by the remote system and may differ accordingly. You can preview the results using the mls command, mls remote-files -. glob does not enable mget and mput to transfer directory subtrees. You can transfer subtrees using tar archives that you later extract.
hash	Display hash signs ("#") during a file transfer. One # is displayed for each data block transferred. The size of a data block is 1024 bytes.
mget *remote-files*	Perform any specified file name expansion in *remote-files* on the remote system. Then execute a get operation for each file name generated. File name expansion is performed as indicated by glob. File names are processed according to case, ntrans, and nmap settings.
mput *local-files*	Perform any specified file name expansion in *local-files* on the local system. Then execute a put operation for each file name generated. File name expansion is performed as indicated by glob. File names are processed according to ntrans and nmap settings.
newer *file-name [local-file]*	Perform a get operation to transfer a file from the remote system, only if the modification time of the remote file is more recent that the *local-file* specified on your local system. If no local file is specified, then a file of the same name is used. If the file does not exist on the current system, the remote file is considered newer.
prompt	Toggle interactive prompting for multiple file transfers using mget or mput. Interactive prompting is on by default. If turned off, you are not prompted for individual files. With mput and mget, all matching files are transferred, and with mdelete all matching files are deleted. *(continued)*

Table 31. FTP Options and Commands *(continued)*

---

proxy *ftp-command*	Allows file transfers between two remote systems. The first proxy operation should be an open command to connect to the second remote system. You can then execute Ftp commands on the second system using the proxy command. Close the connection with a proxy command followed by a close command. Proxy open operation does not define new macros and a proxy close will not erase macros. get and mget transfer files to the second system first. put and mput transfer files from the second system to the first. Execute an Ftp command on a secondary control connection. proxy ? lists help information. Depends on support of the Ftp protocol PASV command by the second system.
put *local-file [remote-file]*	Transfer local file to the remote system. If file name for remote-file is not unspecified, the *local-file* name is used. ntrans or nmap settings may apply. Transfers use the current settings for type, format, mode, and structure.
recv *remote-file [local-file]*	Transfer files from the remote system. Same as get.
reget *remote-file [local-file]*	Transfer files from the remote system, like get. Will also resume transfer of interrupted file transmissions. If the local file exists and is smaller than the remote file, the local file is presumed to be a partially transferred copy of the remote file and the transfer is continued from the apparent point of failure. Useful for transferring large files.
restart *marker*	Restart immediately following get or put at the indicated marker. On UNIX systems, marker is usually a byte offset into the file.
runique	Toggle storing of files on the local system with unique file names. If off (the default) then files transferred with the same name as an existing file will overwrite that file. If off, then a new file name is generated, preserving the existing file. The same name with a **.1** appended to it is used. If the resulting name matches another existing file, a **.2** is appended to the original name. If this process continues beyond **.99**, an error message is printed, and the transfer does not take place.
send *local-file [remote-file]*	Transfer files from your local system to the remote system. Same as put.

(continued)

Table 31. FTP Options and Commands *(continued)*

`sendport`	Toggle the use of `Port` commands. By default, Ftp will attempt to use a `Port` command when establishing a connection for each data transfer. The use of `Port` commands can prevent delays when performing multiple file transfers. If the `Port` command fails, Ftp will use the default data port. When the use of `Port` commands is disabled, no attempt will be made to use `Port` commands for each data transfer.
`sunique`	Toggle storing of files on remote system under unique file names. If off (the default) then files transferred to the remote system with the same name as an existing file will overwrite that file. If off, then a new file name is generated, preserving the exiting file. The same name with a **.1** appended to it is used, and so on.

MACROS, MAP, HELP, AND TRANSMISSION PARAMETERS

`$` *macro-name [args]*	Execute the macro *macro-name*. Macros are defined with the `macdef` command. Arguments are passed to the macro unglobbed.
`form` *format*	Set the format for the file transfer form. The default format is "`file.`"
`help` *[command]*	Display a list of Ftp commands. If command is specified, displays help information about that command.
`macdef` *macro-name*	Define a macro with the name *macro-name*. Enter Ftp command for the macro on the following lines. End the macro definition with an empty line. There is a limit of 16 macros and 4096 total characters in all defined macros. Macros remain defined until a `close` command is executed. Macros can take arguments that are referenced in the macro definition with a `$` and the number of the argument. The `$i` implements a loop on the macro, repeating it once for each argument entered, with `$i` referencing each argument in turn. You can quote `$` in the macro definition by preceding it with `\` to enter the `$` character. `\\` will enter a backslash character.
`nmap` *[in-pattern out-pattern]*	With no arguments, turns off file mapping. With *in-pattern* and *out-pattern* arguments, `nmap` specifies translations to be performed. File names matching the *in-pattern* are translated into the *out-pattern*. Elements of the original pattern name are referenced in the *in-pattern* and *out-pattern* templates using *$num* references. Useful when connecting to non-Unix remote systems with different file naming conventions. *(continued)*

Table 31. FTP Options and Commands *(continued)*

`ntrans` *[inchars [outchars]]*	With no arguments, the file name character translation mechanism is unset. With arguments, characters in remote file names are translated if there is no specified target file name. Characters in a file name matching a character in *inchars* are replaced with the corresponding character in *outchars*. If the character's position in *inchars* is longer than the length of *outchars*, the character is deleted from the file name. Useful when connecting to non-Unix remote systems with different file naming conventions.
`status`	Display the current status of Ftp.
`struct` *[struct-name]*	Set the file transfer structure to *struct-name*. The default is `"stream."`
`system`	Display the type of operating system used on the remote system.
`type` *[type-name]*	Set the file transfer type. If no arguments, the current type is displayed. The default type is network ASCII.

`tar` *options files*	Back up files to tape, device, or archive file.
`tar` **Options**	
`c`	Create a new archive.
`r`	Append files to an archive.
`u`	Update an archive with new and changed files. Add only those files that have been modified since they were archived or files that are not already present in the archive.
`w`	Wait for a confirmation from the user before archiving each file. Allows you to selectively update an archive.
`x`	Extracts files from an archive.
`m`	When extracting a file from an archive, do not give it a new time stamp.
`f` *archive-name*	Save the tape archive to the file *archive-name* instead of to the default tape device. *archive-name* can be either a file or another device such as a tape or disk. The default device is held in `/etc/default/tar` file.
`v`	Display each file name as it is archived.
`z, - -gzip, - -ungzip`	Filter the archive through gzip.
`Z, - -compress, - -uncompress`	Filter the archive through compress.
`- -use-compress-program` *prog*	Filter the archive through *prog* (must accept `-d` option).
`d, - -diff, - -compare`	Find differences between archive and file system.

Table 32. File Backups: `tar`

Table 33. Zip Archive and Compression

-A	Adjust self-extracting executable archive.
-b *path*	Use the specified path for the temporary zip archive.
-c	Add one-line comments for each file.
-d	Remove entries from a zip archive.
-D	No entries created for directories in zip archives.
-e	Encrypt the contents of the zip archive using a password that is entered on the terminal in response to a prompt.
-f	Replace (freshen) an existing entry in the zip archive only if it has been modified more recently than the version already in the zip archive. Does not add files new files to the zip archive.
-F	Fix the zip archive. Used if part of the archive is missing.
-g	Grow (append to) the specified zip archive, instead of creating a new one.
-h	Display the zip help information.
-i *files*	Include only the specified files.
-j	Store just the name of a file without the path, and do not store directory names. By default, zip stores the full path (relative to the current path).
-J	Strip any prepended data from the archive.
-k	Attempt to convert the names and paths to conform to MS-DOS.
-l	Translate the Unix end-of-line character line feed into the MS-DOS carriage return and line feed.
-ll	Translate the MS-DOS end of line, carriage return, and line feed into Unix line feed.
-L	Display the zip license.
-m	Move the specified files into the zip archive; actually, this deletes the target directories/files after making the specified zip archive.
-n *suffixes*	Do not compress files named with the given suffixes.
-o	Set the "last modified" time of the zip archive to the latest (oldest) "last modified" time found among the entries in the zip archive.
-q	Quiet mode; eliminate informational messages and comment prompts.
-r	Travel the directory structure recursively.
-t *mmddyy*	Do not operate on files modified prior to the specified date, where *mm* is the month (0–12), *dd* is the day of the month (1–31), and *yy* is the last two digits of the year.
-T	Test the integrity of the new zip file.

(continued)

-u	Replace (update) an existing entry in the `zip` archive only if it has been modified more recently than the version already in the `zip` archive.
-v	`verbose` mode or print diagnostic version info.
-x *files*	Explicitly exclude the specified *files*.
-X	Do not save extra file attributes (file times on Unix).
-y	Store symbolic links as such in the `zip` archive, instead of compressing and storing the file referred to by the link.
-z	Prompt for a multiline comment for the entire `zip` archive. The comment is ended by an end of file, ^D.
-#	Regulate the speed of compression using the specified digit #, where -0 indicates no compression (store all files), -1 indicates the fastest compression method (less compression), and -9 indicates the slowest compression method (optimal compression, ignores the suffix list). The default compression level is -6.
-@	Take the list of input files from standard input.

Table 34. Archie Commands and Options

ARCHIE CLIENT COMMAND

`archie` *options string*

OPTIONS

`-e`	Exact pattern match (default).
`-c`	Search file names for occurrence of pattern.
`-s`	Search file names ignoring case.
`-r`	Pattern is a regular expression.
`-t`	Sort the results by date.
`-h` *hostname*	Query the host name Archie server.
`-m`*num*	Limits the maximum number of results (matches).
`-N`*num*	Estimate number of results of a query (default 0).
`-L`	Lists the known Archie servers.
`-V`	Verbose; display messages during long search.
`-o`*filename*	If specified, place the results of the search in *filename*.

VARIABLES

`ARCHIE_HOST`	Holds the address of the Archie host to use for Archie client queries, if different for host, compiled in the client.

ARCHIE PUBLIC SERVER COMMANDS

`prog`	Search file names for occurence of pattern.
`list`	Lists the known Archie servers.
`site`	List files at a particular host.
`mail`	Mail results of search.
`quit`	Log out from Archie server.
`help`	Display help.
`set` *variable value*	Set Archie variables.
`show`	Display current values of Archie variables.
`unset`	Remove a variable.

ARCHIE SERVER VARIABLES

`autologout` *num*	Number of minutes that Archie waits idle before automatically logging you out of the Archie server. The default is 15 minutes.

```
set autologout 10
```

`mailto` *address*	Mail address to which results are sent.
	`set mailto chris@mygame.com`
`maxhits` *num*	Limit the maximum number of results (matches).
	`set maxhits 10`
`pager`	Use the default pager utility such as `pg` or `more` to display your results.
	`set pager`
	`unset pager`
`search` *option*	Type of search.
	`set search subcase`

SEARCH OPTIONS

`sub`	Pattern search within file names.
`subcase`	Pattern search that distinguishes between upper- and lowercase letters.
`exact`	Exact pattern match.
`regex`	Use regular expressions.
`sortby` *option*	Type of sort for output.
	`set sortby `*`filename`*

SORT OPTIONS

`none`	No sort.
`filename`	Sort the results alphabetically by file name.
`hostname`	Sort the results by host name.
`time`	Sort the results from most recent date.
`size`	Sort the results from largest size.
`rfilename`	Reverse alphabetical file name sort.
`rhostname`	Reverse alphabetical host name sort.
`rtime`	Sort the results from oldest date.
`rsize`	Sort the results from smallest size.
`status`	Issue status reports on searches as they are performed.
`set status`	
`unset status`	
`term` *terminal-id*	Type of terminal you are using.
	`set term vt100`

archie.au	139.130.23.2	Australia
archie.univie.ac.at	131.130.1.23	Austria
archie.belnet.be	193.190.198.2	Belgium
archie.bunyip.com	192.77.55.5	Canada
archie.cs.mcgill.ca	132.206.51.250	Canada
archie.funet.fi	128.214.248.46	Finland
archie.cru.fr	129.20.254.2	France
archie.th-darmstadt.de	130.83.22.1	Germany
archie.ac.il	132.65.208.15	Israel
archie.unipi.it	131.114.21.15	Italy
archie.wide.ad.jp	133.4.3.6	Japan
archie.kornet.nm.kr	168.126.63.10	Korea
archie.sogang.ac.kr	163.239.1.11	Korea
archie.nz	140.200.128.20	New Zealand
archie.icm.edu.pl	148.81.209.5	Poland
archie.rediris.es	130.206.1.5	Spain
archie.luth.se	130.240.12.23	Sweden
archie.switch.ch	193.5.24.1	Switzerland
archie.ncu.edu.tw	192.83.166.12	Taiwan
archie.doc.ic.ac.uk	193.63.255.1	UK
archie.hensa.ac.uk	129.12.200.130	UK
archie.unl.edu	129.93.1.14	USA (NE)
archie.internic.net	198.49.45.10	USA (NJ)
archie.internic.net	204.159.111.101	USA (VA)
archie.internic.net	204.179.186.65	USA (NJ)
archie.rutgers.edu	128.6.21.13	USA (NJ)
archie.ans.net	147.225.1.10	USA (NY)

Table 35. Archie Server Sites

Table 36. WAIS Commands, Files, and Options

OPTIONS

-s *sourcename*	Select source name for search.
-S *sourcedir*	Specify a source directory. Default is ~/wais-sources.
-C *sourcedir*	Specify a common source directory. Default is /usr/lib/wais-sources.
-h	Help message.

COMMANDS

j, **down-arrow**, ^N	Moves down one source.
k, **up-arrrow**, ^P	Moves up one source.
J, ^V, ^D	Moves down one screen.
K, **escape** v, ^U	Moves up one screen.
#*num*	Position to source number *num*.
/*string*	Searches for source *string*.
spacebar *or* .	Selects current source.
=	Deselects all sources.
v *or* ,	Views current source information.
enter	Performs search.
s	Selects new sources (refresh sources list).
w	Selects new keywords.
X, -	Removes current source permanently.
o	Sets and shows swais options.
h, ?	Shows this help display.
H	Displays program history.
q	Leaves this program.

WAIS INDEX FILES

.doc	Information about the document, including the size and name.
.dct	Dictionary file with list of each unique word cross-indexed to inverted file.
.fn	List of all files created for the index.
.hl	Table of all headlines; headlines are the titles and are displayed in the retrieved results. *(continued)*

Table 36. WAIS Commands, Files, and Options *(continued)*

.inv	The inverted file containing a table of words, a ranking of their importance, and their connection to the indexed documents.
.src	A source description file that contains information about the index, what system it is located on, the topic it deals with, who maintains it, etc.
.status	Contains user-defined information.

WAISINDEX OPTIONS

`-a`	Appends index to an existing one.
`-contents`	Indexes the contents of a file (default).
`-d` *pathname*	Specifies a path name for index files.
`-e` *logfile*	Redirects error messages to *logfile*.
`-export`	Adds hostname and TCP port to source description files to allow Internet access.
`-l` *num*	Sets logging level: 0, 1, 5 and 10. 0, nothing; 1, errors and warnings; 5, Medium priority messages; 10, everything.
-mem	The amount of memory to use during indexing.
`-M`	Links different types of files.
`-nocontents`	Indexes only the header and file name, not the contents.
`-pairs`	Treats capitalized words as one term.
`-nopairs`	Treats capitalized words as separate terms.
`-pos`	Include word's position information.
`-nopos`	Do not include word's position information.
`-r`	Recursively indexes subdirectories.
`-register`	Registers indexes with WAIS Directory of Services.
`-t`	Specifies the type of document file.
`-T`	Sets the type of document.

`filename`	Text type that uses the file name as the headline.
`first_line`	Text type that uses the first line in the file as the headline.
`one_line`	Text type that indexes each sentence.
`text`	Text type that uses the path name as its headline.
`ftp`	Contains Ftp code for accessing other systems.
`GIF`	GIF image file.
`PICT`	PICT image file.
`TIFF`	TIFF image file.
`MPEG`	MPEG file.
`MIDI`	MIDI file.
`HTML`	HTML file (Web page).
`mail_or_rmail`	Mailbox file.
`mail_digest`	Email using the subject as the headline.
`netnews`	Usenet news.
`ps`	Postscript file.

Table 37. WAIS Document File Types

Table 38. Gopher Commands and File Types

---

gopher [-sb] *options hostname*

OPTIONS

-p *string*	Specifies a specific selector string to send to the root-level server on startup.
-t *string*	Sets the title of the initial screen for the Gopher client.

GOPHER MENU ITEM QUALIFIERS

.	File.
/	Menu (directory).
\<CSO\>	CSO name server.
\<TEL\>	Telnet connection.
\<?\>	Database with keyword search.
\<CSO\>	CSO name server.
\<Picture\>	Image file, such as **gif** or **jpeg**.
\<Movie\>	Video, such as **mov** or **avi**.
\<HTML\>	Web page (HyperText document).
\<Bin\>	Binary file.
\<PC Bin\>	DOS binary file.
\<HQX\>	Macintosh binhex file.
\<MIME\>	Multi-purpose Internet Mail Extensions file.
\<)	Sound file.

MOVING TO AND SELECTING MENU ITEMS

k	**up-arrow**	Move up to previous menu item.
j	**down-arrow**	Move down to next menu item.
num		Move to *num* item in menu.
l	**right-arrow enter**	Select the current menu item.

SEARCHING A MENU FOR AN ITEM

/*pattern*	Search menu items for pattern and move to first item with that pattern.
n	Repeat previous search of menu items.

OPERATIONS PERFORMED ON MENU ITEMS

=	Display information about a menu item.
s	Save the current item to a file.
S	Save the current list of items to a file. *(continued)*

Table 38. Gopher Commands and File Types *(continued)*

m			Mail the current item to a user.
p			Print the current item.

MOVING THROUGH MENU SCREENS

>	+	**spacebar**	Move to next menu screen.
<	–	b	Move back to previous menu screen.

RETURN TO PREVIOUS MENUS

u	**left-arrow**	Move back to previous menu.
m		Return to top main menu.

BOOKMARK COMMANDS

a	Add selected item to bookmark list.
A	Add current menu to bookmark list.
d	Remove a bookmark from the bookmark list.
v	Display bookmark list.

OPTIONS, QUIT, AND HELP COMMANDS

q	Quit Gopher.
Q	Quit Gopher without prompt.
?	Help.
O	Display and change options for Gopher.

ENVIRONMENT VARIABLES

PAGER	The client will use that to display files to the user.
GOPHER_HTML	The program to display Web pages (HTML).
GOPHER_MAIL	The program to send mail with (must understand -s option).
GOPHER_PLAY	The program to play sound from a pipe.
GOPHER_TELNET	The program to contact Telnet services with.
GOPHER_PRINTER	The program to print from a pipe.

GOPHER FILE TYPES

0	Text file.
1	Gopher directory.
2	CSO phone book server.
3	Error.
4	Binhex Macintosh file, HQX.

(continued)

Table 38. Gopher Commands and File Types *(continued)*

5	Binary DOS file.
6	Unix uuencoded file.
7	Full-text index (Gopher menu file).
8	Telnet session, includes the remote host's address.
9	Binary file.
g	GIF image file.
h	HTML file.
I	Graphic image file (other than GIF).
M	MIME multipart mixed message.
P	Adobe PDF file.
s	Sound file.
T	TN3270 Telnet session.

`http://`	HyperText Transfer Protocol for Web site access; uses HyperText Transfer and World Wide Web protocols, HTTP and WWW.
`gopher://`	Access Gopher site. Uses Gopher protocol.
`ftp://`	File Transfer Protocol for anonymous Ftp connections; uses File Transfer Protocol, FTP.
`telnet://`	Makes a Telnet connection; uses Telnet protocol, TELNET.
`mailto:`	Send email; uses Simple Mail Transfer Protocol, SMTP.
`wais://`	Access WAIS site.
`nntp://`	Read Usenet news using Net News Transfer Protocol, NNTP.
`news:`	Read Usenet news.
`file:`	Local file.

Table 39. URL Protocols

`.html`	Web page document formatted using HTML, the HyperText Markup Language.

GRAPHICS FILES

`.gif`	Graphics, using gif compression.
`.jpeg`	Graphics, using jpeg compression.

SOUND FILES

`.au`	Sun (Unix) sound file.
`.wav`	Microsoft Windows sound file.
`.aiff`	Macintosh sound file.

VIDEO FILES

`.QT`	Quicktime video file, multiplatform.
`.mpeg`	Video file.
`.avi`	Microsoft Windows video file.

Table 40. Web Resource File Types

Table 41. HTML Codes for Web Pages

BASIC TAGS

<HTML>	Web page. Place <HTML> as the first entry in your Web page and </HTML> as the last.
</HTML>	End of Web page.
<HEAD>	Head of Web page. The head segment of a Web page; includes any configuration entries and the title entry.
</HEAD>	End of head.
<TITLE>*title text*</TITLE>	The title of the Web page; this will be used in hotlists to identify the page easily.
<BODY>	Text of Web page. The body of the Web page; this is the material that is displayed as the Web page.
</BODY>	End of Web page body.
<ADDRESS>*Address of creator*<\ADDRESS>	Internet address of Web page creator.
<BASE=*Href "Web page path name"* >	Path name of Web page that serves as base path name for any relative path names on that page.

FORMAT

<H*n*>*Heading title*<\H*n*>	Headers; *n* is sequential subhead level, as in <H1> for top level, <H2> for subheads, etc.
<P>*paragraph text* </P>	Paragraphs.
<CENTER>	Center text.
 	Line break.
<PRE>	Preformatted text. Displays the following text as it appears with no formatting.
</PRE>	End of preformatted text.
<HR>	Displays a line across the page.
<CLEAR>	Forces break in text.
<B>*bold-text*</B>	Bold text.
<I>*italic-text*</I>	Italic text.
<TT>*typwriter-text*</TT>	Typewriter text.
<CODE>*code-text*</CODE>	Code text.
<CITE>*citation-text*</CITE>	Citation text.
<EM>*emphasis-text*</EM>	Emphasis text.
<STRONG>*emphasis-text*</STRONG>	Strong emphasis text.
<KBD>*keboard-text*</KBD>	Keyboard text.

(continued)

Table 41. HTML Codes for Web Pages *(continued)*

<VAR>*variable-text*</VAR>   Variable text.

IMAGES

<IMAGE SRC="*file.gif*">	Image to be displayed in Web page.
ALIGN="*position*"	Positions images or text on the Web page; position can be bottom, top, left, or right.
WIDTH=	Sets width for display of image.
HEIGHT=	Sets height.

ANCHORS

<A*Anchor tag* /A>*displayed text* </A>	Anchor tag associated with displayed text in the Web page.
<A HREF="*URL address*">*displayed text* </A>	URL reference; ties the specified text to the URL address. Clicking on specified text in Web page will jump to that URL's Web page.
<A HREF=#*Anchor text*>*displayed text*</A>	A named anchor reference. Clicking on displayed text will jump to the NAME anchor defined with the Anchor text following the #. The # is used with NAME to reference NAME anchor entries.
<A NAME=*Anchor text*>*displayed text*</A>	Specifies displayed text as destination for a named anchor reference.
<A NAME=*Anchor text*><H*n*>*Heading* <\H*n*></A>	Makes a heading a destination for a named anchor reference in the Web page.
ID=*Anchor text*	Uses ID instead of NAME to create anchor text in the Web page.
<H*n* ID=*Anchor text*>*Heading text*<\H*n*>	Uses ID to make a heading an anchor text.
<A HREF=*URL address*><IMAGE SRC="*file.gif*">< /A>	URL address tied to the specified image displayed on the page.
<LINK REL=*Relationship* HREF="*URL reference*">	Creates a link to other Web pages making up the Web site; displays buttons at top and bottom of Web page with relationship described by REL.

(continued)

Table 41. HTML Codes for Web Pages *(continued)*

REL=*Relationship*	Relationship of current Web page to others:
	Previous HRL for previous Web page.
	Next HRL for next Web page.
	Home HRL for home page.
	Banner HRL for banner displayed for all Web pages.

LISTS

<LH>*List header* </LH>	Name for the list.
<LI>*List item text*</LI>	List item entries.
<UL>	Unordered list.
</UL>	End of unordered list.
<OL>	Ordered list, usually numbered.
</OL>	End of ordered list.
<DL>	Definition list; a list of terms and an explanation of each called a definition; a term is a word that you specify.
</DL>	End of definition list.
<DT>*Definition term* </DT>	Term for a definition list entry.
<DD>*Definition*</DD>	Text associated with a definition term.

TABLES

<TABLE>*Table entries*</TABLE>	Displays a table.
<TC>*Table caption* </TC>	Table caption.
<TR>*Table row* </TR>	A table row entry.
<TH>*Table head* </TH>	Table heading.
<TD>*Table cell* </TD>	A table cell entry.

FORMS

<FORM> *Form entries* </FORM>	Display forms specified.
<INPUT NAME=*name* TYPE=*type* VALUE= *"value"*> *label*	Creates a form for input. NAME is the name of the object that holds the input value. TYPE is the type of input form. VALUE is the initial value displayed in the form.
TYPE=*type*	Type of the input form:
	text Text box.

(continued)

Table 41. HTML Codes for Web Pages *(continued)*

	check box	Check box; use same name object for check boxes used for the same choice.
	radio	Radio button; use same name object for radio buttons used for the same choice.
	submit	Submit button; used to submit entered data on the page.
	reset	Reset button; used to reset forms to initial default values.

<SELECT>
Select options
</SELECT>   Create drop-down menu of possible choices.

<OPTION NAME=*name* > *Option-title*
        Creates an entry for a drop-down menu. Used within the SELECT tag to specify option entries for drop down menu.

<TEXTAREA NAME=*name* ROWS=*num* COLS =*num*>

default-text
</TEXTAREA>   Create text area form to handle free text of several lines that can be edited. The form includes slider bars on the side and bottom. The *default-text* is displayed initially.

CONFIGURATION

BGCOLOR=*rrggbb*   Background color; hexadecimal number representing color; *rr* = red, *gg* = green, *bb* = blue; all 0s = no color (black); all 1s = white, FFFFFF. It is set in the BODY tag. <BODY BGCOLOR=137HF2>.

TEXT=*rrggbb*   Color of text; it is set in the BODY tag.

BACKGOUND=*file.gif*   Picture to use as background for Web page; it is set in the BODY tag.

ENTITIES

&lt;	<
&gt;	>
&amp;	&
&quot;	"

rwho	Displays all users logged into systems in your network.
ruptime	Displays information about each system in your network.
ping	Detects whether a system is up and running.

rlogin *system-name*

> Allows you to login remotely to an account on another system. It has an -l option that allows you to specify the login name of the account.
>
> > $ rlogin mygame
> >
> > $ rlogin mygame -l justin

rcp *sys-name* : *file1 sys-name* : *file2*

> Allows you to copy a file from an account on one system to an account on another system. If no system name is given then the current system is assumed.
>
> > $ rcp mydata mygame:newdata

-r
> The rcp command with the -r option allows you to copy directories instead of just files.
>
> > $ rcp -r newdocs mygame:edition

rsh *sys-name Unix-command*

> Allows you to execute remotely a command on another system.
>
> > $ rsh mygame ls

Table 42. TCP/IP Remote Access Commands

Table 43. UUCP Commands and Options

PATH MAIL ADDRESSES

system ! login-name Path mail address for System V (UUCP).
```
rose!mytrain!dylan
```
system \ ! login-name Path mail address for C-shell (UUCP). Escape the exclamation point.
```
rose\!mytrain\!dylan
```

UUNAME AND UUCICO COMMANDS

uname	Display system name.
−m	Machine type.
−n	Network node hostname.
−r	Operating system release.
−s	Operating system name.
−v	Operating system version.
−a	All information.
uuname	Lists the systems to which yours is connected.
−l	Display local system name.

uucico *options remote-system*

Dials into and connects to a remote system; this is a systems administration action performed only as the root user
```
$ uucico -r -x rose!
```

UUCICO OPTIONS

-r1	Starts in master mode (calls out to a system); implied.
-s	If no system is specified, calls any system for which work is waiting to be done.
−r0	Starts in slave mode; this is the default.
-f	Ignores any required wait for any systems to be called.
-l	Prompts for login name and password using "login:" and "Password:".
-p *port*	Specifies port to call out on or listen to.
-C	Calls named system only if there is work for that system.
-x *type*	Turns on debugging type; the number 9 turns on all types. Types are abnormal, chat, handshake, uucp-proto, proto, port, config, spooldir, execute, incoming, outgoing. *(continued)*

Table 43. UUCP Commands and Options *(continued)*

---

uuxqt   Program called by uucico to execute uux requests.

UUTO **AND** UUPICK **COMMANDS**

uuto *filename address*

                         Mail command for sending large files to another system.

                         $ uuto mydata gameplace!larisa

UUTO OPTIONS

  -m   Notify sender when file was sent.

  -p   Copy file to spool directory and send the copy.

uupick   Mail command that receives files sent to you using uuto. You are
                         sequentially prompted for each file.

UUPICK **COMMANDS**

  m *dir*   Move file received to your directory.

  a *dir*   Move all files received to your directory.

  d   Delete the file received.

  p   Display the file received.

  enter   Hitting **enter** leaves file waiting.

  q   Quit uupick.

  *   List uupick commands.

  !*cmd*   Execute a Unix command, escaping to your shell.

uucp, uustat, **AND** uux **COMMANDS**

uucp *sys-name*!*filename*   *sys-name*!*filename*   Copies files from one system to another.

                         $ uucp mydata gameplace!justin/newdata

UUCP **OPTIONS**

  -m   Notify the user when a uucp job is completed.

  -n*user*   Notify the remote user when a uucp job is performed.

  -C   Copy file to spool directory and send that copy.

  -c   Do not copy file to spool directory (default).

  -f   Do not create destination directories.

  -g   Specify grade of service (high, medium, low).

uustat   Lists current uucp jobs. With the -k option and the job number, you
                         can delete a uucp job.

                         $ uustat

                                                                        (continued)

Table 43. UUCP Commands and Options *(continued)*

UUSTAT **OPTIONS**

-a	List all jobs for all users.
-u*user*	List all jobs for specific user.
-s*system*	List all jobs for specific system.
-k*jobid*	Kill a uucp job.
-c	The queue time for a job, use with -t .
-t*sys*	The transfer rate for a system.
-q	Display status of jobs.

uux   Remotely execute a command on another system. File names and command name must be preceded with an exclamation point.

```
$ uux !cat gameplace!mydata
```

UUX **OPTIONS**

-z	Notify user the job is successful.
-n	Suppress notification of job's success.
-C	Copy file to spool directory and operate on that copy.
-c	Do not copy file to spool directory (default).
-g	Specify grade of service (high, medium, low).

CU **AND** CT **COMMANDS**

cu   Remotely log in to an account on another system (call Unix).

```
$ cu gameplace
```

CU **OPTIONS**

-s	Specify baud rate (transmission speed) such as 300, 1200, 2400, 4800, or 9600.
-c	Select local area network to be used.
-l	Select communications line to be used.
-e	Set even parity.
-o	Set odd parity.
-h	Set half-duplex.
-b*n*	Set byte size to 7 or 8: -b7 or -b8.
-n	Prompt for telephone number instead of entering it on the command line.
-t	Connect to terminal with auto-answer modem like the ct command does.

(continued)

Table 43. UUCP Commands and Options *(continued)*

CU **COMMANDS**

~!	Temporary return to local system
	$ ~[mytrain]!
exit	End use of local system and return to remote.
	$ ~[mytrain]!
~%	A one command escape to local system
	$ ~[mytrain]% cd newdocs
~% take *remote-file*	Copy a file from remote system to local system.
	$ ~[mytrain]% take mydata
~% put *remote-file*	Copy a file from local system to remote system.
	$ ~[mytrain]% put windata
ct	Remotely connect from your system to a terminal through an auto-answer modem (connect terminal). The ct command takes as an argument a telephone number of the terminal. It has several options for specifying transmission features such as baud rate and parity.
	$ ct 9999999
-s	Baud rate
	$ ct -s57600 9999999

Index

.cap, 369
.elmrc, 83
.maillog, 19
.mailrc, 58
.names, 371
.netrc, 317
.newsrc, 239
.signature, 134, 147
  newsreaders, 148
.telnetrc, 294
.tin, 235

A

Addresses, 14, 264–279, 471
  domain addressing, 16, 264, 544
  domain name service, 271
  IP addresses, 269
  network, 264
  nameserver, 272, 274
  path addressing, 15, 432, 579
  URL, 378, 573
Aliases
  Elm, 82
  mailx, 58
anchor, 453
anonymous ftp, 308, 453
Archie, 333–344, 454
  archie, 334
  client, 334
  commands, 343, 564
  options, 336, 569
  server sites, 339, 566
  servers, 338